The History
of Christian Doctrine

The History of Christian Doctrine

REVISED EDITION

E. H. Klotsche

With additional chapters by
J. Theodore Mueller and David P. Scaer

BAKER BOOK HOUSE
Grand Rapids, Michigan

Reprinted from the 1945 edition
published by the Lutheran Literary Board
Paperback edition issued 1979 by
Baker Book House Company
ISBN: 0-8010-5404-4

PHOTOLITHOPRINTED BY CUSHING - MALLOY, INC.
ANN ARBOR, MICHIGAN, UNITED STATES OF AMERICA
1979

AN APPRECIATION

Dr. E. H. Klotsche was in the midst of readying his manuscript on "THE HISTORY OF CHRISTIAN DOCTRINE" for publication when, on February 11, 1937, he was suddenly and unexpectedly called to rest from his labors. Those who knew this thorough workman felt that it would be a loss if such a manuscript were not made available for the study of professors, pastors, students, and laymen, and Mrs. Marie Klotsche, the widow of the author, was approached in the matter. She very graciously consented to allow the Midwest and the Wartburg Synods of the United Lutheran Church in America to publish this work *AS A MEMORIAL TO HER HUSBAND*. Dr. Klotsche had been a member of the first mentioned Synod while Professor at Western Seminary in Fremont, Nebraska, and of the latter Synod when he took up his professorial duties at the Chicago Lutheran Seminary in Maywood, Illinois. We are thankful to Mrs. Klotsche and family for their helpfulness.

Other books from the consecrated heart of the author include such publications as *"Christian Symbolics"*, *"Luther's Influence in Song and Church Music"* (Dr. Klotsche was an excellent musician), and *"Outline of the History of Doctrine"*. Although it is several years since his death, we feel that this book will be a very welcome addition to the literature of the Church. It is truly an eloquent presentation of an important theme.

The last chapter, about 5,000 words, was written by Professor J. Theodore Mueller, Concordia Seminary, St. Louis, Missouri, a friend of the author. We here include a word of appreciation for his kind service. This chapter brings the work up-to-date, and we feel that with it the reader is given a satisfactory overview of the major theological thought, inclusive of the latest developments.

R. R. BELTER.

Burlington, Iowa.
June 15, 1945.

FOREWORD

When the Lutheran Literary Board, through the manager, asked the undersigned to write the Foreword to Dr. Klotsche's History of Christian Doctrine, he gladly complied with this request, for he knew the late Professor E. H. Klotsche, Ph. D., D. D., both personally and through his books as a humble child of God and a true believer in Christ, his Savior whom he wished to glorify by all he taught and wrote. Also this book of his is written in the heart-warming simplicity of a sincere Christian who desires only to assist in rooting men a little deeper in the divine knowledge by which the praise of God is magnified among men and His kingdom is enlarged.

There are, of course, many ways of writing a History of Christian Doctrine. Dr. Klotsche chose a very direct and unpretentious way, giving to the Church at large a book which, without any great and boastful claims, sets before the readers the elementary truths of this branch of sacred theology in an intelligible and lucid way. So conceived and written, it has a rare charm of its own and will be gladly received, we are sure, by those who wish to deepen their knowledge of Christian theology. Thousands knew Dr. Klotsche as a loving friend, a thorough scholar, and a fearless witness to the divine Truth.

May God's richest blessing rest upon this book as it goes forth to instruct and to testify, to the glory of our precious Lord and Redeemer.

JOHN THEODORE MUELLER.

Concordia Seminary,
St. Louis, Missouri.

CONTENTS

GENERAL INTRODUCTION

Page

A. *Christian Doctrine* 1
    1. Its Definition
    2. Its Presupposition
    3. Its Development

B. *History of Christian Doctrine* 2
    1. Its Definition and Office
    2. Its Source and Method
    3. Its History

HISTORICAL INTRODUCTON

A. *The Gentile Background of Early Christianity* 5
    1. The Religion of Greece and Rome
    2. Zoroastrianism
    3. Mystery Religions
    4. Greek Philosophy

B. *The Jewish Background of Early Christianity* 9
    1. Palestinian Judaism
    2. The Jewish Diaspora

C. *The Early Christian Proclamation* 14

FIRST PERIOD

ORIGINATION AND DEVELOPMENT OF DOCTRINE IN THE PATRISTIC AGE

CHAPTER I

THE CONCEPTION OF CHRISTIANITY ACCORDING TO THE WRITINGS OF THE APOSTOLIC FATHERS

.... 17

    1. First Epistle of Clement
    2. The Shepherd of Hermas
    3. Epistle of Barnabas
    4. Ignatius
    5. Epistle of Polycarp
    6. Papias
    7. Didache
    8. Second Epistle of Clement
    9. General Estimate

CHAPTER II

THE CONCEPTION OF CHRISTIANITY ACCORDING TO THE GREEK APOLOGISTS

Page

A. _____ 23

    1. Epistle of Diognetus
    2. The work of Quadratus
    3. Aristides
    4. Melito
    5. Claudius Apollinaris
    6. Miltiades
    7. Athenagoras
    8. Theophilus of Antioch
    9. Tatian
    10. Flavius Justinus

B. *The Christianity of the Greek Apologists* _____ 25

CHAPTER III

PERVERSIONS OF CHRISTIANITY — JEWISH CHRISTIANITY — GNOSTICISM

A. *Jewish Christianity* _____ 28

    1. Ebionites
    2. Elkesaites
    3. The Pseudo-Clementine Writings

B. *Gnosticism* _____ 29

    1. Rise of the Gnostic Heresy
    2. The First Traces of Gnosticism
    3. Saturninus
    4. Basilides
    5. Valentinus
    6. Encratites, Ophites
    7. General Characteristics of Gnosticism

CHAPTER IV

REFORMATORY MOVEMENTS DIRECTED AGAINST CATHOLIC CHRISTIANITY

A. *Marcion's Attempt at Reform* _____ 36

    1. Marcion's Relation to Gnosticism
    2. Marcion's Doctrinal Views

B. *The Montanist Reaction* _____ 37

    1. Montanus
    2. Montanists
    3. Opposition to Montanism

CHAPTER V

AUTHORITATIVE STANDARDS OF THE ANCIENT CATHOLIC CHURCH

Page

A. *The Ancient Catholic Church* 40

B. *Rule of Faith* 41

C. *Canon*
      1. History
      2. Inspiration
      3. Interpretation

CHAPTER VI

THE BEGINNINGS OF SCIENTIFIC THEOLOGY IN THE ANCIENT CHURCH

A. *In the Eastern Church* 46

      1. Alexandrian Catechetical School
      2. Alexandrian Theology
      3. Origen
      4. Epitome of Origen's System
      5. School of Antioch

B. *In the Western Church* 52

      1. Tertullian
      2. Tertullian's Theology
      3. Cyprian
      4. Irenaeus
      5. Hippolytus

CHAPTER VII

THE PROBLEM OF THE TRINITY

A. *The Deity of Christ and Monarchianism* 58

      1. The Deity of Christ
      2. Monarchianism
      3. Dynamic Monarchianism
      4. Modalistic Monarchianism
      5. The Church's Opposition to Monarchianism

B. *Arianism and the Homoosia of the Son* 62

      1. Decisive Factors in Doctrinal Development
      2. Arianism
      3. Opposition to Arianism
      4. The Council of Nice

C. *Further Development and Final Settlement of the Arian Controversy* 66

      1. The Arian Controversy from 325 to 381
      2. The Doctrine of the Holy Spirit
      3. The Niceno-Constantinopolitan Creed

CHAPTER VIII
The Christological Problem

Page

A. *The Divine-Human Personality of Christ* 71
B. *Fundamental Differences in Attempting to Solve the*
   Christological Problem 72
   1. The Alexandrian School
   2. The Antiochian School
C. *The Christological Conflict and Settlement of Controversy* 75
   1. Nestorius and Cyril
   2. Theodoret and Eutyches
   3. The Councils of Ephesus and Chalcedon
D. *Christological Movements After the Council of Chalcedon* 78
   1. Monophysitism
   2. Monotheletism
   3. Christology of John of Damascus

CHAPTER IX
The Anthropological Controversy

A. *Freedom and Grace* 83
   1. Eastern and Western Anthropology
   2. Pelagius
   3. The Teachings of Pelagius
   4. Augustine
   5. Augustine's Doctrine of Sin and Grace
B. *Settlement of Doctrinal Conflict* 93
   1. Conflict between Augustinianism and Pelagianism
   2. Extreme Augustinianism in Conflict with
      Semi-Pelagianism
   3. The Doctrinal Decisions of the Council of Oarange

CHAPTER X
Conception of the Sacraments in the Ancient Church

A. *Sacraments in General* 97
B. *Baptism — Confirmation* 98
C. *Repentance* 100
D. *Lord's Supper* 103
   1. As a Sacrifice
   2. As a Sacrament — (a) realistic view
                        (b) symbolical view
                        (c) metabolic view

CHAPTER XI
Conception of the Church in the Patristic Age

A. *Episcopacy and Rome's Supremacy* 109
B. *The Donatist Controversy* 112
C. *Augustine's Conception of the Church* 113

SECOND PERIOD

DEVELOPMENT OF DOCTRINE IN THE MIDDLE AGES

CHAPTER XII

PRE-SCHOLASTIC PERIOD: DOCTRINAL CONFLICTS — PRAXIS OF REPENTENCE AND PAPAL CLAIMS

Page

A. *General Characteristics of this Period* _____ 116

B. *Doctrinal Controversies* _____ 118

    1. Iconoclastic Controversy
    2. Filioque Controversy
    3. Adoptionist Controversy
    4. Controversy on Predestination
    5. Controversy upon the Lord's Supper

CHAPTER XIII

CHARACTERISTIC FEATURES AND GENERAL TENDENCIES OF THE SCHOLASTIC AGE

A. *Scholasticism* _____ 127

    1. Realism
    2. Nominalism
    3. Conceptualism

B. *Mysticism* _____ 130

C. *Chief Representatives of Scholasticism and Mysticism* _____ 131

    1. First Period — 1100 – 1200
    2. Second Period — 1200 – 1300
    3. Third Period — 1300 – 1500

CHAPTER XIV

DOCTRINAL DEVELOPMENT IN THE SCHOLASTIC AGE

A. *Theology* _____ 139

B. *Christology* _____ 139

C. *Atonement* _____ 140

D. *Anthropology* _____ 142

    1. Original State
    2. Original Sin
    3. The Sinlessness of Mary
    4. Freedom and Grace
    5. Justification
    6. Faith — Merit — Good Works

CHAPTER XV

DEVELOPMENTS OF THE DOGMA OF THE SACRAMENTS
IN THE SCHOLASTIC AGE

Page

A. *Sacraments in General* 147
    1. Number of Sacraments
    2. Definition and Efficacy of the Sacrament

B. *The Separate Sacraments* 149
    1. Baptism
    2. Confirmation
    3. Eucharist
    4. Penance
    5. Extreme Unction
    6. Ordination
    7. Matrimony

CHAPTER XVI

HIERARCHICAL CONCEPTION OF THE CHURCH AND EFFORTS AT REFORM

A. *Hierarchical Conception of the Church* 157
    1. The Church
    2. Papal Claims

B. *Efforts at Reform* 158
    1. Reform Councils
    2. Scholastics
    3. Humanists
    4. Cathari and Waldenses
    5. Forerunners of the Reformation

THIRD PERIOD

DEVELOPMENT AND FIXATION OF DOCTRINE THROUGH
THE REFORMATION AND COUNTER - REFORMATION

CHAPTER XVII

THE DOCTRINAL VIEWS OF LUTHER AND HIS PLACE IN
THE HISTORY OF DOCTRINE

A. *The Main Stages of the Development of Luther's Doctrinal
Views* 163
    1. When Luther entered the Monastery
    2. Luther in the Monastery
    3. Luther continued his Study of Theology
    4. The Ninety-Five Theses
    5. The Leipzig Disputation
    6. Three Monumental Works
        a. Address to the Christian Nobility
        b. The Babylonian Captivity of the Church
        c. On the Liberty of a Christian Man
    7. Luther and Erasmus

CHAPTER XVII, Continued   Page

B. *Luther's Doctrinal Views Presented in Systematic Order* 169
    1. Rule and Standard of Doctrine
    2. God
    3. Christ
    4. The Work of Christ
    5. Man
    6. Justification Effected by Faith
    7. The Holy Spirit
    8. Baptism
    9. Lord's Supper
   10. The Church
   11. The Ministry
   12. Ecclesiastical Rites and Usages
   13. Relation of Civil Government to the Church
   14. Eschatology

CHAPTER XVIII

ZWINGLI'S REFORMATORY IDEAS AND HIS PLACE IN
THE HISTORY OF DOCTRINE

A. *Zwingli's Reformatory Ideas* 188

B. *The Controversy upon the Lord's Supper* 190

C. *Zwingli's Influence on Doctrinal Development* 192

CHAPTER XIX

LUTHER'S VIEWS AS EXPRESSED IN THE AUGUSTANA AND ITS APOLOGY

A. *Augsburg Confession* 194

B. *The Doctrinal Statements* 195

CHAPTER XX

MELANCHTHON'S DOCTRINAL VIEWS AND HIS PLACE
IN THE HISTORY OF DOCTRINE

A. *Melanchthon's Significance for the History of Doctrine* 202

B. *Brief Summary of Melanchthon's Religious Ideas* 202

CHAPTER XXI

CONTROVERSIES IN THE LUTHERAN CHURCH AFTER LUTHER'S
DEATH SETTLED BY THE FORMULA OF CONCORD

A. *General Survey of Doctrinal Development to the Adoption
of the Formula of Concord* 205

B. *Separate Controversies Settled by the Formula of Concord* 206
    1. Interimistic or Adiaphoristic Controversy

CHAPTER XXI, Continued

2. Majoristic Controversy
3. Antinomistic Controversy
4. Osiandristic and Stancarian Controversy
5. Synergistic Controversy
6. Flacian Controversy
7. Crypto-Calvinistic Controversy
8. Descensus Controversy
9. Predestination Controversy

CHAPTER XXII

SECTS OF THE SIXTEENTH CENTURY IN OPPOSITION TO
THE CHURCH'S DOCTRINE

Page
220

CHAPTER XXIII

CALVIN'S THEOLOGY AND HIS PLACE IN THE HISTORY OF DOCTRINE

A. Sovereignty of God 227

B. Scriptures 230

C. Anthropology 231
    1. Man
    2. Man's Conversion

D. Christ 234
    1. Christ's Person
    2. Christ's Work

E. Justification and Sanctification 235
    1. Justification
    2. Regeneration or Sanctification

F. The Church 238

G. The Means of Grace 241
    1. The Word
    2. The Sacraments

H. Calvin's Place in the History of Doctrine 243

CHAPTER XXIV

CALVINISM — THE ACCEPTED DOCTRINE OF THE REFORMED CHURCH

A. The Later Reformed Confessions 245

B. Influence of Calvin's Theology upon Protestantism in
    England 246

C. Arminianism versus Calvinism 247

D. School of Saumur versus Strict Calvinism 249

CHAPTER XXV

SCHOLASTIC THEOLOGY EXALTED TO THE POSITION OF ECCLESIASTICAL DOGMA BY THE COUNCIL OF TRENT

Page

A. *Purpose and Significance of the Council of Trent* 251
B. *The Dogmatic Decisions of the Council of Trent* 252
    1. Scripture and Tradition
    2. Original Sin
    3. Justification
        1. Preparation for Justification
        2. Justification Itself
        3. Good Works
    4. Sacraments
C. *The Tridentine Profession and the Catechisms* 267

CHAPTER XXVI

TRIUMPH OF JESUIT THEOLOGY OVER AUGUSTINIANISM AND THOMISM AND COMPLETION OF THE DOGMA OF THE ROMAN CATHOLIC CHURCH

A. *Jesuitism versus Augustinianism* 270
B. *Dogma of the Immaculate Conception* 272
C. *Definition of Papal Power and Infallibility* 273
D. *Old Catholic Church* 277

CHAPTER XXVII

THEOLOGY IN GREAT BRITAIN
(During the Seventeenth and Eighteenth Centuries)

287

CHAPTER XXVIII

THE ERA OF THE ENLIGHTENMENT IN GERMANY

305

CHAPTER XXIX

CHRISTIAN THOUGHT AND THEOLOGY IN GREAT BRITAIN
(During the Nineteenth Century)

332

CHAPTER XXX
THE CHRISTIAN DOCTRINE IN ITS MODERN SETTING
J. T. Mueller, Ph.D., Th.D.

Page
.... 335

Positive Confessionalism in Germany 336
The Barthian Movement 339
The Scandinavian Response 341
Church Group Interests in England 342
The Russian Soul-Search 343
Three Trends in America 346
The Revolt of Modernism Against Positive Truth.... 346
The Awakening of Neo-Thomism 347
The Neo-Orthodox Half-Way Challenge 348

CHAPTER XXXI
THEOLOGICAL DEVELOPMENTS SINCE WORLD WAR II
David P. Scaer, Th.D.

.... 350

Neo-orthodoxy 350
Karl Barth 350
Emil Brunner 354
Rudolf Bultmann 355
Paul Tillich 356
Secular Theology 358
John A. T. Robinson 359
Thomas J. J. Altizer 359
Harvey Cox 360
Joseph Fletcher 360
Theologies in Flux 362
Theology of Hope — Moltmann 362
Theology of History — Pannenberg 363
Liberation Theology 364
Process Theology 364
Developments Within Roman Catholicism 365
The Ecumenical Movement 370

Bultmann: His Method and Its Influence Page
  on New Testament Study 375
   Bultmann's Method 375
   Post-Bultmann Era 377
   Redaction Criticism 377
The Survival and Revival
  of Conservative Theology 378
English Bible Translations 383
Theology at the Beginning of the 1980s 385

GENERAL INTRODUCTION

A. NATURE, SCOPE, METHOD AND DIVISIONS OF THE HISTORY OF DOCTRINE.

The History of Doctrine is a department of Historical Theology. Its concern is to explain the rise and describe the historical development of theological thought. It is still a matter of dispute, whether the History of Doctrine shall close with the completion and symbolical fixation of the ecclesiastical dogma, or delineate the historical processes of doctrinal thought down to the present time. The conception and definition of what constitutes a Christian doctrine will determine the scope of our discipline.

"Doctrine" in the narrower sense of the term and "dogma" coincide in their meaning and may within certain limits be used interchangeably. Dogma is doctrine formally stated and authoritatively laid down by the church. Accordingly the History of Dogma is the record of the gradual development and definite shaping of the contents of Christian faith into doctrinal statements or dogmas. The majority of European writers on our discipline both, Protestant and Catholic, insist on a History of Doctrine, in the strict sense of the term, i. e., a History of Dogma. It traces the gradual development of theological thought from its rise in the post-apostolic age to its final dogmatic formulation. For the Eastern Orthodox Church it closes with the second Council of Nice (787), for the Roman Catholic Church with the Vatican Council (1870), for the Lutheran Church with the Formula of Concord (1580) and for the Reformed Church with the Synod of Dort (1619) and the Westminster Assembly (1649).

"Doctrine" in the broader sense of the term is that which is taught; what is held, put forth as true, or supported by a teacher, a school or a sect. In this sense "doctrine" denotes teaching as distinguished from "dogma" which denotes only such teaching as is part of the confession of the church. Thus we speak of the "doctrines" of the New Testament and the "dogma" of the Trinity. In the present work we use the term "doctrine" both in its narrower and broader sense and therefore give a broader scope to the History of Doctrine. There is doctrinal development also after the fixation of the ecclesiastical dogma, and new theological tendencies which are of signal interest manifest themselves down to the present time. Accordingly, the concern of the History of Doctrine is to present the movement of Christian thought from the birth of Christian theology to its latest phases.

The once customary method of dividing the History of Doctrine into General or Synthetic and Special or Analytic History has been

1

abandoned by all recent European writers on our subject. The General History would exhibit, under successive periods, the history of Christian dogma as a whole, while the Special History, under like divisions, would treat the matter under the topics of Systematic Theology. This method lacks real unity, inevitably involves repetitions and does not admit of a strictly historical treatment of the subject.

In describing the historical development of theological thought the History of Doctrine is very closely connected with the history of the church. We may therefore distinguish four chief periods of our discipline parallel with those of Church History:

I. Rise and Development of Doctrine in the Patristic Age.

II. Preservation, Transformation and Development of Doctrine in the Scholastic Period.

III. Development and Fixation of Doctrine through the Reformation and Counter Reformation.

IV. Aspects of Doctrine in the Modern Era.

But while Church History narrates the external course of controversies, the History of Doctrine is confined to the dogmatic interest and busies itself with the internal process and development of doctrinal controversies. It is not merely the recital of the definitions of the church's doctrine. The mere chronicling of isolated facts is not history at all. The History of Doctrine treats the developing process of the church's doctrine as an internal organism. It forms the historical background of Dogmatics which exhibits the church's doctrine in definite propositions and systematic order.

B. HISTORY OF THE HISTORY OF DOCTRINE.

The discipline of the History of Doctrine is of a comparatively recent date. The ancient church was productive as regards the contents of the doctrinal system, but had a dogmatical rather than historical interest in the development of Christian doctrine. The medieval church merely received the transmitted beliefs as a sacred tradition to be accepted without doubt and reverenced as beyond improvement, and therefore had no real interest in delineating the historical process of the development of dogma. In the Reformation period the great conflict between the Lutheran Reformers and the defenders of the Roman Catholic faith gave rise to polemic theology and necessarily stimulated historical researches into the doctrines of the church. But the investigation of the history of doctrines was not yet effected. It was not till the middle of the seventeenth century that the first genuine attempt to give an account of the historical development of the church's doctrine was made, in a work by the Jesuit scholar, Dionysius Petavius, entitled *De theologicis dogmati-*

bus, Paris, 1643-50, and somewhat later by the Oratorian Thomassin, in his *Dogmata theologica*, 1680-89. In the Lutheran Church the history of the doctrines in dispute was discussed in the *Magdeburg Centuries*, an ecclesiastical history of the first thirteen centuries, and in the great systematic and polemic works of Chemnitz, Gerhard, Quenstadt, in which, however, stress is laid upon the agreement with ecclesiastical antiquity and not upon the historical development of dogma.

The German church historian and biblical critic, J. S. Semler, whom Tholuck pronounced "the father of the history of doctrines," was the first to show in his *Historical Introduction to Baumgarten's Glaubenslehre*, 1762, that the History of Doctrine must be separated from ecclesiastical history. According to Semler our science is merely a historical report of the various subjective opinions that men in various periods entertained concerning the Christian faith. Wilhelm Munscher, influenced by Semler's thought, wrote *Handbuch der christlichen Dogmengeschichte*, 4 vols., 1797-1809, and *Lehrbuch der christlichen DG*, 1811, ff.

Of other works upon our science we mention only the following : Baumgarten-Crusius, *Lehrbuch der christl. DG*, 1832, and *Compendium*, 1840. Applying Hegel's conception of development (thesis, antithesis and synthesis) F. Chr. Baur presented the vast material of our discipline in the form of a naturalistic development. His system, received with enthusiasm in his day, is almost entirely abandoned today. Besides several monographs on particular doctrines, Baur published *Lehrbuch*, 1847, and *Vorlesungen uber die christl. DG.*, 1865-67. A. Neander's *Christl. DG.* was published after his death by J. L. Jacobi in 1857. K. R. Hagenbach's *Lehrbuch der DG.*, 1850, (6th ed. by K. Benrath, 1886), is not a pragmatic history but rather a conglomerate of valuable information upon our subject.

From the standpoint of evangelical Lutheranism are the works of Th. Kliefoth, *Einleitung in die DG.*, 1839; H. Schmid, *Lehrbuch d. DG.*, 1860, ed. 4, revised by Hauck; Kahnis, *Die luth. Dogmatik*, vol. 2, *Der Kirchenglaube, historisch-genetisch dargestellt*, 1864; G. Thomasius, *Die christl. DG.*, 1874-76, new ed. by Bonwetsch and Seeberg, 1886-89. Thomasius makes the Lutheran Confessions the goal of the doctrinal development.

A. Harnack, *Lehrbuch d. DG.*, 1886-90; 1909-10, and *Grundriss d. DG.*, 1893, with strong theological tendencies of the Ritschlian School — maintains that the greatest group of Christian dogmas was "created by the Greek spirit upon the soil of the gospel." The church's dogma was, in the main, completed about 300 A. D., received authoritative recognition in the fourth and fifth centuries and was as such accepted by Roman Catholics, but undermined by a

deeper conception of faith in the Protestant Church. Dogma is
obsolete now and the church today cannot but surrender the ancient
dogma. Fr. Loof's *Leitfaden zum Studium d. DG.*, 1889-1906, is
written from the same general point of view as the work of Harnack.
Reinhold Seeberg, *Lehrbuch d. DG.*, 1913-23, 4 vols., and *Grundriss
d. DG.*, 1901; the pre-eminence of the author in the field of original
research, the conservatism of his views and the lucid presentation
of the subject make Seeberg's *Dogmengeschichte* a work of extra-
ordinary merit. F. Wiegand's *Dogmengeschichte* in two volumes,
1912 and 1919, presents a brief history of the ecclesiastical dogma.

Roman Catholic works, of a more recent date, on the History of
Doctrine are by Klee, *Lehrb. d. DG.*, 2 vols., 1837 ff., and Schwane,
DG., 3 vols., 1862 ff., and 1892 ff., in Germany. In France, Fr.
Bonifas, *Histoire des Dogmes de l'Egl. chret.*, Paris, 1889, and J.
Tixeront, *Histoire des Dogmes*, 3 vols., Paris, 1905 ff. As for Italy
we mention the lectures on the beginnings of Christianity by the
Barnabite scholar Semeria, especially his *Dogma, gerarchia e culto
nella chiesa primitiva*, Roma, 1902. *I Criteri Theologici-La Storia
dei Dommi etc.*, Torino, 1888, by Can. Salvatore di Bartolo, is not a
history, but a rational defence of the Catholic dogma, especially
infallible church, Scripture and tradition; it contains, however, a
store of historical information.

Of American authors we mention *A History of Christian Doctrine*
by William G. T. Shedd, 2 vols., 9th ed., 1889, a discussion of the
leading topics of Christian doctrine down to the Socinian and
Arminian systems, from a Calvinistic point of view. *History of
Christian Doctrine* by Henry C. Sheldon, 2 vols., 4th ed., 1906, and
History of Christian Doctrine by G. P. Fischer, 1896 and 1922, trace
the history of theology down to the present time. *An Outline of
the History of Doctrines* by E. H. Klotsche, 1927, is a brief history of
dogma in the strict sense of the term. Volume I, *Early and Eastern*,
of *A History of Christian Thought* by Arthur Cushman McGiffert,
appeared in March, 1932. In 1933 this was followed by volume II,
The West, from Tertullian to Erasmus. Owing to the author's death
a third volume, to continue the History of Christian Thought, has
not appeared.

English translations: Hagenbach, *Textbook of the History of
Doctrines*, transl. by H. B. Smith, 2 vols., 1861; also in Clark's
Foreign Theol. Library, 3 vols., 1880. Neander, *Lectures on the
History of Chr. Dogmas*, transl. by J. E. Ryland, 2 vols., 1882.
Harnack, *History of Dogma*, transl. by Neil Buchanan, 7 vols.,
London, 1895-1900; and *Outlines of the History of Dogma*, transl.
by Edw. K. Mitchell, New York, 1893. Seeberg, *Text-Book of the
History of Doctrines*, transl. by Charles E. Hay, complete in two
volumes, 1905.

HISTORICAL INTRODUCTION

A. THE GENTILE BACKGROUND OF EARLY CHRISTIANITY.

The incarnation of the Son of God for the salvation of the human race marks the central point in the history of mankind (Gal. 4:4). The whole course of previous preparation, both for Jew and Gentile, was completed with this great event. To sketch briefly and only in outline this process of preparation is the purpose of this Introduction. The historical study of Christian doctrine requires chiefly acquaintance with the great religious and intellectual movements and their preparatory or disturbing influences on Christianity. Here we must assume a thorough knowledge of the history of religion and philosophy upon the part of the reader. Acquaintance with the great philosophical and religious movements immediately preceding the Christian era is necessary, if we are to understand Christ's message and his mission. A careful study of the religious and intellectual state of both, Gentile and Jew, in its relation to early Christianity will also enable us to state precisely the extent of Hellenizing and Judaizing influence upon Christian beliefs.

I. At the time when Christianity had its birth and first triumphs *the religion of Greece and Rome* was exceedingly varied. It embraced everything from the most subtle mystic speculations of the Orient down to the crassest forms of indigenous superstitions. The fabrications of pagan superstition and idolatry pervaded every department of life (see I Cor. 8 and 10; Acts 17; I John 5:21). And yet in the midst of all the strange cults and absurd superstitions there is to be noted, especially in the last days of the Roman republic, a longing for deliverance from the existing state of turmoil and confusion, and even the expectation of a deliverer, some great king, or savior-god, who is to bring in a new era of peace and happiness. However, the kingdom of peace that was to come was conceived of as a kingdom of this world and the expected savior should deliver his people from all the distress of the present time. In the Augustan age this savior-god was seen primarily in the Roman emperor, and the deliverance hoped for was a deliverance not from moral but from physical evil; hence the ever-growing significance of the temples of Asclepius, the god of healing.

II. In contradistinction to the indigenous cults the Oriental religions, especially those of ancient Iran, seemed to satisfy the religious cravings of many. We mention here particularly that religion in which we note striking points of contact with the religion of the Bible, *Zoroastrianism*. It is true, Zoroaster's religion is a dualism, teaching that Ormazd, the god of light and goodness, carries on a ceaseless war against Ahriman and the hosts of evil spirits who

dwell in the darkness. But it must also be admitted that no other
ethnic religion has so clearly grasped the ideas of guilt and merit,
good and evil. Nowhere else among the ethnic religions do we
notice such a sure hope of a final triumph of moral goodness over
the moral evils in the world. On the works of men here on earth a
strict reckoning will be held with punishment for the wicked and
reward for the good. Ahriman and all evil spirits and wicked men
shall be cast into hell for an age-long punishment, while the "good
kingdom" will be established in heaven and on earth. Besides belief in a future judgment, separation of the righteous from the
wicked, immortality, heaven and hell, devil and demons, we find
in Zoroastrianism also the idea of a future savior; in fact, there will
be three saviors, each appearing at an interval of a thousand years
and each born of a virgin mother.

III. The similarity of pagan ideas to Christian beliefs is still
more obvious in the so-called *mystery religions*. These appealed
mightily to the deeper religious feelings of a world-weary humanity.
They not only fixed attention upon the great problems suggested by
the enigma of death, future life, deliverance from the present world,
need of purification, considered an offended deity, but actually
seemed to offer a solution. In the mystery religions the intellectual
apprehension of a supposed truth was aided by the mysteries which
interpreted the secret meaning of that truth, lifted the soul above
the world in the experience of salvation and initiated into the region
of divine wonders. Through secret rites or mysteries the "mystes"
(literally "one whose eyes are closed") or "initiate" was led to the
vision of the unseen and spiritual, to a direct union with God. The
mysteries were means of salvation, some of which resembled the
Christian sacraments. Besides purification ceremonies and sacramental rites we hear in the mystic cults also of a man-god incarnate,
his suffering, death and resurrection. The *Hilaria*, which commem-
orated the death and resurrection of Attis, were celebrated March
25, i. e., about the time of our Easter.

We have briefly sketched some of the theories and practices of
the pagan religions and mystery cults. That there is an apparent
similarity of these to Christian beliefs and usages cannot be denied,
and the conclusion has been drawn that Christianity is a syncretistic
religion and that it did not gradually become such during the early
centuries of the Christian era, but was syncretistic from its very
beginning. Here, however, a few questions arise, which must be
answered. Those, who hold that the chief doctrines and practices
of Christianity were inspired by the mysteries or modelled on Gentile originals, have never answered, or even attempted to answer,
these questions: If the Christian dogma was "created by the Greek

spirit upon the soil of the gospel," if Christianity is merely a religion among others, the same thing only under a different name, how shall we explain the fact that Christianity as a religion overcame and triumphed over all other religions? If Christianity is a syncretistic religion, how do we explain the fact that its adherents everywhere and always were fully conscious of being altogether different from the adherents of other religions? If Christianity does not essentially differ from other religions, how is it that it came in conflict not only with the established religion of the Roman empire, but with every other religion as well, and within three centuries had driven them all from the field? Wherein lies the overcoming power of Christianity? Certainly not in that which it has in common with other religions, but in that in which it essentially differs from them.

Both, Christianity and the Gentile religions, promise a salvation. But here, man's salvation is God's work alone, and there, it is man's own achievement. Here, man is by nature sinful, unclean, lost, hopelessly lost; there, man is by nature good, divine, and capable of making himself worthy of communion with the deity. Here, it is a gracious God who goes after the lost; there, it is man who approaches the deity after having purified himself. Here, it is God who forgives sin; there, it is man who purifies and cleanses himself. The idea that God forgives sin, that he "cleanseth us from all unrighteousness," and thus removes the barrier which separates man from God, was absolutely foreign to the Greek mind. The end and purpose of the Christian sacrament is stated in these words: "for the forgiveness of sins," and he who feels and knows his own unworthiness is a worthy recipient of the sacrament. But a mystery for the forgiveness of sins would have been an absurdity to the Greek mind. The mystes had to purify himself before he was admitted to the vision of the *sacra*. And as far as the similarity of the savior-god is concerned, the difference likewise outweighs by far the similarity. In the mysteries we have a "Passion-Play," a seeming suffering and death of some mythical being. In the Christian religion we deal with realities, with an actual suffering and death of a person who really lived, suffered and died. The same is true as to the alleged resurrection of the savior-gods of the mystery religions.

Whatever may be the explanation as to the similarity of Gentile ideas to Christian beliefs, this can be said with certainty that the alleged Gentile elements in Christianity did not affect its nature. In the New Testament neither Christ, nor Paul, nor any of the evangelists or apostles, have ever mentioned, or alluded to, the mystery religions. The eating of meat offered in sacrifice to idols, to which Paul refers in I Cor. 8, has nothing to do with the mysteries. To maintain that Paul's Christianity was inspired by, and modelled on, the mystery religions is absurd. The apostle knew himself to be in opposition to Jew and Gentile alike. His message, Christ the crucified, was a stumbling-block to the Jews and sheer folly to the Greeks.

IV. The thinking and educated, who were aware of the falsehood and folly of the popular religion, betook themselves to various systems of *Greek philosophy,* in which they believed they found an explanation of the universe around them and a true guide to human life. In a corrupted and effeminate age many, no doubt, received a high moral impulse in the popular philosophy of Stoicism which developed some of the noblest characters that the heathen world had known. The Stoic held that virtue is the only good. Virtue consists in living according to nature, i. e., according to divine reason in which all men participate, for all have God in themselves; cf. Paul's quotation from the Stoic poet Aratus, Acts 17 : 28, "we are his offspring." The human soul, a part of God, is imprisoned in the body and will finally be returned to that universal soul from whence it sprang. Since the world is the work of divine wisdom, permeated by the divine spirit and governed by divine law, it is man's duty to conform freely to whatever destiny may be his. Even moral evil is necessary to the establishment of consonance with the law of nature. In case of necessity man may terminate an existence which has missed its aim. On the one hand, the religious ethical system of Stoicism presents one of the noblest creeds devised by unassisted human reason; on the other hand, some of its leading tenets were not less pernicious than erroneous, taking away the strongest motives to virtue.

The profoundest and noblest philosophical system of all was Platonism. Plato, usually reckoned the greatest thinker in the province of philosophy, discovered whatever the mere light of nature could reveal, and tended, in some sense, to prepare men's minds for Christianity. No heathen taught a purer conception of God than Plato did. God is the one supreme being, perfect, self-existent, self-sufficient, infinitely good, and the author of good only. He made the world because he is good. "Free from all envy he desired that all things should be as like himself as possible" (Timaeus, 30, A). Wherever Plato speaks of gods in the plural, he has in mind inferior deities who possess immortality as derived from the Supreme God. Man's nature is akin to deity and capable of bringing himself as far as he can into harmony with God. Man's soul is immortal. Before it came into the body it preexisted in the being of God. There is to be a future state of retribution.

The teachings of Plato, however approaching to truth and perfection, are not without serious defects and imperfections. With all the perfections which the Platonists ascribed to the deity, they held that it was confined to a certain place. Evil originated in matter which is possessed of invincible malignity and corruption, which even divine power has not been able to reduce entirely to order. It must be gotten rid of by bodily mortification. Sin is the result of ignorance, a state of infirmity or disease in the soul, rather than one of radical corruption and positive guilt. By successive transmigrations on earth and suffering in purgatory the soul is purged from sin and prepared for a happy future life. There is no resurrection of the body. It is only by death of the body that the soul can arrive at its perfection.

Besides the high and noble philosophies of Stoicism and Platonism we would mention here Epicureanism with its atheistic and materialistic tendency, and the Middle Academy of the second and third centuries B. C. with its infidelity and skepticism. The Epicureans taught that happiness or pleasure is the chief good and the only possible end of rational action. Fatalism is rejected. Man can control himself, and the life of pleasure to be genuine must be a life of prudence, honor and justice. The soul is mortal. The gods, if they exist, neither do nor can extend their providential care to human affairs. On the basis of the uncertainty of human knowledge the skeptics questioned the existence of the gods, the immortality of the soul, and the superiority of virtue to vice. Christian writers of the early centuries not infrequently used the arguments of the skeptics to prove the unreliability of human reason and the necessity of a revelation for any valid knowledge.

The state of mind which these various philosophical systems had produced may be characterized as confusion and uncertainty together with a yearning for truth and assurance. These philosophies were more or less the attempts of thinkers seeking God, "if haply they might feel after him, and find him" (Acts 17:27). At the same time they revealed the practical truth that "the world by wisdom knew not God" (1 Cor. 1:21).

B. The Jewish Background of Early Christianity.

I. *Palestinian Judaism.* After the cessation of prophecy the observance of the Law, both in divine worship and in daily life, became a most important factor in the development of Judaism. The exile with its great sufferings had taken away from Israel its former inclination toward idolatry. It was its strict adherence to the law that now preserved Israel, surrounded by paganism, from pagan contamination. Nevertheless there came a deep spiritual decline. Especially since the Maccabean wars Israel's observance of the law degenerated into pure legalism and formalism. The sect of the Pharisees aimed at keeping Israel separate from the surrounding heathenism, and its own members from everything defiling. To this end they enjoined upon the people the strictest observance of the Mosaic law and the "halacha," or "the traditions of the elders"— the Jewish oral laws supplementing or explaining the law of the Scriptures. The halachic interpretation (midrash) developed into an elaborate artificial system in which the spirit of the law was frequently sacrificed and great weight attached to the performance of rites and ceremonies and punctilious attention to matters of outward conduct. Through this external observance, the Pharisees held, man is made righteous before God. Under the influence of the Pharisaic system with its lack of a real consciousness of sin, its righteousness of dead works, its narrow-minded pride of nationality and its carnal anticipations of Messianic times the Jews rejected their true Messiah.

The pronounced opponents of the Pharisees were the Sadducees — so called perhaps from Zadok, the supposed founder of the sect, or from "zaddikim", "the righteous." They were composed largely of the priestly aristocracy, whereas the Pharisees were drawn mainly from the ranks of the common people. They were politically and doctrinally opposed to the Pharisees. They sympathized with the Romans and the Herodians and were not beloved by the people; they had influence only among the wealthy classes. They rejected the traditions of the elders to which the Pharisees attached supreme importance. The Sadducees regarded as binding only the written law of Moses. They denied the resurrection of the body, future rewards and punishments, and the existence of angels and spirits. While the Pharisees accentuated God's preordination, the Sadducees postulated the freedom of the will. Man is the master of his own destiny. The Sadducees were hostile toward Christ and his apostles. It is nowhere explicitly stated that any of them joined the early church. After the destruction of Jerusalem they disappear from history.

A third sect, the Essenes, (the derivation of the name is uncertain) were a sort of monastic order among the Jews of Palestine from the second century B. C. to the second century A. D. They had in common with the Pharisees their veneration for Moses and the law, their strict observance of the Sabbath and rites of purification, and their tendency toward fatalism. Hence some consider Essenism as a pure product of the Jewish mind. There are, however, elements in Essenism which can be explained only from extra-Jewish, probably Phythagorean or Oriental influences. The sect was organized on a rigid communistic basis and practiced the strictest asceticism, abstaining from marriage and despising riches no less than pleasure. According to Josephus they addressed their ancient prayers to the sun "as if they made a supplication for its rising."

They also repudiated animal sacrifices and animal food and elected their own priests.

It has been maintained that there are certain striking traits in common between the Essenes and the early Christians as, for example, the community of goods and abstention from marriage. But holding property in common was with the early Christians a matter of Christian liberty, whereas it was compulsory with the Essenes. The same is true in regard to celibacy. Moreover, Josephus states that the Essenes renounced marriage, because they had a low opinion of the character of women. Paul (I Cor. 7:25 ff.) recommends celibacy "by reason of the present distress," and regards a single life as in itself better and happier only if the individual possesses the same gift for it which the apostle had (ib. 1:7 ff.). There are, however, obvious points of resemblance between Essenism and medieval monasticism, as the novitiate, obedience to the superior of the order, communicating to none the secrets of the order, celibacy, community of goods, strict observance of all rules relative to fasting, working, and religious exercises. Foakes-Jackson, in his *History of the Christian Church*, 8th ed., 1927, p. 12 f. presents a striking comparison of the three Jewish sects: "The object of the Sadducee was to conform himself to the world, that of the Pharisee to live in yet separated from it; but the Essene introduced a new principle destined to have a very powerful influence on the subsequent development of Christianity. His ideal was to form a Kingdom of God isolated from the world."

From the fact that Jesus often attacked the Pharisees and Sadducees, but never the Essenes, it has been inferred that Jesus himself was an Essene. This, however, is mere conjecture and belongs to the realm of unfounded hypothesis.

Besides the three religious parties described above, there were groups of pious individualists who cultivated the Messianic hope of Israel. With a pessimistic estimate of self and the universe, and with no faith in the present, they were constantly looking forward to the consolation of Israel and the coming of the kingdom of God. They aimed to solve the difficulties connected with the righteousness of God and the suffering condition of his righteous servants on earth, and comfort the faithful by prefiguring the future triumph of the Messianic kingdom in which the poor and the outcast would share equally with the great ones of the land. Their literature begins about 250 B. C. and continues to 100 A. D. It consists of the so-called *Apocalyptic Writings,* the more important of which are: *Baruch, Enoch, Ascension of Isaiah, Book of Jubilees, Assumption of Moses, Testaments of the Twelve Patriarchs, Fourth Book of Esdras, Sibylline Oracles* — a medley of fragmentary poems, Jewish and

Christian, containing visions, and polemics against polytheism, *Psalms of Solomon*, and *Odes of Solomon* discovered recently and published by J. Rendel Harris, in 1909.

II. *The Jewish Diaspora*. While Palestinian Judaism has its important place in New Testament history, the Jewish Diaspora must not be overlooked. Numerous synagogues existed outside of Jerusalem and among the Jews of the Diaspora. In Acts 15 : 21 it appears that they had existed for many generations "in every city." The synagogue in the Diaspora filled a greater place in the communal life than the synagogue on Palestinian soil, for there the temple enjoyed a predominant position. The synagogue became the centre of prayer and worship with reading and explanation of the law and instruction in the prophetic word and in history. Through its missionary influence upon a great number of Gentiles the synagogue in the Diaspora proved of great use to the church. The proselytes of righteousness, who had accepted the Jewish faith, and the "God-fearers" who were accustomed to monotheistic ideas, morally trained, and familiar with the promises of the Old Testament, were well prepared for the reception of the gospel which offered fulfillment in place of promise. Besides the great number of synagogues the Greek translation of the Old Testament, the Septuagint, offered the heathen who cared for it, an opportunity of becoming personally acquainted with the peculiar character of Judaism.

At the same time the Jews of the Diaspora were necessarily influenced by their Gentile neighbors. The multitude of exiles who had planted themselves permanently in Babylonia maintained more intimate fellowship with the exclusive Rabbinism in Palestine, but in the countries to the West, Asia Minor and especially Egypt, where the Jewish population was thickest, we notice a curious blend of Judaism and Greek culture. Most of the Jews in Alexandria and its neighborhood so far forgot Hebrew that the Old Testament had to be translated into Greek. And with the language of Hellas they appropriated much of Hellenic culture with the result that Judaism of Diaspora, i. e., Hellenistic Judaism, became a type by itself distinctly different from Palestinian Judaism. It is true, the Jews of the Diaspora amid Gentile surroundings held fast to their Judaism and regarded their faith in one holy God, his promises to them, and above all their law, as superior to all earthly wisdom, but they were ready to give up some Jewish customs, some religious usages and ceremonies, and came to lay more and more stress on the moral side of their religion as expounded by the prophets in particular.

About the middle of the second century B. C. there arose at Alexandria a peculiar type of Jewish theology, a combination of Judaism and Greek philosophy. One of the earliest of the Jewish-

Alexandrine philosophers, who aimed to reconcile and identify Greek philosophical conceptions with Old Testament teaching, was Aristobulus (c. 160 B. C.), of whose philosophical commentary on the Pentateuch fragments have been preserved by Clement of Alexandria, Eusebius and other Christian writers. A notable monument of Hellenistic Judaism is the apocryphal book called *The Wisdom of Solomon.* The author, a Greek-speaking philosopher, influenced by Plato and the Stoics, presents true wisdom as it were an hypostasis beside God: Wisdom is a breathing of the power of God, an effulgence of his glory; it works, orders and renews all things (c. VII-IX).

The leading exponent of the Jewish Alexandrine religious philosophy was Philo, a contemporary of Christ (b. about 20 B. C., d. about 42 A. D.). He taught that God is an abstract Being, comprehending all, yet uncomprehended, without quality and movement. Accordingly there is a wide gap between God and matter. But between God and matter there is an intermediate world (corresponding to Plato's world of ideas) consisting of innumerable mediating potencies, either personal beings, such as angels and demons, or active powers, ideas, or self-revelations of God. All intermediate entities are comprehended in the divine *Logos* or Reason of God. He proceeds from God whereas all mediating beings proceed from the *Logos.* He is the instrumentality, through which the world was made. The Philonic *Logos* is not the Word or *Logos* of the fourth Gospel. Following the Stoic doctrine of God as the *Logos* or Reason operative in the world Philo does not conceive of the *Logos* as a person, nor as bearing any relation to the Messiah, nor as becoming incarnate.

Like his doctrine of God and matter, Philo's doctrine of man is strictly dualistic, and is mainly derived from Plato. Man's higher soul came from the creative, living breath of God pure, untainted by sin, but his lower soul as well as his body, were the creation of several angelic potencies or demiurges, and subject to the possibility of sinning. Accordingly the body is a prison and a fountain of sin and all evils. Salvation is, therefore, deliverance from bodily appetites and sense-perception. The supreme end of man's ethical development is the ecstatic vision of God. To attain this end man needs the assistance of God without whom he cannot walk in the ways of wisdom and virtue.

All this Philo deduces from the Scriptures by the allegoric method of exegesis. The dualism of his system is also seen in his method of interpreting the Scriptures. In them he notices a double sense, the literal or immediate sense, fit only for the weaker minds, and the allegorical or mediate sense, open only to cultured believers.

The literal sense is the outer integument which the allegorical sense penetrates and fills as the soul does the body. Allegorical interpretation was used already by Aristobulus with the purpose of putting upon the Old Testament teachings, especially the anthropomorphic utterances about God, a sense which would appeal even to Greek readers. It had also been practiced in the rabbinical schools of Palestine before Plato's date.

Philo's literary labors show us a systematic attempt to harmonize Greek culture with Jewish faith. This end and object Philo did not attain. Nevertheless, his religious philosophy was of far-reaching significance for Christianity and exerted a profound influence upon the early Christian theology.

C. The Early Christian Proclamation.

The teaching of our Lord and his apostles constitutes the authentic source of Christian doctrine. A close investigation of this teaching enables us to distinguish several types of doctrine under which the systems of the New Testament writings may be discussed. There is the Teaching of Jesus according to the Synoptists and according to John; then there is the Petrine and Pauline and Johannine type of doctrine. It is the concern of New Testament Theology to investigate, in a purely historical manner, the forms of doctrine of each single writer of the New Testament, and clearly to set them forth in their unity and harmony. The History of Doctrine is concerned not so much with the variety of the Biblical forms of teaching as with the elements which are common to all New Testament writers and from which the later doctrines of the church have been derived and by which they have been established.

The elements which constitute the common basis of the New Testament doctrine may be summarized as follows:

The central point of the initial teaching of our Lord is described in general as "the gospel"— glad tidings —"the gospel of God," or "the gospel of the kingdom of God" or "of heaven." These designations of the kingdom imply that it is not a product of development from below, but has its origin in the world above. It is a gift of God, not an achievement of man. The founder of the kingdom of God is the promised Messiah, the Christ who appears on the scene of his ministry with the message: "The kingdom of heaven is at hand." He is not only the founder of the kingdom of God but its very foundation. He does not only proclaim the truth and show the way of life to men: He is the way, the truth, and the life, the living embodiment of God's saving truth. As the "Word," the divine Logos, he revealed and declared the Father's will. He came not to destroy, but to fulfill the law and the prophets. But the tradition of the elders he rejected. As the only begotten Son of God he has ever been and ever remains the object of the Father's love and the sharer of his nature, majesty and work. Accordingly he lays claim to a homage and reverence, which without idolatry cannot be rendered to any creature. With the testimony of Jesus himself agrees the testimony of the apostles. To them Jesus is nothing less than God incarnate. The entrance of the divine Son of God into the world to take upon himself our nature could not but be supernatural. He is not the son of a man, but "the Son of Man"—a favorite self-designation of Jesus indicating not merely his perfect humanity but emphasizing in contrast with his present humiliation his heavenly nature and origin and his future glory. His vicarious living and dying has the definite aim of redeeming humanity from the guilt and dominion of sin and thereby restoring to man the fellowship with God which he had forfeited through the disobedience of the first Adam. His triumphant rising from the death, thus vicariously endured, is the divine evidence that his death was the means of our reconciliation with God. After his going to the Father he exercises his unlimited power from on high for the salvation of men, imparting to them life and righteousness and gathering them into the kingdom of God. In the Holy Ghost, who is clearly distinguished from the Son as well as from the Father, Christ comes and remains ever with his own until in the consummation of the ages he shall be revealed in yet higher glory.

Conditions of entrance into the kingdom are a definite change of mind, a break with the sinful past, i. e., repentance together with faith as the consciousness of the divine authority and power of Christ. This is to be ratified by submission to the rite of baptism which is described as the new birth "of water and of the spirit" or "the washing of regeneration." Accordingly men become children of God, "sons of God" in the higher, spiritual sense, not directly, but through their relation to Jesus himself. "As many as received him, to them gave he power to become the sons of God, even to them that believe on his name" (John 1:12). They are justified before God by faith without the deeds of the law. Justifying faith is not merely intellectual belief, but the renewal of heart, a new relation between God and man. Renewal of heart which manifests itself in love to God and men marks the character of the members of the kingdom. They form together a spiritual community, living Christ's life over again. And in that community "there is neither Greek nor Jew, circumcision nor uncircumcision, Barbarian, Scythian, bond nor free: but Christ is all and in all" (Col. 3:11).

The Old Testament writings are acknowledged as the divinely inspired Scriptures. The words of Christ together with the teachings of the apostles are of binding authority. By baptism all believers are being separated from the heathen and Jewish world and closely united to their Lord and to each other. By the ever new proclamation of his death in the Supper of the Lord they evermore continue their fellowship with him and with one another.

The blessings of salvation begin here and are completed in the future with the coming of the Lord. This will be followed by the resurrection of the dead, the universal judgment, and an irrevocable decision on the last day. Then the children of darkness will be forever separated from the righteous and receive a just retribution, and the tried fidelity of the subjects of the kingdom will be recompensed with the full reward of grace.

FIRST PERIOD

ORIGINATION AND DEVELOPMENT OF DOCTRINE IN THE PATRISTIC AGE

CHAPTER I

THE CONCEPTION OF CHRISTIANITY ACCORDING TO THE WRITINGS OF THE APOSTOLIC FATHERS

A. The written testimony of the early ecclesiastical teachers are the *Writings of the Apostolic Fathers,* who were, or may reasonably be supposed to have been, the personal associates of the apostles or of those who had been taught by the original apostles. Their writings are as follows :

1. *The First Epistle of Clement* is an official communication from the Roman congregation to the church at Corinth, written about 97 by Clement of Rome who was according to tradition one of the first bishops of Rome and a disciple of Peter. The occasion of the epistle was a dissension at Corinth; its object, to restore harmony to the divided church.

2. *The Shepherd of Hermas* (so called, because the angel of repentance in the form and habit of a shepherd is the leading character in the book) appeared in Rome, according to the ancient tradition, about 140-145. It is divided into five Visions, twelve Mandates and ten Similitudes. Its main object is to call the church to repentence; hence numerous exhortations of a moral sort are given, such as warnings against impurity and love of pleasure, and against apsotasy in the present times.

3. An *Epistle* from Alexandria in Egypt bears the name of *Barnabas;* its date has been much debated (70; 96-98; 117-118). That it was written after the destruction of Jerusalem and the temple, is evident from chapter 16 of the epistle, which alludes to that event, and before the second devastation and reconstruction under Hadrian (120). Its central problem is the relation of Judaism to Christianity. In its spirit it is strongly anti-Judaistic going even so far as to deny any historical connection between the two.

Its method is extremely Alexandrine. The contents of the book as well as its language suggest that the writer was not Barnabas, Paul's fellow-apostle, but possibly some unknown namesake of Paul's companion, probably a converted Jew from Alexandria.

4. The most famous of the Apostolic Fathers is *Ignatius,* the martyr Bishop of Antioch, and yet very little is known of his life except its noble ending. Our trustworthy information is chiefly derived from the letters which he wrote about 110 on his journey from Antioch to Rome where he suffered martyrdom. Six of them were addressed to various churches, to the Ephesians, Magnesians, Trallians, Romans, Philadelphians, Smyrnians; one of them to Polycarp. These *Seven Epistles of Ignatius* are now, after long and sharp contests, pronounced genuine. They are a testimony to the unity of the church analogous to the unity of the divine and human in Christ, and visibly exhibited, so it is held by Ignatius, in the episcopate.

17

5. The date of the *Epistle of Polycarp* of Smyrna, a disciple of the apostle John, depends upon the date of the Ignatian letters which Polycarp mentions in his epistle (13). It is now generally fixed between 112-118. The epistle was written to the Philippians to accompany the transmission of those Ignatian letters which Polycarp had in his hands.

6. *The Exposition of the Oracles of the Lord* in five books published by *Papias*, Bishop of Hierapolis, about 125, is known only through a few scanty fragments in later writers, chiefly Irenaeus and Eusebius.

7. *The Didache or Teaching of the Twelve*, was written about 100-120, probably in Alexandria. Its only Greek manuscript of 1056 was discovered in 1873 by the Greek bishop Philotheos Bryennios, in the library of the Jerusalem Monastery in Phanar, the Greek quarter of Constantinople, and published by the discoverer in 1883. The book divides itself into three parts. The first part (1-6) — ethical — contains a body of catechetical instructions in Christian conduct, treated under the scheme of Two Ways, the way of life and the way of death. The second part (7-15) — disciplinary — treats of church ritual and discipline. The third part (16) — eschatological — sounds a solemn warning to watchfulness in view of the second coming of Christ.

8. The so-called *Second Epistle of Clement* is not really an epistle, but a moral instruction or homily, probably delivered in Corinth; it is the earliest extant Christian homily by an unknown author, about 150.

9. Of the so-called *Praedicatio Petri* (110-130), a spurious work, only fragments are extant.

B. These writings furnish us an insight into the faith of the Christian church between A. D. 90-150. Their doctrinal contents form the starting point for the presentation of the History of Doctrine. The following is a *Summary Account of the Doctrinal Contents* of these writings.

The Apostolic Fathers affirm their belief in the One God, the Creator of the world. He is almighty and merciful, Lord and Father; "the Unseen but beholding all things; uncreated, who made all things by the word of his power; needing nothing, whom all things need and for whom they exist" (Praed. Petri in Clem. Al. strom. 6:5); who takes up his abode in the hearts of his chosen people, the Christians, and guides their lives (Magn. 1; Eph. 3:11; Smyrn. 4; Barnabas 16).

Christ, the Son of God, was with the Father before the creation of the world (Barn. 5). Hermas expressly asserts the personal preexistence of the Son before the incarnation (Sim. 9:12), although elsewhere he identifies the pre-existent divine nature of the Son of God with the Holy Ghost (ib. 5:6; 9:1). Harnack maintains that Hermas here gives "clear-expression" to Adoptionist theology. Like Hermas, the writer of the Sec. Ep. of Clement identifies Christ with the Holy Ghost (9:5). In the rather obscure, probably interpolated passage (14) he assumes the premundane existence of Christ and the Holy Spirit, but seems to regard them as creatures of the Father. The center of Ignatius' theology is Christ as God Incarnate. "There is One God who manifested himself through Jesus Christ his

Son" (Magn. 8). The union of the divine and human natures is expressed in the strongest possible way : "There is only one physician, of flesh and of spirit, generate and ingenerate, God in man, true Life in death, Son of Mary and Son of God, first passible and then impassible, Jesus Christ our Lord" (Eph. 7). Against the Docetae, who held that Christ's body was merely a phantom or appearance, Ignatius laid great emphasis on the reality of the humanity of Christ. Even after the resurrection he was in the flesh (Smyrn. 1-3). We further notice that Ignatius is the first writer outside the New Testament to assert that Christ was born of a virgin, for he describes "the three great mysteries of Christianity" as "the virginity of Mary and her child-bearing and likewise also the death of the Lord" (Eph. 19). These three mysteries are said to be "hidden from the prince of this world" (ib.). We have here, no doubt, the germ of the later doctrine of the deception of Satan. Like Ignatius, Polycarp emphasizes against the Docetae the reality of Christ's humanity; "every one who shall not confess that Jesus Christ is come in the flesh, is antichrist" (7).

In connection with the baptismal formula and otherwise the Apostolic Fathers use the designation of God as Father, Son, and Holy Ghost, but make no attempt distinctly to discriminate between the person of the Holy Ghost and that of the Father and the Son.

The mission of the Son of God is man's purification from sin (Hermas, Sim. 5:6). At the same time Christ is preeminently regarded as law giver and teacher of divine knowledge (ib. and 2 Clem. 3:1, 4; 17:1). Our redemption is effected through his blood which brought the grace of repentence to the whole world (1 Clem.). Clement does not grasp the saving efficacy of Christ's death in its full Biblical significance (see c. 36). According to Barnabas Christ appeared in the flesh and suffered upon the cross to the end "that he might destroy death and show forth the resurrection of the dead," but especially "that we might be sanctified by the remission of sins" (5). In no other post-apostolic writing has the Pauline doctrine of atonement been so faithfully reproduced as in this epistle. Ignatius' conception of Christ's mission is closely related to the Johannine doctrinal type. Christ became man in order to reveal God to men, "for Christ is the mind *gnosis,* of the Father" (Eph. 3) and "his word, *logos,* (Magn. 8), and to establish "the newness of everlasting life" through "the abolition of death" (Eph. 19). Our life has its origin in the death of Christ (Magn. 9). Christ is our life not only in that he brought eternal life to men, but in that he personally dwells in the believer as the life-giving power (Eph. 3:11; Magn. 1: Smyrn. 4). He dwells in us; we are his temples; he is in us as our God (Eph. 15). Accordingly Ignatius calls himself Theophoros, "a God-bearer," and the Ephesians "God-bearers," "temple-bearers," "Christ-bearers," "bearers of the Holy One."

In the Catholic church Ignatius sees the continuation of the mystery of the incarnation. The church exhibits under earthly conditions the indwelling of God and Christ in her. Ignatius is the first known writer to employ the term "catholic church." "Wherever Christ is, there is the catholic church" (Smyr. 8). Ignatius has here in mind not the individual congregation but the church universal comprising all churches founded and instructed by the apostles in person. But the individual congregation is a copy of the church universal. What the apostles are to the church universal that are the presbyters to the individual congregation. The presbyters are types of the apostles (Trall. 2:3; Magn. 2:6: Eph. 6), while the bishop is "a type of the Father" (Trall. 2), or of "the Lord himself" (Eph. 6). As the universal church has Christ as its center, so the individual congregation has its center in the bishop. Ignatius lays great stress upon the function of the episcopate. He does not refer to the episcopate as a universal office, but as a center of unity for the local church. The ideal of church unity can be attained only by due respect for "the bishop and the presbytery and the deacons" (Philad. 7). "Be obedient to the bishop and to one another . . . that there may be union of flesh and of spirit" (Magn. 13). Second, Clement sets forth a peculiar view of the relation between Christ and the church, a relation which the Gnostic Valentine would have styled a *syzygy*. Alongside of the premundane spiritual being, Christ, there stands a kind of feminine aeon, the church, which is spiritual, which was created before the sun and the moon. Christ and the church form a spiritual entity. "The male is Christ and the female is the church" (14). The Apostolic Fathers distinguish sharply between the Christian church and Judaism which represents an antiquated stage of development. Writing to the church of Magnesia, Ignatius says: "If even unto this day we live after the manner of Judaism, we avow that we have not received grace (8). It is monstrous to talk of Jesus Christ and to practice Judaism, for Christianity did not believe in Judaism, but Judaism in Christianity" (10). Ignoring altogether the progressive method of God's dealing with his people and the historical development of the plan of salvation Barnabas maintains that the Christians are the only true covenant people and that the covenant with Israel was never really concluded (4:14). In his mystical allegorical interpretation of typical Jewish institutions he goes so far as to say that the explanation and observation of the Mosaic law by the apostate people are mere errors caused by "an evil angel" (9).

Salvation is applied to men by Baptism as a means for the forgiveness of sins, the Word of God as the message of salvation, and the Eucharist (Didache 7) as a means to immortality. Ignatius describes the Eucharist as "the flesh of our Savior Jesus Christ, which flesh suffered for our sins" (Smyrn. 6) and styles the Eucharistic bread "the medicine of immortality and the antidote that we should not die" (Eph. 20). The Didache designates the Eucharist as "spiritual food and drink" (10).

Faith, which is knowledge of God and confidence in him, apprehends salvation. The Pauline idea of Justification by faith and the inner relation of faith and works is generally obscured in the writing of the Apostolic Fathers. Faith marks only the first step. This must be followed by the moral development of the individual. In First Clement we notice a blending of Paul's doctrine of faith and James' doctrine of works, while Second Clement repeatedly and emphatically declares that good works are necessary to salvation. Barnabas (2) holds the same view. Sin forgiven in Baptism remains in man as a power. But there is forgiveness even for the gravest sins after Baptism, except apostasy (Hermas, Sim. 9:19) which is to be followed by a new conversion (ib. 31). We notice here the starting point of the later Catholic discrimination between venial and mortal sins. The relation of faith and good works is also here very imperfectly understood. Eternal life is given as a reward for doing God's will (ib. 5:1; 6:1; 8:2; Mand. 4:2). Hermas teaches not only the merit of good works, but also works of supererogation (Sim. 5:3). In martyrdom he sees a sin-atoning virtue (Vis. 3:2: Sim. 9:28). He ascribes extra merit to celibacy, though he allows second marriage (Mand. 4:1, 4). In this passage as well as in Sim. 5:3 — "if thou do any good thing outside the commandment of God thou shalt win for thyself more exceeding glory"— we have an allusion to the later doctrine of the evangelical counsels. The writer of the Didache conveys implicitly the same idea: "If thou art able to bear the whole yoke of the Lord, thou shalt be perfect; but if thou are not able, do that which thou art able" (6). He quotes with approval, as also does Barnabas (19), the counsel: "If thou hast ought passing through thy hands, thou shalt give a ransom for thy sins" (4).

The end of all things is thought to be very near. The Son of God, our eternal Highpriest, now exalted at the right hand of the Father, will come as judge of the quick and the dead (Polyc. 2; 6; 12). There will be a resurrection of the body and "in this body we shall receive our reward" (2 Clem. 9:1, 5). Those who disobeyed Christ's commandments (6:7), or "denied him by their words or their deeds" shall be "punished with grievous torments in unquenchable fire" (17:7), while the righteous" shall have rejoicing throughout a sorrowless eternity" (19:4). The idea of the final judgment must be for Christians a strong motive to keep the commandments and cling to the fellowship of the church (Barn. 1; 4; 21). Before the end lies the millennial kingdom which Barnabas and especially Papias picture in glowing colors. We have it also on the authority of Eusebius (Hist. eccl. III. 39, 12) that Papias maintained the personal reign of Christ upon earth preceding the end of the present dispensation.

C. GENERAL ESTIMATE.— From the beginning the church was in full possession of the Christian truth, for it had the twofold heritage of the apostles : (1) the oral testimony concerning Christ through which alone the church was founded and build up at first, and (2) the evangelical and apostolical writings given through the Holy Spirit to be an authoritative and infallible canon for the further development of the church. Yet, the church in the sub-apostolic age did by far not reach the depths and heights of the truth set forth in this twofold testimony. Even though face to face with the oral and written testimony of the apostles, the Apostolic Fathers have not fully caught the apostolic meaning and have often obscured most distinctive features of the gospel; for example, salvation through grace alone, faith and forgiveness of sins suffer some eclipse, while the gospel is made a new law and good works are often regarded as a condition of salvation. The marked difference between them and the New Testament writers is one of kind, not of degree, and bears testimony to the divine origin of the writings of the evangelists and apostles.

In order to explain this theological "retrogression" it must be borne in mind that with the full possession of divine truth there were not at once given the full intellectual apprehension and the definite form of the expression of revealed truth. It is here where the human factor in the development of Christian doctrine becomes apparent. Moreover, in this period the unique religious authority of the New Testament canon was not yet clearly seen by all. Not all books of the New Testament were universally received, while various other writings had attained to an equal authority with the canonical books of the New Testament. Even some of the writings of the Apostolic Fathers, such as the Shepherd of Hermas and the epistles of Barnabas, Clement and Polycarp, enjoyed, for a time, quasi-canonical authority and were frequently read in the meetings of the churches. Toward the end of the second century, however, they were dropped from the recognized body of canonical Scriptures. It must also be remembered that Christianity, as something essentially new, entered a world that was foreign to its nature, and that especially the Gentile Christians found it difficult to comprehend fully and at once the apostolic proclamation of the gospel.

CHAPTER II

THE CONCEPTION OF CHRISTIANITY ACCORDING TO THE GREEK APOLOGISTS

A. It was in defending Christian truth against the assaults of paganism and Judaism from without, and against the opposition of Gnosticism from within, that the church had to unfold and ultimately establish Christian truth. Hence the study of Christian thought leads us from the purely practical literature of the Apostolic Fathers to the reflective theology of the Apologists. *The Greek Apologists* first of all defended Christianity against the attacks from without. Some of their apologies for Christianity are still extant, while others are known to us only by reputation, or by fragments cited in other writings.

1. One of the earliest apologies is to be found in the *Epistle to Diognetus*, about 150. It is often classed with the writings of the Apostolic Fathers. The unknown author who styles himself "a disciple of the apostles" aims to give to the addressee, a heathen of high social position and culture, information as to the Christian belief in God and worship of God.

2. Another of the earliest of the ápologies is the work of *Quadratus,* bishop of Athens. According to Eusebius his apology which is lost was presented to the emperor Hadrian on occasion of his presence in Athens in 125 or 126. Quadratus claims to be a disciple of the apostles.

3. *Aristides,* an Athenian philosopher and contemporary with Quadratus, addressed his work either to Hadrian, or according to the Syriac version of the apology, to Antoninus Pius. The original has perished, but we have the apology in three recently discovered versions, Armenian, Syrian, and Greek.

4. *Melito,* "the philosopher," bishop of Sardis, addressed an apology to Marcus Aurelius. From the scantiness of the material of this apology, preserved only in Eusebius' writings, one cannot estimate justly Melito's importance for the History of Doctrine, though from his numerous works we know he took an interest in the dogmatical questions of his time, championed orthodoxy and upheld apostolic tradition.

5. *Claudius Apollinaris,* bishop of Hierapolis in Phrygia, a contemporary of Melito, wrote an apology addressed to the same emperor. It is lost as well as the apology written by — —

6. *Miltiades, an Athenian* philosopher and rhetorician. Eusebius

attributes to Miltiades exhaustive treatises against both Jew and pagans, and an apology for his faith addressed "to the rulers of the world"— probably Marcus Aurelius and Lucius Verus.

7. Another Christian philosopher, *Athenagoras*, by report an Athenian, addressed his work Apology or Intercession in behalf of the Christians, also to Marcus Aurelius, about 177. In elegant language and polished style the author defends not only Christianity, rebutting charges of atheism, cannibalism and sexual promiscuity, but also makes a vigorous and skilful attack on the folly and vanity of paganism and on the shamefulness of obscene myths.

8. Of the writings of *Theophilus of Antioch* (d. about 181) there have been preserved the three books to Autolycus, an educated heathen friend of Theophilus. The first book is apologetic defending the belief in God and the Christian hope of the resurrection. The second is polemic combating heathen belief as well as philosophical speculation. The third book points out the inferiority of heathen literature when compared with the Old Testament Scriptures as the ancient source of the knowledge of God. He makes but few references to any of the writings of the New Testament.

9. The apologetic work entitled "Address to the Greeks" by the Assyrian *Tatian* belongs to Tatian's catholic period. He attempts to prove the reasonableness and high antiquity of Christianity. To this end he shows the worthlessness of paganism including Greek mythology and philosophy. Utter contempt for everything Greek characterizes the Address to the Greeks. The writer prefers to be "a disciple of the philosophy of the barbarians," i. e., Christians.

10. The greatest among the Greek Apologists of the second century is *Flavius Justinus*, surnamed "Philosopher and Martyr," born of Hellenic parents about 100 at Flavia Neapolis (the ancient Sichem) in Samaria. A thorough acquaintance with the various philosophical schools, Peripatetics, Pythagoreans, Stoics and Platonists, brought home to Justin the conviction that the true knowledge was not to be found in them. It was at this time that he met a mysterious venerable old Christian, who entered into a conversation with him and led him from the Greek philosophers to the Hebrew prophets, from metaphysics to faith in Christ. Thus Justin found the way to true knowledge, or, in his own words, "I found this philosophy alone to be safe and profitable." After his conversion he retained the philosopher's mantle and went about from place to place to proclaim Christianity as the only true philosophy. On his second stay in Rome he engaged in a public disputation with the Cynic Crescens, and in the end died there a martyr's death. To form an opinion as to Justin's theology we must turn to his two Apologies and to his Dialog with the Jew Trypho. In the two

Apologies he sought to convince the emperors how unjust and how unreasonable were the persecutions of the Christians. In his Dialog he refutes the objections of the Jews and shows that Christianity is the new law for all men, and proves from Moses and the prophets that Jesus is the Christ.

B. In outlining *the Christianity of the Greek Apologists* we follow in the main the teachings of Justin, "the most influential and important for the forming of Hellenically modified Christianity and the founder of Christian theology" (Moeller, Hist. of Chr. Church, I, p. 173). Justin always remained a philosopher. He regarded his conversion as a passing from an imperfect to the perfect philosophy. Thus he sees the truths of the Christian religion to a certain extent foreshadowed through the seminal Logos, of whom all men partake, in the religious philosophies — truths which in Christianity are guaranteed by the manifestation of the Logos in the person of Christ (Apol. II. 8:10). Accordingly he maintains the salvability of the heathen who lived "with the Logos;" they are Christians even though they have been thought atheists, as among the Greeks Socrates and Heraclitus and men like them (Apol. I. 46; II. 10). All philosophical wisdom and all prophetic inspiration came from the same origin, the Logos. By way of typological and allegorical exegesis he finds even in the Old Testament everywhere references to Christ. The Old Testament covenant was, as a mere historical fact, imperfect and insufficient, but the truths typified in the law and foreshadowed in the prophets were great and glorious.

The Apologists were content to speak of Christ's redemptive work in simple scriptural and general language without further attempt at an explanatory doctrinal statement. They all agree that belief in the significance of Christ's suffering and death forms an essential part of the common Christian faith. By his sufferings and death Christ freed mankind from sin and death. The ninth chapter of the Epistle to Diognetus has a beautiful passage on redemption such as we find in no other early Christian writing outside of the New Testament:

"He Himself took on Him the burden of our iniquities. He gave His own Son as a ransom for us, the holy One for transgressors, the blameless One for the wicked, the righteous One for the unrighteous, the incorruptible One for the corruptible, the immortal One for them that are mortal. For what other thing was capable of covering our sins than His righteousness? By what other one was it possible that we, the wicked and ungodly, could be justified, than by the only Son of God? O sweet exchange! O unsearchable operation! O benefits surpassing all expectation! that the wickedness of many should be hid in a single righteous One, and that the righteousness of One should justify many transgressors"!

But in defining the work of Christ the Apologists more or less emphasize that Christ became our teacher, lawgiver and exemplar.

It is in keeping with their conception of Christianity as a new philosophy that not Christ's redemptive work, but the teaching of Jesus, holds the central place in their thoughts. Christ became the teacher of the new doctrine and the promulgator of the new law, as he had already shown himself before his incarnation. (Dial. 18).

As to the person of Christ the Apologists hold in substance the common orthodox doctrine upon this subject, although they use Stoic and Philonic phraseology. "The ineffable Father and Lord of all . . . remains in his own place . . . he is not moved or confined to a spot in the whole world. How, then, could he be seen by any one, or how could he communicate with anyone?" Justin answers: God produced of his own nature a rational power, his agent in creation, who also became man in Jesus (Dial. 61. 100. 128; Apol. II. 6). Justin identifies the historical Christ with the rational force operative in the universe, yet he represents the relation between the Son and the Father as a relation of personal intercourse, though the Son seems not to become fully personal until the creation of the world was about to take place (Dial. 61. 62. 127. 129). Accordingly Justin affirms the subordination of the Son in the most positive manner (*ib*. 61. 62; Apol. II. 6). According to Tatian the Logos sharing in the rational power of the Father in the beginning of the world — "becomes the first-begotten work of the Father" (Cohort. 5). Athenagoras saw in the Logos the prototype and the energizing principle of things (Suppl. 10). With Theophilus the Logos is the reason immanent in God; as such he had always existed in the bosom of God; he is the counsellor of God (Autol. 10). When God determined to create the world he sent forth the Logos from himself and so he is the first-begotten and only begotten of God (*ib*.). Theophilus is the first to distinguish the internal Logos from the Logos expressed. At the same time the Logos is the first creature of the Father and subordinate to him. Aristides strongly asserted the deity of Christ and his birth of the virgin Mary. The passage of the Apology in which he describes the person and the work of Christ contains striking correspondences with the second article of the Apostles' Creed: "Christ is the Son of the Most High God, having by the Holy Spirit come down from heaven, born of a Hebrew virgin. He took flesh and revealed himself in the human nature as the Son of God . . . being pierced with nails by the Jews, after three days he rose from the dead and ascended to heaven. . . ."

The Apologists also asserted their belief in the Trinity as an article of the common faith, Theophilus being the first to use the term "Trias" (II.15), but they did not attempt to define the relation of the divine persons to one another.

Man is able to fulfill the law of Christ, since God created him free. Even after the fall man is free to decide for God through faith and repentance. Despite the stress which the Greek Fathers laid upon the freedom of the will, they also with one accord emphasized grace as necessary to salvation.

The means by which one becomes and remains a Christian are the reading of the prophets and the gospels, preaching and exhortation, Baptism and the Lord's Supper. Baptism is indispensable to salvation; it brings forgiveness of sin (Just. Apol. I. 61). Without explaining how Christ is present in the Eucharist, or how the elements become his body and blood, the Apologists maintained that in the Eucharist there are two things, the earthly and the heavenly. Bread and wine are so conjoined with the heavenly Word that they may be styled his body and blood.

Belief in the resurrection of the body also forms an essential part of the common faith of the church. According to Athenagoras sin consists entirely in sensuality; hence his doctrine tends to asceticism, and yet he maintains the resurrection of the body in the most material sense. In his treatise *De resurrectione,* to which he refers toward the end of his Apology, he attempts to prove the truth of the resurrection from the wisdom, power and justice of God as well as from the destiny of man. Theophilus and Justin denied that man was created with an immortal nature. Adam was neither mortal nor immortal, but capable of either mortality or immortality, receiving immortality as a reward if he aspired after it by obeying the divine commandments, and becoming the author of his own ruin if he disobeyed God (Autol. II. 19. 24. 27; Dial. 5. 6.). After the resurrection, both the righteous and the wicked shall receive their just reward (Just. Ap. 1. 20; II. 7).

Justin is confident that his teaching is that of the church with the exception of his belief in a millennium. Upon this point, he admits, Christians differ (Dial. 80. 81). He believes in an earthly Jerusalem and depicts Christ's reign on earth in the glowing colors of the millenarians.

Such is the theology of the Greek Apologists. They themselves being Gentile Christians and under the influence of the civilization of the age were bent on harmonizing Christian truth with Hellenistic philosophy, and sought to convince outsiders that Christianity is the highest wisdom and absolute truth. As they conceived of Christian truth as a new improved philosophy they failed to give Christianity its full value as the religion of salvation.

CHAPTER III

PERVERSIONS OF CHRISTIANITY
JEWISH CHRISTIANITY — GNOSTICISM

A. JEWISH CHRISTIANITY.— Over against Judaising tendencies in the Christian church the Conference of the Apostles emphasized the independent, spiritual and universal character of Christianity (Acts 15). Nevertheless, there were still many Jewish Christians who at least in the case of Jewish Christians demanded strict observance of the ceremonial law as necessary to salvation. Even in the great conflict of Paul with the Judaisers the Jewish element was not banished altogether from the Christian church.

1. After the fall of Jerusalem the Palestinian Jewish Christians separated from their non-Christian fellow countrymen and settled in the territory east of the Jordan. A considerable portion of these held to the old conservative position of primitive Jewish Christianity. This group is known as the *Ebionites* (Heb. *byonim,* poor people), originally a common name for all Jewish Christians, adopted by this group signifying their poverty. There is no sufficient ground for dividing the Ebionites into two separate and distinct groups, the Ebionites proper and the more moderate Nazarenes, for both names are applied by the Fathers to the same people, i. e., Jewish Christians. We may, however, distinguish different types of Jewish Christianity. *The more moderate* Ebionites accepted the virgin birth of Jesus and did not hold the observance of the law as obligatory upon Gentile Christians. *The more rigid Ebionites* declared Jesus to be the son of Joseph and Mary, demanded the observance of the law of all Christians alike, rejected Paul as an apostate from the Mosaic law, accepted and used only a Hebrew Gospel of Matthew and held extreme millenarian ideas.

2. Toward the end of the first century we find a considerable group marked by rigorous Essenic asceticism and Gnostic speculations. They are known as the *Elkesaites*. They accepted as a revelation the Book of Elkesai. It was claimed that an angel of Terrifying dimensions accompanied by the Holy Spirit, as a female angel of the same nature, had given the book to Elkesai. It taught that Christ, who had often appeared at earlier periods, was an angel born of human parents. The law is not annulled. Especially necessary are Sabbath observance and circumcision. Baptism is to be repeated for the purification from all sins and the healing of wounds and diseases. The book also authorizes the practice of astrology and magic.

3. *The Pseudo-Clementine Writings, Homilies, Recognitions and Epitome*, throw some light upon this phase of Jewish Christianity. The tendency of this literature is to show the essential identity of Christianity with Judaism. There is one God, the creator and righteous judge of the world, although in another place (Hom. 2.15 ff.) the world is said to have emanated from God, who is the All. Christ is the true prophet. He is not God, but the son of God, since he sprang from a change in God. The death of Christ does not mean salvation to our author. Christ's resurrection is not mentioned. Man made in God's image has free will. Circumcision is given up. Bloody sacrifices are rejected. The eating of flesh is forbidden. Frequent ablutions are recommended or commanded. Marriage is forbidden, but early marriages are commended to avoid fornication. Side by side with Christian and Jewish elements we find, especially in the Homilies, pantheistic and dualistic and strong ascetic tendencies, showing kinship with the great religious syncretism in the church called Gnosticism.

4. *Over against the syncretistic Jewish Christianity the Christian Apologists* laid emphasis upon the unique and universal character of Christianity. They showed from Scripture itself the true relation of the two dispensations to each other and proved, especially from Old Testament prophecies and types concerning the Messiah, that Jesus was the true Messiah, and harmonized his deity with monotheism by means of the doctrine of the Trinity. Ebionite tendencies exerted no further influence on the development of Christian doctrine and were finally absorbed by Mohammedanism.

B. GNOSTICISM.—The second form of the perversion of Christianity during the first Christian centuries was Gnosticism.

1. In order to understand the great Gnostic movement in the ancient church we must bear in mind *the syncretistic tendency of the age*. Skepticism had undermined and finally dissolved the traditional religious beliefs of the ancient world. The influence of Oriental elements made itself strongly felt in Greek and Roman culture. Pagan ideas were eagerly absorbed, interpreted through, and harmonized with, philosophical ideas. In conformity with the spirit of the age the great ideas of Christianity were also compared and harmonized with Hellenistic and Jewish philosophy, and Oriental theosophy. In Ebionism we have already noticed the syncretistic tendency of the age to force Christianity into the legalistic particularism of Pharisaism. In Gnosticism the syncretistic tendency was to amalgamate Oriental theosophy and Hellenistic philosophy with Christianity in order to establish a universal religion. As many a Jew when he embraced the Christian religion wished to introduce Judaism into Christianity, so many a heathen wished to carry with

him ethnic ideas dear to him and mingle them with Christian elements.

The Gnostic teachers drew from Pagan sources no less than from the sacred books of the Jews and the Christians. But the highest source of knowledge with them was a secret tradition of their own which they set up against the open popular tradition of the church. Christian Gnosticism is usually characterized as an intellectual tendency chiefly concerned with philosophical speculation which has for its end and object the reconciliation of Christian revelation with reason. The word "gnosis"—knowledge—seems to point in the same direction. It is true, the Gnostics drew largely from the philosophical systems of Plato and the Stoics and connected with their doctrines the charm of mystery claiming for themselves a deeper knowledge or gnosis of divine things than was accessible to the uninitiated. But at the same time, in their tasks to solve the problems of religion, they were not only guided by speculative but by practical motives as well. They sought to save man's soul by imparting not only philosophical, but also intuitive, experimental knowledge making man actually realize the divine life in personal experience through the formulas and forms of the mysteries. The means by which they sought to solve their problems were chiely derived from Oriental religions. Gnosticism, therefore, is an essentially heathenish movement with a Hellenistic philosophical tendency within the pale of Christianity.

2. *The first traces of Gnosticism* are found already in the apostolic age. Gnostic ideas threatened especially the churches in Asia Minor and Crete as is evident from the Epistle to the Colossians and Ephesians, the Pastoral Epistles, 2 Peter, Jude and the Revelation of John. The heresies indicated in these New Testament writings seem largely Jewish in origin and combine ideas from Jewish and heathen sources with Christian truth. In dealing with the solution of evil they arrived either at dualistic asceticism (Col. 2:21-23; 1 Tim. 4:1-3; Tit. 1:15), or immoral antinomianism (1 Tim. 6:4, 5; Tit. 1:10-16; 2 Pet. 2:1-4; Jude 4, 16; Rev. 2:6, 15, 20 ff.). The false teachers mentioned in Jude and the Nicolaitans of the Apocalypse probably based their licentious views on Gnostic speculations. The heretics, against whom Paul warns, worshipped angels (Col. 2:18), intermediaries between God and man, such as appear in the system of Gnosticism, and allegorically explained the resurrection as something past already (2 Tim. 2:18). Others denied the deity of Christ and the incarnation. This form of heresy is combated in the writings of John (1 John 2:22, 23; 4:3; see also Ignatius, Trall. 11:2; Philad. 6:60.

It is generally believed that this was the heresy of *Cerinthus* who taught that Jesus, the offspring of Joseph and Mary, was like his fellow men, tainted with sin, though "more righteous, prudent and wise than other men." The Christ, however, was at baptism joined with him and these two continued together. Before the passion Christ left Jesus again and became pure spirit (Iren. I. 26, 1:III. 2, 1). According to Irenaeus (III. 3, 4) the apostle John met Cerinthus in Ephesus in a bath-house and perceiving him within rushed out without bathing, exclaiming, "Let us fly, lest even the bath-house fall down, because Cerinthus, the enemy of the truth, is within." Ignatius describes this heresy as heterodoxy and warns the Ephesians to avoid these false teachers as they would wild beasts (7.1). They are "deceivers, not Christians, but Christ-be-trayers;" they tend to represent Christ's earthly career and sufferings as only seeming (Docetism), not real (Trall. 9.10; Smyrn. 1.6). For this reason "they abstain from the Eucharist. ., because they confess not the Eucharist to be the flesh of our Savior Jesus Christ" (Smyrn. 7. 1). They deny the resurrection and the judgment (*ib.* 2; also Polycarp ad Phil. 7.1).

To the same period belongs *Simon Magus* whose teaching, min-gled with astrology and the arts of magic, gradually took on the form of an elaborate Gnostic system. According to Acts 8: 10 his followers considered him "that power of God which is called great," i. e., the chief emanation from the deity and so entitled to divine worship. Justin Martyr, himself a native of Samaria, relates (Apol. I.26, 56; Dial. 120) that almost all Samaria honored Simon as the highest God and his female companion, Helena, as God's first thought. Irenaeus gives more detail concerning Simon and his adherents. Helena is the mother of all things, by whom in the be-ginning Simon had conceived the idea of making angels and arch-angels (Haer. I.23). Here we notice the Gnostic conception of syzygies taken from naturalistic cosmogonies which make the pro-creation of all things proceed from the male and female elements. As regards morality Irenaeus points out the sect's contempt for the moral law which proceeded from the world-creating angels and not from the highest God. Those who place their trust in him and Helena, no longer regard the precepts of the prophets, but being free live as they please; for men are saved through his grace, and not on account of their own righteous action. Irenaeus further tells us that the followers of Simon both led profligate lives and prac-ticed every kind of magic. They also worshipped images of Simon under the form of Jupiter and of Helena under that of Minerva.

The adherents of Simon developed the Gnostic system of their master. Simon's successor, Menander, who was also a Samaritan, transplanted it to Antioch. In the closing paragraph of the same chapter Irenaeus represents his doctrine as being the same as that of Simon, only that it was Menander this time who was the savior of the world. "His disciples obtain the resurrection by being baptized into him, and can die no more, but remain in the possession of immortal youth."

3. *The most prominent exponents of Gnosticism* were Saturninus, Basilides and Valentinus. Saturninus or Satornilos, a pupil of Menander, was the most prominent leader of the Gnostic movement in Syria. His Gnosticism is distinguished from that of Simon in that Saturninus lays no claim to divinity, knows nothing of celestial syzygies and insists on ascetic severity. He does not teach explicitly the principle of dualism. He represents the God of the Jews and Satan as antagonistic beings, but says nothing as to Satan's part in the cosmic process.

One of the most conspicuous exponents of Alexandrian Gnosticism was Basilides, who taught at Alexandria in the time of Hadrian. The fundamental theme of his doctrine is the question concerning the origin of evil and how to overcome it. He solves his problem by forms of Oriental gnosis taken chiefly from Iranian dualism. From this there is an advance to the more Greek antithesis of soul and body, spirit and matter. He teaches both development from below upwards and emanation from above downwards. On the one hand he emphasizes the principle of development making everything strive from the worse to the better. On the other hand he teaches that the 365 heavens with their spirits had emanated from the supreme God and that the powers from whom this world originated were the lowest emanations of the supreme God.

The most prominent and influential Gnostic teacher was Valentinus or Valentine. Little is known of the events of his life. He was brought up and educated in Alexandria. He taught in Rome about the middle of the second century.

4. *Valentine's system* is known only as described in detail and refuted by his opponents, where his teachings are scarcely distinguished from those of his pupils. We will give therefore an outline of the teachings of Valentine and his school:

Valentine starts from the unbegotten, ineffable, incomprehensible, supreme Being which he calls Bythos or Abyss. Alongside of Bythos stands Sige or Ennoia as his consort or syzygos. From Bythos and his Siege emanated the Aeons in fifteen pairs with the difference of sexes. Every such marriage union of Aeons is designated "syzygy." These fifteen pairs of Aeons together with the Father of all formed the Pleroma, the plenitude of divine powers. From the passionate striving of the last Aeon, Sophia, to unite with Bythos itself, arises an untimely being, Achamoth or the Desire of Wisdom. A rupture is taking place in the Pleroma. Being expelled from the Pleroma, Achamoth communicates the germ of life to matter and forms the Demiurge of physical substance. Thus produced, the Demiurge creates the world, in which three kinds of substance are mixed, pneumatic, psychic, hylic. All hylic natures are under the dominion of Satan, all psychic, under that of the Demiurge, while Achamoth directs those that are pneumatic. In the meantime a sixteenth pair of Aeons arises, Christ and the Holy Spirit. They are to restore the disturbed harmony in the Pleroma, Then all the Aeons combine in emanating a new aeonic Being, the Savior, or higher, heavenly Christ, who is to be the future husband of Achamoth. The Messiah, the lower, earthly Christ, is sent by the Demiurge to his chosen people, the Jews. The heavenly Christ is united with him in baptism till the crucifixion. The Messiah is crucified by the Jews but does not suffer, since he has merely an apparent body. The heavenly Christ unites with himself the pneumatic natures and separates them and the psychic from the hylic. The pneumatics are led to perfection by knowledge (gnosis), the psychic by faith (pistis). Ultimately he leads Achamoth back with the pneumatics into the Pleroma, while the psychic, i .e., the Demiurge and his pious ones occupy the middle place; but the hylic will perish in fire which shall destroy them and all matter. Accordingly the latter are annihilated, while the pneumatics and the psychic are irrevocably predestinated to eternal life. Absolute predestination had an important place in all the schools of Gnosticism and it should be observed that it first appeared in Christianity under the garb of heresy.

Irenaeus tells us (I.6, 4) that the Valentinians feel themselves under no necessity to attain by their deeds to the spiritual nature; they possess it inherently. Even the Demiurge, who sins, though only through ignorance, is to be raised to the borders of the Pleroma, for he inherently possesses relative truth.

Valentine had a large number of followers, who variously altered his system according to their own caprice. His school which split into an Oriental and Italian branch, produced many distinguished teachers. Among them we mention Heracleon, of the Italian school, the first known commentator of the Gospel of John.

5. To this period belongs *Tatian,* at first a disciple of Justin Martyr, at last settled in Gnosticism. His adherents were called, from their ascetic life, Encratites (Self-disciplined), or Hydroparastatae or Aquarii, from the use of water instead of wine in the Lord's Supper, which practice was condemned by Clement of Alexandria, Cyprian and Chrysostom. It is interesting to note that modern Prohibitionists have resorted to the same heretical practice. The Ophites or Naasseni were a Gnostic sect who revered the serpent as the symbol of the hidden divine wisdom. Some identify the Ophites with the false teachers mentioned in the Epistle of Jude.

6. *General Characteristics of Gnosticism.* Gnosticism addressed itself to the same problem which lay at the foundation of all Oriental religions — the relation of finite man to the infinite God. How can an imperfect world proceed from a perfect God? What is the relation of spirit to matter? How did evil enter the world? What is evil? Almost all early thinkers were driven by these questions into some form of dualism. There are, they said, two worlds in sharp contrast with one another, the worlds of the good and of evil, the worlds of light and of darkness, the spiritual world and the material world. Matter is eternal and is identified with evil; it cannot be traced to God as a spirit. From the supreme God, the absolute and infinite Being, the ineffable One, is to be distinguished the creator of the world and lawgiver of the Old Testament.

The present world came into existence by a process of emanation or evolution. Fallen divinities, or spirits, sank down into the world of matter, or evil which, previously insensible, was animated into life and activity. There is a natural and gradual unfolding of the divine potency, or an emanation from the divine Being according to the law of sexual polarity (syzygy). The products of emanation are called Aeons which are thought to be the media of creation, development and redemption of the world. The lowest and weakest of these Aeons, the Demiurge, is the creator of the world.

One of the highest Aeons appears as the Redeemer in whom the celestial Aeon and the human person are clearly to be distinguished. Dualism stamped itself upon the very person of Christ. In the different Gnostic systems we find a manifold confusion as to Christ's person, but they all agree that Christ was not God Incarnate in whom both natures are united in one person. Jesus is either a mere man with whom, for a time, the Aeon Christ unites himself. Or he is a heavenly Aeon which assumed a body formed of psychical substance. However, it was only the psychical Christ who suffered and was crucified; or he was human in appearance only, having no real human nature, but a wholly spiritual one. His sufferings were only apparent. Christ's mission was not to atone for the sins of the world, but to bring deliverance of the captive spiritual elements from matter by the imparting of knowledge. The means of this deliverance are mystical rites, gnosis and asceticism. This gnosis brings redemption in that it frees the pneumatic from the material world and aids him to find his way to the upper world at death.

Mankind is divided into three different classes and so fitted for different destinies. The church is the congregation of the pneumatics or spiritual men, who are capable of gnosis. The psychical are capable only of pistis and will therefore obtain a lower degree of eternal bliss. The hylic or carnal are left in hopeless subjection to the powers of Satan.

The Christian eschatology as a whole is rejected. There is no room for the resurrection of Christ, nor the resurrection of the dead. The only thing to be expected from the future is the complete deliverance of the spirit from matter and its final return into the Pleroma.

Gnosis was also said to lead to moral purification and a perfect life. Perfection shows itself in the contempt of the material world — the practical consequence of Gnostic dualism. This led some to adopt in theory and practice strict ascetic abstinence. Others, convinced that they were free from and above matter and that therefore nothing could harm them, fell into wild libertinism.

With all this, Gnosticism perverted Christianity, basing it on ancient Oriental theosophy. In the second century Gnosticism became the gravest of all dangers to Christianity. Substituting heathen speculation it claimed to be the universal religion. It promised spiritual renewal, without true repentance, through outward asceticism. It allured many by the charm of mystery connected with its doctrines.

7. *Summary of the Church's Opposition to Gnosticism.* The church most successfully met the great movement of Gnosticism and prevailed against it. The anti-Gnostic Fathers, particularly Irenaeus, Tertullian and Hippolytus rejected:

(1) The separation of the creator of the world from the supreme God, and maintained that God is at once Creator, Preserver and Redeemer.

(2) The dualistic separation of matter and spirit. Good and evil cannot be explained by two antagonistic natural endowments. This would do away with man's responsibility. According to the Gnostics sin was a physical necessity. The Apologists showed that it was a free act of man.

(3) The Docetic views of the Gnostics, and laid stress on the necessity of the Incarnation of the Logos.

(4) The Gnostic conception of the resurrection, and championed the resurrection of the flesh.

Indirectly Gnosticism was one of the most powerful factors in the development of Christian doctrine. Since the Gnostics used the standards of the church and professed to accept the common belief of the Christians, the church was led to insist more and more upon its Bible, to determine with greater distinctness what Christianity is and to define more clearly the fundamental doctrines of the church.

CHAPTER IV

REFORMATORY MOVEMENTS DIRECTED AGAINST CATHOLIC CHRISTIANITY

A. MARCION'S ATTEMPT AT REFORM.—Marcion of Sinope in Pontus came to Rome about 140, where he gained influence in the congregation. Here he also became acquainted with the Syrian Gnostic Cerdo whose speculations influenced the doctrinal views of Marcion. Soon his doctrines raised opposition. He withdrew from the catholic church, about 144, and established in Rome a community of his own. He won an immense number of converts. By a vigorous propaganda his doctrines soon spread "throughout the whole race of men," as Justin Martyr puts it.

1. *Marcion's Relation to Gnosticism.* Marcion is often, mistakenly, reckoned among the Gnostics. With the Gnostics he had in common dualism, although he started from very different premises, and asceticism, but he was not a Gnostic dreamer. Abstract questions on the origin of evil or on the essence of the Godhead interested him little. He was guided not by metaphysical but soteriological motives. He therefore laid the stress on the pure gospel and faith rather than on knowledge as necessary to salvation. His idea was not to be found, as other Gnostic teachers had done, a school for the learned and privileged. He proposed to reform the whole church through a return to the gospel of Christ and to Paul. He wanted a Christianity untrammeled and undefiled by association with Judaism.

2. *Marcion's Doctrinal Views.* Marcion maintained that there was no agreement possible between the revelation of Jesus Christ and the teaching of the Old Testament. In the writings of Paul he found the irreconcilable antagonism between law and gospel, justice and grace, Judaism and Christianity. His work in which he expounded these views is called Antitheses. This antagonism between the Old Testament and the New Testament formed the fundamental idea of his system. It led him to reject the Old Testament and to believe that Paul was the only true apostle, whereas the other apostles had corrupted the gospel. He therefore created his own New Testament canon, admitting, besides a mutilation of Luke's Gospel, only an "Apostolicon," containing ten Epistles of Paul. From these he had first eliminated all alleged Judaizing elements. Marcion's Gospel begins with the words: "In the fifteenth year of the emperor Tiberius God descended in Capernaum and taught on the Sabbath."

36

His theology is dualistic; his Christology Docetic. To explain the antagonism between law and gospel, Old and New Testament, he introduced a second God, the Demiurge who was the creator of the world and the lawgiver, under whose curse the whole race fell, since no one could keep the law. Then a higher God, hitherto unknown, of free grace resolved to redeem the condemned race of men. He sent the Redeemer, the "Saving Spirit" who, according to Marcion, was a manifestation of the true and good God. He had neither birth nor growth, but assumed the appearance of a full-grown body. The Demiurge became angry with him and caused him to be crucified. He died, however, only a seeming death. Not all men will be saved, but only those who attach themselves to the gospel. They are to live in the strictest asceticism, particularly celibacy. Only the soul shares in salvation. Accordingly there is no resurrection of the body. Nor did Christ rise again, but he went down into Hades where he liberated those who rejected the God of the Jews, such as Gentiles, even Sodomites and Egyptians, while the legally pious of the Old Testament are destined to receive either an inferior happiness or utter reprobation.

3. In combating Gnosticism *the church's opposition* was at first especially directed against Marcion and his adherents. Almost every Apologist from Justin onward takes some notice of him. The danger threatening from Marcionites was the greater, because of their severe morality and their ardor in braving persecution, which was equal to that of the orthodox. Moreover, their master's doctrine, though mixed with error, was more closely related to true Christianity than that of Gnostics.

Marcionite societies maintained themselves in the East as late as the sixth century, their doctrinal views having been modified by Christian influences though more often perverted by Gnostic speculations.

B. The Montanist Reaction.—1. *Montanus,* a mutilated devotee of the worship of Cybele, became a Christian and appeared as a prophet and reformer of Christianity in Pepuza in Phrygia, about 157, while Gratus was Proconsul in Asia. The chronology is uncertain; the date given by Eusebius is 172. Joint with him were two prophetesses, Prisca or Priscilla and Maximilla, two wealthy women of high social position, who left their husbands.

Montanus believed himself to be a passive instrument of the divine spirit. In the suppression of self-consciousness and submission to the Spirit as a will-less instrument he saw the proof of perfect prophecy. In teaching, he spoke of himself as "the Lord God Almighty." When he spoke, it was the Paraclete himself who spoke. "Man is a lyre and I play upon him as a plectron. . . I am the Lord the Almighty" (Epiph. 48.4, 11, 12, 13; 49.1). Since this type of prophecy was unlike that recorded in the New Testament the Montanists rightly called it "new prophecy." His followers regarded Montanus as the incarnation of the promised Paraclete. Others, who could not accept this view, derived the Montanistic revelations from Satanic inspirations.

2. *The Montanists* did not consciously dissent from the dogmatic statements of the church. In opposition to the false universalism of Gnosticism they insisted that Christianity alone is the true religion. Their interest centered in practical life instead of theoretical speculation. They aimed at reform of the church's practice. Claiming possession of the primitive gifts of the Spirit and insisting upon freedom of utterance under the influence of the Spirit Montanism was a strong vindication of the priesthood of all Christians and a protest against the deadness of officialism and ecclesiastical authority. It must further be borne in mind that with the increase of the church's membership there came an accession of earthly interests. The lively expectation of the Parousia gave place to other views. The Montanists proclaimed the near approach of the age of the Holy Spirit and of the millennial reign in Pepuza, upon which they expected the descent of the New Jerusalem, whence they were somtimes called Pepuziani. Tertullian, himself a Montanist, pictures in glowing colors to his excited imagination the glory of the Millennium in "the city built by the hand of God, which the Apostle also calls the New Jerusalem coming down from God out of heaven."

In opposition to the church's worldiness the Montanists pointed to the end of this age as being near at hand. The expectation of this great event should determine the entire life of the Christians. Hence strict fastings were enjoined. Virginity was strictly recommended and second marriages were disapproved. Flight in persecution was forbidden and martyrdom not only encouraged but extraordinarily exalted. With regard to gross sins after baptism the Spirit declared through the new prophets: "The church has power to remit sin, but I will not do it lest others offend" (Tert. De pud. 21). Only martyrdom can atone for mortal sins. The followers of the Paraclete called themselves spiritual Christians in distinction from the psychic, the adherents of the secularized church.

The Montanist movement or "Phrygian heresy" spread to the West and was regarded with favor in Southern Gaul, Rome, and especially North Africa where Tertullian became the most conspicuous convert to Montanism.

3. *Opposition to Montanism.* Montanism cannot be treated as heresy in the same way as Gnosticism, for it remained in harmony

with the church on the fundamental points of doctrine. However, as is usually the case with ecstatics and visionaries, the Montanists fell into such extremes of exaggeration that there arose a sharp opposition to the new prophecy. Their extremest opponents were the so-called Alogi, or deniers of the Word. They rejected the Apocalypse and along with it the Gospel of John on account of its promise of the Paraclete. In this way they sought to undermine the foundation of Montanism.

The church rejected the doctrine of the Montanists that the Paraclete had not come until now as unbiblical, and their legalistic requirements as destroying Christian liberty. Over against the Montanist proclamation of a new era of prophecy and the continuity of revelation the church authoritatively declared that revelation was closed and prophecy was at an end. The conflict, therefore, had an important influence upon the fixation of the New Testament canon.

Montanism was gradually suppressed and finally driven out of the church. The followers of Tertullian were won back to the church by Augustine. After the fourth century the emperors repeatedly enacted laws against the sect which disappeared with the sixth century.

It is interesting to note how Montanistic tendencies have since reappeared in the course of the history of the church, from Novatianists and Donatists in the ancient church, the Anabaptists and chiliastic Enthusiasts in the Reformation period, down to the Irvingites and Adventists of the present day.

CHAPTER V

AUTHORITATIVE STANDARDS
OF THE ANCIENT CATHOLIC CHURCH

A. THE ANCIENT CATHOLIC CHURCH.— The church founded by Christ was from the beginning the communion of believers who have fellowship with Christ and with the brethren. From the first the different congregations were united by the bond of a common faith. But when danger of division in the church was threatening from heresies and sects there was naturally an increased incentive to strengthen the bond of unity in faith. Consequently the source of the common faith, the Scriptures and the apostolic tradition, gained more and more normative authority. When heretics attacked or misinterpreted Scripture, one would repair to the apostolic testimony and interpretation as found and preserved within the churches which the apostles had founded, such as Jerusalem, Antioch, Ephesus, Alexandria, Corinth, Thessalonica, Rome. Especially the traditions of the church at Rome were early held in high esteem. Agreement with Rome's traditions would guarantee the trustworthiness of traditions, and the communion of all those who shared the same faith and confession, constituted the one, apostolic, catholic church.

Another important factor in the transformation of the general conception of the church was the growing influence of the episcopacy as the indispensable link for connecting the church with Christ. The uninterrupted succession of the bishops guaranteed the valid transmission of the apostolic tradition, and secured the unity of the episcopacy and through it the unity of the church. The church, then, was no longer the communion of believers, an object of faith, but an outward organism of which the bishops were the representatives. What is true in regard to the church as the communion of believers, that out of the church no one can be saved, was now referred to the visible body, the outward organization of the church.

We notice this transformation in the general conception of the church at the beginning of the third century, though its first beginnings may be traced to Irenaeus, who already attached great importance to the episcopate, attributing to it a sure gift of grace for the custody of the truth, or even to Ignatius who laid great stress upon the function of the episcopate in the interest of unity in the church.

B. Rule of Faith.—A brief summary of saving truth was soon laid down in the so-called Rule of Faith (regula fidei), which at different times in different churches assumed different shape and form. The common substance of the various rules of faith, however, points to a common source which was none other than the triune formula of baptism, Matt. 28: 19. This triune original early expanded into a brief statement of fundamental Christian truths. The formula thus enlarged was used as the baptismal confession of faith in the Triune God and served as a basis of catechetical instruction. Out of the baptismal confession grew, no doubt, the so-called Apostles' Creed.

It is generally agreed that the oldest form of the Apostolicum is the Old Roman Symbol which as early as 250 was used in the religious service of the Roman church. There it was held in high esteem and believed to be derived directly from the twelve apostles and brought to Rome by Peter. It was thus designated at Rome as apostolic in the strict sense of the word, and no additions to it were permitted. Later, however, the creed was gradually enlarged by several additions until at the beginning of the sixth century it reached its final form. Its original form cannot be reconstructed with any degree of certainty. This is to be explained from the fact that under the influence of the Secret Discipline (arcani disciplina) of the church the creed was committed to memory, not to writing. The Apostolic Symbol would thus be kept secret in the ceremony of baptism.

C. Canon.—1. *History.* During the first decades of the church's history, when eyewitnesses of the events of our Lord's life and death and resurrection, and companions of the apostles could personally testify to the gospel message, the necessity would not exist for a collection of the records of Christ's life and doctrine or of the instructions of the inspired teachers of the church. But when at the end of the first century one and another of the early witnesses passed away, the oral traditions became corrupt and conflicting, and men were forced to rely on the writings of the apostles and their companions for an authoritative account of the words and deeds of the Master and his first disciples.

Moreover, heretical parties, like the Gnostic sects, Marcionites and Montanists, used in their own interest the standards of the church, Scripture and tradition, misinterpreted and corrupted the New Testament and rejected the Old. This, too, demanded a clearer definition of what constituted the authentic documents of the Christian revelation.

On the strength of the testimony of Christ and his apostles for the divine authority of the Old Testament canon the church from the beginning recognized the Old Testament as authoritative Scripture. The church accepted without dispute the conclusions of the Jewish Synod at Jamnia, about A. D. 90, where the limits of the Hebrew canon were officially and finally determined. Because of the universal use of the Septuagint the Fathers also often recognized as Scripture what we regard as Apocrypha. Jerome (d. 420), however, declared decidedly for the Hebrew canon (*ep. 32 ad Marcellam, et passim*).

At what time the books of the New Testament were collected into a distinct volume and became known to the church in that collected form, is not certainly known, but there is no doubt that it was very early. The so-called Muratorian Canon, composed about 170 or 180 (publ. by the Italian archeologist L. A. Muratori, 1740), contained a list of the New Testament books except the Epistle to the Hebrews, 1 John, 1 and 2 Peter and the Epistle of James. From this as well as from the canon of Marcion we may conclude that about the middle of the second century there was used in the churches a collection of New Testament books to which a canonical character was assigned. These were the four Gospels, Acts, thirteen Pauline Epistles, 1 Peter, and 1 John; they are known as *homologoumena* or protocanonical. . . The Epistle to the Hebrews, James, 2 Peter, 2 and 3 John, Jude and the Revelation were universally received after long hesitation; they are usually called *antilegomena*, or sometimes deuterocanonical books. In the East it was especially through the efforts of Origen, Eusebius and Athanasius, that the boundary of the New Testament canon was settled; in the West, through the powerful influence of Augustine. The synod held at Hippo Regius, in 393, gave the first express definition of the New Testament canon in the form in which it has ever since been retained. This was ratified by the synods held at Carthage, in 397 and 419, under the lead of Augustine.

The doubts regarding the canonicity of the disputed books were based upon the uncertainty as to their apostolic origin. To determine the canonicity of a given book two tests were applied: (1) Was it of apostolic origin? Or, if not, did its author sustain such a relation to apostles as to place his book on the same level with the writings of the apostles? (2) Were its contents in keeping with apostolic teaching? To settle these questions one had to consult the tradition of the church, especially that of the apostolic mother churches. It was not till this had been done that councils stepped in to recognize and accept the results that had been thus obtained. It was, therefore, not from the authoritative decision of a council that the canonical books won their position and general reception, but from the common recognition everywhere of the unimpeachable evidence upon which their apostolic origin was established. By the mature examination, deliberate judgment, and general consensus of the Christian church under the directing providence of God the canon of the New Testament was formed in the same gradual manner as the canon of the Old Testament.

Although tradition played an important part in fixing the canon, yet it was not placed above the canonical Scriptures. The two continued, no doubt, to be regarded as the same in substance. In refuting the pagan errors of the Gnostics who rejected some of the books of the Scripture, and distorted the rest by their false interpretation, the church often had to repair to tradition in order to maintain the true Scriptures and the true exposition of them. But in the Arian controversy, for example, the question was not of excluding some pagan element but of encountering an adversary who like orthodox theology itself stood on Biblical ground and whose opposition invited appeal to the written oracles rather than to tradition. In general, the contents of Scripture and of catholic tradition were considered to be essentially coincident. Where, however, Scripture conflicted with tradition, Scripture was to be followed. Where tradition conflicted with tradition, either Scripture decided or that tradition which possessed the three criteria of valid doctrine: *universitas, antiquitas,* and *consensio,* i. e., it must have been accepted everywhere, always and by all. This final definition of the idea of true tradition was given by Vincent of Lerinum (434) in his Commonitorium: *Magnopere curandum est, ut id teneamus, quod ubique, quod semper, quod ab omnibus creditum est* (c. 2).

2. *Inspiration.* The ancient Church Fathers emphasized the divine origin of the Scriptures as proof of their being the sufficient and infallible source of divine truth. The inspiration of the canon as a whole as well as of each individual book was presupposed, but as to its nature we find already in the writings of the early teachers of the church various views or theories.

The Fathers accepted the inspiration of the Old Testament after the Greek and Jewish mode of conceiving it, which represented the human mind as entirely passive in it. Athenagoras (Apol. 7. 9) maintained that the writers of the Old Testament were in a state of ecstasy or trance, and were unconscious of what they wrote or spoke. We have an example of this theory in the Alexandrine-Jewish legend of the composition of the Septuagint by seventy, or more exactly, seventy-two inspired writers translating independently, but miraculously attaining identical results. According to Philo human consciousness ceases with the prophetic illumination — "the understanding that dwells in us is ousted on the arrival of the divine Spirit."

The Apostolic Fathers and the Apologists, so far as they express any theory, approximate to Philo's conception. The prophets were only passive, though not unconscious instruments in the hands of the revealing God; his pens rather than his penmen. Every word was given them by God (Just. *Apol.* 36). The soul of the inspired writer is compared to a musical instrument which the Holy Spirit uses, as the flute-player breathes into the flute (Athenag. *Apol.* 9); or a harp or lyre, and the Holy Spirit the plectrum (Just. *Cohort.* 8). Although the church was averse to the Montanist view that the state of inspiration is a state of ecstasy in which sensation and self-consciousness are wholly lost, yet the general tendency was to regard the sacred writers as passive organs and inspiration as extending not merely to the contents but also to the form employed (Iren. II. 28, 2). Only in this way, the Fathers thought, was the infallibility of the divine revelation secured. There were, however, among the Fathers some who recognized besides the divine agency also a human factor in the production of the apostolic writings. Irenaeus (III. 7) already made the quality of Paul's style depend on his mental characteristics. According to Origen (*c. Cels.* VII. 4 ff.) inspiration elevates and quickens the natural faculties of the agent. There are also degrees of inspiration among the sacred writers. Origen also distinguishes between the substance of revelation, which is always true, and the language in which the writers clothe their revelations, between the divine and the human element in the Scriptures.

In the School of Antioch, under its founder Lucian, before 311, and especially under the influence of its chief leader, Theodore of Mopsuestia (d. 428), the human side in the production of Biblical revelation was made prominent. Augustine, though not blind to the human side of the Scriptural writings, stressed Biblical inerrancy so emphatically that he seemed to exclude any human factor in the composition of the Scriptures (*Ep.* 82; *Serm.* I). Gregory the Great called the writers of the Scriptures the *calami* of the Holy Spirit and maintained the strictest theory of inspiration (*Mor. praef.* I. 1. 2). The difference in style and diction of the various writers compelled critical scholars like Chrysostom (*in Matt. hom.* I) and Jerome (*in ep. ad Gal.* III. 5) to recognize the human element in the Scripture, but they never questioned the fact of the inspiration of the divine word.

The Fathers of the ancient church, then, were all agreed that the Scriptures were inspired, but differed in their views as to the "how." Some maintained that the state of inspiration is the state of ecstasy, or at least a state from which all human agency is to be excluded. Others recognized the human element in the Biblical writings though they never questioned the divine origin nor the inerrancy of the Scriptures.

3. *Interpretation.* In interpreting the Scriptures it was only natural to consult tradition, i. e., the testimony of those who followed the apostles. In opposition to heresies it became customary to give connected statements of the main points embraced in the traditional teaching and to interpret Scripture through the Rule of Faith, the chief certificate of true apostolic teaching. This did not preclude sound exegesis; it only precluded interpretation *contra regulam.* When heretics began to interpret and distort Scripture, there was naturally an incentive to compare Scripture with Scripture, and to seek that interpretation which agreed best with the body and texture of the sacred volume.

It was in Alexandria that Christian teaching very early assumed the form of a regular catechetical institution. In Scriptural interpretation, however, the Alexandrian School followed Philo in his allegorizing method.

The Fathers of Antioch adhered to hermeneutical maxims insisting more on the grammatico-historical sense of the Scriptures than on their moral and allegorical meaning.

The contemporary exegetical productions of the Latin Fathers were neither as extensive nor as important as those of the East.

Allegorical interpretation was a most palpable fault in early exegesis throughout the Greek Church, and the Latin Church was by no means altogether free from it.

CHAPTER VI

THE BEGINNINGS OF SCIENTIFIC THEOLOGY IN THE ANCIENT CHURCH

A. IN THE EASTERN CHURCH.

1. The Apologists had treated Christianity chiefly as a body of teachings relating to religion and morals. This intellectual interest was still more prominent in the *Alexandrian Catechetical School,* originally designed for the instruction of pagans and Jews who turned to Christianity, but soon developing itself into a school of theology for the training of Christian teachers and preachers. It was at various times under the headship of highly distinguished men.

The first known superintendent of this school was Pantaenus, a converted Stoic, a native of Sicily, about 185. Little is known of him. None of his writings have been preserved. We can only judge of him by his pupil and future successor Titus Flavius Clement, a pagan by birth, of comprehensive scholarly and philosophic culture. He left the school in the Severian persecution, 202, but subsequently returned to Alexandria and died there about 220.

The principal works of Clement are his *Prôtreptikos* or Exhortation to the Heathen, an apologetic treatise in three books, intended to win pagans to Christianity. It points out the immorality and unreasonableness of heathenism and contrasts with the latter the truth as taught in the inspired Scriptures, recognizing, however, the elements of truth in pagan poets and philosophers. His *Paedagogus* or Instructor is an ethic of treatise addressed to those already won for Christianity, intended to be a guide for the formation and development of Christian character and for living a Christian life. The *Stromateis* or Miscellanies, seven books, are of a dogmatic character, though without any systematic order, as the full title of the work indicates: *Miscellaneous collections of speculative (gnostic) notes bearing upon the true philosophy.*

Clement was followed by Origen (d. 254), who was leader in the school to 232. Through him it reached the highest attainments in speculative theology. Under the leadership of his pupil Heraclas (d. 248) and Dionysius (d. 265) it continued to flourish until under the headship of the blind but learned Didymus (d. c. 400) the school, shaken already by the Arian controversy, lost more and more of its influence and finally became extinct.

2. *Alexandrine Theology.* In order to form a correct opinion as to the peculiar theology which proceeded from this school, it must be remembered that this theology stands in its origin in closest relation with Greek speculation and scholarship. Alexandria was the home of the Philonic theology, Gnostic heresy, and Neo-Pythagorean and Neo-Platonic philosophy. The catechetical school assumed

already under the headship of Pantaenus a very learned character and became a sort of theological seminary. Clement, though not an adherent of one particular school, but well acquainted with the current systems of philosophy, borrowed ideas from several systems. Origen followed more the track of Platonism. He had been a pupil of Ammonius Saccas, the founder of Neoplatonism. Both Clement and Origen set a very high value on philosophy. They saw in it a preparation for Christianity and a means by which to attain to a deeper knowledge for Christian doctrine. Accordingly the Alexandrine theologians made it their task to set forth the truth of Christianity through Hellenistic philosophy and to show that Christianity is the highest philosophy. Therefore the Alexandrine teachers distinguished between pistis, the simple confidence in the facts of revelation, a kind of faith sufficient for the renewal and salvation of man, and gnosis, a deeper insight into the mysteries of revelation. Faith in the heart must precede the philosophic cognition of Christianity; it is perfected by knowledge. Faith is the outward acceptance of Scriptural truth in the literal sense. But gnosis is the inward apprehension and comprehension of truth in the spiritual sense. This is the true gnosis in opposition to the false gnosis of the Gnostics. Yet in their attempts to reconcile Christianity with philosophy these orthodox Gnostics like their heretical brethren were often led to phantastic speculations. Like them, too, they distinguished sharply between an exoteric knowledge, communicated and intelligible to the general body of followers, and an esoteric knowledge, designed for, and understood by, the specially initiated alone. The higher spiritual knowledge and intuition, however, stand in closest connection with the exercise of a perfectly pure life, i. e., emancipation from sensuality.

The object of both faith and knowledge is the Logos. Around the Logos centered the speculations of the Alexandrine theologians. They blended the Logos idea of the fourth Gospel with that of Philo and the Alexandrine-Jewish philosophy. The Logos is the Divine Reason, the Mediator between God and world, the organ of all revelation in history. Hence he was in the world before the incarnation. All that is true and beautiful in the Greek philosophers must be traced to the activities of the Logos before his incarnation. We notice here the Stoic conception of the Logos as the seminal reason diffused in all beings possessed of reason. Accordingly Greek philosophy contained already Christian elements and was therefore a preparation for the Christian truth. This Logos, viewed as the sum of all reason and truth, became incarnate in Christ and therefore Christianity is the true philosophy and absolute truth.

3. *Origen* formulated these ideas into a system in his great and comprehensive work *De principiis* or On First Principles, the earli-

est systematic treatise on doctrinal theology, which has come down to us, with the exception of a few Greek fragments, in the translation of Rufinus. Origen was both a philosophical idealist and an orthodox traditionalist. As a speculative philosopher he transmuted the whole contents of the faith of the church into ideas permeated with Neoplatonism and thus often indulged in vain and unauthorized speculations. As an orthodox traditionalist he held very positively to the faith of the church, so that there seems to be no adequate reason to doubt his substantial orthodoxy. His doctrines called forth vehement opposition as well as vehement defence. Being excluded from communion with the church on account of his foreign speculations, his self-mutilation and his violation of the church's laws, Origen left Alexandria, 231, for Caesarea in Palestine, but his doctrine remained, interpreted by his convert and pupil Dionysius. The churches in Palestine, Arabia and Achaia paid no attention to his excommunication. Origen continued to fill the office of presbyter in Caesarea and opened a new philosophical and theological school, which soon outshone that of Alexandria. Thither repaired the most distinguished students, such as Gregory, afterwards surnamed Thaumaturgus, and many others. At the opening of the Decian persecution Origen was arrested, dragged to the rack, thrown into prison and condemned to the stake. Nothing daunted his courage. Having regained his liberty by the death of the emperor, he survived the end of the persecution for two or three years. He died at Tyre (253 or 254) at the age of sixty-nine.

In his work *De Principiis*, before stating his own doctrinal conclusions, he refers to the teachings of the church, the Rule of Faith, and the Scriptures. The Scriptures, however, are to be interpreted spiritually. Origen applied Plato's distinction of body, mind and spirit to the Scriptures, admitting in them a somatic or literal, a psychic or moral, and a pneumatic or spiritual or symbolical sense. The third sense is open only to "the perfect," the cultured believer. Origen believed that the apparent discrepancies of the Evangelists can be explained only by means of the spiritual sense. For his allegorical method he appealed to Prov. 22:20-21.

In the first three books of his *De Principiis* he presents the whole content of his teaching. In the first book he treats of God, the Logos, the Holy Spirit, reason and the angels; in the second, of the world and man, the incarnation of the Logos, the soul, the resurrection of the body, and the punishment of the wicked; in the third, of the freedom of the will, sin and redemption. In the fourth book he treats of the divinity of the Scriptures and deduces rules for their interpretation, concluding with a recapitulation of the entire system.

Of his immense literary output a comparatively small portion has come down to us. Of his books which remain, we shall chiefly use in our present discussion, besides his *De Principiis* and his exegetical writings, his well-known apologetic work, *Contra Celsum*, written in defence of Christianity against the attacks of Celsus, a philosopher.

4. *Epitome of Origen's System.* God is an incomprehensible, unchangeable and spiritual Being, the absolute causality of all that is good. He is good and just in all his works and ways, "one and the same, a just and good God, . . . he confers benefits justly, and punishes with kindness; since neither goodness without justice, nor justice without goodness, can display the real dignity of the divine nature" (*de pr*. I. 1. 5; II. 5. 3; *c. Cels*. VIII. 8. 21). God is always active and therefore he exists never alone. God and the world are co-eternal. He is the cause of the world, but he is conceived of as a personality; he is the Creator, Preserver and Governor of the world. Accordingly creation is not a Gnostic emanation, but an eternal act of God, i. e., in eternity past (*de pr*. I. 2. 10; II. 3; III. 5. 4; *c. Cels*. III. 49).

The Logos is the mediator of all divine agency. He is the mediator between God and the world (*ib*. VI. 60; II. 9; *de pr*. I. 2. 8). As God is the cause of the world, so he is the begetter of the Son. The Logos proceeds from the Father as the will proceeds from the mind of man. This does not imply a partition or division of divine essence nor a sensuous emanation from the essence of the Father. The Logos is generated of the Father and this generation is eternal (*ib*. I. 2. 4. 6. 10). The immutability of God requires the eternity of the Logos; "there was not a time when he was not." He is the Son and of the same essence with God, *homoousios*, and yet himself a separate hypostasis (*ib*. I. 2. 9. 10). "We worship, therefore, the Father of truth, and the Son, who is the truth; and these, while they are two, considered as persons and subsistences, are one in unity of thought, in harmony and in identity of will" (*c. Cels*. VIII. 12). In relation to God, the Son is a copy of the original and as such inferior to that. Though co-eternal and co-substantial with the Father, the Son is at the same time called "a second God" (*ib*. V. 39). He is "made God," not *the* God, but simply God, *theos*, with the article omitted (*in Johann*. II. 2). He is said to be "a creature" (*ib*. I. 22; *de pr*. I. 2. 1). In one place (*c. Cels*. V. 37) he is even called "the most ancient of all creation." The Father is above him as the Son is above the creation.

We observe then that in Origen's teaching on this topic Athanasian and Arian views are blended. In later times both the orthodox and the Arians appealed to his teaching.

The same view of subordinationism we notice again in the relation of the Holy Spirit to the Father and the Son. Though like the

Son he has a personal existence and is uncreated, yet since all things
have come into existence through the Logos it follows that the Holy
Spirit is the first of the spirits begotten of the Father through the
Son (*in Johann.* II. 6; *de pr.* I. 3. 3, 5). There is also a subordination
as to the sphere of his operations. The influence of the Father extends to all, since all derive their existence from him. The Logos
is active in all rational beings; the Holy Spirit alone in the souls of
the saints (*ib.* I. 3. 5, 8).

The Holy Spirit was the first product of the Logos. But from
eternity the Logos also created, prior to the creation of matter, a
limited number of finite spirits, originally all alike, whose freedom
of will was inseparable from their existence. "This freedom of the
will incited each one either to progress by imitation of God or
reduced him to failure through negligence. And this is . . . the
cause of the diversity among rational creatures, deriving its origin
not from the will or judgment of the Creator, but from the freedom
of the individual will." Because of their apostasy the material
world was created as a school of discipline and purgation for the
fallen spirits (*ib.* II. 9. 6, 8.), who became souls, i. e., they "cooled
down" from that natural and divine warmth into souls (Origen derives *psyche* from *psychao*) and were clothed with material bodies
as a punishment for their sin. They are now passing through a
disciplinary process in order to be restored to their pre-existent
condition (*ib.* II. 1, 1-4; 8, 3; 9, 8; III. 5, 4).

Since, according to Origen, souls were stained with sin by voluntary choice in a former state and thus entered into the world in a
sinful condition, and since even in this life sin is a voluntary election
of evil, there is no place in his system either for unconditional predestination or for original sin, i. e., inherited sin.

In order to save fallen men it was necessary for the Logos to
become incarnate. He assumed human nature and was God and
man (*c. Cels.* III. 28; VII. 17), the God-man, *theanthropos* (*de pr.*
II. 6, 3). But how could the Logos, who is of the same essence with
the Father, appear on earth? Origen answers: There was a pure,
unfallen, pre-existent spirit, who grew into an indissoluble union
with the Logos, and thus merited to become in due time the human
soul of Christ (*ib.*). This is in fact not a real incarnation, but only
an indwelling of God in man (*ib.* IV. 3; *c. Cels.* I. 66. 68). It was the
body or the soul of Christ that suffered, not the Logos (*ib.* II.16;
IV. 15; VII. 16). After the ascension the human was absorbed in the
divine (*in Johann.* 32. 17).

Christ's redemptive work is chiefly that of a teacher, lawgiver
and exemplar. It extends to all, first through the natural and revealed law, and then through the gospel which is conceived of as

essentially a new law (*c. Cels.* III. 7. 62; IV. 4. 22. 32). There is a deeper revelation in the gospel through the mysteries, i. e., the sacraments, for such as are spiritually prepared to receive them (*in Johann.* VI. 17). The sacraments are symbols. Baptism is a symbol of the purifying power of the divine Logos (*in Luc. hom.* XXI). The elements in the Eucharist are symbols of the word of Christ (*in Lev. hom.* VIII. 5), which nourishes and delights the heart. Christ is all this for us because he has first delivered us from the powers of evil and reconciled us to God. Christ's sacrifice for us, his suffering and death, have therefore also a prominent place in his redemptive work (*c. Cels.* I. 54; II. 23. 44; VII. 57). His death is conceived of not only as a sacrifice for sin offered to God, but also as a ransom paid to Satan. Jesus had committed his divine spirit to the Father, but offered up the human soul for a ransom. Satan, however, found himself defrauded and was not able to retain the ransom paid him, as is proved by the resurrection. Thus through Christ's victory Satan lost all right over humanity (*ib.* II. 47; VIII. 54. 64; *in Johann.* XVI. 8). The final object and end of Christ's work is the deliverance of the Spirit from its unnatural union with the sensual. Accordingly the Christian Gnostic must aim at attaining not only a higher degree of knowledge, but a complete freedom from the passions (*c. Cels.* I. 26; VI. 68; VII. 48; VIII. 55; *in Lev.* XI. 1). Origen's attitude toward the pleasures of sense explains his strong opposition to the sensuous conception of a millennium on earth (*de pr.* II. 11. 2, 6).

Immediately at death the righteous enter paradise, a state of blessedness, but where they are still under training advancing from knowledge to knowledge until they meet Christ. The wicked pass through a process of purification by the fire of punishment, fire being a symbol of the pain of conscience (*ib.* II. 10. 4; 11. 4, 5; *c. Cels.* VI. 72). Finally all created spirits, including Satan and the demons, are purified and restored to live in full vision of the Godhead. However, a shadow is cast upon this restoration of all things by Origen's fear that incalculable free will may again depart from God (*ib.* IV. 6; VIII. 72; *de pr.* III. 6. 3, 6).

Despite many inconsistencies and errors in Origen's theological system — (allegorical interpretation, eternal creation, pre-existence of souls, free will of man, relation of Son to Father, co-essential and subordinate; denial of original sin, Christ's death a ransom to Satan, spiritualizing of sacraments, intermediate state, final restoration of all) — his theology prepared the way for the later dogmas, such as those of the Trinity, Holy Spirit, person of Christ, eternal generation and incarnation of Christ. All the later parties in the church learned from and found something congenial in his writings. In stating Christianity in terms of philosophy Origen did not furnish milk for babes. But it was just in this form that his theology succeeded in striking the death blow against heretical Gnosticism.

5. After the death of Origen there sprang up a great school in Syria which soon developed into a chief centre of theological influence, the *School of Antioch*. It owed its origin, no doubt, to the impulse given by Origen to theology, but in the course of its development it became independent of, and indeed frequently opposed to, the school of Origen.

The presbyter and martyr Lucian (d. 311), who had great influence as an exegete and metaphysician, is generally regarded as the founder of this school. He adhered to Paul of Samosata even after the latter had been condemned. Arius and his most distinguished friends and later the Nestorians claimed descent from the school founded by Lucian. The most celebrated representatives of the Antiochian School were Diodorus of Tarsus (d. 378) and "the three great Antiochians," Theodore of Mopsuestia (d. 428), John of Antioch, better known as Chrysostom (d. 407) and Theodoret, bishop of Cyrus in Syria (d. 457).

The School of Antioch, from its first, gave its main attention to the critical, grammatical and historical interpretation of the Scriptures. In contrast with the dogmatic allegorical interpretation prevailing in the Alexandrian School, the Antiochenes based interpretation on the given grammatical and historical conditions. They looked to reason rather than to authority to explain and develop dogma. As in their exegetical labors they aimed at doing justice to the human factor in the production of Biblical revelation, so did they likewise in their theological and Christological efforts lay the stress on the human element in the person of Christ. They took little account of the divine element and consequently saw in Christ preeminently a teacher and exemplar.

B. In the Western Church.

The Western theologians did not, like the Greek Fathers, conceive of Christianity as a new philosophy, but as a new life, or a new relation between God and man. Therefore they did not set a true gnosis against a false one, but emphasized tradition as the actual possession of truth in the church. Faith was to them not, in the first place, knowledge of the divine truth, but the way to the salvation of the soul.

1. The most prominent representative of the Western School was *Tertullian* (160-c. 230), a man of great originality and genius, distinguished by a lively imagination, wit, keenness and varied learning. He was the son of a heathen centurion at Carthage, re-

ceived a scholarly education and devoted himself at first to the study of oratory and Roman jurisprudence. Once a Christian he was determined to be so with all his soul. Having experienced the renewing and transforming power of Christianity in his own life he conceived of Christianity as something entirely new in the world and altogether different from human wisdom. He embraced Montanism, probably at the time of the persecution under Septimius Severus, most likely touched by the moral strictness of the Montanists. From his Montanistic point of view he advocated in an age of laxity strict moral discipline in the church. Toward the bishop of Rome he assumed a very independent attitude, while at the same time he remained a zealous advocate of the catholic faith.

His writings cover the whole theological field of the time. We mention here only the more important. They may be divided into two groups : (1) apologetic and polemic: *Apologeticus, De testimonio animae, Adversus Judaeos, Ad nationes, Adversus Marcionem, De praescriptione hereticorum, Adversus Valentinianos, Adv. Hermogenem, Adv. Praxeam, De carne Christi, De resurrectione carnis, De baptismo,* etc. (2) practical and disciplinary : *De pudicitia, De monogamia, Ad uxorem, De virginibus velandis, De jejuniis, De pallio, De cultu feminarum, De exhortatione castitatis,* etc.

2. *Tertullian's Theology.* Tertullian is after Augustine the greatest of the ancient church writers of the West. He may properly be called the father of Latin theology and of the Latin church language.

In his writings he maintains the divine authority of the Scriptures, but also their insufficiency, since heretics at any time may pervert them, and asserts the authority of tradition and appeals to the Rule of Faith (*de praescr.* 13; 14; *Apol.* 19; 39).

In direct contrast to the mystic idealism and metaphysical speculation of the Alexandrians Tertullian maintains a determined realism with a strong tendency to materialism. "Incorporeal" is with him the same thing as "non-existent" (*de carne Chr.* XI). Man is at once soul and body (*de test. an.* IX). Tertullian rejects Origen's idea of pre-existence of the soul, as well as the Pythagorean theory of metempsychosis. Nor is the human soul separately created in each individual born (creationism), but it is transmitted from parent to child, propagated by generation as *per traducem,* along with the body (*ib.* XIX-XXXI). Traducianism most easily explains the propagation of original sin by generation (*ib.* XXVII). "Still there is a portion of good in the soul, of that original divine, and genuine good, which is its proper nature. For that which is derived from God is rather obscured than extinguished" (*ib.* XLI). In his sinful state man still possesses freedom of the will (*c. Marc.* II.6; *Apol.* XII). God himself has corporeity though he is a spirit; hence man could be created in his likeness (*adv. Prax.* XII).

In distinction from the Logos of the philosophers Tertullian maintains that the Logos is a real subsistence (*Apol.* XXI). Against the Patripassianism of Praxeas he designates him a person distinct from the Father, and the Spirit distinct from both the Father and the Son (*adv. Prax.* XII. XXV). These three are one substance, but not one person (*ib.* IX). Tertullian does not hold Origen's theory of the eternal generation of the Son, but states that he had a beginning (*adv. Hermog.* III). The Logos assumed his form and mode of life, when God said: "Let there be light" (*adv. Prax.* VI. VII).

The doctrine of the Holy Spirit is not clearly stated by Tertullian. In the statement of the Trinity he asserts the identity of nature but holds to a marked subordination of the Son and the Spirit to the Father. "The Spirit indeed is third from God and the Son, just as the fruit of the tree is third from the root, or as the stream out of the river is third from the fountain, or as the apex of the ray is third from the sun. Nothing, however, is alien from that original source whence it derives its own properties. In like manner the Trinity flowing down from the Father . . . does not at all disturb the monarchy, whilst it at the same time guards the state of the Economy" (*ib.* VIII). By the economic Trinity Tertullian means the successive Trinity.

The pre-existent Logos became man when he was born of the Virgin Mary (*De carne Chr.* XIII; XVI-XVIII; XX). He assumed actual human flesh, together with a human soul (*ib.* VI; XV; XVIII). The divine and human are combined in a unity of one person (XIII). But the divine nature abides unchanged in the midst of changing circumstances (III). He suffered and died in his humanity (XXIX). The divine nature is not capable of suffering (*ib.*). Tertullian does not define the work of redemption but merely affirms it (V; *adv. Marc.* VII; VIII; *de pud.* VI).

We are born again in the water of baptism which is necessary to salvation (*de bapt.* XII), unless its omission be supplied by martyrdom (*ib.* XVI). A truly sanctifying virtue is inherent in the baptismal water (V; VIII). For the Eucharist Tertullian does not claim any inherent virtue, but regards it a symbol of the broken body of Christ (*adv. Marc.* IV. 40). Sins committed subsequent to baptism may be forgiven. By repentance the offended God may be appeased (*de paen.* IX). Baptism and repentance are therefore called the "two planks" on which the sinner may be saved from shipwreck (XII). In c. VIII and IX Tertullian points out three constituent elements of true repentance: heartfelt sorrow, confession of sins, and satisfaction. The entire life of the believer and his relation to God is put on a mere legal footing. The gospel is the "new law" (*de praescr.* XIII; *monog.* VII; VIII). God is preeminently the lawgiver and judge who metes out righteous punishment to the transgressor (*de exhort. cast.* II; *c. Marc.* I.26). Accordingly the fundamental relation of man to God is that of fear (*de paen.* VII; *ad ux.* II. 7). Yet by true repentance man can earn for himself God's favor in baptism (*de paen.* VI) "We are not washed in order that we may cease sinning, but because we have ceased" (*ib.*). For this reason Tertullian wishes baptism to be deferred in the case of little children, who are not yet able to fulfil the spiritual conditions required to give full efficacy to the sacramental grace (*de bapt.* XVIII).

We should not only fulfil the precepts of the law, but if possible also its counsels, such as "counsels of innocence, chastity, justice and piety" (*c. Marc.* II.17; *ad. ux.* II.1), in order to become holy and righteous and "to repay to Him what He has paid for us" (*de pat.* XVI; *de res.* VIII). We should do all this with the divine recompense constantly in view. "A good deed has God as its debtor, just as an evil one has too" (*de paen.* II).

The frequent recurrence, in Terullian's writings, of such legal terms as: merit, reward, punishment, penalty, satisfaction, compensation, payment and the like, are in keeping with his legalistic conception of Christianity. His conception of Christian truth and life is in the main that of the later Catholic Church.

3. After Tertullian, *Cyprian,* bishop of Carthage (d. 258), the champion of episcopacy, had great influence in North Africa. His teachings were of special importance in reference to the doctrine of the church, church government and discipline, while the writings of the Latin Fathers Commodianus, Lactantius and Arnobius were of little or no significance for the later development of Christian doctrine.

4. *Irenaeus.* One of the most distinguished authors and theologians representing both the Eastern and Western Churches was Irenaeus, a disciple of Polycarp. He spent the earlier years of his life in Asia Minor. At the time of the persecution of the Gallic Church under Marcus Aurelius (177) he was presbyter, later bishop, at Lyons (d. about 202).

Irenaeus keeps the safe middle path between Eastern and Western theology. In his *Refutation* of the false Gnosis, *Adversus haereses*, in five books, of which only fragments remain in the original Greek, but which exists in full in a literal and crude Latin translation, he rejects the fanciful and arbitrary Gnostic speculation and maintains the realistic substance of Christianity. The foundation upon which he bases his arguments consists in the episcopate as the safeguard of truth, the canon of the Old and New Testaments and the Rule of Faith (III. 3).

His conception of Christ and his redemptive work rises above that of Tertullian. He does not attempt to offer a metaphysical construction of the great mystery of the Trinity. He looks upon the Logos not as the Reason but as the Word of God, as did the writer of the fourth Gospel. The divine Word is the full revelation of the Father; he is at once the truth and the life (II. 30. 9; IV. 6. 5 ff.; 20. 7). Irenaeus refuses to offer an explanation of the mode of the generation of the Son; of this we know nothing (II. 28, 6; 13, 8). We know the Son as always co-existing with the Father (II. 30, 9; III. 18, 1). The world was created by the Word out of nothing (II. 2, 1, 5; 11, 1, 2). The eternal Logos became a real man assuming not only the body but also the soul (III. 22, 1); thereby he united all flesh to God. He recapitulated as it were in himself the whole human race (III. 16, 6; 18,·1, 7; 22, 2). Irenaeus makes the incarnation more than a superior mode of revelation, or divine illumination. The chief object of the incarnation is redemption of the fallen race. He speaks of a propitiation, a ransom, but not as a prize given to Satan. Redemption through the *incarnate Christ* is given the central place in Irenaeus' system. Redemption, according to him, is the victory of the holy obedience of the head of the new humanity over the power of sin, death and devil. Hence Irenaeus maintains in all its reality the human nature of Jesus Christ as the representative of humanity (III. 20).

5. *Hippolytus*, a pupil of Irenaeus, was presbyter of the church at Rome under the Roman bishops Zephyrinus (199-217) and Callistus (- 222). He was distinquished for his learning and eloquence, took an active part in all the doctrinal and ritual controversies of his time, but came to great discord with the Roman bishops, especially with Callistus, on account of their subverting the discipline of the church by extreme leniency to offenders, and their favoring Patripassian opinions. The result was a schism, and Hippolytus appeared as an anti-bishop at the head of a schismatical party at Portus near Rome. About 225 he was banished with the Roman bishop Pontianus to Sardinia for his Christian confession, where it would seem that both of them died. From the fact that his memory has ever since been celebrated in the church as that of a holy martyr, we must suppose that before his death Hippolytus returned into the bosom of the catholic church.

His numerous works, all written in Greek, embrace the sphere of exegesis, homiletics, apologetics and polemics, chronography and ecclesiastical law. Most of them are preserved only in fragments. The most important of his polemical writings is the *Refutation of all Heresies*, previously only known by its first book, *Philosophumena*, and falsely ascribed to Origen. Of its ten books the second and third are lost. Of his dogmatic works that on *Christ and Anti-christ* has been almost entirely preserved.

For his theology Hippolytus is indebted to Irenaeus whom he follows in the main, but differs from him in his conception of the church. Irenaeus sees in the church of Rome the church with which all Christendom must agree, or to which all other churches must resort (III. 2). Hippolytus was a decided antagonist of the contemporary Roman bishops, both for doctrinal and disciplinary reasons. He constantly warns against retrogression to Jewish sacerdotalism and theocratic rule. In his theology he follows Oriental speculation and for this reason does not, as his master did, bring into light the harmony of the human and the divine in Jesus. Like Tertullian he maintains the production of the Word at the moment of creation (*c. Noet.* 10; *Refut.* X. 33).

At the end of the second and the beginning of the third centuries we find the church maintaining the true character of Christianity over against the opposition from without and within. The church is well grounded in the common confession of faith appealing to oral tradition and the canonical Scriptures as the two equally authoritative sources of truth. We have had occasion to observe the various attempts of the teachers of the ancient church at a scientific presentation and theological formulation of the divine truth. The church's theology is now well prepared to enter upon the task of the theological elaboration and dogmatic formulation of the church's doctrines.

CHAPTER VII

THE PROBLEM OF THE TRINITY

A. The Deity of Christ and Monarchianism.

1. *The Deity of Christ.* The ancient church occupied herself first with the solution of the problems of theology in the strict sense of the term as the doctrine of the essence of God. She approached the problem not from speculative motives as though she had in the first place to deal with the questions pertaining to God the Father, or the Trinity. The church concentrated her interest first of all on the doctrine of the person of Christ; and here it was the deity of Christ that first engaged the church's attention. In the attempts to reconcile Christ's deity with the idea of monotheism the church had also to give theological definitions concerning the Father, the Holy Spirit and the Trinity.

The deity of Christ was not the goal but the starting point of theological development. The church did not accept and believe the doctrine of the deity of Christ because and after the teachers of the church had set forth and defined that doctrine, but from the beginning the church believed in the only begotten Son of God. The Rule of Faith as well as the Apostolic Fathers asserted the true divinity and the true humanity of Christ. So did the Apologists. Not only did they acknowledge the divine person of Christ without any limitation, but they attempted to answer such questions as, Who is Christ the Lord? What is his relation to God the Father? Linking Christian theology with philosophical theology of antiquity the Apologists answered: Jesus Christ is the divine Logos; he is of the very essence of the Father. Their provisional answer, however, did not solve the problem implied: The problem of the Trinity of the divine persons in the unity of the Godhead, and that of the union of the divine and human natures in the person of Christ. A solution of the former was attempted in the Monarchian and Arian controversies; of the latter, in the Christological controversies.

2. *Monarchianism.* The assertion of the district personality and the perfect equality of the Father and the Son demanded a clear definition. In the attempt at defining the two it could easily come to this that the one was emphasized at the expense of the other.

Toward the end of the second century there arose within the Church two tendencies opposing the doctrine of an independent personal subsistence of the Logos and identifying the divine in

Christ with God himself. The opposition arose out of fear that this doctrine endangered the absolute unity or *monarchia* of the Godhead. The theory was therefore styled Monarchianism.

According to their different conceptions of the person of Christ the Monarchians fall into two classes. In order to hold fast to the unity of the Godhead the one abandons the Deity of Christ, holding Christ to be a mere man chosen of God, in whom the Holy Spirit dwelt in a (quite) unique sense (Dynamic or Adoptionist Monarchianism). It resembles the Ebionite view. The other, maintaining Christ to be a manifestation of God himself abandons the personal distinctions and confounds the persons of the Father and the Son (Modalistic Monarchianism). It resembles the Docetic view.

3. *Dynamic Monarchianism.* The first representative of Dynamic Monarchianism was Theodotus, the Fuller, who came to Rome from Byzantium about 190 A. D. He held that Jesus, though born of a virgin was a mere man yet one of highest virtue and piety. His Deity was only a power (*dynamic*), communicated to him at his baptism. There, the Christ, otherwise called the Holy Spirit, descended upon him in the form of a dove. Thus he received the power to work miracles. Some of the Theodocians held that he never was made God, while others maintained that this prerogative became his after the resurrection from the dead. Pope Victor condemned such doctrines and excommunicated Theodotus. Similar views were also held by Theodotus, the Money Changer, about 210, and Artemon, about 235.—In this class of Monarchians are improperly reckoned the *Alogi...* They rejected the doctrine of the Logos, but did not deny the deity of Christ.

This type of Monarchianism was more fully developed by Paul of Samosata, the worldly, splendor-loving patriarch of Antioch, 260-272. He held that Jesus was a mere man miraculously born. Inspired by the Logos he gradually rose to divine dignity, so as to be worthy of the name of God. Paul's Monarchianism is of the Adoptionist type. His theory may be summed up as follows: Father, Son and Spirit are the one God. Both, the Logos and the Holy Spirit, are impersonal. The Logos, who may be called Son or Wisdom, is an impersonal attribute of the Father and can never become a concrete manifestation. The Son is therefore not in an 'hypostasis,' i. e., a distinct subsistence or person, but he is always in God just as man's own reason (*logos*) is always in the heart of man. As divine wisdom dwelt in the prophets, and in a still higher degree in Moses and many others, so it dwells in a unique way in the man Christ. Hence the "Logos from above" is the "Christ from below." The man Christ, then, is another than the Logos. Christ was not before Mary, but received from her the origin of his being. But from his birth he was anointed with the Holy Spirit whereby a union of Christ with God was effected, a moral union in the will and in love, that was carried to such a perfection that he was adopted by God and exalted to divine dignity. He inherited the name which is above all names, the prize of love and affection vouch-safed in grace to him.

4. *Modalistic Monarchianism.* The modalistic Monarchians stressed the true divinity of Christ and, since they held fast to the unity of the Godhead, they confounded the persons maintaining that the names "Father" and "Son" were only different designations of the same subject. This type of Monarchianism was the more dangerous, since the church also taught and emphasized the deity of Christ and the homoousia.

The first prominent representative of this type of Monarchianism was Praxeas, a confessor from Asia Minor, who brought this doctrine to Rome about 190, whence it also spread to North Africa. He taught that Christ was only a theophany. The Father became Son, the Father was born, the Father suffered (Patripassianism). While in Rome, Praxeas also procured the condemnation of Montanism. Hence Tertullian sarcaustically charged him with having accomplished two tasks for the devil: "he drove away prophecy and he brought in heresy; he put to flight the Paraclete, and crucified the Father" (*c. Prax.* I).

In support of his theory Praxeas constantly appeals to such passages as Is. 45:5 "I am the Lord and there is none else, there is no God beside me." John 10:30 "I and the Father are one." John 14:9 "he that hath seen me, hath seen the Father;" v. 11 "I am in the Father and the Father in me." That Jesus says v. 12 "I go unto my Father," is of no consequence to Praxeas. There is a certain inconsistency in Praxeas' view, as in the one person he distinguishes two, Father and Son, "it is the Son indeed who suffers, the Father is only his fellow-sufferer — *filius patitur, pater vero compatitur*" (*ib.* XXIX). This passage reveals a leaning toward dynamic Monarchianism. Others conclude from it that Praxeas was not a Patripassianist.

The Patripassian view obtained fresh support in Rome under Zepyrinus and Callistus about 215 from Noetus, a native of Smyrna, and his disciples Epigonus and Cleomenes. If we may trust the account of his opponent Hippolytus, Noetus held that "when the Father had not been born, he was justly styled Father; and when it pleased him to undergo generation, having been begotten, he himself became his own Son, not another's" (*Ref.* IX. 10). Christ is himself the Father and the Father himself was born and suffered and died. The same person bears the name of Father or Son, as circumstances require (*ib.* X. 23).

A more conciliatory Patripassian view was expounded in the East somewhat later, about 240, by *Beryllus,* bishop of Bostra in Arabia. He distinguished between the divine person which is strictly one, the Father, and the deity of Christ which was not his own but that of the Father committed to him in the incarnation (Euseb. *h. e.* VI. 33). This view forms a connecting link between the Patripassians and the Sabellians who also held that the Son did not pre-exist as a divine person distinct from the Father and that the Father after the incarnation assumed the special mode of existence as Son.

Sabellius, of Libyan origin, spent some time at Rome early in the third century. He did not only identify the Father with the Son, but developed and elaborated a regular Trinitarian system. The unity of the Godhead has been active in three apparently consecutive manifestations, in that of the Father as Creator and Lawgiver; in that of the Son as Redeemer, from Christ's incarnation; and in that of the Spirit as the Giver of Light, from the day of the ascension. Accordingly, the Father is the same as the Son, and the Son the same as the Spirit, three names thus being attached to one and the same Being. This Being is also named Son-Father. And yet God was not Father and Son and Spirit at the same time, but assumed three distinct successive forms of manifestation comparable to the tripartite nature of man, body, soul and spirit, or to the sun which manifests itself as a heavenly body, as a source of light and a source of warmth. As Christ possessed personality only in his historical appearance in the flesh, that personality neither existed previous to his incarnation, nor does it continue to exist now in heaven.

5. *The Church's Opposition to Monarchianism.* The church recognized the errors of both forms of Monarchianism and rejected especially the heresy of Paul of Samosata. He was excommunicated and deposed at a synod at Antioch, probably 268. The sentence did not take effect until late in 272. Sabellius' influence was more strongly felt in the East than in the West. In Rome he was excommunicated by Callistus, but his party continued to exist there for a considerable time afterwards. In the East his doctrine, which underwent various modifications, was violently controverted by many bishops, notably Dinonysius of Alexandria. In opposition to Monarchianism the Eastern Church stressed the union of the Son with the Father, while the Western Church asserted the personality of the Son distinct from the Father. In the West Tertullian took the lead contending against Praxeas. In refuting Monarchianism he had to stress the distinct personality of the Son, but at the same time he had to hold fast to the unity of the Godhead. Two co-

ordinate divine persons would seem to destroy the divine unity, but a second person proceeding from and subordinate to the first seemed less antagonistic to unity. Hence to meet this double demand Tertullian and the writers who followed him, fell into the subordinationist' error. In the East we note a different thought in connection with the doctrine of Christ's deity. Clement of Alexandria emphasized the essential unity of the Godhead to such an extent that although he affirmed the distinction of Father and Son (*Protr.* I), he also, in some passages, obliterated the personal distinction. The Logos is co-existent with the Father and is said to undergo no change (*strom.* III. 7; VI. 9); hence Clement rejected the distinction between the internal Logos and the Logos expressed. Origen went a step forward. He harmonized the distinct personality of the Son with the divine unity in that he maintained the timeless, eternal generation of the Son. God is eternally a Father, and "as the light cannot be without its brightness, so God can never have been without the Son, the brightness of his majesty" (*de pr.* I. 2. 4). And yet the Father is God in the most eminent sense, while the Son, though co-eternal with the Father, is God in a derived sense.

This view of subordinationism led to new misunderstandings and far-reaching controversies. On the other hand, the first attempts were made at a scholarly interpretation of the traditional doctrines of the church, to wit, the Son's deity and unity in essence with the Father, and the distinct personality of the Son. But there still remained the difficult task of reconciling the two conceptions. The church had yet to pass through a long struggle of opposition and controversies until these doctrines were clearly defined and formulated and as such officially accepted.

B. ARIANISM AND THE HOMOOUSIA OF THE SON.

1. *Decisive Factors in Doctrinal Development.* During the period in which the church was agitated by the great controversies upon the doctrine of the deity and personality of Christ, theological scholarship was exceedingly flourishing and prolific. The great theologians of the Eastern Church, such as Athanasius (d. 373), the Three Cappadocian Fathers: Gregory of Nazianzus (d. 390), his older friend, Basil the Great (d. 379), and Basil's younger brother, the deep thinker, Gregory of Nyssa (d. 394), and in the West, Hilary of Poitiers (d. 367), opposed a tendency that would introduce rationalistic, mythological and polytheistic elements into Christianity, and defended the central doctrine of Christianity with piety as well as with intelligence.

The factors decisive in the formation of doctrine were also in this period tradition and Scripture; the latter more in theory recognized as the supreme authority, while the praxis under the growing influence of the synods laid emphasis on tradition.

To understand the doctrinal movement of this period we must also call to mind that the antagonism of the two rival schools in theology governed much of the history of doctrine: The School of Alexandria which laid great emphasis on the divinity of the person of Christ, and the School of Antioch which stressed the reality of the human in the person of Christ.

Another decisive factor in the doctrinal history of this period was the interference of the state in doctrinal controversies of the church.

2. *Arianism.* Arius, a Libyan by birth, of Antioch by training, a pupil of Lucian, was a presbyter and teacher in the church of Alexandria when the Arian controversy began, about 318. Strongly influenced by a deistic conception of God's relation to the universe that God cannot be known, or comprehended, or conceived by the human mind, and not only by men, but also not even by his only-begotten Son, Arius, since 318, gave prominence to his peculiar views in opposition to Sabellianism as well as to the church's doctrine of the unity of essence of the Son with the Father. The dominant idea in his view was that there is only one Being to whom be-ginningless existence can be ascribed, i. e., God. To maintain that the Son is beginningless would mean to establish two Gods equal to each other. The Son has a beginning; there was a time when he was not. The Father created the Logos out of nothing by his own will. In the incarnation the Logos assumed only a human body and took the place of the rational human spirit. According to Arius neither true humanity pertains to the Son, for he is without a human soul; nor true divinity, for he is without the essence and attributes of God. Though a created being the Logos is the most exalted of all creatures: (1) He is prior in existence to all creatures, the first of created beings; (2) God created him as the medium in the creation of the world; all other things are made through him; (3) he is supreme in rank, yet "of an alterable nature," but "he remains good by his own free will;" in anticipation of his sinless life he is called the Logos, the Son, the Only-begotten, or even God. At the same time he is not God in the full sense of the word, but God foreseeing his victory over temptation gave him his dignity according to his divine favor, as he gives to all others.

The monotheism of Arius can hardly be distinguished from that of the pagan philosophers, and the rank assigned to Christ by Arius is really that of a demi-god.

Arius, excommunicated about 321, disseminated his doctrines in sermons and theological conferences and in an entertaining half-poetic work, called *Thalia,* containing songs for sailors, millers and travelers. He gained many adherents in Egypt and found sympathizing friends in Palestine and Syria, especially among those bishops who, like him, had passed through the school of Lucian.

3. *Opposition to Arianism.* Arius' first opponent was the Alexandrian bishop, Alexandria, who met Arius with strenuous resistance. Against the Arian error that the Son has only a temporal nature and existence he insisted very fully upon the eternity of the Logos. Since all things were made through the Logos, the Logos cannot himself have come into existence in time.

The most valiant of the champions against the Arians and one of the most illustrious defenders of the Christian faith was Athanasius, bishop of Alexandria. Thought his works belong mainly to a later period, yet he was constantly by the side of Alexander and had already a great influence over him. Possessed of a great heart and a great intellect, inspired with an enthusiastic devotion to Christ, and inflexible in his conception of the Christian faith, he defended in his Four Discourses against the Arians — *Orationes quatuor contra Arianos* — the essential divinity of Christ as the only true foundation of redemption and salvation.

Other writings of Athanasius stating his teaching in opposition to Arianism are : *Apologia contra Arianos; Expositio fidei; De decretis synodi Nicaenae; Apologia de fuga sua; Historia Arianorum ad monachos; Ad Serapionem de morte Arii; De synodis Arim. at Seleuc.; Apologia ad Constantium; Ad episcopos Egypti et Libyae.* His two essays, *Adversus gentes* and *De incarnatione Verbi Dei,* belong to the ante-Nicene period and are without any special relation to the Arian controversy.

In denouncing Arianism Athanasius points out (1) God who needs a medium in order to come into direct touch with a creature would also need a medium in order to get into touch with the Son who, as created, can in no sense be God (*or.* II. 25. 26; *de decr.* VIII). (2) If the Logos is created and foreign to the divine substance, he cannot reveal to us the Father, and we cannot behold in him the Father (*or.* I. 35). (3) The assertion of Christ's deity on the one hand, and the denial of unity of essence with the Father on the other, lead inevitably to polytheism (*ib.* III. 15. 16) and (4) make men worship both a creator and a creature (*ib.* I. 8. 38. 42; *de decr.* II); but above all (5) the doctrine that the Son is a created being destroys the very essence of Christianity, since redemption from sin and death and union with God in faith demand that God has become man, has been incarnated (*or.* I. 35; II. 67. 70; IV. 20).

In stating his own positive arguments Athanasius starts with the conception of the One Essence in the Godhead. There is but One Divine Substance, or Nature, or Being (*or.* IV. 1). But this One Divine Being existed from all beginning as Begetting and Begotten, as Father and Son, so that we cannot conceive of God as the Father without the Son, or of the Son without the Father. The Son is "outside the things created by the purpose" of God. He is God's Son by nature and not by an act of will (*or.* III. 59-64). The Begotten is not dissimilar to the Begetter, but his very image (*ib.*). Athanasius re-asserts Origen's conception of the timeless generation of the Son (*or.* I. 27; III. 66). The Father and the Son are two persons of one and the same essence (*de decr.* III. 22. 23). The Son is, therefore, of the same substance with the Father, *homoousios,* co-essential — co-eternal, immutable (*ib.* XXIII. 12; *de synod.* X L), but at the same time as begotten, distinct from the Father (*expos. fid.* II; *or.* III. 4).

Thus with the whole force of his mighty personality Athanasius laid bare the fallacies and specious sophistries of Arius and his adherents. This, and the fact that he asserted the essential eternal divinity of the Son as the only true foundation of redemption, constitute the importance of Athanasius in the history of doctrinal development.

4. *The Council of Nice.* The doctrine propounded by Anthanasius gained the victory. At the Council of Nice or Nicaea in Bithynia, 325, the homoousia of the Son was accepted and became a dogma of the church. Besides a large number of presbyters, deacons and acolytes, more than two hundred and fifty bishops, according to Eusebius, assembled there. Athanasius (*ep. ad Afr.* 2) speaks of three-hundred and eighteen delegates, a number which has ever since dominated the tradition, whence the council is frequently referred to as the assembly of the Three Hundred and Eighteen. The delegates were mostly from the East. Among the deacons was Athanasius. The most distinguished representative from the West was Hosius, bishop of Cordova in Spain, the emperor's confidential adviser. He had persuaded the emperor, Constantine the Great, to convene the council. He also acted as chairman of the council. The Arian party, led by Eusebius of Nicomedia, presented a confession of faith. This was rejected with indignation. Even the eighteen signers of this confession, with the exception of two, did not dare to adhere to it. Then the middle party, led by Eusebius of Caesarea, presented an indefinite confession, a Caesarean form of the Apostles' Creed. In it Christ was called "God of God, light of light, life of life, the only-begotten Son, the first-born of all creation, begotten of the Father before all the ages." This creed was favorably received by the emperor, but, very likely under the influence of Hosius and the other homoousian bishops, he suggested the addition of the *homoousion.*

This furnished the basis for the third group of Alexander and

Athanasius. They changed the Eusebian formula, which dated from a period anterior to the outbreak of the Arian struggle and consequently had no direct reference to the controversy of the hour, and gave it a decidedly anti-Arian character: "Very God of very God, begotten, not made, of one and the same substance with the Father." An anathema was added against the Arians: "And those who say, 'Once he was not,' and 'before his generation he was not,' and 'he came to be from nothing,' or those who pretend that the Son of God is of 'other substance or essence,' or 'created,' or 'alterable,' or 'mutable,' the Catholic Church anathematizes."

This formula was finally accepted and signed by nearly all the Bishops. Besides Arius, only two bishops, Theonas of Marmarica and Secundus of Ptolemais, refused to sign it and were banished with Arius to Illyria. Eusebius of Nicomedia and Theognis of Nicaea signed the creed but not the damnatory clause. For this they were deposed and for a time banished by the emperor. The works of Arius were condemned to be burned and his adherents branded as enemies of Christianity.

C. FURTHER DEVELOPMENT AND FINAL SETTLEMENT OF THE ARIAN CONTROVERSY.

1. *The Arian Controversy from 325 to 381.* Though the doctrine of Athanasius was unconditionally endorsed at Nice, the Nicene Creed did not bring peace and unity in the church. The symbolical formulation aroused the opposition of those bishops who had subscribed with reluctance the orthodox formula, particularly the obnoxious 'homoousion.' The influential Eusebius of Nicomedia and Theognis of Nicaea returned from their exile and agitated powerfully against the adherents of the "homoousion." The opposition to the Nicene decision was, moreover, strengthened by the fact that the emperor's view was completely reversed under the influence, as it appears, of his sister Constantia, a disciple of Eusebius of Nicomedia. The Eusebians acquired for a time the ascendency in the empire and effected at a synod at Tyre, 335, the deposition of Athanasius who after the death of bishop Alexander, 328, had become bishop of Alexandria. The emperor banished him to Treves, 336. The Eusebian chiefs and the emperor declared themselves in favor of the re-admission of Arius. Preparations were made for the solemn restitution of Arius to the fellowship of the church at Constantinople, when Arius suddenly died, 336, at the age of over eighty years. His death seemed to have exercised no influence worth speaking of on the course of events.

In 337 Constantine died. The influence of the Arian party grew still more under Constantius, second son of Constantine the Great. Eusebius of Nicomedia was made bishop of Constantinople (338) and led in the opposition to Athanasius and the orthodox West. On the death of Constantine, Athanasius had returned, but was deposed a second time, in 339. Strife and confusion continued in church and state. Council was held against council; creed was set up against creed; anathema was hurled against anathema. The pagan historian Ammianus Marcellinus says of the councils under Constantius : "The highways were covered with galloping bishops." Gregory of Nyssa tells us, how every nook and corner of Constantinople, the markets, the streets, the baths and the shops were filled with dogmatic disputes.

After the removal of Athanasius the Eusebians were in control in the East and tried to win over the Western theologians. In the confessions or formulas, adopted at the synods of Antioch, 341 and 344, they approached the Athanasian view as closely as possible, but avoided the 'homoousion' and asserted the generation of the Son by an act of the Father's will (see Athan. *de syn.* 22-26). The ninth chapter of the fifth confession, known as the *Prolix Exposition* or *Macrostic, might be considered as a paraphrase of the* "homoousios," yet it also condemns the Athanasians — "those who irreverently say that the Son has been generated not by choice or will" (*ib.*).

The position of the Arians was considerably strengthened and that of Athanasius weakened in that two friends of Athanasius one-sidedly emphasizing the "homoousion" approached Monarchianism. Marcellus, bishop of Ancyra, opposed not only the Arian doctrine of Christ's inferiority, but also its polytheistic coloring. A rigid defender of monotheism and the divine unity he maintained that God is a monad which is potentially indivisible, but extends to a triad. The Logos is a power immanent and, therefore, eternal in God, but proceeds from the Father as power in action to accomplish the work of creation and redemption. Only as Logos incarnate can He be called the Son of God. But even after the incarnation God and the Logos are not to be separated and the eye of faith, accordingly, sees the Father in Christ (John 14:9), and when the Savior's work ends the Logos will be wholly reunited with God and the monad will again exist as it existed before the creation of the world. Thus Marcellus obliterated the personal distinctions in the Trinity and, since he taught that the Logos assumed an impersonal human nature, the two natures in Christ (Epiph. *haer.* 72. 4; also Athan. *or.* IV). A council held at Constantinople, in 336, condemned his doctrine and deposed him from his office. The third Antiochian formula of 341 condemned the opinions of Marcellus, who is classed with Sabellius and Paul of Samosata. Athanasius (*ut supra*), too, attacked the views of Marcellus without naming him.

Marcellus' pupil, Photinus, bishop of Sirmium, approached still

nearer to Samosatenism. He also denied a hypostatic distinction of
the Logos from the Father and maintained that Christ was only a
supernaturally begotten man in whom the Logos dwelt. Not only
the Eusebians at the synods of Antioch, in 344, and Sirmium, in 351,
but also the Nicene theologians at a synod at Milan, in 345, rejected
Photinus' doctrine (see *First Sirmian Confession,* Athan. *de syn.* 27).

Constantius, though a Eusebian, complied for political reasons
with the request of his orthodox brother, the Western emperor
Constans, to call a general synod in order to settle the controversy.
Accordingly a council met at Sardica — the modern Sofia in Bulgaria
— in 343, but instead of bridging the chasm between the East and
the West it ended in complete separation. The Orientals demanded
the deposition of Athanasius and Marcellus. The Occidentals
found the charges against Athanasius baseless and pronounced also
Marcellus orthodox. The Western bishops remained at Sardica.
The Eastern bishops left the council and assembled separately at
Philippopolis. The latter reasserted their Antiochian formula; the
former had to give up Photinus, but adhered to their creed. Athanasius was recalled, in 346, and in 348 it seemed as if orthodoxy
had triumphed. But the death of Constans, in 350, changed the
situation.

Aided by Constantius the Eusebians had for a long time the
upper hand taking for their catchward "homoiousios," the Son is of
like but not of the same essence with the Father. They were
therefore called Homoiousians or Semi-Arians. Athanasius and his
adherents who held fast to the "homoousios," were condemned and
banished, and at Arles, 353, and Milan, 355, the Western bishops
were compelled to recognize their condemnation. Among those
who resisted this were Lucifer of Calaris, Hosius of Cordova, Li-
berius of Rome and Hilary of Poitiers. Athanasius, thus deposed,
fled and found refuge among the monks and hermits of the desert.

But it was just this success that led to the downfall of Arianism.
Aetius, a deacon of Antioch, and Eunomius, bishop of Cyzicus,
keen and ruthless dialecticians, taught that the Son was of a different substance, (*heteroousios*), and unlike the father (*anomoios*),
and created out of nothing (*ex ouk onton*). They were therefore
called Eunomians, Heteroousiasts, Anomoeans, Exoukontians. A
synod at Seleucia even adopted the formula that the Son is unlike
the Father not only in substance but in all things. This led to a
split among the Eusebians themselves.

There were now the Homoians who came to stand near to the
original position of Arius, and the Homoiousians or Semi-Arians
who stood nearer to the Nicene Creed. Council followed upon
council until the decided Arians with the Homoians supported by

the two bishops Ursacius and Valens, in the second Sirmian formula, 357, declared that no more mention be made of either "homoousios" or "homoiousios" (Athan. *de syn.* 28; Socrates II. 30). This formula was accepted by many Western men, and even by Hosius. Thereupon the conservative Semi-Arians, at the council of Ancyra, 358, under the leadership of Basil of Ancyra, condemned the Arian heresy and affirmed that the Son is like the Father in nature and not only in power. In 359 the double council at Ariminum where the Western bishops assembled, and at Seleucia where the Eastern bishops met, aimed, on the one hand, at the restoration of the Nicene Creed, on the other hand, it affirmed the homoiousia, until under the dictatorial influence of Constantius a modified homoian formula was adopted (Socr. II. 37. 39. 40).

Again the situation changed on the accession of Julian the Apostate (361-363), who never troubled himself about party disputes. This was salutary for the development of the Nicene theology. Athanasius again returned from banishment and sought to unite all really non-Arian elements. The conciliatory spirit which, under his guidance, characterized the council at Alexandria, 362, also contributed to the uniting of the middle party with the Homoousians. Moreover, the influence and violence of the Arians and the fanaticism of emperor Valens (364-378), himself an Arian who persecuted the Homoousians and Semi-Arians alike, brought these two parties closer together. After the death of Athanasius (373) the Three Cappadocians defended the Nicene Creed and did much to secure its prevalence. Thus the victory of the Nicene orthodoxy was already achieved. In 381 Emperor Theodosius the Great convened the second ecumenical council at Constantinople which declared its approval of the Nicene Creed.

2. *The Doctrine of the Holy Spirit.* The simple statements of the Apostles' and the Nicene Creeds of the belief in the Father, Son and Holy Ghost, as well as the testimony of the ancient church teachers concerning the three persons of the Godhead show that the church from the outset believed in the existence, office and personality of the Holy Spirit. But it was not until the fourth century, in the light of the affirmation of Christ's full divinity, that the problem of the personality and divinity of the Holy Spirit were made prominent. Even the Nicene Creed, although the views of Arius were just as erroneous in respect to the Holy Spirit as in respect to the Son, contained no definite statement on the subject, but simply said, "We believe in the Holy Ghost." The doctrine of the Son's divinity was the first in the logical order, and it would not have been wise to complicate matters by contending about the divinity of the Holy Spirit at that time. But when Semi-Arians under

Macedonius, bishop of Constantinople, continued to pronounce the
Holy Spirit a creature, like the angels, subordinate to the Son,
Athanasius and the synod of Alexandria, in 362, defended the
homoousia of the Spirit as the only true doctrine.

The followers of Macedonius were called Macedonians or Pneu-
matomachians. In opposition to them the Three Cappadocians also
championed the divinity and hypostatical character of the Spirit.
In 381, at the general council of Constantinople, the Pneuma-
tomachians were condemned and the doctrine of the Spirit's divinity came to a substantial triumph. The council confirmed the
Nicene Creed with the addition of ascribing implicitly the
"homoousion" to "the Holy Ghost, the Lord and Giver of life, who
with the Father and the Son together is worshipped and glorified,
who spake by the prophets."

3. *The Niceno-Constantinopolitan Creed* is distinguished from
the old Nicene Creed, apart from small variations in the first two
articles and the omission of the anathema, by additions after the
words "Holy Ghost" in the third article, which were made in order
to reject the heresy of the Macedonians and the Semi-Arians who
like these denied the divinity of the Holy Ghost. The Creed itself,
however, cannot be traced to the council at Constantinople. It
existed at an earlier date. It is really the baptismal confession of
the church at Jerusalem, probably approved by the council of
Constantinople and later incorporated in the acts of the council.
It was first quoted at the council of Chalcedon, 451, as "the faith
of the One hundred and Fifty Fathers" where it also received
symbolical recognition together with the old Nicene Creed or "the
Faith of the Three hundred and Eighteen Fathers."

CHAPTER VIII

THE CHRISTOLOGICAL PROBLEM

A. The Divine-Human Personality of Christ.— In stating the relation of Christ's divine-human person to Father and Spirit it became also necessary to define the humanity and divinity of Christ and state their relation to each other in his one person. Hence the Christological problem presented itself already during the Arian controversy.

1. *From the outset the church believed in the divine-human Redeemer.* The Apostles' Creed, the ante-Nicene Rules of Faith, the Nicene Creed, all confess the divine-human character of Christ as the chief object of the Christian faith. His divine-human personality forms the basis of his mediatorial work.

But now the question arose as to the true unity of divinity and humanity in the one person and as to the distinction of divinity and humanity in the one person, so that there be no mixture of natures. Over against Docetism the church was called upon to defend the reality of Christ's human body. At the same time the question arose: What is the relation of the human soul of Christ to the divine Logos? The question became more complicated since trichotomy, the threefold division of the human nature into body, soul and spirit, had become current. An answer to this question was given already by Origen who held that Christ's soul was like all others, pre-existent, but pure and unfallen. It grew into an indissoluble union with the Logos who thus took upon himself human nature and became God-man. In this way Origen maintained the personal union of the divine-human in Christ, a union of the divine with a rational soul. It was, however, not until a century later that a renewed attempt at a scientific solution of the problem was made.

2. *Apollinaris,* bishop of Laodicea (d. c. 392), a keen opponent of Arianism and a zealous champion of the homoousia, with his logical and dialectical training subjected the doctrine to a fresh, scientific examination. In order to meet the objection of the Arians that the assumption of a perfect human nature with a rational soul is a substitution of two persons for the single Christ, and to present a union of the two natures in the God-man, Apollinaris taught that Christ assumed a human body with its life principle or animal soul, while the Logos took the place of the higher rational principle. According to Apollinaris two perfect wholes cannot be united in

71

one person. If Christ were perefect man, he could not be un-changeable and without sin, for where there is a complete humanity there is sin; and his human nature could not be an object of adora-tion. By means of this theory Apollinaris maintained the true unity of .the divine and human in Christ, but he thereby also destroyed Christ's complete humanity, for God assumes into per-sonal union with himself a fundamentally defective and mutilated humanity. Apollinaris substituted a God clothed with flesh (*theos sarkophoros*) or a man inspired of God (*entheos anthropos*) for a real God-man (*theanthropos*).

This view of Apollinaris being in conflict with essential postu-lates of the Christian faith called forth decided opposition. If Christ is not true man he cannot be a sufficient representative of humanity. Only if Christ assumed human nature in its entirety could he be example and redeemer. Apollinaris was opposed by Athanasius and Gregory of Nyssa. Local synods at Rome (377, 378) and Antioch (378) testified against this doctrine. At the sec-ond ecumenical council at Constantinople, 381, Apollinarianism was condemned and the two natures were maintained.

The Christian belief in Christ's complete humanity and his absolute divinity had thus been stated. The church had now to enter upon the solution of the Christological problem: How can two personal natures exist in one person?

B. Fundamental Differences in Attempting to Solve the Christological Problem.— In attempting to harmonize a plurality of natures with personal unity it naturally happened that the one was emphasized at the expense of the other and thus either the distinction of the two complete natures or their intimate union was surrendered. This twofold error arose in the two leading *Schools of the East, the Alexandrian and the Antiochian.* Both maintained Christ's humanity and divinity, and the unity of his person, but the Alexandrians insisted upon the union, the Antiochians upon the difference of the two natures. The Alexandrians were chiefly interested in Christ's deity, the Antiochians in his humanity. The former held that there is a miraculous co-mingling of the two natures, so that the two coalesce in one, i. e., the human is in some inexplicable way fused into oneness with the divine; the latter mechanically distinguished and separated the two natures, so that there is not a complete union but only a permanent association of the two.

1. The *Alexandrian School* continued in the spirit of Athanasius and greatly subordinated the human to the divine and insisted upon a complete union of the divine with the human. Athanasius

would not recognize a mere indwelling of the Logos in Christ, but taught that the Logos, who was God from all eternity, became very man. "He became man, and did not come into man . . as in former times the Logos was used to come into each of the saints" (*or.* III. 30). "The Logos bore the infirmities of the flesh, as his own, for his was the flesh: and the flesh ministered to the works of the Godhead, because the Godhead was in it, for the body was God's" (*ib.* 31). It is therefore correct, in a certain sense, to speak of the sufferings of the Logos. It is likewise correct to speak of "the crucified God," of "worshipping the man Jesus," and of Mary as "Theotokos," i. e., "God-bearer," for the Logos also participated in the incarnation (*c. Apoll.* I. 4. 6. 12; *or.* III. 14. 29. IV. 32). Thus the Logos became the head, representative and proxy of mankind. In fact God himself had entered humanity. By means of the union of the Godhead with the manhood in his person was made possible the leading back of mankind to God.

The Cappadocians, following the track of Athanasius, likewise laid the greatest stress on the union as a transformation of the human into the divine, though they were willing to discriminate *in abstracto* two natures. This tendency is especially noticeable in the simile of Gregory of Nyssa: "As a drop of vinegar mingled with the sea is transformed and becomes part of the sea water, so the flesh of Christ was transformed and lost all its natural properties by union with the divine infinitude" (*c. Eunom.* V).

Cyril of Alexandria (d. 444) was more definite and asserted a unity of the hypostases, "one nature of the divine Logos made flesh; neither as a mixture nor compound" (*c. Nest.* II. 11). There are two natures "in theory alone," but after the incarnation there is but one incarnated nature of the divine Logos. Since there is but one person, there is thus also in Christ a communion of attributes. But since the Logos-person, who has assumed the impersonal human nature, is immutable and impassible it can be said that "God became man," that "God suffered," if only it be added, "according to the flesh." Hence it is also dogmatically correct to speak of Mary as "Theotokos," Mother of God. (*ib.* I. 6; II. 3. 10; IV. 6; V. 4).

In studying the development of ecclesiastical orthodoxy we are concerned with Cyril chiefly as a dogmatic theologian. There can be no doubt that he was sincere in his opinions. His character, however, was markedly deficient in the graces of the Christian life. Schaff (*Hist. of the Chr. Church,* I. 944 f.) says of him: "Cyril furnishes a striking proof that orthodoxy and piety are two quite different things, and that zeal for pure doctrine may coexist with an unchristian spirit. In personal character he unquestionably stands far below his unfortunate antagonist. The judgment of the Catholic historians is bound by the authority of their church, which, in strange blindness, has canonized him." Cyril's polemic and dogmatic writings were of great importance for the history of doctrine. He wrote Twelve Anathemas or dogmatic propositions against the Christological errors of Nestorius, and, in addition to these, five other books against Nestorius; also an apologetic against Theodoret. Here may be mentioned also his treatise in dialog form on the Trinity and another on the incarnation.

The Theotokos became the catchword of the Alexandrian School. It met the postulates of the Christian piety of the church that God became man and partook of the infirmities of the human nature, and that the latter became partaker of God and immortality. The term Theotokos was favorably received because of the growing tendency to pay homage to the Virgin Mary.

2. *The Antiochian School* distinguished sharply between Christ as Son of God and Christ as Son of man giving the human nature of Christ a more distinct recognition. As critics and masters in grammatico-historical exegesis the Antiochians were especially interested in the character of the historical Christ as portrayed in the Gospels. They laid much stress upon the freedom of man as a condition of moral excellence. And what is true of man in general must be true equally of the man Christ Jesus. They regarded therefore Christ's human nature as developing much in the same free way as that of man in general.

In order to preserve the integrity of the two natures they asserted only a combination of the two personal natures through their unity of will; and in their combination the two natures are one person. It is not a natural, but a moral union. The man Jesus desires what God desires. The union began at the conception. It differs from the union of God with the prophets and saints in that God operates in Christ as in his own Son. This union has become an indissoluble one, the indwelling Logos conducting Jesus to perfection which is attained through the ascension of Jesus. As the divine cannot be said to have really become man, divine honor is due to Christ in reference to his divinity, and to his humanity inasmuch as his human nature shares in the honor, glory and dominion which belong to the Logos. Mary, the Mother of the man (Anthropotokos), can, properly speaking, not be called Theotokos, since God did not become man. She can only in a metaphorical sense be called Mother of God, since God was in the man who was being born.

Thus the Antiochians preserved the reality and completeness of

Christ's human nature, but endangered the unity of the person, for they held that there is only a moral, relative union between two persons. They differed from the Samosatenians only in that they maintained that the Logos in Christ is a person.

C. The Christological Conflict and Settlement of Controversy.

1. *Nestorius and Cyril.* The two Schools came to a positive collision in the persons of Nestorius, bishop of Constantinople, and Cyril, bishop of Alexandria. The immediate occasion of the great controversy arose from a declaration of Nestorius, in 428, that Mary did not give birth to divinity, but to man, the instrument of divinity, and that therefore Mary is not to be called Theotokos, God-bearing, but Theodochos, God-receiving, and Anthropotokos, Man-bearing, or Christotokos, Christ-bearing. Following Antiochian Christology Nestorius admitted the full deity and the full humanity of Christ, but put them into loose mechanical conjunction. The defect in his Christology does not relate to the distinction of the two natures, but to the union of the two in one person. They are not united in a single self-conscious personality. The Logos dwells in the man Jesus as in a temple. In Christ are two, if we regard the natures; one, if we consider the dignity. "I divide the natures, but I conjoin the reverential adoration." Nestorius objected to the sharing of each nature in the peculiar properties of the other; hence the Logos did not participate in the sufferings of the human nature of Christ.

The teachings of Nestorius met with considerable opposition in Constantinople, Alexandria and Rome. Cyril of Alexandria and pope Coelestine united in opposition. At a Roman council in 430 Coelestine condemned Nestorius, giving him ten days to recant. His condemnation in the East was brought about by Cyril. He sent forth twelve anathemas against the Christological errors of Nestorius, who in turn responded with twelve counter-anathemas. Cyril maintained that according to Nestorius we would be redeemed by the suffering of a mere man, and that the worship of one, who is not by nature God, is man-worship. Nestorius charged Cyril with confounding the two natures and annulling the immutability of God.

To settle the growing conflict emperor Theodosius II summoned a general council to meet at Ephesus, on Whitsunday, 431. The council was opened, despite the protest of Nestorius, before the arrival of the Antiochian bishops. The anathemas of Cyril were accepted as orthodox and Nestorius was condemned and declared deposed from all clerical office on the very first day of the council. Meanwhile the Oriental bishops reached Ephesus and opened a counter-council under John, bishop of Antioch, excommunicated Cyril's followers and deposed Cyril and his chief adherent, Memnon of Ephesus, because they had illegally opened the council. Nothing was said as to Nestorius or his doctrine. Since John of Antioch refused to confer with "the deposed and excommunicated persons," both parties addressed themselves to the emperor, who first approved the action of both parties, but later inclined to the Alexandrians. Cyril and Memnon were restored to their bishoprics, while Nestorius voluntarily entered a cloister at Antioch.

Thus the third ecumenical council accomplished nothing in the way of positive construction of Christology except that it was known that the majority, 159 bishops, sanctioned the teaching of Cyril as in accordance with the Nicene doctrine.

2. *Theodoret and Eutyches.* In order to restore peace, efforts were made by the Antiochians to prepare a union symbol, into which each party could read its own Christology. The formula, apparently prepared by Theodoret, excluded both extremes. Cyril's theory of the one nature and the Antiochian idea of a combination of the two natures, as also Apollinarianism, for Christ is said to be perfect man of a rational soul. It asserted the two natures, the one person, the union of the two natures and the Theotokos. John of Antioch consented to the condemnation of Nestorius who died in 440. The Nestorians were persecuted and fled into the Persian empire where they established a separate church.

The proceedings against Nestorius kept the contending parties quiet only for a while. The zealous Orientals were not satisfied with the compromise made; and Cyril, whose dogmatic position was censured by the Orientals, did not cease to attack his opponents. In 444 he died. His successor Dioscurus, a violent man and still more unscrupulous in his struggle for supremacy, widened the breach by oppressing the Nestorians and denouncing their doctrine wherever an opportunity presented itself.

His archimandrite, the veteran monk Eutyches, who stood at the head of the Alexandrian party at Constantinople, also vehemently opposed the doctrine of Nestorius. He even accused the Unionists of Nestorianism and in his opposition went so far as to affirm that after the incarnation there is only one nature, that of the incarnate Word, and that therefore Christ's human body was essentially different from other human bodies. His doctrine was in consequence condemned by Eusebius of Dorylaeum, a follower of Cyril, at a synod presided over by Flavian at Constantinople, in 448.

3. *The Councils of Ephesus and Chalcedon.* Having rejected

Nestorianism as well as gross Monophysitism orthodoxy seemed to steer a safe middle course between the two extremes. But Eutyches and the Egyptian party, whose interests were at stake, did not feel willing to acquiesce in the decision. At a council held in Ephesus, 449, under the presidency of Dioscurus of Alexandria, Eutyches was reinstated. Eusebius and Flavian, his chief opponents, and others were deposed and the Antiochian doctrine of the two natures was condemned as Nestorianism. Pope Leo's celebrated epistle — commonly called the *Tome* — to Flavian in support of the doctrine of the two natures in one person was ignored. The sanction of the council was obtained from the emperor by means of falsified acts. Because of the disorderly, rude and tyrannical manner in which the council was conducted pope Leo styled it *latrocinium* or Robber Synod. Dioscurus was victorius over Old and New Rome, but the triumph did not prove lasting.

Theodosius II. died in 450, and his sister Pulcheria and her husband Marcian who succeeded, were for political reasons hostile to the fanatical Alexandrian bishop and sided with Leo. The latter was anxious to secure the annulling of the proceedings of the Robber Synod and finally succeeded in procuring a new general council. It was held not in Italy under his leadership, as he had desired, but at Chalcedon, not far from Constantinople on the Asiatic side, in 451. Nevertheless, the pope claimed for his delegates the right to preside at the council and insisted that any act that failed to receive their approval would be invalid. The decrees of the Robber Synod were annulled and Dioscurus was deposed and degraded. Though Leo's letter to Flavian was not given dogmatic authority it was adopted in refutation of Eutychianism, while two synodical epistles of Cyril against Nestorius were adopted in refutation of Nestorianism.

The council affirmed the doctrine of the inseparable and indivisible union, without confusion, of two perfect and complete natures, the human and the divine, in the one person of Christ. The Creed framed by the council reads as follows:

"Following the holy Fathers we with one consent teach (men) to confess one and the same Son, our Lord Jesus Christ, the same perfect in divinity and the same perfect in humanity, very God and very man, of a rational soul, and a body, consubstantial with the Father according to the Godhead, and consubstantial with us according to the manhood; in all things like unto us, without sin; begotten before all ages of the Father according to the Godhead; and in these last days for us and for our salvation, born of the Virgin Mary, the Mother of God, according to the manhood; one and the same Christ, Son, Lord, Only-begotten, to be acknowledged in two natures, unmingled, immutable, indivisible, inseparable; the distinction of the natures being by no means obliterated by their union, but rather the peculiarity of each nature being preserved, and being united in one person and one hypostasis, not parted or divided into two persons, but one and the same Son and Only-begotten, God the Word, the Lord Jesus Christ; as the prophets of old time have spoken concerning him, and the Lord Jesus Christ himself has taught us, and the Creed of the holy Fathers has delivered to us."

The Chalcedonian Creed may rightly be called "the ripest fruit of the Christological speculations and controversies of the Ancient Church." It points out with sound religious judgment the extremes that must be avoided and after the manner of a symbol gives clear expression to the pious Christian convictions of the age, but it is far from offering a solution of the Christological problem. Consequently, the Chalcedonian decision did not stop the controversy.

D. CHRISTOLOGICAL MOVEMENTS AFTER THE COUNCIL OF CHALCEDON.

1. *Monophysitism.*— The Alexandrians, and with them the adherents of Eutyches, saw in the Chalcedon decree of two natures only another form of Nestorian duality of persons in Christ. They arose in opposition everywhere in the East,— in Palestine Theodosius, in Egypt Timotheus Aelurus, and in Syria Petrus Fullo. As advocates of only one nature in Christ they acquired the name of *Monophysites.* They were also known as *Theopaschites* (from *theos* and *paschein* 'to suffer') because they held that in Christ's passion God suffered. The history of the Monophysite conflicts, which were often violent and acrimonious in the extreme, can here be sketched but briefly.

After long and vehement struggles the Monophysites gained the upper hand when in 475 Basiliscus the Usurper ascended the imperial throne. Basiliscus took up their cause and rejected the Chalcedonian Creed in his *Encyclion,* 476, and about 500 bishops signed the document. His son-in-law and successor Zeno strove to compromise matters. In his famous edict, the so-called *Henoticon,* 482, Nestorians and Eutychians were condemned, the twelve anathemas of Cyril accepted and the Chalcedon Creed ignored. This effort to allay the agitation was quite in vain. Pope Felix III. saw the prestige of Rome involved in this slighting of the Chalcedon Confession and his predecessor Leo's epistle. A breach with Rome ensued which lasted for 35 years, 484-519. Justin I. ascended the throne in 518, and in the following year the negotiations with Rome were reopened. The Henoticon was quietly abandoned and community re-established between the Churches of Rome and Constantinople. But this measure proved unable to subdue the Monophysites. Justinian I. (527-565) soon realized that forcible suppression of the Monophysites was futile and, greatly influenced by his wife Theodora, attempted a different policy, that of reconciling the Monophysite separatists with the church. Recognition was

given to the formula "God crucified for us," first introduced by
Petrus Fullo into the liturgical Trisagion. This formula met with
the approval of the Scythian monks. In order to please the Monophysites Justinian took some action against the doctrines of the
Antiochian School which was especially obnoxious to the Monophysites. He therefore issued, in 544, an edict, the so-called *Three
Chapters,* in which he condemned (1) Theodore of Mopsuestia and
his writings, (2) the anti-Cyrillian writings of Theodoret of Cyros
in defense of Nestorianism, and (3) the letter which Ibas of
Edessa, friend of Nestorius (d. 457), is said to have written to the
Persian bishop Maris.

The edict was favorably received by the majority of the Eastern
bishops. The few who refused to subscribe their assent were
deposed and banished. But among the bishops of Illyria, Dalmatia
and North Africa the edict met with determined resistance. Thus
was kindled the so-called *Three Chapter Controversy* which, destitute of all doctrinal interest, agitated the church for eight long
years. Of this fruitless but violent controversy it has been rightly
said that "it has filled more volumes than it is worth lines." It
was finally decided to settle this dispute at a general council.
In 553, the fifth ecumenical council at Constantinople ratified the
emperor's edict, recognized the council of Chalcedon, condemned
Origen, and adopted the doctrine of the Theopaschite supplement.

But the Monophysites were not yet reconciled to the church.
They still continued in their opposition to the orthodox creed.
Their influence, however, was weakened since they had become
divided among themselves. The Severians, followers of Severus,
bishop of Antioch, stood nearest to the Christology of Cyril. They
fully recognized the reality of the two natures in Christ, but insisted
that they became indissolubly united so that there was only one
new theandric energy.

An opposite tendency was that of the Julianists, followers of
Julian, bishop of Halicarnassus. They adhered to Eutyches and
held that Christ's body was so inseparably united with the Logos
as to be free from natural infirmities, such as hunger, thirst, weari-
ness, sweat, tears, bleeding. When Christ hungered and thirsted
he did so, not of necessity, but because he willed it.

Both tendencies differed as to whether or not the body of Christ
was incorruptible even before the resurrection. The Severians
denied it and taught that Christ's body was like ours, created and
corruptible, *phtharton.* They were therefore nicknamed *Phthar-
tolatrae, Corrupticolae,* worshippers of the corruptible. The Julianists held that Christ's body was, from the moment of the union with

the Logos, incorruptible and of the same character as after the resurrection. They were called *Aphthartodocetae* or *Phantasiasts*. An extreme school even maintained that Christ's body, from the time of the union, was uncreated. They were therefore called *Actistae*. After the Monophysite ideas in regard to the body of Christ had been carried to the extreme, the argument was also extended to Christ's human soul. The Severians, led by Themistus of Alexandria, said that it was like ours, limited in knowledge; hence their name *Agnoetae*.

The Monophysites who had passed into a state of permanent schism, maintained themselves in the East as separate sects, even to this day, under various names — the Jacobites in Syria, the Copts in Egypt, the Abyssinians and Armenians.

2. *Monotheletism.* The Monophysite movement, especially in Egypt and Syria, was still too powerful to be subdued; it had to be managed. Emperor Heraclius (610-641), pressed hard as he was, on the one side by the Persians, on the other by the Saracens, had a vital political interest in winning back for the church and the empire the excommunicated and persecuted Monophysites. During his stay in Armenia, while on his expedition against Persia, in 622, he learned from Paul, the head of the Severians there, that what was particularly repugnant in the definition of Chalcedon was the implication of two wills in Christ. To reunite the Monophysites with the catholic church the emperor, supported by Sergius, patriarch of Constantinople, employed the formula of the "new theandric energy" in Christ. This aroused the opposition of Sophronius of Jerusalem, who designated the new doctrine as rank Apollinarianism. Sergius placed the situation before pope Honorius, who expressed himself in accord with the patriarch's position, and stated that "the controversy over one or two energies should be abandoned and left to the grammarians; the use of either expression savors either of Nestorianism or Eutychianism . . . We confess also one will of the Lord Jesus Christ" (Mansi X. 992 ff.; XI. 529 ff). Sergius, therefore, prepared the so-called *Ecthesis* — Exposition of Faith — which was signed by the emperor in 638. It states that neither one or two energies are to be spoken of and that there is only one will, in Christ. The document was not acceptable to Honorius' successors, Severinus and John IV. In Italy and North Africa it met with violent opposition led by Maximus the Confessor. This caused Constans II. to withdraw the edict and to substitute for it his own *Typos* or *Precept* enjoining silence as to the matter in dispute. The reply of the Western Church was that Monotheletism was anathematized as inconsistent with Chalcedon, that both the Ecthesis and the Typos, and their authors were con-

demned, and that *Dyotheletism*, the doctrine of two wills in Christ was formally defined and accepted by the first Lateran synod held by Pope Martin I. in 640. Both Martin and Maximus were dragged off to Constantinople, exposed to cruel persecutions, and finally succumbed.

When under Constans' successor the controversy once more revived and the understanding between Rome and Constantinople was again interrupted, the new emperor, Constantine Pogonatus, found it necessary to summon a general council — the first Trullan (so called, because it met in the domed hall *troullos* of the imperial palace) or sixth ecumenical council at Constantinople, in 680. In 679, at a synod under Pope Agatho at Rome, it had been agreed to stand by the decision of the Lateran synod. Agatho held that the will is attached not to the person but to the nature and, therefore, where there are two natures there are two wills. He gave his judgment on the doctrine in his official letter communicated to the council at Constantinople. The council adopted the doctrine of the two wills and two energies, but decided that the human will must always be considered as subordinate to the divine. Pope Honorius as well as the Monothelete patriarch of Constantinople, who had been condemned in Agatho's letter, were also anathematized by the council.

Monotheletism was still cherished by the Maronites, (probably so called after their leader Maro) who resided on Mount Lebanon and in parts of Syria, until the Crusades. Then they abandoned their distinctive opinions and united with the Church of Rome. They still retain their Syriac liturgy and some distinctive practices, e. g., administering the Eucharist in both kinds.

3. *The Christology of John of Damascus.* It cannot be said that the council of Constantipole solved the difficult questions of detail as to the two natures of Christ in the unity of his person; on the contrary, the problem became still more difficult. If the will is a property of the nature, the question arises : How far can two wills be without two persons willing?

·In his *Exposition of the Orthodox Faith,* which constitutes the third division of his principal work *The Fountain of Knowledge,* John of Damascus (d. after 754) spoke for the Greek Church the final word in Christology. His object was to secure the unity of the two natures in the unity of one personality. To exclude the idea of a double personality, he held that the Logos-hypostasis became also the hypostasis of the potential man. This potential man is not without hypostasis, nor of own independent subsistence, but enhypostatic in the Logos-hypostasis (*de fid. orth.* III. 9). There

is, then, one hypostasis for both natures (11). Accordingly Christ
has two natural wills and energies (13-15). There is no room for
the idea of one will (14), or one composite nature (2). This unity
of the hypostasis involves a *perichoresis* or communication of
properties (3). But this communication proceeds only from the
side of the divine nature which interpenetrates, pervades and de-
fies the receptive and passive human nature (7). The human will
in Christ has become the organ of the divine will (17. 18).

Thus the Damascene maintains and explains the Chalcedon
formula, but does it in the spirit of Cyril. Though he presses the
reality and full validity of the two natures, the drift of his teaching
is in the Apollinarian and Monophysite direction.

CHAPTER IX

THE ANTHROPOLOGICAL CONTROVERSY

A. FREEDOM AND GRACE.

1. *Eastern and Western Anthropology.* At the beginning of the fifth century, during the Christological conflicts in the East, there arose quite unexpectedly and unforeseen a violent controversy in the Western Church, the so-called anthropological controversy. The point in question was the relation of the human will to divine grace in regeneration.

From the first the Christian church acknowledged the universality of human sinfulness and the need of divine grace in Christ in order to deliverance from it. But the ancient Fathers set forth, with very little perspicuity the relation of the human will to divine grace. They emphasized divine grace as necessary to salvation and, at the same time, held that by virtue of our liberty we may do good works. They stated the doctrine of sin, free will and grace in this general form. We notice, however, as early as the second century, a marked difference of opinion in the Ancient Church, both Eastern and Western, which showed itself in two great tendencies. The Greek Fathers owing to their speculative conception of Christianity strongly advocated the doctrine of free will as able to turn from sin by exercise of its own inherent energy. The theologians of the Western Church were distinguished by their practical tendency in contrast with the speculations of the former and conceived of Christianity not as a new philosophy or as the doctrine of the true God, but as a new life with God through Christ, and, consequently, laid greater stress on the depravity of man and the importance of grace. These two tendencies were growing during the succeeding centuries. They did, however, not clash until a one-sided emphasis was laid on one of the two factors: human freedom or divine grace. This was done in the controversy between Pelagius and Augustine.

2. *Pelagius,* a British monk, well educated, of a shrewd and crafty turn, according to his birth and matter-of-fact temperament an Occidental, in his religious views following the doctrinal tendencies of the Eastern Church, strict and austere in morality, came to Rome about the beginning of the fifth century, where he preached repentance. His interests were primarily ethical; hence his insistence on the freedom of the will and human responsibility. Guided by monkish ideals he believed that holiness could be ar-

rived at by rigor of discipline. Overrating the moral power of man
he imagined that he could do more than the law required. He had
no use for Augustine's sentence: *Da quod iubes et iube quod vis,*
"Grant what thou commandest and command what thou wilt."
His peculiar views were distinctly stated in his brief commentary
on the Epistles of Paul. They might not so speedily have attracted
attention had they not been adopted by Coelestius, who had been a
Roman lawyer, but embraced Christianity and became an ardent
follower of Pelagius.

In 411 the two friends went over to Africa where they met
Augustine. Pelaguis soon sailed for Palestine, while Coelestius
remained in Carthage with a view to ordination. But in 412, before
a synod at Carthage, Paulinus, a presbyter of Milan, charged
Coelestius with holding six or seven errors which were founded on
this that Adam's sin had injured only himself, and that new-born
children are in the same state as Adam before the fall. Coelestius
was excommunicated.

In Palestine Pelagius aroused attention by a letter to Demetrias,
a high-born maiden, who had decided to be a professed virgin.
The letter, written at the request of the mother of Demetrias, has
much excellent advice, but reveals also the peculiar views of
Pelagius. His opinions were at first favorably received in the East,
for the Eastern Church had not been affected by the Augustinian
views; yet, Augustine's influence also withstood him there. Orosus,
a Spanish priest, came from Augustine to warn Jerome against
Pelagius. Jerome, himself a Western theologian, agreed with
Augustine in the doctrine of the universal corruption of sin, but
taught the freedom of the will and conditional predestination. He
wrote against Pelagius, but the synod at Jerusalem, in 415, declined
to pronounce against him. Jerome now sought to procure a condemnation of Pelagius, but the synod at Diospolis (Lydda), in the
same year, pronounced Pelagius to be in agreement with catholic
teaching. The North African Church, however, resented the
Oriental decisions and in the following year sent up from their
synods at Carthage and Mileve an appeal to Pope Innocent I., who
decided the question in favor of the African Church. His successor
Zosimus, a man of little theological knowledge and without independent judgment, first testified to the orthodoxy of both Pelagius
and Coelestius, but when he saw that the African bishops were
too firm in their convictions and too independent to alter their
course of conduct (synod of Carthage, 418), he began to give way
and finally drew up his famous *Epistula Tractoria* inviting all the
bishops of Christendom to subscribe a condemnation of Pelagian
opinions. Eighteen Italian bishops refused, among them Julian of

Eclanum, both in character and ability the most prominent leader of the Pelagian party.

The Eastern Church confirmed the decision of the West. The council of Ephesus, in 432, passed against the Pelagians without specifying their errors. The East never took the question at issue into thorough consideration. It was a Western controversy.

3. *The Teachings of Pelagius.* Over against Augustine's affirmation of the bondage of the will with no power of self-deliverance, Pelagius insisted that man is able to do all that God commands, else God would not have commanded him to do that which is good. Man has this ability, for he is free, i. e., able to choose good or evil. We are born neutral, characterless and with no bias toward good or evil. This freedom constitutes man's natural endowment and is therefore inamissible, and is accordingly found in the heathen as well as in the Christian. There were some men, even before the appearance of Christ, who did not commit sin. Explaining Rom. 5:12 Pelagius says that this actual sin has not been transmitted from the first man to other persons by natural descent, but by imitation, and that 'all' does not mean 'all without exception,' but is to be taken relatively for the majority. Pelagius goes even so far as to maintain the possibility of an entirely sinless life, though he does not maintain that there is a man without sin.

There is, therefore, according to Pelagius no such thing as original sin, or propagation of sin by the act of generation, for sin is not a fault of nature. It consists only in separate acts of the will. As a creationist Pelagius held that each soul is the product of a special creative act of God and there is no chance for the transmission of sin from soul to soul. If sin were a fault of nature, our sin would be chargeable on God, the Creator. Nor would deliverance from sin be possible, for our essential nature cannot be taken away from us. New-born infants are in the same condition as Adam was previous to the fall. Children who die in infancy, being untainted by sin, are saved without baptism. Baptism in their case has not any sin-remitting effect but only transfers them from a good to a better state consecrating them, who are already innocent and uncondemned, to be members of Christ. Pelagius, however, did not deny that baptism gives remission of actual sins to adult persons. As there is no original sin there can be no guilt and no punishment of original sin. Even temporal death is no part of the punishment of sin, because Adam was created mortal, so that he would have died whether he had sinned or not. The universality of sin is to be accounted for by the force of temptation, the influence of example and of habit, and the sensuous and worldly character of man.

Since it is the human will which takes the initiative and is the determining factor in the salvation of the individual it follows that divine grace is not absolutely but only relatively necessary to attain holiness. It renders its attainment easier to man. By divine grace Pelagius means primarily the endowment with reason and free will. Then, to check the ever-growing habit of sinning, God gave the law until in the preaching and example of Christ the gift of God's grace was completed. Pelagius vacillates considerably in his statements in regard to grace. In one place he says that grace is "necessary not only for every hour, and for every moment, but also for every act of our lives" (Agustine, *gratia Chr. II*), in another he maintains that grace is given "in order that men may more easily accomplish that which they are commanded to do by free will" (*ib.* XXX) to which Augustine rightly adds that the phrase "more easily" tacitly suggests the possibility of accomplishing good works even without the grace of God (*ib.*). This grace is intended for man, but man must make himself worthy of it by an honest striving after virtue.

Christ, the Son of God, became man to be our teacher and perfect example. As we imitated Adam's sin, so are we to imitate Christ's holiness. Good works decide whether any one is good. The standard of good works is the Word of God as law which must not only be known but also fulfilled. There is no difference between law and gospel, for the law is as good a means of salvation as the gospel.

The anthropology of Pelagius is essentially naturalistic and rationalistic. Pelagius falsely separates the individual from the connection of the race. He locates good and evil in the separate acts of man. There is no such thing as a sinful character or a sinful nature. The freedom of the will, of which Pelagius makes so much, is only the liberty of indifference or the power of contrary choice. It is not real, but formal freedom. The great importance he attaches to the natural power of man makes divine grace unnecessary and Christianity practically useless.

4. *Augustine.* The anti-type of Pelagius, so far as personal experience and religious nature are concerned, was Augustine. He was born, 354, at Thagaste in Numidia. His father, Patricius, was still a pagan at the time of his sons' birth. From his Christian mother Monica Augustine received his first religious impressions and yet he grew up without any profession of Christian piety. There was a time in his life when the religious impressions of his childhood were almost obliterated. His evil desires developed early. He informs us in his *Confessions* (II) that in his younger

years he was guilty of many serious moral offenses. He admits that, in the wild life he lived, he was unhappy and without peace. Despite his fervid, sensuous temperament and youthful aberrations, Augustine was from the first an earnest student and a seeker after truth. Cicero's *Hortensius,* a work in praise of philosophy which has not come down to us aroused in him an eager desire for nobler things. "This book, in truth, changed my affections, and turned my prayers to Thyself, O Lord, and made me have other hopes and desires. Worthless suddenly became every vain hope to me; and, with an incredible warmth of heart, I yearned for an immortality of wisdom, and began now to arise that I might return to Thee" (*Conf.* III. 4). But, strange to say, he was attracted at first not by the church of his mother, but by the half-heathen religion of Mani. At the age of nineteen he became a disciple of the sect of the Manichaeans attracted by their rigorous life and their claim to possess the true knowledge of God and of the mysteries of the world (III. 10). The sect was divided into two classes, the *electi* or the perfect Manichaeans, and the *auditores* or the secular Manichaeans. To the former, marriage was forbidden; to the latter, it was permitted conditionally as a matter of necessity. Augustine was admitted into the class of *auditores* and continued for nine years to be a fervent member of the sect, but did not find the satisfaction of his spiritual longings. Disgusted particularly with their phantastic philosophy of nature and their doctrine of evil as a substance, and as having its seat in matter instead of free will, he severed his connection with the Manichaeans. At this time he fell into despair of all truth (V. 7.10). It was the Neo-Platonic philosophy which next led him into a new world of thought. The dualism of the Manichaeans was replaced by the monism of the Neo-Platonists. From this philosophy he learned that only the good is the substantial, the truly existent, while evil is but the absence of good, a mere negative (VII. 11-17). Though Neo-Platonism had gradually changed his metaphysical convictions, yet he still regarded Christianity as something only for the common man who could not rise to the heights of philosophy. It was at this time that he fell under the influence of Ambrose, bishop of Milan. Ambrose's allegorical interpretation of the Old Testament helped Augustine in understanding "the old Scriptures of the law and the prophets which when taken literally seemed most absurd" (VI. 4). Augustine heard Ambrose preach, at first, only from admiration of his oratory, but soon attracted by the content of the sermons. Severe inner struggles followed. He turned to the Epistles of Paul, which showed him what he needed. Determined to renounce the old life with its pleasures of sense he experienced at the same time the terrible power of sin and his own inability to overcome his sinful desires. The seventh chapter of Romans appealed to him with special force, for in the spiritual struggles in the soul of man as here described by Paul, he recognized his own (VIII. 5). The details of the history of his conversion, as told by Augustine himself in the eighth book of his *Confessions*, are well known,— when, in a garden of the Villa Cassiciacum, in September of the year 386, he flung himself under a fig tree and poured out his heart to God and seemed to hear the divine voice of a child: "Take up and read," and, on his doing so, his eyes fell upon the verse: "Put ye on the Lord Jesus Christ and make no provision for the flesh to fulfil the lusts thereof." "No further would I read," says Augustine, "nor did I need; for instantly, as the sentence ended — by a light, as it were, of security infused into my heart,— all the gloom of doubt vanished away" (VIII. 12. 29).

This revolutionary experience of Augustine, which we have been accustomed to call his conversion, meant to him the renunciation of everything that is not God and the complete surrender of his will to the will of God. "For Thou didst so convert me unto Thyself, that I sought neither a wife, nor any other of this world's hopes" (VIII. 12. 30). "When I shall cleave unto Thee with all my being, then shall I in nothing have pain and labor; and my life shall be a real life, being wholly full of Thee" (X. 28). Thus his profound moral struggles, his growing consciousness of sin, the example and prayers of his mother, the testimony of the church especially that of Ambrose, and above all the Epistles of Paul, had directed him to salvation in Christ alone.

From his first entrance upon a Christian life Augustine occupied himself especially with the study of the Pauline Epistles. Himself a living witness of saving grace he found in the Pauline teaching an expression of his own inward experience. His experience and Luther's, both resemble Paul's.

As may be supposed, owing to his own experience of salvation, he was prone to place man's depravity and moral bondage in striking contrast with the sovereign grace of God. It was only natural that this tendency should grow in strength as he engaged in the Pelagian controversy.

Of chief importance for our discussion are the following writings of Augustine: Prior to the Pelag. controversy: *De libero arbitrio. Confessiones*, XIII books. *Liber de 83 quaestionibus. Quaestiones ad Simplicianum.* In connection with the Pelag. controversy: *De peccatorum meritis et remissione*, III books. *De spiritu et littera. De perfectione institiae hominis. De natura et gratia. De gestis Pelagii. De gratia Christi et de peccato originali*, II books. Against Julian, *Contra Julianum*, VI books. *De nuptiis et concupiscentia*, II books. *Contra duas epistolas Pelagianorum*, IV books. **Opus imperfectum** *contra Julianum,* VI books. Against the Semipelagians, *De praedestinatione sanctorum. De dono perseverantiae. De gratia et libero arbitrio. De correptione et gratia.* Also, *Enchiridion. De civitate dei,* and *Letters* and *Sermons.*

5. *Augustine's Doctrine of Sin and Grace.* Starting from the proposition *omne bonum aut deus aut ex deo*—"all good is either God or from God" (*lib. arb.* III. 13. 36). Augustine recognizes no moral goodness and righteousness in any creature save in communion with God through holy love which God's grace must first impart. Accordingly he asserts that (a) *the original state* of man was a state of *natural perfection,* in which man possessed the divine image which consisted in wisdom, positive righteousness or holiness and immortality, a state in which man was positively good and free (*civ. dei,* XIV. 10. 11). Man in his original state possessed also the gift of grace (*de corrept. et grat.* XI. 29. 31. 32). By this grace Augustine means the supernatural assistance (*adiutorium*) indispensable to all creatures, even to the good angels, for their perseverance in good (*ib.* 32). We notice here already the germ of the Scholastic doctrine of the *donum gratiae super-additum.* Man's freedom was not a mere formal freedom, a power of contrary choice, but real freedom, a determination and inclination to goodness (*op. imp.* V. 6). Yet man's freedom was concreated and therefore relative, not absolute. The latter is the freedom of God who is destitute of the power of sinning (*de nat. et gr.* 49. 57). Whether Adam should become absolutely free, like God and the holy angels, depended upon the use which he should make of his freedom during the period of probation. Adam was accordingly not in the state of absolute freedom where sin and death were no longer possible — *non posse peccare et mori* (*ib.* 33) — a state within his reach through the divine assistance, *adjutorium, of the* "first grace" (*ib.* 31), but in a state of relative freedom with a possibility, but not a necessity, of sinning and dying — *posse non peccare et non mori* (*ib.* 33).

(b) *All this Adam lost in the fall,* the heinousness of which cannot be exaggerated. Not only was Adam expelled from paradise, but he also lost his fellowship with God and accordingly was smitten with mortality. Ignorance took possession of his soul. The *adiutorium* of divine grace and his true freedom were lost. The freedom of the will now amounted simply to a freedom to sin. The harmony of man's nature was destroyed and the inclination of the will toward the good perverted and turned toward evil. Augustine sees Adam's sin not in the mere outward act of the eating of the fruit but in disobedience to God's commandment. In pride and selfishness Adam abandoned his love to God and began to love himself. The very essence of Adam's sin was the love of himself.

amor sui. This evil will, the love of self, preceded the outward act. "Our first parents fell into open disobedience, because already they were secretly corrupted; for the evil act had never been done had not an evil will preceded it" (*civ. dei* XIV. 13. 14).

(c) *All these features of the fallen Adam have now passed over to his posterity.* Augustine considered the human race as one compact mass, a collective body, responsible in its unity and solidarity. All men were in Adam, the first transgressor, and are by birth what he became by disobedience, and thus his moral character becomes theirs. Adam not only became a sinner, but also begets sinners. Adam's sin is propagated not by way of imitation, but by propagation sin passed from Adam to his descendents and thus every one participated in original sin, for nature and the vice of nature are simultaneously propagated. Accordingly also the penalty pronounced upon Adam passes over to his posterity. Thus the human race has become a mass of perdition (*massa perditionis*), and is condemned in him. From this universal condemnation infants are not excluded, since they also belong to the mass of perdition; "if there were in men nothing but original sin, it would be sufficient for their condemnation" (*pecc. mer. et rem.* I. 12. 15).

Augustine does not explain the unbroken transmission of the corrupt nature of man by any of the current theories as to the origin and propagation of souls. He rejects Origen's theory of pre-existence and reaches no conclusion as to traducianism or creationism, for this is a question "on which no assistance can be rendered by clear and certain proofs of the Holy Scriptures" (*ib.* II. 36). He merely asserts that the production of children is not possible without sinful concupiscence. By this he does not mean to condemn marriage which is good in itself, though virginity is to be preferred, but he maintains that lust, *concupiscentia,* is operative in every natural generation. This carnal concupiscence is transmitted, in every instance, from parents to children, even where the parents are regenerate persons. By regeneration only the guilt of original sin is removed, not the sin itself. "This mysterious verity" Augustine illustrates by a parallel supplied by nature: "As a wild olive grows out of the seed of the wild olive, and from the seed of the true olive springs also nothing but a wild olive . . . , so what is born in the flesh, either of a sinner or of a just man, is in both instances a sinner" (*nupt. et conc.* I. 21).

(d) *No human power but only the grace of God can deliver man* from this state of total depravity (*civ. dei* XXII. 22. 4). Even in paradise before the fall divine grace was needed. How much more since the fall! It is true, the divine image in man is not altogether lost by Adam's sin. "The little spark of reason, *scintilla rationis,* which was the image of God in him, has not been quite quenched" (*ib.* XXII. 24). Nor was the freedom of his will altogether destroyed. "For God does not work our salvation in us as if he were working in insensate stones, or in creatures in whom nature has placed neither reason nor will" (*pecc. mer. et rem.* II. 6). But since after the fall man's freedom amounts only to a freedom to sin, man is totally unable to do good (*c. duas ep. Pel.* II. 5. 9). For this reason even the good works of the heathen are not to be regarded as virtues, but as vices (*civ. dei* XIX. 25). From this follows that all human work is excluded and divine grace is made the sole cause of man's recovery. Divine grace is not a personal spiritual relation, but a creative energy which generates that freedom of the will which is entirely lost in the natural man and exerts its influence upon man's will making it capable of doing good.

We notice here the influence of Augustine's Neoplatonic conception of sin as a negation, a privation and weakening of man's spiritual power. Grace is accordingly God's activity upon the will and intelligence giving them a new direction. Therefore grace consists not so much in the forgiveness of sin, which marks only the beginning of the renewal, as in the communication of moral powers.

Since divine grace is the sole originating cause of the entire process of regeneration it may be spoken of as *gratia operans* or *praeveniens* and *gratia co-operans et subsequens;* the former as the creative power of God which generates a new will in man; the latter operating in the renewed heart of man, whereby he is qualified to perform good works. There are several degres of grace which mark the several stages in the process of regeneration: (1) *Renewal* begins with baptism which effaces guilt for the past, working particularly the forgiveness of the guilt of original concupiscence and, in the case of adults, the forgiveness of sins actually committed. But concupiscence, though weakened, remains in the baptized. It is, however, no longer sin, since God no longer so accounts it. (2) The next stage of Christian life is *faith* which is a gift of God. According to Augustine faith is not that trustful attitude of the heart which apprehends forgiveness of sin. It is first of all belief in the revealed truth and as such precedes knowledge and is the key to it. On the other hand we advance through faith to knowledge and insight, for knowledge is the reward of faith. Faith also manifests itself in longing and praying for the renewing grace of God. (3) Thus faith becomes *faith which works by love.* And it is this faith, to which self-surrender and love are united, that justifies. Augustine clearly understands and faithfully presents Paul's *sola gratia,* but he lacks the clear Pauline conception of *sola fide,* the relation of faith to works. Nevertheless, he does not speak of the merit of works as a ground of acceptance with God. Rewards which men receive from God are not so much rewards as free gifts. It is his gifts that God crowns, not our merits. (4) The crowning act of grace is *the infusion of love* or the in-breathing of a new and good will. Justification, then, is not a forensic act but a process, a transformation of an ungodly into a righteous man, so that he becomes actually righteous and is able to perform righteous works. This transformation is effected by shedding abroad love in our pardoned hearts by the Holy Spirit who inspires holy desires and endows with new moral powers (*enchir.* 117). And this process of transformation marks the entire Christian life, for concupiscence "still remains, until our entire infirmity be healed by the advancing renewal of our inner man, day by day, when at last our outward man shall be clothed with incorruption" (*nupt. et conc.* 25. 28).

(e) With all the emphasis laid on the divine agency in the work of regeneration *man's freedom* is not denied. In his *De gratia et libero arbitrio* and *De correptione et gratia* Augustine expressly maintains that divine grace does not exclude human freedom. *Nemo credit nisi volens,* no one believes unless he wills. But if we remember that according to Augustine it is God who effects that man may will, we see at once that a real freedom is thereby excluded. And if grace lays hold of man there can be no resistance, for when God wills to save any one, no will of man resists him. The fact, then, that some are saved and some are not, Augustine explains on the ground of predestination which is the cause of salvation. In consequence of an eternal decree, and without any reference to the future conduct of man (*de praed.* 13. 37), God elected a fixed number (*corr. et gr.* 13. 39) — a substitution of the number of the fallen angels (*enchir.* 29) — out of the mass of perdition to become vessels of his mercy, and left the rest as vessels of his wrath to a just condemnation (*corr. et gr.* 13). The predestinated are made partakers not only of regenerating grace, but also of the gift of perseverance (*donum perseverantiae*). Perseverance, like faith, is the gift of God bestowed only on the predestinated (*praed.* 18. 37). Not all believers are predestinated. The unpredestinated or "foreknown," even if they appear true Christians, will not be saved, because they have not been elected (*dono pers.* 8. 19), while others, even outside the Christian church, have been saved, simply because they were predestinated (*ep.* 102; *praed.* 9. 17). There is no assurance of salvation possible, since "no one is certain and secure of his own predestination and salvation" (*Corr. et gr.* 13. 40). But the saints who will persevere should not trouble themselves with the question whether they are in the number of the predestinated, "since it is well for them not to be high-minded but to fear" (*ib.; dono pers.* 8, 19).

Though Augustine speaks of those as "predestinated to eternal death" he does not say that the reprobation of the wicked is the cause of sin. In answer to the objection that it is unjust in the case of those, who are alike guilty to pardon one and punish the other, Augustine replies that in the reprobate God reveals his justice, as in the elect his mercy (*ib.* 8). For the former fell and sinned by their own will, the latter persevered by the will of God. If all men were saved, the justice due to sin would not be discerned. If none were saved, the benefit of grace would not be known (*civ. dei* 2112). In maintaining unconditional predestination and irresistible grace Augustine had no other object in view but to make divine grace the sole cause of man's salvation.

B. SETTLEMENT OF DOCTRINAL CONFLICT.

1. *Conflict between Augustinianism and Pelagianism.* Pelagius' positions were obviously in conflict with those of Augustine and it was only natural that a violent controversy ensued. Although Pelagianism found sympathizers both in the East and the West, yet there could be little doubt that Augustinianism, at least in the West, would win the day.
of the regenerate proved Pelagius' views as erroneous. It was easy

Pelagianism conflicted seriously with the Christian consciousness of the necessity of redemption and salvation through Christ alone. The testimony of the Scriptures as well as the personal experiences for Augustine to show that the position of Pelagius was anti-scriptural. It was easy for him to show that Pelagius' theory of the free will of man was untenable, for if fallen man were free, Christ would have come into the world in vain. If man can overcome sin by his own strength, it would be useless for him to pray for the remission of sins. If children are not sinful, they would not need baptism.

The errors of Pelagius were condemned both in the East and in the West. But not all who approved the condemnation of Pelagius were in accord throughout with Augustine. His doctrines of absolute inability, irresistible grace and unconditional predestination, were combated by many distinguished theologians, especially in Gaul, endeavoring to pursue a middle course. They were first called "remnants of the Pelagians"— *Reliquiae Pelagianorum* — or*"Mass-ilians,"* from their principal seat Marseilles, in Southern Gaul. Much later, since the sixteenth century, they were called, yet not in strict propriety —"Semi-Pelagians," for they might just as well be termed "Semi-Augustinians."

2. *Extreme Augustinianism in Conflict with Semi-Pelagianism.*
Some of the monks of Adrumetum in North Africa were driven to
despair, others moved to indifference, or even licentiousness by
Augustine's predestinarian teaching, while still others held that the
free will is assisted by the grace of God in the work of regeneration.
In his two treatises *De gratia et libero arbitrio* and *De correptione
et gratia* Augustine seems to have successfully relieved the difficulties of the monks.

Contemporaneously with this occurrence violent opposition to
Augustine's doctrine of predestination arose in Southern Gaul, especially in Massilia. The leader of the Massilians was a Scythian
monk, *John Cassian,* a disciple of Chrysostom. Other advocates of
the Semi-Pelagian theory were Vincent of Lerins, Gennadius of
Massilia and Faustus of Reji. The Massilians distinctly repudiated
Augustinian predestination, "because it introduces a fatal necessity,
it cripples moral energy and plunges men either into despair or
licentiousness." They maintained that in the plan of salvation all
mankind were included and that predestination was based on the
foreknown "merit of faith and perseverance." (see Aug. *ep.* 225.
226).

Augustin, who had received an account of this from Prosper
Aquitanus and a certain Hilary, addressed to the Massilians two
tracts: *De praedestinatione sanctorum* and *De dono perseverantiae,*
but emphasizing the most objectionable points Augustine did not
succeed in convincing his opponents.

The Massilians strenuously opposed the Pelagian doctrine of
man's complete moral ability, as well as Augustine's, of man's complete moral inability. Their intermediate position between Augustinianism and Pelagianism, which coincides in all essential points
with that set forth by Cassian in the thirteenth Colloquy of his
Collationes patrum, and *De coenobiorum institutis,* may be briefly
sketched as follows: (a) Adam's fall entailed death and corruption
of nature upon his posterity (original sin). (b) Original sin does
not eliminate the free will, but weakens it, nor does it involve complete impotence, but only moral infirmity. (c) The natural man
is accordingly neither morally dead (Augustine), nor morally
healthy (Pelagius), but morally sick and weakened. (d) He
needs, therefore, divine grace as the co-operative agency of the
human will in conversion (coll. XIII. 13). Accordingly the main
share in our salvation is to be ascribed not to the merit of our own
works, but to heavenly grace (*ib.* 18). (e) Sometimes it is the
divine agency as in the cases of Paul and Matthew, sometimes it is
the human agency (Zacchaeus) which begins the work of regeneration (*inst.* XII. 14. 18; *coll.* XIII. 11). (f) There is no uncondi-

tional election to eternal salvation. Predestination is based on fore-knowledge. Those who perish, perish against God's will, for He willeth all men to be saved (*ib.* 7).

After Augustine's death, *Prosper* became the leading representative of Augustinian anthropology. In his treatise against Cassian, *Contra Collatorem,* he defended the Augustinian doctrine of grace, concealing the difficulties. But despite all his energy he was not able to ensure the victory of Augustine's doctrine in Marseilles. Neither did the scheme which the author of *De vocatione gentium* — incorrectly ascribed to Prosper — set forth, solve the problem. He attempted to disguise the severity of the Augustinian position by distinguishing between general and special grace, the latter only being effectual.

While the adherents of Augustine tried to settle the dispute by explanatory treatises, the Massilians, on the other hand, continued their assaults upon the advocates of Augustiniansim. In the anonymous work *Praedestinatus,* composed by a Massilian, "the horrible doctrines taught by a predestinarian sect" were presented in the baldest form. Vincent of Lerins in his *Commonitorium* shows that the "novelty" of Augustinianism does not stand the true catholic test of doctrine: *quod semper, quod ubique, quod ab omnibus creditum est.* The Massilian presbyter Gennadius, who continued Jerome's *De viris illustribus,* reveals his Semi-Pelagian attitude by his derogatory verdicts on Augustine's doctrine of predestination.

The ablest advocate of the Semi-Pelagian view in the last half of the fifth century was the highly-esteemed Bishop Faustus of Reji (d. 495). At a synod of Arles in 475 and, soon after, at Lyons he gained the victory over the presbyter Lucidus, who had championed certain hyper-Augustinian propositions: that the foreknowledge of God appoints men to death, that Christ did not die for all, and that a "vessel unto dishonor" can never become a "vessel unto honor." At the request of these synods Faustus wrote his *De gratia,* in which he denounces alike Pelagius whom he characterizes as *pestiferus,* and Augustine, though he calls him *quidam sanctorum.*

For several decades Semi-Pelagianism continued to be the prevailing form of doctrine in Gaul. But in the attempt to seek an intermediate position Semi-Pelagianism really reacted too far in the direction of Pelagianism. Moreover, the popes of Rome expressed themselves against Semi-Pelagianism and held to the Augustinian doctrine ignoring, however, Augustinian predestination. The North African Bishop Fulgentius of Ruspe (d. 533), in his treatise *Contra Faustum* championed the strict Augustinianism in the name of sixty African bishops. Associated with them were those Scythian monks (p. xxx) who combated Nestorianism as well as Pelagianism and Semi-Pelagianism. After a variety of fortunes a mild Augustinianism obtained acceptance everywhere, even in Gaul, where Caesarius of Arles, Prosper Aquitanus and Hilary of Arles, as also Avitus, archbishop of Vienne, were its decided advocates.

3. *The Doctrinal Decision of the Council of Orange.* Although at the synod of Valence, in 529, Caesarius' views upon the doctrine of grace were assailed in his absence he re-affirmed them before the council at Arausio (Orange), in the same year. His views together with the sentences of pope Felix IV. which in the main were derived from Prosper's, were made the basis of the decrees of Orange, designated to put an end to the Semi-Pelagian controversy.

In twenty-five canons the synod of Orange rejected Pelagianism and adopted a moderate Augustinianism. It asserted that by Adam's sin, he himself and all his posterity, were injured in body and soul. Original sin was defined not on its positive but rather on its negative side as the moral inability of the natural man to do good. The necessity of divine grace was affirmed. All moral human activity depends upon grace, but grace is not irresistible. Baptism is the vehicle of grace. The election of grace is recognized but unconditional election is not mentioned and predestination to evil is expressly anathematized.

To these twenty-five canons the synod added a concluding confession. The following are some of the leading propositions of this confession: By the fall free will has been so bent and weakened that without prevenient grace no one can love God, or believe on Him, or do good for His sake, as he ought. Even the Old Testament saints had their faith only through God's grace. By grace received through baptism, all may by the assistance and co-operation of Christ, perform what is necessary for their soul's salvation. We do not believe that God has predestinated certain individuals to evil, *ad malum;* if there are any who believe such an evil thing, we condemn them with all detestation. In every good work we do not begin; but God, without any merit preceding on our part, inspires in us faith in and love of Himself, so that we may believingly desire the sacrament of baptism, and after baptism, by His help, perform those things which are pleasing to him.

Boniface II. (d. 532), in accordance with the measures adopted by his predecessors, approved the resolutions of Orange, in 530 or 531 (Mansi VIII. 735 ff.).

CHAPTER X

CONCEPTION OF THE SACRAMENTS IN THE ANCIENT CHURCH

The ancient church produced no dogma of the sacraments. We find, however, in the writings of the ancient Church Fathers numerous passages bearing on the doctrine of the sacraments in general and baptism, confirmation, Lord's Supper and the practice of repentance in particular.

A. CONCEPTION OF THE SACRAMENTS IN GENERAL.— In the first centuries of the Christian church the words *sacramentum*, used in the Western Church, and *mysterion*, used in the Eastern Church, were applied in ecclesiastical usage to anything sacred or consecrated, to anything which had a secret or hidden meaning. After Tertullian the term sacrament was applied to any significant Christian rite and soon became especially associated with baptism and the Lord's Supper. The first of the Fathers who gave careful attention to the definition and doctrine of the sacraments was Augustine, though he, too, uses the word sacrament in a wider sense, applying it to matrimony, holy orders, exorcism at baptism, etc. Leo the Great and Gregory the Great used the word with similar vagueness.

Augustine wrote no systematic treatise on the sacraments, but in his writings we find a number of passages relative to the defiinition, meaning and necessity of the sacraments. He defines a sacrament as a visible sign of an invisible grace. Sacraments are, therefore, symbols, yet not merely symbols but also vehicles of divine grace of which they present the emblem. The visible signs become what they are through the word. "The word is added to the element, and there results the sacrament, as if itself also a kind of visible word" (*in Johann*. 80. 3). The efficacy of the sacrament does not rest in the outward observance of the sacrament, but in the divine inwardly effectual act which does not always accompany the human transaction. We observe here the influence of Augustine's theory of predestination.

Sacraments impart to the recipient divine grace provided he believes and lives in the church. Speaking of the efficacy of baptism Augustine says: "Whence has water so great an efficacy, as in touching the body to cleanse the soul, save by the operation of the word; and that not because it is uttered, but because it is believed" (*ib.* 80. 30). Referring to those who have received baptism in heresy, Augustine says: "Let them hasten to the unity and truth of the Catholic Church, not that they may have the sacrament of washing, if they have been already bathed in it although in heresy, but that they may have it to their health" (*de bapt.* V. 8. 9).

B. BAPTISM AND CONFIRMATION.

1. *Baptism.* From the very outset great significance was attached to baptism. The Greek Fathers considered it as indispensable to salvation, so necessary that even a child cannot be saved without it. It gives pardon of sin previously committed. Sins committed after baptism are purged by disciplinary sufferings. Baptism brings salvation, gives assurance of eternal life, imparts the Holy Spirit and all his graces. The great emphasis laid on baptism is also shown by the various terms in which the Greek Fathers speak of baptism. They call it a seal, the illumination, the laver of saving water, the cleansing, the completing act in the appropriation of Christianity. Following Justin Martyr who contrasts the regeneration, by water in baptism with the natural birth by ordinary generation, the Fathers taught the doctrine of baptismal generation.

After Tertullian the Fathers thought of a real connection of the Spirit with the water of baptism, but differed in their views as to the mode in which the effects of the sacrament are communicated, whether with the application of the water, or through the action of the cleansing power imparted to the water itself. The beneficial effect of baptism, in case of adult candidates, requires a right inner disposition and purpose.

From the earliest times it was held that while its effects may be lost, baptism cannot be repeated. Infant baptism was practiced early in the church. The earliest witness to the prevalence of this practice is Irenaeus who says that Christ came to save all "who through Him are born again to God — infants, and children, and boys, and youths, and old men" (II. 22. 4). Origen spoke approvingly of infant baptism as a well-established custom of the church (*in. Lev.* VIII). *On Rom.* 5:9 he says that the church has received from the apostles the tradition to give baptism to little children. By opposing infant baptism Tertullian proved that it was customary in his day. He opposed infant baptism on the ground of inexpediency of placing infants under the heavy responsibilities which the recipient of baptism takes upon himself (*de bapt.* 18). According to Cyprian children should be baptized as soon as possible though not necessarily on the eighth day after their birth (*ep.* 58.2).

In the writings of the Fathers we find no dogmatic specification

as to the mode of administering baptism. The practice of immersion in baptism was undoubtedly universal in the early church. Yet the Didache, written not later than the early years of the second century expressly permits affusion. Cyprian maintains that also those are to be accounted legitimate Christians who were not washed, but sprinkled or affused, with the saving water (*ep.* 75. 12). The Fathers were concerned not so much about the mode of baptism as about its effect.

According to Augustine baptism is indispensable to salvation, for men can be saved only within the church to which baptism is the only entrance. Accordingly unbaptized infants are lost, although the condemnation allotted to them is the mildest possible of all. As to the dying thief who was saved without baptism, Augustine conjectured that he was baptized with blood instead of water or that he had been baptized on some former occasion. Like Origen, Augustine regarded martyrdom as a substitute for ordinary baptism. Baptism is the sacrament of the remission of sins. It frees from the guilt of original concupiscence and also from further sins actually committed, although these may be atoned for through repentance. But penitential works could not bring foregiveness to man if he were not baptized.

Baptism, like ordination, imparts to the recipient an abiding, indelible character, and therefore these two sacraments are not to be repeated in the catholic church (*c. Parm.* II. 13. 20). From the abiding character of the sacrament must be distinguished its gracious effect which does not follow the recipient if he does not live in the church (*ib.* 11. 24; *de bapt.* V. 8. 9).

Since sacraments impart divine grace only to the believer, who lives within the church (*in Johann.* 80. 3), Augustine taught that infants who have no faith in themselves are benefited by the faith of the church which presents them to God in baptism making a confession of faith in their stead (*ep.* 98. 2. 3; *de pecc. mer.* III. 4. 7). "An infant, although he is not yet a believer in the sense of having that faith which includes the consenting will of those who exercise it, nevertheless becomes a believer through the sacrament of that faith. For as it is answered that he believes, so also he is called a believer not because he assents to the truth by an act of his own judgment, but because he receives the sacrament of that truth" (*ep.* 98. 10).

There was not yet any recognized church doctrine as to the character and significance of the sacrament of baptism. But Augustine had laid the foundation of the Roman Catholic conception of baptism.

2. *Confirmation.* Closely connected with the act of baptism were the laying on of hands and anointing. These usages, which at first marked the completion of the act of baptism, gradually came to be regarded as a separate sacrament. The laying on of hands became less prominent than the anointing. Hence this sacrament was called the sacrament of chrism, or unction. Later in the Western Church it was known as the sacrament of confirmation. Ambrose addressing the catechumens, who had just been baptized and anointed, describes the significance of this rite as follows: "You received the seal of the Spirit . . . God the Father sealed you, Christ the Lord strengthened (*confirmavit*) you, and gave the earnest of the Spirit in your heart" (*de myst.* VI. 29. 42). Augustine calls the anointing the sacrament of chrism "which is indeed holy as among the class of visible signs, like baptism itself" (*c. litt. Pet.* II. 239).

C. REPENTANCE.— In closest relation to baptism stands repentance. It is preparatory to baptism, the sacrament of foregiveness and regeneration. But even the regenerate is not free from sin. Is there foregiveness for post-baptismal sin?

1. In the early church a distinction was made between repentance preparing for baptism, and repentance to obtain forgiveness of sins committeed after baptism. Hermas proclaimed in accordance with a special revelation the possibility of a second repentance for the believer. But for the sin of apostasy there is no pardon. Martyrdom, however, secures forgiveness of all sins.

The aim of the penitential praxis was to preserve the dignity and purity of the church and to purge the sinner more and more from sin. To this end he must be disciplined. Soon the idea developed that the sinner ought to make satisfaction to God whom he had offended (Tert. *poen.* 10). In fact the three constituent elements of the Roman sacrament of penance, contrition, confession and satisfaction, are already found in Tertullian (*ib.* 8). The person hearing confession was to be an experienced and devout Christian, either clerical or lay (Origen, *in Ps.* 37). In the Western Church only a priest could hear confession. This spiritual adviser by divine authority either remitted or retained the sins of the sinner.

Thus the church in the first two centuries granted "this second and only (remaining.) repentance" (Tert. *poen.* 9). The penance of the baptized Christian was therefore called *secunda tabula* or *planca post naufragium,*— a second plank grasped by a shipwrecked man after which there was no third chance to be readmitted into the church (*poen.* 12). After a prescribed period of rigorous, humiliating, public penance and the pronouncement of the divine forgiveness there occurred his readmission into the church, after which he must still perform certain external acts by way of satisfaction; and if he fell away, he could not be restored. Irenaeus, however, points out an exception to this universal practice in the case of the Syrian Gnostic Cerdo: "Coming frequently into the church and making public confession, he thus remained, one time teaching in secret, and then again making public confession; but at last having been denounced for corrupt teaching, he was excommunicated from the assembly of the brethren" (III. 4. 3).

2. It seems that about A. D. 200 this second repentance was granted in all cases of grave sins, including apostasy, murder and adultery. Tertullian had only reluctantly accepted the theory of the second repentance (*poen.* 7). After he had joined the ranks of the Montanists he gave it up together with its authority Hermas, "that apocryphal Shepherd of adulterers" (*de pud.* 20). In chapter 19 (*ib.*), after a rather arbitrary exegesis of 1 John 5:16, he makes the distinction between venial sins or sins of weakness, "sins of daily committal to which we all are liable," and mortal sins which are "irremissible" and "for which it is not permitted even to make successful intercession." Tertullian gives seven mortal sins: Murder, idolatry, fraud, apostasy, blasphemy, adultery and fornication.

It cannot be denied that the then existing penitential discipline had its defects and inconsistencies. Especially were the opinions divided regarding the second repentance in case of fornication and apostasy. Pope Callistus (217-2220) sought to establish a more logical system. He published a new penitential order, according to which the second repentance was to be granted in case of fornication and adultery. Tertullian and Hippolytus opposed him without success. The new penitential order introduced by Callistus was favorably received also outside the Roman Church. At the middle of the third century it had become universal.

After the Decian persecution, when multitudes of backsliders, *lapsi*, desired to be restored to the church, the question whether the second repentance should be granted also in case of apostasy, became a pressing one. Cyprian who originally, like Tertullian, utterly opposed the restoration of the lapsed, modified his views as to readmitting the lapsed to communion after long penitence, in prospect of death. In expectation of a new persecution the second repentance which up to this time had been granted only to those in immediate peril of death, was now extended to all the lapsed. However, the final decision as to their restoration rested with the bishop. An assembly of bishops at Carthage in 252 approved these regulations of church discipline laid down by Cyprian.

Soon after his election to the bishopric Cyprian met with opposition on the part of five presbyters who were dissatisfied with Cyprian as being unworthy, because of his flight during the persecution, to rule over men who had endured torture with heroic constancy. The controversy on the restoration of the lapsed resulted in a schism. The dissatisfied party instigated by Novatus chose a deacon of their own, Felicissimus, and set up Fortunatus as bishop of their party. Their motto was "to bring back and recall the lapsed into the Church" (ep. 39.5). They refused the episcopal decision in the case of readmission and restored the lapsed without any discrimination.

Soon after the African schism there arose a schism in Rome in consequence of an election of a bishop. Cornelius, who was nominated as bishop of Rome, showed great indulgence towards the lapsed. Against him rose up one of his presbyters, Novatianus, and was chosen bishop by the opposition. His adherents considered themselves as the Pure or 'Kathari,' a congregation of actually holy men. Hence they refused communion with the church at large which had defiled itself by readmitting the lapsed, and rebaptized those who came over to them from other communions. Novatian admitted the possibility of mercy for the fallen and therefore exhorted them to repentance, but denied the possibility of their ever being received back into the church (ep. 51. 28). The Novatian schism perpetuated itself in various provinces of the West and the East for some generations.

4. Augustine accepted the customary distinction between venial or daily sins, and damnable or great sins. Accordingly he distinguished a twofold repentance after baptism: (1) repentance for the lighter daily sins which are purged away through alms and prayers and fasting; (2) repentance for grave sins. Those who are guilty of these must make confession to the bishop who will advise as to an appropriate satisfaction (serm. 6. 12; 4.10). All those who remain in the church will be saved regardless of the deficiencies of their moral character which will be repaired by "suffering a punishment of fire, lasting for a time proportionate to the magnitude of their crimes and misdeeds, but they shall not be punished with everlasting fire" (ench. 67).

5. About the end of the fourth century public penance was more and more abandoned in the East, but continued in the West though under less and less rigorous discipline. Public penance had no longer reference to apostasy, murder and adultery but to all grave sins. Consequently, the object of penance, reconciliation with the church, was more and more identified with reconciliation with God.

The penance was regarded as the discharge of a liability due to God or the church. It was the duty of the bishop to determine the quality and duration of the penance, but the penitents were allowed to perform their penances in secret, and only at the end were they publicly readmitted by the bishop into the' fold. Gradually the office of readmitting penitent sinners was left to be discharged by priests. The fundamental elements of the Roman sacrament of penance, *compunctio* or *contritio, confessio* and *satisfactio,* were clearly set forth by Gregory the Great.

D. THE LORD'S SUPPER.— Already in the ancient church we notice two distinct features in the celebration of the Eucharist, (1) what the congregation presented to God in prayer or devotion, the sacrifice, and (2) what the congregation received from the Lord, the sacrament. Accordingly the doctrine of the Lord's Supper may be treated under the twofold aspect, as a sacrifice and as a sacrament.

1. *The Lord's Supper as a Sacrifice.* The sacrificial conception of the Lord's Supper in the first Christian centuries is worthy of notice, since it contains the germ of the later doctrine of the sacrifice of the mass.

Justin Martyr and Irenaeus speak of an offering in the Lord's Supper and prize it over against the sacrifices of the Jews and Gentiles as the fulfilment of Mal. 1:11 ". . . in every place incense shall be offered unto my name, and a pure offering," (*dial.* 41. 117; *haer.* IV. 18. 3. 6). By this they mean in the first place the bread and wine which with other gifts of the congregation were rendered to God as a 'thank-offering' and were therefore called oblationes. The bishop or an appointed official received the bread and wine as gifts and presented them to God with the prayer of thanksgiving, the *eucharistia,* which was also styled an "offering," or a "sacrifice," and soon the term passed over to the entire rite.

The eucharistic prayer at first contained thanksgiving for both the natural and spiritual gifts of God. Both Justin and Irenaeus mention a twofold object in the presentation of bread and wine: a memorial of the gifts of creation and of the redemptive sufferings of Christ. All this is yet consistent with the universal Christian priesthood. To the Fathers of the second century the eucharistic offering is a congregational thankoffering, not priest offering, nor a sin-offering. But when Justin says that the presiding official taking the eucharistic element "offers thanks" and "that the food which is blessed by prayer of word spoken by him, is the flesh and blood of that Jesus who was made flesh" (ap-I. 65. 67), or when Tertullian applies to the Eucharist as a whole the expressions "sacrifice," "offering," or "to offer" (*de cult. fem.* II. 11; *virg. vel.* 9), there is but a short step to Cyprian's idea that as Jesus our high priest offered himself as a sacrifice to his Father, so the human priest takes Christ's place, and imitates his action by offering in the church a true and full sacrifice to God the Father (*ep. ad Caecilium,* 62. 14). Cyprian puts the priest in the place of the congregation and represents him as offering Christ's body and blood for the sins of men. The thank-offering for creation and redemption had thus become a repetition or showing forth anew of the self-sacrifice of Christ. Moreover, in the thanksgiving prayer special mention was made of those who brought the oblations. Prayer was also made for the departed on the day of their death. Tertullian is the first to speak of "sacrifices" or "offerings" for the dead (*de monog.* 10; *de exhort. cast.* 11; *de cor.* 3). It is, however, not known how these "oblations for the dead" were made and what their relation to the eucharistic offering was, but there can be no doubt that thus was formed the germ of the Catholic idea of masses for the dead.

Since the fourth century we notice in the writings of the Greek Fathers the conception of the Eucharist as an unbloody, propitiatory sacrifice which is efficacious for the living and the dead. According to Cyril of Jerusalem the benefits of "the sacrifice of propitiation" extend not only to all the living "who stand in need of succor" (*cat.* 23. 8), but preeminently to the dead; "it will be a very great benefit to the souls, for whom the supplication is put up, while that holy and most awful sacrifice is set forth" (*ib.* 9). "We, when we offer to Him our supplications for those who have fallen asleep, though they be sinners, weave no crown, but offer up Christ sacrificed for our sins, propitiating our merciful God for them as well as for ourselves" (*ib.* 10).

Chrysostom saw in the eucharistic sacrifice a purely priestly function. "As the wise men from the East saw their Savior in the manger, so do we see Him on the altar and in the hands of the priests (*in Matt. hom.* 83; *de sacerd.* 3, 4. 5). He also regarded the sacrifice and the communion, as two separable acts and condemned the practice of leaving the service before the communion (*hom.* III. in *Eph.* 4).

The sacrificial conception of the Lord's Supper is also found in Ambrose (*resurr.* 46) and Augustine. The latter speaking of the sacrifice of the mass wishes the sacrifice of the church to be a daily imitation of Christ's sacrifice on the cross. Christ "is both the Priest who offers and the Sacrifice offered" and "the Church which being His body, learns to offer herself through Him" (*de civ. dei* X. 20). Augustine also asserts that the sacrifice of the altar and alms of the faithful on earth are of great service for the departed (*ench.* 10).

Since then the idea of the eucharistic sacrifice has held a prominent place in both Eastern and Western Christendom. After Augustine it was Leo the Great (*ad Dioscurum, ep.* IX. 3) and especially Gregory the Great who found the whole significance of the
Lord's Supper in the sacrifice of the mass which is particularly
efficacious for the purpose of rescuing the souls of the departed
from purgatory (*dial.* IV. 55. 58; *hom. in ev.* II. 27. 7-9; 37. 7).

2. *The Lord's Supper as a Sacrament.* Although the Lord's
Supper was very early regarded under two aspects, as a sacrifice
and as a sacrament, yet the ancient church laid the emphasis not
on what man offered God, but on what he received from Him.

Since the days of the apostles the ancient Christians saw in the
eucharistic elements not merely symbols but a communion with the
body and blood of the Lord. However, in explaining the sacramental union of the terrestrial and celestial, the views of the Fathers
differed widely. We recognize within the first five centuries three
views as to the relation of the elements to the body of Christ. We
may style them the realistic, symbolic and metabolic views.

(a) A *realistic conception* of the sacramental union was held
by Ignatius, Justin, Irenaeus and also Tertullian. In one passage
(*apol.* I. 66) Justin speaks of a change or transmutation in the elements, from which it has been inferred that he taught transubstantiation. But he does not say that the change in bread and wine is a
change of essence. All he seems to mean is that as the divine Logos
is present in the incarnate Christ, so is he also mysteriously present
in the Eucharist. Justin has in mind chiefly the gracious effect
which the Eucharist has, rather than the nature of the elements.
The same idea that bread and wine in virtue of the act of consecration are pervaded by the body and blood of Christ appears with
Irenaeus. He also holds that the reception of the body of Christ
has the effect of preparing the resurrection body in the person of
the believer. With all this Irenaeus does not teach transubstantiation, for after the consecreation there are still "two realities, earthly
and heavenly!"

Tertullian sometimes uses expressions as if the bread and wine
were only symbolical signs, "the bread by which he represents
his own proper body" (*c. Marc.* I. 1): or he makes the words of
institution "this is my body" as being equivalent to "the figure of
my body" (*ib.* IV. 40). We must remember, however, that Tertullian intended to prove in opposition to Marcion's Docetism that
without the reality of the body of Jesus there could be no figure.
"A figure . . . there could not have been unless there were first a
veritable body" (*ib.*). On the other hand, expressions of an oppo-

site kind show that he believed that a supernatural element was connected with the outward sign, "the body receives the body and blood of Christ, in order that the soul may be nourished by God" (*de. resurr. carn.* 8).

(b) In keeping with the spiritualizing tendency of their school, the Alexandrians and also Eusebius held to a *symbolical* conception of the Eucharist. They see in the sacrament a symbol, yet they ascribe an effect to the symbol in itself. Clement regards the Eucharist as an initiation into divine knowledge and immortality (*paed.* II. 2; *strom.* I. 1). Both, Eusebius and Athanasius, commenting upon John 6:61-64, repudiate emphatically the partaking of real flesh and blood. Eusebius also speaks of memorializing the sacrifice of Christ "by symbols both of the body and of the saving blood." These Greek Fathers approached the Calvinistic doctrine of a spiritual real fruition of Christ's life in the Eucharist.

Origen, fully aware that his view deviated from the commonly received one, declared that the only effectual thing in the Eucharist is the word of Christ, of which the elements are a symbol. He approached the view of Zwingli that the sacrament is a memorial without mystical elements. Eating Christ's body and drinking his blood mean to Origen receiving Christ's word (*in Matt. serm.* 85). They are accordingly not confined to the Eucharist. The only difference between the hearing of the Word of God and the Eucharist is that in the latter a symbol is added to the Word. According to Gregory of Nazianzus the elements are symbols or antitypes of the real, historic body of Christ and of the salvation effected through him (*or.* 17. 12). Basil likewise gives a spiritual meaning to the eating the flesh and drinking the blood (*ep.* 8. 4).

In the West Cyprian and Augustine held to the symbolic view. Although Cyprian calls the Eucharist "the body and blood of Christ (*ep.* 53.2), he nevertheless favors a symbolical interpretation of the words of institution. He considers the mixing of the wine with water essential, for it symbolizes the union of Christ with his church, the wine representing the blood of Christ, the water representing the people (*ep.* 52. 13). To Augustine the elements are visible signs of an invisible grace. He recognizes in the sacrament no actual presence of Christ's body which is in some place in heaven after the manner of a real body, but according to his divine nature Christ is everywhere entirely present like God. It is true, Augustine often uses expressions which sound realistic, naming the consecrated elements the body and blood of Christ, speaking of receiving the body and blood of Christ. Herein he may have followed universal custom. The expressions themselves must be interpreted in the light of his own explanation: "It is only in a certain manner that Christ's body is Christ's body" (*ep.* 98. 9).

(c) At the close of the fourth century we notice a third view which connected with the symbolic offering a change of the elements into the body and blood of Christ (*metabolic view*). As has been already indicated, the doctrine of transubstantiation was not entertained by Justin and Irenaeus. But Cyril of Jerusalem in his "mystagogical catecheses" enunciates the idea of a *metabole* or transformation of the bread and wine into the body and blood of Christ. What Cyril means by transformation is not a change of the substance of the elements (22.6), but a change of the significance of the elements in which Christ upon the consecration is miraculously dwelling (23.7). Cyril does not think of the partaking of real flesh and blood. In continuation of the passage quoted above (22.9) he says: Strengthen thou thine heart by partaking thereof as spiritual." Expressing the same view as Cyril, Gregory of Nyssa in his catechism (37) speaks of a transformation or transelementation (*metastoicheiosis*). The bread is by its consecration by the priest transformed into the body of the divine Logos. Chrysostom seems to go further than Cyril and Gregory. In his fervid rhetoric he speaks of the presence of Christ in terms which sound so material as to indicate the presence of the actual body of Christ in the Eucharist. But he does not mean a change of substance any more than he holds to a literal transubstantiation of the baptismal water where he employs the same term in which he expresses the change of the eucharistic elements (*cat.* 34). In a letter to the monk Caesarius, of which only a fragment is extant, he states that the consecrated bread "is worthy to be called the appearance of the Lord's body, although the nature of bread remains in it."

Though the early Greek theologians approached to the doctrine of a positive change they did not teach transubstantiation, for they presupposed that the substance of the elements remains although these undergo an inner change or transformation in so far as the Logos unites himself with them, whereas in transubstantiation it is essential that the elements be replaced.

The doctrine of a real change was held at a later period by John of Damascus (c. 750), and through him this doctrine became the common property of the Greek Church. He argued that it is wrong to say that the elements are mere antitypes of Christ's body and blood after as before consecration and maintained a real change, *metabole,* and remaking, *metapoiesis,* i. e., bread and wine are changed into the body and blood of Christ. Not that Christ's ascended body comes again to earth in any manner in the eucharistic form, but the eucharistic body which results from the change is that born of the Virgin Mary (*fid. orth.* IV. 13). The Damascene, too, did not teach the later Roman doctrine of transubstantiation. His *metabole* is rather a transformation through assumption. As Christ once assumed the body born of the virgin, so now in the Eucharist he assumes the bread and wine. The change is analogous to that by which food is assimilated and changed into our flesh.

When from the fourth century Greek ideas had a stronger influence in the West the metabolic view of the Eucharist was also favorably received there by leading theologians. Ambrose, though nowhere asserting the real presence of the actual body and blood, speaks (*de myst.* 9. 52) of the mysterious efficacy of the holy prayer by which the sacramental elements are transformed, *transfigurantur*, into the flesh and blood of Christ. To illustrate the change wrought in the elements he refers to the transformation of Moses' rod and the waters of the Nile (*ib.* 51). The eucharistic food, however, is not corporeal but spiritual (*ib.* 58).

Augustinian theology checked the development toward transubstantiation in the West, but as a result of the growing tendency of the age toward the marvelous and the magical, the church departed more and more from his own symbolic-spiritualistic view and drifted irresistibly in the direction of the amazing dogma of tran-substantiation.

It is interesting to note that pope Gelasius I (496) — speaking *ex cathedra* and in matters of faith — pronounced decidedly against transubstantiation. "The sacrament of the body and blood of Christ, which we receive is a divine thing, because through the same we are made partakers of the divine nature, yet the substance or nature of the bread and wine does not cease to be — *non desinit substantia vel natura panis et vini* — and assuredly the image and the similitude of the body and blood of Christ are celebrated in the performance of the mysteries" (Mirbt, *Quellen z. Geschichte d. Papstums*, p. 86).

CHAPTER XI

CONCEPTION OF THE CHURCH IN THE PATRISTIC AGE

A. EPISCOPACY AND ROME'S SUPREMACY.— When errors and conflicts threatened division in the early church the need to strengthen the bond of the unity in faith was strongly felt. But then already the mistake was made of confounding the inward and the outward unity, to connect the internal communion with Christ with the outward fellowship consisting in a definite form. The uniting band was no longer faith in Christ but the external organization. The tendency to find the unity in faith guaranteed in the outward organization of the church and above all in the Roman episcopate is particularly noticeable in the great Christological and anthropological controversies. The Roman popes increasingly exercised their influence in deciding doctrinal questions. They did it on the ground that they had the doctrine of Peter and that as Peter's successors they were its only transmitters. The church no longer expresses common fellowship of believers with God through Christ; it is now an institution of salvation, a visible body under the control of the episcopacy. The separation between clergy and laity becomes more and more marked. The clergy forms a hierarchical corporation with the bishop of Rome as its visible head.

The first germ of this perversion may be traced to Ignatius and Irenaeus. Ignatius contrasts the catholic church of which Christ is the head with the individual local church, the head of which is the bishop. The individual congregation is subject to its bishop, who stands in the place of Christ with his presbyters about him like the apostles. Irenaeus attributes to the bishops, because they "possess the succession from the apostles," a sure gift of grace for the custody of the truth, *charisma veritatis* (IV. 26. 2). Ignatius sees in the bishop a vicar of Christ; Irenaeus, a successor of the apostles. The Ignatian episcopacy is congregational; there is no distinction of rank or order among the bishops, each bishop being the head and centre of a single congregation. The Irenaean episcopacy is diocesan with distinctions of rank or order, the bishops of the original apostolic churches enjoying a certain preeminence in point of honor. Irenaeus attributes to the Church of Rome a special preeminence as being founded jointly "by the two most glorious apostles, Peter and Paul;" hence "it is a matter of necessity that every Church should agree with this Church, on account of its preeminent authority."

Before his conversion to Montanism Tertullian held the same view as Irenaeus, only that he clearly distinguished between bishops and presbyters (*de praescr. haer.* 32), while Irenaeus used the words "bishop" and "presbyter" interchangeably. Afterwards, as a Montanist, he broke with the episcopal hierarchy and combated the pretensions of the Roman bishop. Christ, he argued, gave the keys to Peter, and not to the bishops, and the true successors of Peter are the spiritually-minded.

Cyprian goes a step further in attributing sacerdotal function to the bishops. The bishop conducts the worship as "the priest of God." Priest and bishop are synonymous terms with Cyprian. In the Lord's Supper the priest represents Christ and offers the body of Christ. The worshippers are not priests; they offer oblations. But the bishop is *the* priest; he offers a sacrifice (*ep.* 62. 14). According to Cyprian the church is an outward organism founded by Christ, of which the bishops are the pillars. As successors of the apostles (*ep.* 26) they are the conservators of apostolic grace and authoritative interpreters of apostolic truth (*ep.* 62. 1. 17; 73. 10).

The apostolic succession as understood by Cyprian is much more than the merely historical matter-of-fact succession of the apostolate which is seen both in Irenaeus and Tertullian. According to Cyprian "the bishops do really represent, not the apostles, but Christ. As the apostles were the representatives of Christ to the first generation and received from Him power to forgive sins, so each succeeding generation possesses representatives of Christ, who have the same power to forgive sins" (T. M. Lindsay, *The Church and the Ministry in the Early Centuries*, p. 312). "If with Ignatius the bishop is the centre of Christian unity, if with Irenaeus he is the depository of the apostolic tradition, with Cyprian he is the *absolute vicegerent* of Christ in things spiritual" (J. B. Lightfoot, *Dissertations on the Apostolic Age*, p. 204). Hence Cyprian mentions but does not emphasize "vicarious ordination" by which "all chief rulers" in the church "succeed to the apostles" (*ep.* 68. 4). What he emphasizes is that the bishop is God's representative appointed directly by God.

The bishops are necessary to the very being of the church, which without them is without the saving grace for the giving of which the church exists. Hence outside the church no one can be saved, *extra ecclesiam nulla salus* (*ep.* 72. 21). No one "can have God for his Father, who has not the Church for his mother" (*de unit. eccl.* 6). Cyprian regards the united episcopate as the chief means of expressing and conserving the unity of the church. He sees the unity of the church in the unity of the bishops in one episcopate, and every believer is to be in communion with the one episcopate through his own bishop; "they are the Church, who are a people united to the priest, and the flock which adheres to its pastor. Whence you ought to know that the bishop is in the Church and the Church in the bishop; and if any one be not with the bishop, that he is not in the Church" (*ep.* 68. 8). "The Church is founded upon the bishops and every act of the Church is controlled by these same rulers" (*ep.* 26. 1). What Cyprian means is "that as each bishop sums up in himself the church over which he presides, the whole Church of Christ practically exists in the whole of the bishops, and the harmonious action of the whole Church can be expressed through the common action and agreement of all the bishops" (T. M. Lindsay, *ut supra*, p. 314).

Cyprian contended for upholding outward unity against the Novatians to whom he denied the possibility of salvation on the ground of their schism, and the validity of whose baptism he refused to admit. Referring to Novatian he says, "he who is not in the Church is not a Christian" (*ep.* 51. 24).

Cyprian finds the origin and foundation of the unity of the church in its being built upon the one Peter, Matt. 16:18 (*unit. eccl.* 4). He does not attribute to Peter a higher authority than to the other apostles. Christ granted to the other apostles and to the post-apostolic bishops the same power originally given to Peter (*ib.* also *ep.* 74. 16). When Cyprian says that "Rome from her greatness plainly ought to take precedence of Carthage" (*ep.* 48. 2), or when in his epistle to Cornelius he calls the Roman Church "the chief Church, *principalis ecclesia*, whence priestly unity takes its source" (*ep.* 54. 14), he does so from respect for the mother see. He certainly does not acknowledge any supremacy or authority of the Roman bishop over or apart from his co-bishops. This is clearly shown from the context of the epistle itself as well as by Cyprian's persistent opposition to the Roman bishop Stephen on the question of heretic baptism (see *ep.* 74. 17), and his invariable testimony to the ecclesiastical parity of all bishops.

Owing to its apostolic associations Rome enjoyed, already in the second century, an extensive authority. It was the only *sedes apostolica* in the West. In all disputes and controversies it was the practice in all parts of the Western Church to apply to Rome for guidance, or to appeal to it for ultimate decision. And since Rome almost always supported the due maintenance of orthodox doctrine, it rose in authority. The synod of Sardica, 343, recognizing Pope Julius I as the strongest support of the Nicene party, accorded to

him, as an individual, the right of supreme jurisdiction over the
metropolitan bishops. On the basis of that decree Innocent I
(*d.* 417) laid claim to a supreme right of adjudication in "all the
more grave and momentous cases" (*Mirbt. Quellen, p.* 62). The
political position of Rome in the empire, and the support given to
the Church of Rome by the emperor very greatly helped this tendency. In 445, the edict of emperor Valentinian III gave Leo I
the supreme judicial and legislative right in the West: "Let that
be a law to all: whatever the authority of the Roman see has sanctioned or shall sanction" (*ib.* p. 77).

At the outset, the councils acknowledged the papal claim to
primacy as based only upon human authority. Leo, however,
claimed that the Church of Rome had obtained the primacy through
no synodical decrees but from Christ himself. Matt. 16:18, which
Cyprian had applied to all the apostles and hence to all bishops,
Leo applied to Peter exclusively and to the pope as his sole successor (*serm.* 3. 3, 4; 62. 2; *ep.* 10; 33, *ad syn. Ephes.*). The councils
did not blindly accept the papal claim, and no doctrinal infallibility
was imputed to the bishop of Rome (cf. sixth ecum. council, 680,
and pope Honorius I.). While in this period the pope was accorded
a certain primacy in honor, he was not accorded a constitutional
supremacy over the whole church. Nevertheless, the bishops of
Rome claimed supremacy over the entire church and exercised it
increasingly in the West from the fifth century.

B. The Donatist Controversy.— The doctrine of the church —
not so much as the polity but as the life of the church is concerned—
received its deepest and fullest exposition in the Donatist Controversy. Donatism sprang from the same roots as Novatianism, and
in its history it had in many things the same character. The persecution of Decius gave birth to Novatianism; the Diocletian persecution to Donatism. The Novatians insisted upon a church of actually
holy men and consequently held that the lapsed should not be received again into communion with the church. The Donatists,
like the Novatians, insisted on absolute purity in the church but
laid the stress especially on the purity of the priests. If they are not
blameless, they cannot cleanse others. How can they give to others
what they do not possess themselves? The validity of sacerdotal
acts depends upon the personal character of the agent and, therefore, sacraments administered by *traditores* (those who had delivered up their copies of the Scriptures under the compulsion of the
Diocletian persecution) are null and void.

The schism originated in the church of Carthage, whence it
spread over the whole province. In 311, Caecilian, who held mod-

erate views as to the *traditores,* was elected bishop of Carthage and consecrated to the office by Felix, bishop of Aptunga, whom the strict party denounced as a *traditor.* On that ground the consecration was declared invalid. Majorinus was elected counter-bishop. Donatus the Great was his successor. It was formerly believed that the leading representative of the anti-Caecilian party was Donatus of Casae Nigrae and that from him the name of the sect was derived. It is now known that the two names denote one and the same person, Casae Nigrae being the birthplace of Donatus the Great.

The Donatist movement was practically confined to Africa. Outside of Africa Caecilian was generally recognized as the legitimate bishop. The emperor Constantine, who was drawn into the matter by the Donatists, sided with the Caecilian party. Under his influence the synod of Arles, 316, decreed that the validity of sacramental functions is not dependent upon the worthiness of the administrators. But the absolutely uncompromising spirit of the Donatists frustrated all efforts to allay the controversy. Donatism existed for more than a century. After 411 the sect was suppressed by law and finally disappeared from the church's history.

C. AUGUSTINE'S CONCEPTION OF THE CHURCH.— At the beginning of the fifth century Augustine entered the contest with the Donatists. The two questions that had given rise to the schism — (1) whether a church by tolerance of unworthy members within its pale lost the essential attributes of purity and catholicity, and (2) whether the character of a bishop affected his official acts,— led Augustine to develop his conception of the church and the sacraments.

The marks of the true church according to Augustine are its unity, purity, catholicity and apostolicity. He granted that ecclesiastical discipline must be exercised, but repudiated the Donatistic test of ecclesiastical validity, namely, ideal perfection which is not possible here on earth. Over against the Donatists who failed to distinguish between the invisible and visible church Augustine maintained that the church is a *corpus mixtum (de doctr. chr.* III. 32. 45). Tares must be left to grow with the wheat (*de bapt.* V. 21. 29; *c. litt. Petil.* III. 2. 3); the presence of the unworthy does not unchurch the worthy. The wicked and heretics are *in* the house but they are not *the* house of God (*de bapt.* VII. 51. 99); they are *in communione sanctorum* only in so far as they are *in communione sacramentorum (de doctr. chr.* III. 32. 74). They may be members of the visible church, the *corpus mixtum,* but only the good and holy, "the saints predestined before the foundation of the world," constitute the true inner church, the *corpus verum (de bapt.* V. 27. 28).

The church is the true body of Christ not because it is spotless, but because of the Spirit and all-pervading and all-uniting love that are in the church and its members. But the Spirit of love is present only in the catholic (*c. litt. Petil.* II. 78. 172), apostolic church which is spread throughout the whole world (*ib.* 38. 91), and which has remained in connection with the church of the apostles whose successors the bishops are (*c. Cresc.* III. 18. 21; *in Johann. tr.* 37. 6). Augustine refers to the Roman Church as one "in which the supremacy of an apostolic chair has always flourished" (*ep.* 43. 7), but he knows nothing of an infallible authority vested in Peter or his successors. On the contrary, he describes "the Christian Society" as one "which, by means of the Apostolic Sees and the succession of bishops, is spread abroad in an indisputably world-wide diffusion" (*ep.* 232. 3). The church, which is spread throughout all the world, had its beginning not at Rome but at Jerusalem (*c. litt. Petil.* II. 55. 126).

Upon the Catholic Church depends the individual faith. Separation from the Catholic Church is a renunciation of the Spirit of love, and union with the Catholic Church is essential to salvation (*unit. eccl.* 2. 2; *ep.* 141. 5; *de bapt.* IV. 1). "Whoso is not in this Church, does not now receive the Holy Ghost" (*in Johann. tr.* 32.7). Though Augustine laid not as much stress as Cyprian upon the divine right of the episcopate, nevertheless, he made the belief of the individual Christian depend upon the authority of the Catholic Church. He went even so far as to declare that he believed the gospel only on the authority of the Catholic Church. "For my part, I should not believe the gospel except as moved by the authority of the Catholic Church" (*c. ep. Manich.* 5). His belief that everything really and permanently good is found in the Catholic Church, the *civitas dei*, led him to the conviction that the state is bound to protect and uphold the church and even to employ force against heretics "to compel them to come in," Luke 14.23 (*ep.* 93. 2, 5; 138. 2, 14; *de correct. Don.* 7. 6. 24).

In his conception of sacraments administered by unworthy persons Augustine followed the decrees of the synod of Arles, 316. Optatus of Mileve held the same views as Augustine. Sacraments are gifts of God, holy in themselves and not through men (Optatus, *de schism. Don.* II. 1; V. 4). The validity of the sacrament cannot be made depend on the moral condition of the administrator, "for the gift of the sacrament is not his, but God's" (*c. litt. Petil.* 30. 69). Hence the validity of baptism by heretics and of ordination by *traditores* was maintained (*c. ep. Parm.* II. 13. 28). Accordingly, baptized heretics returning to the Catholic Church are not to be rebaptized. But as long as they remain "outside in the plain sacrilege of schism" they "cannot possibly be saved" in spite of the validity of "all that they possess of the holy sacraments." The Catholics still designated the Donatists "brethren." Optatus calls their church only a *quasi ecclesia*, because it lacks true catholicity and apostolicity (*de schism. Don.* III. 10).

Augustine's conception of the church is deficient in unity. We find in it, side by side, violent contradictions, evangelical and catholic elements. Hence Protestants could appeal to him as the advocate of the evangelical conception of the church as the communion of saints; and Catholics found in him the champion of the Roman Catholic system of hierarchical rule and sacramental grace.

Upon Augustine's doctrine of the church was built by the Roman bishops themselves, especially by Leo I., the structure of the papacy, the bishop of Rome being finally recognized as the head under Christ of the *civitas dei*. The ecclesiastical title *papa*, which in the fourth and fifth centuries was frequently used in the West of any bishop, came gradually to be reserved to the bishop of Rome becoming his official title as the successor of Peter and as such the vicar of Christ, the visible head of the church.

SECOND PERIOD

DEVELOPMENT OF DOCTRINE IN THE MIDDLE AGES

CHAPTER XII

DOCTRINAL CONFLICTS IN THE
PRE-SCHOLASTIC PERIOD
600 – c. 1080

A. GENERAL CHARACTERISTICS OF THIS PERIOD.— The beginning
of the Middle Ages marks a period of transition from the old to the
new. The political structure of the ancient world began to disin-
tegrate. The Saracens and their allies, the Moors, held sway in the
Asiatic and African provinces. The Lombards, the Visigoths, the
Franks and the Anglo-Saxons had established kingdoms in Italy,
Spain, Gaul and Britain. In this great change of circumstances the
Western Church was the medium through which the inheritance
of the ancient world was transmitted and perpetuated among the
barbarian nations.

The movements in the Western Church, however, were without
any marked effect upon the Eastern Church. In the East the empire
continued to exist until towards the end of the Middle Ages, and
the Eastern Church did not develop, as did the Western Church,
during this period, but remained true in every particular to her
ancient character. This was due largely to the peculiar character
of Greek Christianity and also to the imperial despotism with its
policy of enforcing conformity to the accepted standards.

In the West, the church was brought face to face with the
greatest revolution that Europe has ever experienced. But while
the political history of Europe was violently interrupted by the
Germanic invasion, the position of the church was never seriously
affected.

The church entered upon the great task of converting and training
the Germanic nations who adopted Christianity with very little
resistance. They received Christianity from the church as a sacred
tradition to be accepted without doubt and reverenced as beyond
improvement. Accordingly, the new conditions exercised very
little influence upon shaping doctrinal conceptions.

In this period we do not notice any real development of dogma.
The church in the main fortified and defended her dogmatic structure. Augustine had prepared the way for the medieval conception

of Christianity. His ideas, though often misunderstood and misinterpreted, controlled the theology of the church. The task of the theologians, then, was chiefly to gather together the doctrinal materials acquired, to sift them, to preserve them. The theologians of this period are traditionalists drawing on and systematizing the teachings of the Fathers, primarily for polemic purposes and for establishing Augustinianism.

Of this type of theologians we have a striking example in the first representative of medieval Catholicism, *Gregory I.* (590-604). Great as an administrator, but also great as a writer and teacher, Gregory stands on the frontier lines of ancient and medieval times connecting the Graeco-Roman with the Romano-Germanic type of Christianity. Though without originality as a theologian he influenced profoundly the dogmatic development in that he preserved and transmitted to the church the legacy of Augustine.

Leaning entirely upon the great Augustine, Gregory transferred the old doctrine of the church into the new ecclesiastical forms which grew out of national readjustments. He interpreted Augustinian beliefs in a Semi-Pelagian spirit and modified them into forms which made them more available for the uneducated multitudes. Gregory made also a distinct advance upon the older theology in that he defined and incorporated into the doctrinal plan certain religious conceptions which had long been current in the church, but had not hitherto been defined with precision, e. g., the sacrifice of the mass, purgatory, intercession of angels and saints, efficacy of relics, and worship of images (see Mirbt. *Q.* 99-101).

The dwarfed type of Christianity which finds expression in Gregory's writings became the religion of the Middle Ages.

Of Gregory's writings we mention here his *Moralium libri* XXXV, *Regula pastoralis, Dialogorum libri IV, Homiliarum in Ezech. libri II, Homiliarum in Evangelia libri II, Epistolarum libri XIV.* 853 Epistles of Gregory are extant, printed in Migne, publ. separately by P. Ewald and L. M. Hartmann in *Monum. Germ. historiae,* Berlin, 1887-1899.

After Gregory no great teacher, with the exception of Scotus Erigena (d. about 880) in the realm of philosophy and theology, arose in the church until the time of Anselm. Gregory's doctrinal views underwent no actual development. Creed and doctrine were complete; it was only necessary to preserve them intact.

Charlemagne endeavored to attract to his court the best intellects of Europe. Under their guidance theology and culture flourished in the Frankish empire. But since the scholars of the day were content to think what those of old had thought before them they made no actual advance in dogmatics beyond the interpretation of the Fathers. This is shown in all the theological controversies of the age. The task of the medieval theologians was, not to discover truth, but to systematize, harmonize and defend the traditional dogma.

During this period deviations from the authorized faith were in the main local and limited phenomena, e. g., Adoptionism, Gottschalk's twofold predestination, Berengar's antagonism to the doctrine of transubstantiation. The iconoclastic and filioque controversies concern both the Eastern and Western Churches and mark the termination of doctrinal development in the Eastern Church.

B. DOCTRINAL CONTROVERSIES.

1. *Iconoclastic Controversy and Completion of Dogma in the Greek Church.* The prohibition of pictures in churches by the synod of Elvira in Spain, about 306, shows that as early as toward the end of the third century the use and adoration of images had become popular in the church. The tendency steadily advanced especially in the East under the influence of the example of heathen worship as well as under the influence of Alexandrian Christology with its emphasis on the permeation of the earthly nature by the divine. Basil the Great had held already that "the honor paid to the image passes on to the prototype" (*de spir. sancto*, 18. 45). The icon was not only in some way the channel through which the saint was approached, but to it was ascribed a kind of personality of its own, inasmuch as certain pictures were efficacious for certain graces. The writings of the Pseudo-Areopagite, which since the close of the fifth century became so influential in the East, made symbols and mysteries the actual representation of things invisible and laid the dogmatic foundation for a religious veneration of images. Dionysius Areopagiticus was one of those who believed when they had heard Paul preach on Mars Hill, Acts 17.34. According to Eusebius (*h. e.* III. 4; IV. 23) he was the first bishop of Athens. About 500 his name was attached by the Pseudo-Areopagite to certain theological writings by the latter. The mystagogical theology of the Pseudo-Areopagite exerted an enormous influence upon Greek Christianity.

In the West, Gregory the Great disapproved of the action of bishop Serinus of Marseilles who had ordered the destruction of all sacred images in his diocese, and declared pictures to be the books of the uneducated. "What those who can read learn by means of writings, that do the ignorant learn by looking at a picture" (*ep.* 11. 13; Mirbt. *Q.* 99 f.).

In the opposition to image worship emperor Leo the Isaurian took the lead. In 726 he forbade image worship as being a chief hindrance to the conversion of Jews and Mohammedans and opposed to the first commandment. His repressive measures against image worshippers aroused energetic opposition not only in the East but also in the West. Pope Gregory II. harshly reproved the emperor. Gregory III. condemned the enemies of images. Germanus of Constantinople took side with Leo's opponents. John of Damascus defended image worship in three orations. According to the Damascene, communion with God is attained through vision. Herein lies for him the religiously significant motive of the image question. Material things are bearers of the spiritual, the divine. They lead us to the immaterial God. Images are therefore of a sacramental virtue. We revere them not as divine in themselves but as filled with divine grace. We honor them not by divine worship, but by veneration. The veneration of images is divinely sanctioned by the forms of Old Testament worship and supported by the tradition of the church.

Leo's son, Constantine Copronymos, was still more daring in his measures against image worshippers. The council of Constantinople, 754, denounced image worship as idolatry and Monophysite and Nestorian heresy, for images of Christ — since it is impossible to represent his divinity — either confound or divorce his two natures. The only authorized representation of Christ is the Eucharist. Those who resisted the decree of the council, especially the monks, had to feel the severity of the emperor's wrath.

Leo IV. pursued the same course as his father. But after his death, his widow Irene being friendly to images and desirous of obtaining the support of the image venerating party in her position as guardian of her minor son restored image worship and finally, in 787, succeeded in convening the seventh ecumenical council at Nicaea. 300 bishops, among them the delegates of pope Adrian I. took part in that council. It ascribed to the images "affection and respectful reverence," but reserved "true worship" to God alone (Mirbt. Q. 216).

The further outward course of the iconoclastic controversies belongs to the sphere of Church History. Suffice it to say that in the East the prohibition of images was reaffirmed and the persecution of image worshippers reappeared and lasted until about 842 when during the reign of Theodora, widow of emperor Theophilus, the worship of images was restored. The Eastern Church today celebrates annually, on the first Sunday of the Greek Lent, the Feast of Orthodoxy commemorating the Church's triumph over iconoclasm and all other heresies. It was founded after the downfall of iconoclasm in 842 "in honor of the restoration of the holy images to the churches."

After the storms of inconoclasm the Church both East and West settled down again in secure possession of her images. The council of Nice, 787, had restored the cult and defined the dogmatic theory of images. Image worship had become an integral part of the faith. Both Western and Eastern Churches recognize as ecumenical the council at Nicaea, the last council in which they met in unison.

This terminates the doctrinal development in the Orthodox Eastern Church. The doctrine defined by the Church must be accepted and believed to be true. Faith is nothing more than the acceptance of dogma. The mere intellectual apprehension of the truth is aided by the mysteries which interpret the secret meaning of the truth, lift the soul above the world in the experience of salvation and initiate into the region of divine wonders. Hence the tendency to realize the spiritual and eternal in sensuous, corporeal, visible form. The sacred symbols, mysteries, mystic consecrations, saints and their relics and images lead the soul to the vision of the spiritual. This explains why the Greek Church developed no further dogma. Doctrine has its counterpart in ceremonial worship.

In tracing the doctrinal development of the Greek Church we find then that on the one hand, Greek Christianity did not get beyond the range of the theology of John of Damascus. On the other hand, we notice a marked retrogression to the mystagogical theology of the Areopagite. "... it is a peculiar illustration of the irony of history, that the same city, Nicaea, in which the first dogma was framed, was also the birthplace of this last Greek dogma. The two councils of Nicaea mark the course of Greek Christianity — from dogma to images" (Seeberg, *Hist. of Doctr.* I. 306 f.).

2. *Filioque Controversy.*

A controversy supplementary to the Trinitarian conflicts arose at the end of the sixth century concerning the procession of the Holy Spirit. It concerned one of the principal differences between the Eastern and Western Churches.

Inasmuch as neither John 15:26, nor the Apostles' Creed, nor the Constantinopolitan Creed, says anything of a twofold procession, that is, from both the Father and the Son, the Greek Church held to the single procession of the Holy Spirit. This was in keeping with the Greek conception of the Father as the sole fountain, root and cause of the deity (subordinationism). By the single procession of the Spirit is meant the eternal procession, that is, an eternal inner-Trinitarian process, like the eternal generation of the Son, and not the temporal mission of the Spirit —"whom I will send unto you from the Father"— concerning which there has been no controversy between the Eastern and Western Churches. The passage John 15:26 does not support the position taken by the Eastern Church, because it does not speak of the essential relation of the Spirit to the Father, but of the mission or sending of the Spirit.

The Western Church in the interest of the homoousia of the Son and on the ground of true co-ordination since Augustine — *unus deus est ipsa trinitas*, "Father, Son and Holy Spirit are one God"— held to the double procession of the Spirit from the Father and the Son. If the Spirit proceeds from the essence of the Father, he must also proceed from the essence of the Son, for they have the same essence.

To the words of the Constantinopolitan Creed "who proceedeth from the Father" the Latin Church added, without consulting with the Greek Church, the words "and the Son," *filioque*. The addition first meets us in the Athanasian Creed. It was adopted by the third council of Toledo, 589. From Spain it spread into France. The Constantinopolitan Creed in this enlarged form was used in the Frankish Church. The synods of Gentilly, 767, Friaul, 791, and Aachen, 809, sanctioned the use of the addition. Pope Leo III. whose confirmation of the decision of the synod at Aachen was asked for by Charlemagne admitted the dogmatic correctness of the *filioque* but refused formally its introduction into the Creed. On this point, however, the Frankish Church persevered in the course it had already initiated, and despite the opposition it became the official doctrine of the Western Church that "the Holy Spirit proceedeth from the Father and the Son. The Eastern Church has always objected to this insertion. Photius, patriarch of Constantinople (d. c. 891), in his encyclical letter, accused the Church of Rome of various errors and emphasized the *filioque* as one of the greatest errors of the pope. Nicolas I. in turn anathematized the patriarch and his adherents. A council at Constantinople, 869, pronounced against those who should venture to make any addition to the Creed. The course taken by Michael Caerularius, patriarch of Constantinople, who renewed the ancient charges of Photius, resulted in the complete cleavage between the Greek and Roman Churches, 1054.

3. *Adoptionist Controversy.* A Western echo of the Christological controversies of the Eastern Church is found in the Adoptionism of Spain in the latter part of the eighth century. The chief exponents of the Adoptionist view were Elipandus of Toledo and Felix of Urgellis.

Attempting to solve the Trinitarian problem a certain Migetius in Spain had revived Sabellianism in a gross form, teaching that there are three bodily persons in the Trinity, the Father (David),

the Son (Jesus of the seed of David), and the Holy Spirit (Paul),
thus positing a threefold historical manifestation of the one God.
Elipandus, his opponent, vindicating the orthodox idea of the
Trinity, went to the other extreme. He was aided by his much
more gifted friend Felix, bishop of Urgellis. They distinguished
sharply between two modes of sonship in Christ, the natural or
proper, and the adoptive. As the second person of the Trinity
Christ is the only-begotten of the Father. As son of Mary he is the
first-born among many brethren, the adopted Son of God, and called
God. As the only-begotten Christ says, "I and my Father are one."
As the first-born Christ says, "The Father is greater than I."

The Adoptionists did not mean to teach a dual personality since,
from the time of his conception, the Son of man was taken up into
the unity of the person of the Son of God. But the affirmation that
Christ, as to his human nature, was only nominally, not really, God,
and that he suffered only as the adopted man, implied two distinct
persons in Christ.

Though the Adoptionist view was not really Nestorian yet the
distinction between an adopted and a natural Son of God seemed to
the contemporary theologians, who attempted the refutation of the
heresy, like a revival of the error of Nestorius. Nor can it be
proved that the Adoptionists were under the direct influence of the
old Antiochian theology. This theory is based on the assumption
that the so-called "Orthodox Brethren of Cordova," whom Alcuin
holds responsible for the Adoptionist error were a colony of Eastern
Christians of Nestorian tendencies. That Adoptionism is a survival
of the old Germanic Arianism is quite out of question, since the
Adoptionists adhered to the orthodox Trinitarian teaching. Nor
can the Adoptionist movement be explained from the opposition of
Mohammedanism as in part determining the form of men's views
on the doctrine of Christ's person, since the greatest difficulty from
the standpoint of Islam, the Trinity, remains untouched.

At least if it can be said about the Adoptionists that their
attempt to solve the problem of dyophysitism as the Chalcedon
decision had left it, was a failure. Adoptionism displayed the
defective theological culture of the age. The same must be said of
the orthodox theologians who combated Adoptionism. Besides
likening the Adoptionists to the Nestorians and charging them with
dividing Christ into two sons they simply emphasized the fact that
Adoptionism was not in keeping with the teaching of the Fathers
and the church. Although they asserted that Christ is really and
truly the Son of God, even according to his human nature as distinguished from a human person, they nevertheless allowed his humanity to fall into the background as compared with his divinity so that

in reality they presented an altogether divine person, who has assumed impersonal human substance and nature. In the Christology of the assailants of Adoptionism no advance was made beyond that of Cyril who was one of their main authorities. Hence the Adoptionist controversy contributed nothing to the historical development of doctrine.

Adoptionism was rejected and condemned by three Frankish synods, at Regensburg, 792, at Frankfurt, 794, and at Aachen, 799, and also by the popes Hadrian I. and Leo III.

4. *The Controversy on Predestination.*— Augustine's doctrine of predestination was revived in the ninth century by the earnest-minded and learned monk Gottschalk of Orbais. In the majority of instances Augustine had applied the term "predestination" to the heirs of salvation and only incidentally, had spoken of a twofold predestination. Gottschalk, starting from the conception of the immutability of God who from eternity has ordered all his decrees in virtue of his foreknowledge which merely accompanies predestination, contended for a twofold predestination. The immutable God has from all eternity predestinated eternal life to the elect, and the elect to eternal life. And the same immutable God has immutably predestinated everlasting punishment to the reprobate, and the reprobate to everlasting punishment. God did not predestinate to sin, but only to punishment for sin. Christ did not die for all, but only for the elect; and only they constitute the true church. Gottschalk did not differ essentially in his view from the Augustinian scheme. He only carried Augustine's doctrine to its extreme logical conclusions.

While Gottschalk followed the teaching of Augustine, his opponent, Rabanus Maurus, archbishop of Mayence, took Gregory the Great as his guide. To him Gottschalk's doctrine appeared extremely offensive. He opposed it in two violent epistles not without misrepresenting Gottschalk's views and drawing unjust inferences from them; for example, he accused Gottschalk of asserting that God predestinates to sin, and that he forces man to damnation even though he may strive after salvation with true faith and good works. At the synod of Mayence, in 848, convened by Rabanus, Gottschalk's doctrine was condemned as heretical, and he himself beaten and handed over to Hincmar, archbishop of Rheims, who sent him back to his monastery at Orbais. The next year Hincmar summoned him before the council at Chiersy. Gottschalk attempted to justify his ideas, but was again condemned as a heretic, degraded from the priesthood, terribly scourged and shut up for life in a cloister, where he remained firm and steadfast in his opinions till his death (c. 868). Over against Gottschalk's Augustinianism the synod of Chiersy decreed that Christ died for all men, and that God desires all men, without exception, to be saved.

The inhuman treatment which Gottschalk suffered at the hand of Hincmar, and the rejection of Augustine's doctrine of predestination, gave rise to a heated controversy in the Frankish Church. Powerful theologians, such as Prudentius, bishop of Troyes, Ratramnus of Corbie, Remigius of Lyons, and Lupus of Ferrieres, pleaded the cause of Augustinianism and wrote in favor of Gottschalk and against Hincmar. Rabanus and Hincmar, on the other hand, assailed Gottschalk's theory. Both expressed Semi-Pelagian views in Augustinian terminology and applied predestination only to the election to life and based reprobation on foreknowledge. Scotus Erigena, whom Hincmar had called in as an authority, attempted to solve the theological problem by philosophical conceptions and opposed Gottschalk's doctrine on the ground that it was an abandonment of the saving power of God's grace and an abolition of the functions of the free will of man. As evil is only a stage in the development of good, there will be ultimately a universal return to God.

The question was discussed at the council of Chiersy, 853, deciding for Hincmar; and at Valence, 853, and Langres, 859, deciding for the Augustinian teaching and condemning Scotus' theory as "the Scottish mess," and "an invention of the devil."

After renewed attempts at a settlement at Savonnieres, 859, and at Toucy, 860, had proved futile, the dispute was abandoned without any decision having been reached. The last event in this controversy was the publication by Hincmar of a work on predestination, composed in defense of the decision of Chiersy, 853. Augustinianism had lost the day.

5. *Controversy on the Lord's Supper*. A controversy of greater importance arose in the ninth century on the doctrine of the Lord's Supper. Paschasius Radbertus, abbot of the monastery of Corbie, in 831, composed a work *De corpore et sanguine domini,* in which he set forth without any intentional innovation on his part, in unequivocal terms, the doctrine of transubstantiation. After the words of institution are uttered, Radbertus taught, nothing remains, save the body and blood under the outward form of bread and wine. The substance of the elements is changed into the body and blood of Christ, even the same body which was born of the Virgin, suffered on the cross and arose from the tomb. The accidents alone, color, taste and form remain, else were there no room for faith. Besides, the actual eating of flesh would clash with human custom. The effects of participation are remission of daily faults and slight sins, bodily unification with Christ and impartation of an imperish-

able principle of life preparatory to the resurrection. But since this is a spiritual participation of faith, only the believer partakes of Christ's body. Radbertus follows here Augustine's distinction between the sacrament and the virtue of the same. The worthy receive the virtue of the sacrament, the unworthy the sacrament only to damnation, the body and blood being only apparently offered to them.

Radbertus proves the truth of his doctrine from the words of institution "this is my body" which he takes in the crassest literalness, from the testimonies of the Fathers, and from instances of miracles where instead of the bread and wine the body and blood of Christ were presented preceptibly to the senses.

Radbertus' doctrine was in the main features that of the ancient church. On the other hand, it seemed to conflict with the teachings of the Fathers, particularly those of Augustine. Accordingly, it was both favorably received and violently opposed. His opponents were Rabanus Maurus, John Scotus Erigena, and especially Ratramnus, a learned monk of Corbie. The latter in a treatise addressed to Charles the Bald, bearing the same title as that of Radbertus, undertakes to answer two questions strictly connected with Radbertus' doctrine: Whether bread and wine are called body and blood of Christ after a sacramental manner, *in mysterio,* or in the true and proper sense, and whether it is the same body in which Christ was born, suffered and rose from the dead. Bread and wine, he answers, are not the body and blood of Christ in the proper, but only in a secret and spiritual sense, and it is therefore not the historical body of Christ, but the body that is received is the memorial of Christ's natural body. The effect of participation consists in spiritual communion with Christ, or in the communication of the divine Logos.

Although Radbertus' theory still gave offense to many, yet the spiritual and symbolical view of Ratramnus met with an increasingly decided opposition from the spirit of the time. Other theologians of the ninth century, such as Hincmar of Rheims and Haimo of Halberstadt, took the side of Radbertus and taught the theory of transubstantiation. The controversy, however, did not result in a dogmatic definition by the church.

In the dark and confused interval between the ninth and the eleventh centuries the Radbertian theory had gained general acceptance in the church, as may be seen in the controversy to which Berengar of Tour gave rise in the eleventh century. In a letter to Lanfranc, 1050, a monk of Bec and the most celebrated theologian of that age, Berengar reproached Lancfranc because he still adhered to the Radbertian theory which according to Berengar was contrary to reason, unwarranted by Scripture and inconsistent with the teaching of men like Ambrose, Jerome and Augustine. His own view was that bread and wine are not converted into the body and blood, but are merely emblematic of his body and blood. Through the consecration is added to the elements a spiritual power which is apprehended by faith without which the elements remain empty, powerless signs. Christ cannot be corporeally present in the sacrament, because, if so, he must be spatially present and his body must then be at once in the separate communions in various places.

Through Lanfranc's influence Berengar was condemned unheard at Rome and Vercelli, in 1050. The papal legate Hildebrand, at a synod at Tour, in 1054, declared himself satisfied with Berengar's written statement upon oath that the bread and wine after the consecreation are the body and blood of Christ. Trusting in Hildebrand's support and in the justice of his cause he presented himself at a synod of Rome, in 1059, under pope Nicholas II., but overwhelmed by his opponents he was forced to recant and assert that "the true body and blood of our Lord Jesus Christ are not only a sacrament, but in truth touched and broken by the hands of priests and torn by the teeth of the faithful" (Mirbt, *Q*. p. 144). Once back in France and full of remorse for this desertion of his faith Berengar was again compelled to recant at Rome, in 1079. He returned with rage in his heart and retracted his recantation. After another trial he kept silence. He passed the rest of his life in ascetic solitude on the island of St. Come, near Tours, where he died in 1088.

His chief opponents were Lanfranc, Hugo of Langres, Durandus of Troanne and Guitmund of Aversa. They upheld the Radbertian theory and went even beyond Radbertus. Lanfranc distinctly asserted the real presence for the unworthy as well as for the worthy, the latter only with saving efficacy. Guitmund affirmed that the entire body of Christ is in the entire bread and in every portion of the bread.

Radbertus' doctrine as propounded by Berengar's opponents became the doctrine of the church. The term *transubstantiatio* as a dogmatic expression is first found in the first half of the twelfth century, in the sermons of Hildebert of Lavardin, archbishop of Tours (d. 1134).

The fact that the theory of transubstantiation was universally advocated was no doubt in affinity with the reigning spirit of the age. The predominant tendency to sensualize the objects of religious faith, the inclination to the magical in religion, the notion of a sacrificial function belonging to the priesthood, i. e., offering daily the sacrifice of the real body and real blood, all this prepared the way for a general admission of the doctrine of transubstantiation.

CHAPTER XIII

CHARACTERISTIC FEATURES AND GENERAL TENDENCIES OF THE SCHOLASTIC AGE

A. SCHOLASTICISM.— The term Scholasticism is usually employed to denote the scientific theology of the Middle Ages particularly of the period between the eleventh and fifteenth centuries. It derived its name from the great cathedral and monastic schools, *scholae,* which became the centres of medieval learning and speculation. The professional teachers in those schools were called *doctores ecclesiastici.* Since the twelfth century the universities, that of Paris taking the lead, replaced the ecclesiastical schools.

As compared with the theologians of the pre-Scholastic period, whose task it was chiefly to adopt and preserve the traditional beliefs, the medieval Schoolmen gave a comprehensive logical and dialectical presentation of the dogmas of the Catholic Church. The doctrines inherited from the earlier ages were sacred and inviolable. Hence the problem which the Scholastics undertook to solve was simply to support the traditional dogma by the evidences of reason or philosophy, and present the whole mass of dogmas in a schematic and harmonious unity.

If we call to mind the two great influences which shaped medieval thought, namely, the tradition of ancient philosophy and the doctrines of the church, we can easily understand that the Schoolmen so readily applied the logical distinctions of Aristotle to the doctrines of the church thus rationalizing the whole churchly system. But since the dogma established on the authority of the church is absolutely transcendental to human reason, it follows that reason is subject to authority, and that its conclusions are predetermined. Philosophy becomes the handmaid, *ancilla,* of theology. It can be employed only for subordinate purposes to show the reasonableness of the church's doctrine as consistent with philosophy. The mixture of the theological and philosophical interests under the predominance of the former was one of the characteristics of the Scholastic age.

The necessary preliminary for the task of Scholasticism to elaborate a rational system of faith, was the possession of the Christian consciousness. Following Augustine's maxim *fides praecedit intellectum,* "faith precedes knowledge," the Scholastics made faith the necessary beginning of knowledge. Without faith we cannot experience the objects of faith and without such experience we cannot understand them. Hence Anselm said: *Credo ut intelligam,* "I believe that I may understand;" compare with this Augustine's *Ut intelligamus, prius credamus,* "in order to know let us first believe" (*serm.* 89). But after faith has grasped the truth it becomes necessary to demonstrate by reason the truth of what we believe. This demand for rational explanations Anselm carries to such an extent that, at times, he seems to ascribe to reason the power of penetrating even to the mysteries of faith unaided by supernatural revelation. Still more decisively did Abelard give a formal, rational expression of the received ecclesiastical doctrine. He exalted reason to such an extent that he maintained that a thing is believed not because God said so but because it has been proved to be so.

In the attempt to convert what had been an object of faith into logical truth by way of logical reasoning, certain philosophical problems presented themselves to the Schoolmen: What is the relation between the idea of a thing and its reality? between thinking and being? Do words which denote general ideas, *universalia,* designate realities, entities? Or are they mere names, *nomina,* invented to express common qualities of particular things?

The historical occasion of the doctrine of universals is found in Porphyry's *Isagoge* to Aristotle's *Categories,* translated into Latin by Boethius in the sixth century, and much used in the schools of the Middle Ages. In the commentary on his translation of Porphyry, Boethius left the real existence of common conceptions an open question, but in the commentary on Victorinus' Commentary on Porphyry he decided in its favor. Since then the question has often been taken up. From the middle of the eleventh century it was answered definitely by the Schoolmen. According to the answer to this question we may distinguish three different types of Scholastic teaching:

1. *Realism* of the Platonic type regarded universal ideas as realities existing prior to and independent of the individual objects in which they are embodied; *universalia ante rem.* For example, truth and goodness as distinguishable from the thoughts and virtues of particular persons are realities and not mere names or intellectual abstractions. Or, human nature, as distinguished from human individuality, is not merely a product of human reason, but has a real existence. Realism was evidently favorable to the teaching of the church on the dogmas of the Trinity and the Eucharist. Chief representatives of this type of Scholasticism were Anselm, William of Champeaux and Bonaventura.

2. *Nominalism,* the view of the ancient Stoics, maintained that

general conceptions are merely the products of the human reason, *flatus vocis,* intellectual abstractions, *nomina,* derived from the common properties of individual objects; *universalia post rem.* Chief representatives of this type of Scholasticism were Roscellinus, Occam, Biel. Nominalism was a doctrine of sceptics and suspected heretics. On the ground of his nominalism Roscellinus of Compiegne maintained that the Trinity being a merely a subjective conception has no real existence, and laid the stress on the separate reality of the three persons as individuals in such a way as to approach tritheism. In his treatise *De fide trinitatis* Anselm refuted Roscellinus.

3. *Realism* of the Aristotelian type, by modern writers called *Conceptualism,* held that general conceptions are inherent in the objects themselves. They do not exist prior to them, nor do they have any reality apart from the particular objects to which they apply; *universalia in re.* The chief representative of this type of Scholasticism was Abelard. He attempted to mediate between the extreme realism of William of Champeaux and the nominalism of Roscellinus. In opposition to William's contention that universals are the true realities which are present and undivided in each individual object, he insisted that universals have a real existence, but only psychically, as the concepts which unite the individual things. In opposition to Roscellinus he maintained that universals are not only sounds and names but words to express thought. But his mediating conceptualism did not prevent Abelard from coming dangerously near to obnoxious ideas the maintenance of which involved him in life-long persecutions.

Following Aristotle as their model the Schoolmen applied his principles both dialectical and philosophical to the investigation and explication of the church's doctrines.

The characteristic feature in the method of the Schoolmen, since the time of Peter Lombard, consists in this that they present their teaching in the form of commentaries on the Sentences of Peter Lombard, which became the foundation of academic lectures for centuries. Starting a multitude of isolated questions on all the subjects of which they treat they carry out the dialectical method in the minutest detail with its thesis and antithesis, its *pro* and *contra,* and then sum up with a brief decision, *conclusio* or *resolutio.* In this way the Schoolmen believed they could establish and prove the rationality of the dogmas of the church.

The constant effort of Scholasticism to demonstrate Christianity as rational and the rational as Christian seemed at last successful. But the further progress of Scholastic thought shows that Scholasticism had failed in its task to rationalize the doctrines of the church. The failure was due to the contrariety of the two authorities by which the minds of men were governed: in the province of natural reason, the authority of Aristotle; in the Christian province, the authority of the church's tradition. The contrariety between these two authorities naturally led to scepticism. Men refused to admit as truths what could not be proved by dialectics. After Duns Scotus had dissolved the unity between theology and philosophy, the decay of Scholasticism began, soon to end in complete dissolution.

B. MYSTICISM.— By the side of Scholasticsm there appears in the twelfth century another tendency of theology, Mysticism; the former essentially intellectual, formal and philosophical; the latter pietistic and contemplative — two different tendencies, yet not in antagonism with each other. Both accepted the traditional doctrines of the church as sacred and inviolable truths, but while Scholasticism sought to elucidate truth by means of the intellect and develop it by dialectics, Mysticism strove to apprehend truth by the feelings and develop it by inward contemplation.

The cultivation of the inner life led Mysticism to an entire renunciation of worldly things. Hence asceticism, flight from the world — that peculiar element of medieval piety — is a characteristic part of Mysticism. Scholasticism became the handmaid of the hierarchy in carrying to its height the other peculiar element of medieval Christianity, namely, the church theocracy, or the church's control over the world.

That Scholasticism and Mysticism were not antagonistic may be shown from the fact that great Mystics, like the Victorines and Bonaventura, were also Scholastics, and distinguished Schoolmen, like Thomas Aquinas, found a place for Mysticism in their theology. The combination proved mutually helpful. Insisting upon the deep inner life, which is to be found only in the union of the soul with God, Mysticism helped to check the excessive subtlty and speculation of Scholasticism. On the other hand, the scientific distinctness and precision of Scholasticism counterbalanced the subjective tendency of Mysticism which neglected the scientific aspect of religion, professing direct intercourse with the divine Spirit and a knowledge of God and spiritual things unattainable by the natural intellect, and incapable of being analyzed or explained.

C. THE CHIEF REPRESENTATIVES OF SCHOLASTICISM AND MYSTICISM.

1. The *First Period* of Scholasticism extends from the end of the eleventh to the end of the twelfth century. It is the period of the rise of Scholasticism.

Anselm (d. 1109), the pupil of Lanfranc and his successor as prior of the cloister of Bec in Normandy and finally also as archbishop of Canterbury, was the first who clearly set forth and successfully employed the principles of Scholasticism. He may rightly be called the father of medieval Scholasticism, being the most distinguished realistic philosopher of the eleventh century. In him are found the special characteristics of Scholastic thought, that is, a profound conviction of the rationality of revealed truth, and a high estimate placed upon dialectics as a means of proving this rationality. There were also harmoniously co-mingled in him the two elements, the religious and emotional on the one hand, and the speculative and dialectic on the other. Since revealed truth and the human mind are both divine gifts, they cannot be at variance. The sincere inquirer, who brings them into fair comparison with each other, will find that a profound harmony manifests itself in both.

The dogmas of the church are to Anselm identical with revelation itself. Proceeding on the principle, "I believe that I may understand, I do not seek to understand that I may believe," he attempted to give a philosophical demonstration not only of the existence of God, but also of the Trinity and the incarnation. In his *Monologium* he argues in accordance with his realistic philosophy that the idea of God carries the evidence of its reality in itself. In his *Proslogium* he sets forth his celebrated ontological proof for the existence of God. Existence belongs absolutely to the perfect Being than which nothing greater can be conceived, else a still more perfect being could be thought. Only a fool, *insipiens,* would deny that the existence of God could be demonstrated. To the objection of the monk Gaunilo, an Aristotelian realist, who criticized the book in the treatise *Pro insipiente,* objecting that the idea of the lost Isle of the Blest does not prove that it exists or ever had existed, Anselm replied in his *Apologeticus contra Gaunilonem,* but the discussion ended without leading to any definite result.

Anselm's greatest work and one that exercised a marked influence on the form of church doctrine is his treatise on the reason why God became man, *Cur deus homo,* in which he attempts to explain the rational necessity of the atonement.

The first notable representative of the dialectico-critical school of Scholasticism was *Peter Abelard* (d. 1142). His brilliant ability and restless activity made him the central figure in the dialectical discussions of his time. In him the balance was lost between the mystic and the dialectic elements. His principle that "by doubting we are led to inquiring, and by inquiring we arrive at the truth" he illustrated in his famous *Sic et Non — Yes and No,* a book containing a number of theses for each one of which he gathered from the Scriptures and patristic literature apparently contradictory statements. Yet Abelard maintained "the excellency of the canonical authority of the Old and New Testaments." Alleged errors of that canonical authority are due either to a defective text or faulty interpretation. Following his own conviction he demanded free discussion of religious things and opposed the compulsion of authority. "A doctrine is believed not because God has said it, but because it has been proved to be so." Only what is known can be believed. As for his ethics he believed that he could prove the agreement in morals of Greek philosophy and Christianity. Abelard also opposed the extreme realism of his teacher William of Champeaux. His own mediating view by which he hoped to escape the consequences of extreme nominalism as well as those of realism has been distinguished under the name *conceptualism.*

His greatest antagonist was *Bernard of Clairvaux* (d. 1153), the recognized guardian of orthodoxy in France, who led in the final successful assault upon Abelard at the synod of Sens, in 1141. Bernard persistently opposed Abelard as an enemy of orthodoxy and ecclesiastical authority. He describes him as "a monk without a rule, a prelate without a cure, neither keeps his order nor is kept in order by it. He is a man inconsistent with himself, within a Herod, without a John; a thorough hypocrite, having nothing of a monk but the name and habit" (*ep.* 193). "When he discourses of the Trinity he savors of Arius; when of grace, of Pelagius; when of the person of Christ, of Nestorius" (*ep.* 192), and "while he exhausts his strength to make Plato a Christian, he proves himself a heathen" (*ep.* 190. c. 4).

Bernard was a Mystic and at the same time a rigid and disciplined ascetic, a vigorous theologian, an illustrious preacher, and an ardent defender of orthodoxy. His greatness and far-reaching influence lay not in the qualities of his intellect but in the depth and ardor of his piety. His whole mysticism centers in Christ, particularly about his passion. By Christ's work of redemption the church has become his bride (*serm.* 74.5; 69.6). In his sermons on the Canticles Bernard uses very freely the symbolism of marriage. From the forgiveness of sin proceeds the Christian life which must manifest itself in the good works of love (*serm.* 58.3; 85.13). Christ's love awakens a responsive affection in our hearts (*serm.* 11.7; 20.7). Therefore it is necessary for the soul to immerse itself in the contemplation of Christ's suffering and death (*serm.* 3.1; 62.7). Bernard's mysticism is pure and spiritual and free from pantheistic ideas. It is true, we find occasional extravagances of language in his writings, particularly in his sermons on the Canticles, but he distinguishes sharply the union with Christ, to which the pious soul attains, from a consubtantiality, as it exists between Father and Son in the Trinity (*in Cant.* 71.7). Bernard's writings had a far-reaching influence upon posterity. They were the main source of the *Imitatio Christi.* The Reformers saw in him a champion of their favorite doctrine of the supremacy of divine grace.

The school of St. Victor eagerly welcomed and enthusiastically spread the teaching and practice of Mysticism. In *Hugo of St. Victor* (d. 1141) were blended the mystical and the speculative tendencies. In his *Summa sententiarum* which was the fruit of his Scholastic training he endeavored to give a rational presentation of the content of faith, although he maintained that truth cannot be discovered by reasoning, and professed to be guided only by the authority of Scriptures. His *Summa* is a positive counterpart to Abelard's *Sic et Non,* and still more so his *De sacramentis,* the ripest fruit of his intellectual labors. The first part of it treats of the matter of faith, the second of the act of faith. By the act of faith, *affectus,* he means the cultivation of mystical contemplation resulting in religious exaltation to God and union with him. In the latter part Hugo gives a detailed explanation and regulation of the rites of the church.

Richard of St. Victor (d. 1173) more absorbed in Mysticism than his master Hugo, sought to save the traditional dogma, imperiled by the method of dialectics, by recourse to Mysticism.

Robert Pulleyn (d. 1150) on the other hand, in his eight books of Sentences, collected the opinions of distinguished Scholastics on various points of doctrine and tried to reconcile contradictions by the dialectical method and the Aristotelian philosopher.

Peter Lombard (d. 1160), teacher, and later bishop at Paris, known as *Magister Sententiarum,* lives in literary history by his great work *Sententiae patrum,* which became the textbook of the schools, gave rise to endless commentaries and finally obtained the sanction of the church at the Lateran Council, in 1215. It is a collection of doctrinal statements from the Fathers compiled and arranged in such a way as to constitute a scientific whole. It is divided into four books, of which the first deals with the evidence for the existence of God; the second with the nature of man and the doctrine of angels; the third with Christology; the fourth with the sacraments. A moderate dialectics and cautious objectivity characterize Lombard's work.

Beside Peter Lombard worthy of special mention are *Gilbert de la Porree* (d. 1158), *Peter of Poitiers* (d. 1205), and *Alanus ab Insulis* (d. 1203).

Scholasticism of this period also met with adverse criticism. *Walter of St. Victor* (wrote between 1180 and 1190), proceeding on his theory that philosophy and dialectics came from the devil, made an impassioned attack on the dialecticians of his time, calling Abelard, Lombard, Gilbert and Peter of Poitiers "the four labyrinths of France." John Salisbury, bishop of Chartres (d. 1180), "a humanist before the Renaissance," opposed to sophistic Scholasticism a practical common sense, and contrasted the aberrations of his contemporaries with the sound views of the classics, especially those of with Plato and Aristotle.

In spite of the prohibition of the church Aristotle's system took possession of all the leading minds and was pursued with eager interest and enthusiasm in all the leading schools. It even became customary to compare Aristotle, as the *praecursor Christi in naturalibus,* to John the Baptist, the *praecursor Christi in gratuitis.* Men like Albert the Great and Thomas Aquinas reproduced the whole philosophy of Aristotle in a form adapted to the Christian faith.

2. The *Second Period* of Scholasticism embracing the thirteenth century is the period of its bloom. The dialectic spirit obtained a fresh impulse through the influence of the whole Aristotelian philosophy, its dialectics as well as its physics, metaphysics and ethics. The Stagirite's influence on doctrine, however, was mainly a formal one. The material influence was that of the church and of the strictly Catholic spirit. Aristotelian analysis was employed in the defense of the traditional dogma of the church and hence this philosophy came finally to be patronized and protected even by the popes.

Another characteristic feature of this period is that the mendicant friars came forward as the leaders of Christian learning and faith. Nearly all prominent Schoolmen of this period belong to the Dominican or to the Franciscan order. They represented the medieval ideal of flight from the world and entire renunciation of worldly things, and at the same time they were the support of the secularized church and the papal supremacy.

The first theologian of this period, who was acquainted with the whole of the Aristotelian works, was *Alexander of Hales*

(d. 1245), a Franciscan, called *doctor irrefragabilis,* or *theologorum monarcha.* In his *Summa universae theologiae* he developed especially the doctrine of the *thesaurus* and the sacraments.

In a comprehensive way the system of the Stagirite was first employed in the construction of theology by Albert of Bollstadt (d. 1280), universally known as *Albertus Magnus,* teacher at Cologne and General of the Dominican Order of Germany. Albert was a universal genius. His many-sidedness as an author procured for him the title of *doctor universalis,* while his acquaintance with natural science made him a sorcerer in the eyes of the vulgar. His principal theological works are a *Commentary* on the Sentences of Peter Lombard, and also the Sentences in a systematic work called *Summa theologiae.*

In his still greater disciple, *Thomas Aquinas* (d. 1274, known as *doctor angelicus,* Scholasticism reached the zenith of its perfection and power. Thomas was a man of genuine and deep piety, inclining toward Mysticism. As a theologian he was of blameless orthodoxy and at the same time enthusiastic in the prosecution of philosophical investigation. According to Thomas, reason and revelation are two distinct sources of knowledge, but since they both come from the one source of knowledge, the absolute God, they are not contradictory. Christian mysteries are above reason, but not against reason. His chief writings are a *Commentary* on Peter Lombard's Sentences, the *Compendium theologiae, Expositio symboli, the Summa de veritate catholicae fidei contra gentiles,* and the *Summa theologica,* divided into three parts treating of God, man, and the God-man, the third part being completed by Thomas' disciples in accordance with his designs. The method of the work is to state a proposition in interrogative form, then to assail it with objections from the Bible, the Fathers or Aristotle; then follow arguments in favor of the proposition; then follows the decision, subordinate to the dictates of the church. The *Summa,* as the authoritative statement of theology became in the first instance the accepted doctrine of the Dominican Order, and then the official philosophy and theology of the Roman Catholic Church. In his encyclical *Aeterni patris* of August 4, 1879, Leo XIII. directed the clergy to take the teachings of Thomas as the basis of their theological position.

Thomas' friend and Alexander's pupil, the Franciscan, John of Fidanza, better known as *Bonaventura* (d. 1274), presented a marked contrast to his predecessors and contemporaries in that he put the highest value on spiritual illumination. Nor was he merely a meditative thinker; he was also a dogmatic theologian of high rank. Well may he be called "the greatest Scholastic among the Mystics, and the greatest Mystic among the Scholastics." When still a youth, his teacher Alexander Halesius designated him "an Israelite indeed in whom Adam seems not to have sinned," while his contemporaries, in admiration of his angelic purity, bestowed on him the eulogistic title *doctor seraphicus*. His chief dialectical writings are a *Commentary* upon the Sentences, and his *Brevilogium*, one of the best exposition of Christian dogmatics produced by the Schoolmen. His chief mystical and devotional writings are *De septem itineribus aeternitatis* and above all *Compendium itinerarium mentis in deum*. Bonaventura's mysticism was a silent protest against the rationalizing tendency of Scholasticism.

Roger Bacon (d. 1294), English philosopher and scientist, famous Franciscan theologian, called *doctor admirabilis,* criticized sharply the Scholastic method of instruction. He withdrew from the Scholastic methods and devoted himself to the study of languages and experimental research. In the realm of nature he emphasized the importance of experience. In the field of theology he upheld the Scrpitures as the supreme authority and insisted upon reading the Bible in the original.

The chief critic of Aquinas was the Franciscan, *John Duns Scotus* (d. 1308). He forms the close of this period and marks the transition to the last phase of the Scholastic theology. Scotus won the title *doctor subtilis* which well expresses the chief characteristics of his criticism. He lacked the spiritual depth of Aquinas, but in subtlety, in analyzing and developing ideas he surpassed all his predecessors. While Aquinas was a constructive philosopher, Scotus was a destructive critic. To the position of Aquinas that reason and revelation are two distinct sources of knowledge in harmony with one another, Scotus takes exception and maintains that no true knowledge of anything can be obtained apart from theology as based upon revelation. Thus separating philosophy from theology Scotus began the work of undermining the whole undertaking of the Schoolmen who through centuries had labored to overcome the dualism between faith and reason. The ultimate authority according to Scotus is the authority of the church on which even the authority of Scripture depends. Scotus made the authority of the church a positive ecclesiastical law, from which no deviation could be tolerated. This legal conception of orthodoxy characterizes the later Nominalist theology.

With Scotus began the division of the later Scholastics into the two great *conflicting schools of Thomists and Scotists.* The Thomists were Aristotelian, the Scotists more Platonic in their realism. The former followed in the most part Augustine; the latter inclined distinctly to Pelagianism. Hence their diversity on the question of the relation of grace to the human will. The doctrine of the immaculate conception was also one of the great subjects in dispute between the Thomists who opposed it, and the Scotists who supported it. Scotus' most important work is his Commentary on the Sentences of Lombard, known as the *Opus Oxoniense.*

3. The *Third Period* of Scholasticism covering the fourteenth and fifteenth centuries marks its decadence. The opposition of the two rival schools was still further developed. A chief characteristic of this period is the revival of Nominalism, so that to the conflict of the Thomist and Scotist Schools that of Nominalist and Realist was added. A few independent thinkers meet us in this period *Durandus* of St. Porcain (d. 1334), though a Dominican, passed over from Thomism to Nominalism. More eminent was the Franciscan, *William Occam* (d. 1350), *doctor invincibilis* and *venerabilis inceptor.* He was the real new founder of Nominalism which had been in decadence since the days of Roscellinus. Scotus, his teacher, though not yet a Nominalist, had already laid the emphasis not upon the universal, but upon the individual as the higher form of existence. Occam carried his master's criticism further. He asserted that the individual is the only reality and that universals do not exist in things, but only in the thinking mind. Occam denies that any theological doctrines are demonstrable. They rest solely on authority and are to be accepted as revelations made to the church. Even the existence of God is to be accepted as an article of faith. Thus the harmony of reason and faith gives place to the dual nature of truth. This complete severance of philosophy and theology necessarily led to the dissolution of Scholasticsm.

It is also worthy of note that Occam based the authority of the church's teaching on that of the Bible. Popes and councils may err, but Scripture is infallible, for it is inspired by God. It is true, Occam was not aware of the far-reaching consequences of this principle nor did he seem to apply it except in his protest against the secularization of the church, but the principle of scriptural infallibility was theoretically laid down though it was yet far from being practically carried out.

Gabriel Biel at Tubingen (d. 1495) usually styled "the last of the Scholastics," followed the Nominalism of Occam, whose system he reproduced in his *Epitome et Collectorium ex Occamo.*

Besides Nominalism, *Mysticism* contributed its share to the disintegration of Scholasticism. In proportion as the secularization of the church advanced and Scholasticism lost itself in barren, hair-splitting subtleties and scepticism, the spiritually minded sought their satisfaction more and more in Mysticism.

In the Mystic theology of the fourteenth and fifteenth centuries we must discriminate between a more speculative and a more practical tendency. *Speculative Mysticism* undervalued historical Christianity and diverged from the catholic faith into a pantheistic conception of the relation of the creature to God.

Meister Eckhart (d. 1327) described the absorption in God in terms which, literally taken, are pantheistic. He held that the supreme human bliss is a deification whereby man becomes one with God. On the other hand, *practical* or *evangelical Mysticism* directed attention to the fact that religion is a life as well as a truth, and that the church's doctrines are of value only as related to practical piety. This Christian life is to be inculcated and nurtured by the preaching of the word. In these respects Mysticism prepared men in a very real way for a break with the traditional system and paved the way for the Reformation. Mystics of this class were the *Friends of God, Johann Tauler* (d. 1361), *Heinrich Suso* or *Seuse* (d. 1365), *Ruysbroeck* (d. 1381), *Thomas a Kempis* (d. 1471), and *the author of the German Theology*, issued anonymously by the Friends of God at Frankfort, 1350.

Having thus presented the characteristic features and general tendencies of the Scholastic age, we now proceed to the exposition of the doctrines developed during that period.

CHAPTER XIV

THEOLOGY, CHRISTOLOGY, SOTERIOLOGY, ANTHROPOLOGY ACCORDING TO THE SCHOOLMEN

A. THEOLOGY.— Following Augustine, who had defined God as "the only unchangeable substance or essence," Anselm held to the absolute unchangeableness of God. But he went a step further and maintained that God is a thinking Spirit and designated him as the most perfect Being, the ultimate ground and principle of things and thoughts. According to Aquinas God is the 'unmoved mover,' the first cause of everything, the cause of even the free acts of men through predestination, but he is not the author of moral evil. As unmoved mover God is existent only in action. He is pure and perfect actuality, ever thinking and willing, whose final object can be only the absolutely good. God wills good to every being which exists. Therefore love is the fundamental relation of God to the world. Alongside of this conception of God is also found in Aquinas the Areopagite idea that God is an unpredicated, super-substantial being. Dun Scotus opposed Aquinas' theory of de-terminism. Will is the predominant element in his conception of God. The absolute free will of God orders all things. The good is good only because God wills it and for no other reason.

No positive advance in the doctrine concerning the Trinity is to be noted in the teaching of the Schoolmen. Following the sugges-tions of Augustine they refer to the spiritual functions of man as furnishing explanatory analogies, memory, intelligence and will, or intellect, feeling and will. The Mystics, also following Augustine, sought to find the solution of the problem in love, the Father being the subject, the Son the object of love and the Holy Spirit the bond of love between the two.

B. THE CHRISTOLOGY of the Schoolmen is merely a reproduction of the traditional dogma and a demonstration of its logical consis-tency. Abelard was chiefly concerned about the humanity of Christ and emphasized the independence of the finite in the man Jesus. Christ is the man assumed by the Logos and as such he fulfills the will of the divinity dwelling in him. According to the Lombard the immutable Logos assumed the body and soul, but not the person, of a man. The sufferings of Christ were limited to the human nature. Not divine worship, but only veneration is due to Christ's human nature. Scholastic Christology does not overstep the teaching of the Damascene. The person of the Logos assumes the impersonal human nature. Thus Christ is *unum* since his human nature lacks the hypostasis. This unity of the hypostasis involves a *communicatio idiomatum* between the *concreta* God and man (Bonaventura).

C. ATONEMENT.— In the ancient church, both in the East and the West, the Fathers viewed the significance of Christ's death under two aspects, as a ransom in delivering mankind from the bondage of Satan, and as a reconciliation with God through sacrifice. The former was a favorite view with the Fathers. It was set forth in its crassest form by Gregory of Nyssa. But they all agreed that the death of Christ was the most prominent factor in his atoning work, and maintained the piacular and substitutionary nature of Christ's work. This faith, however, had not yet been developed into the form of a strict theory of satisfaction explaining how the justice and the mercy of God are reconciled. The term *satisfactio* occurs first in the writings of Tertullian though its reference there is to the penitence of man rather than the death of Christ.

C. ATONEMENT.— The theory of satisfaction received its first thorough discussion at the hands of Anselm in his *Cur Deus Homo* "Why God became man." It is, in brief, as follows: God's honor has been immeasurably injured. His justice demands satisfaction, either punishment of the sinner, or an equivalent. God, being merciful, chose the latter alternative. The wounded honor of God being infinite, the satisfaction must be infinite. Sinful man *cannot* render adequate satisfaction, yet man, being the transgressor, *must* make satisfaction. Hence satisfaction is only possible through the God-man. The free surrender of his infinitely precious life more than compensated for the injury to God's honor; its merit is infinite. God's justice cannot suffer the merit of Christ to go unrewarded. Having all things Christ can be rewarded only by obtaining the deliverance of man from the penalty pronounced upon him. It is in this way only that God's justice as well as his mercy are preserved.

Anselm's *Cur Deus Homo* opens a new era in the discussion of the doctrine of atonement. The universally accepted theory of redemption as a ransoming from the devil has, of course, no place in Anselm's treatment of the subject. In his famous treatise we notice especially a profound and spiritual conception of sin, a clear consciousness of guilt, a complete disavowal of human merit in the sight of a just God, and an evangelic estimate of the cross of Christ as a means of salvation. Nevertheless, Anselm's theory is not without serious faults. As his entire argument is based upon the old Germanic law, so he also puts the whole relation between God and man on a merely legal footing and gives it no ethical bearing. It is a relation of a subject to his legal ruler. Redemption is based one-sidedly upon the death of Christ, while the rest of his redeeming work almost vanishes out of sight.

In opposition to Anselm's theory which makes the atonement consist in an expiatory act, stands Abelard's theory which places the effect of Christ's sufferings and death wholly in their moral results. It is therefore usually styled "the moral view" of atonement. Abelard, too, discarded the ancient theory that Christ made atonement to Satan. The Devil has no more right over man than a slave has over his fellow-slave whom he has seduced to desert his master and keeps possession of him. There is nothing in the divine love which necessitates expiation or substitutionary sacrifice for past transgression. Can God be reconciled by the slaying of his innocent Son? God sent his Son to sinful men to reveal his love to them. The object of the incarnation and death of Christ was to move men to love by his highest revelation of the divine love. The love thus kindled in man's heart is the ground of the forgiveness of sins, frees from the bondage of sin and enables to fulfill the law which Christ taught and fulfilled, giving thereby the highest example. Christ continues to teach us and make intercession for us.

Abelard's subjective view of atonement duly counterbalances and supplements Anselm's objective theory. Anselm based redemption one-sidedly upon Christ's death. Abelard based it upon the revelation of God's love through Christ and attached no specific importance to the death of Christ.

Bernard combated Abelard's theory. He first opposed the view which Abelard held in common with Anselm, that no satanic claims are met by the sacrifice of Christ, and maintained that Christ brought forgiveness of sins and released from the bonds of the Devil which were righteously permitted by God as a just retribution for sin. Then Bernard assailed Abelard's subjective view of atonement and maintained that Christ is our teacher and example, but his example cannot effect our redemption. It is the blood of Christ which redeems us from sin, death and Devil and brings about the reconciliation of the Father.

In Peter Lombard we find various elements not clearly stated in their mutual relations. He introduces the idea of the merit of Christ. By his suffering and death Christ merited for us redemption from sin, punishment and the Devil and entrance into paradise. The Lombard takes no notice of Anselm, but makes use of suggestions from Abelard. The death of Christ justifies us when by it love is wakened in our hearts. Christ set us free from everlasting punishment by remitting our debt. He delivered us from temporal punishment, which is remitted in baptism and mitigated by penance. The Lombard also adopts the old mythical representation and says that the cross of Christ became a mousetrap and his blood a bait for the Devil.

The later Schoolmen like Alexander of Hales and Bonaventura produced nothing new concerning the doctrine of atonement. They generally combine Anselm's objective view with Abelard's subjective interpretation. Thomas Aquinas, however, deserves particular attention. In distinction from Anselm he denied that satisfaction was the *sine qua non* for the forgiveness of sin. God adopted this method because his justice and mercy could be best revealed through satisfaction. On account of the divine subject in Christ his suffering and activity are infinite. Hence the passion of Christ was not only a sufficient, but also a superabundant satisfaction for the sins of mankind.

Duns Scotus also denied the necessity of satisfaction. It was necessary only because God willed it. Further, he denied Anselm's view that sin is of infinite demerit. He also denied that the suffering of Christ is of infinite value, since the merit of Christ belonged to his human nature. Yet it pleased God to accept Christ's sacrifice as an equivalent for human transgression (acceptilation theory), not from any intrinsic value of it, but because the divine will chose to make Christ's passion the means of the salvation of man. The passion which Christ offers in our behalf to the Father awakens in our hearts love to Christ and God. In his theory of redemption, then, Duns Scotus co-ordinates the objective and subjective aspects of atonement.

Thus the Schoolmen since Anselm and Abelard contributed nothing essential touching the redemptive work of Christ.

D. ANTHROPOLOGY.— 1. *Original State.* In describing the primitive state of man the Scholastics distinguished (1) the original endowment of the first man, what man had in virtue of his original natural constitution. Characteristics of this *status purorum naturalium*, which some Scholastics describe as original righteousness, are the harmony of the natural powers and the absence of concupiscence; and (2) the additional endowment bestowed upon man by grace. This *donum superadditum* was according to some of the Schoolmen the ground of original righteousness. By nature man had power to do good, but this nature was not sufficient of itself to realize the destiny of man. He needed an added endowment of grace to prevent an inner moral contradiction.

The Schoolmen, like the Greek Fathers, used to distinguish

between image and likeness (Gen. 1:26) usually identifying the former with the original and the latter with the superadded endowment of man. Thomas distinguished between the two only in the abstract, but made them coincide in the concrete. The added endowment was given to man at the moment of his creation. Others, like Alexander, Bonaventura and Albert held that it was given to man after creation. They also maintained that man was to earn the superadded endowment for himself by a merit of congruity, i. e., the fitness that God should bestow this gift in response and proportionately to good works performed by man in his original natural state.

2. *Original Sin.* When man lost this superadded gift, no important alteration took place in his nature. Hence Schoolmen, like Anselm and Duns Scotus, defined original sin as something negative, as the lack of original righteousness. The spiritual equilibrium was lost and to that extent man was weakened and no longer inclined toward the good. According to Peter Lombard, Hugo of St. Victor and Thomas Aquinas original sin is not only a negation, but also something positive consisting essentially in concupiscence. But the seat of concupiscence is the flesh (Lombard). The Schoolmen regarding creationism as the only orthodox theory held that the pure human soul separately created by God in each individual born becomes sinful through the union with the corrupted flesh. The rational soul is not transmitted from parent to child, but according to Aquinas the sinful human nature is propogated by generation. Aquinas infers the transference of Adam's sin to posterity from the unity of the organism of the race. "All who are born of Adam may be considered as one man; thus men derived from Adam are members of one body." The results of original sin are alienation of the human will from God, disorder of the powers of the soul and liability to punishment. We are punished, however, for our own sins, and for the sins of our parents only so far as we follow them in their transgressions. Hence children dying unbaptized are not punished but only deprived of the vision of God.

3. *The Sinlessness of Mary.* Although the Schoolmen admitted the universality of sin, yet, owing to the ever growing adoration of the Virgin Mary, they made an exception in her case. They all agreed that Mary was exempt from actual sin, but were divided on the question whether she was conceived without sin (Duns Scotus), or whether she was first tainted by original sin and made immaculate in her prenatal state (Bernard, Alexander, Albert, Bonaventura, Thomas).

The Church Fathers, though many of them exempted Mary from

actual transgression, knew nothing of her freedom from original sin. Paschasius Radbertus was the first to teach that Mary remained free from sin in the womb and entered the world without sin. When in 1140 an attempt was made at Lyons to introduce a festival of the immaculate conception of Mary, Bernard of Clairvaux declared himself decidedly against the idea, although he held to a perfect sanctification of the Virgin before birth. The doctrine of the immaculate conception was likewise rejected by Bonaventura and Thomas. Duns Scotus argued for Mary's exemption from hereditary sin from the first moment of her conception, yet expressed himself with reserve and merely asserted that the immaculate conception was the more probable among the different probabilities. The Franciscans, who were especially zealous in rendering honor to Mary, embraced this view, while the Dominicans rejected it. No formal decision of the question was reached by the church, though the belief in the immaculate conception became increasingly widespread and the tendency of the age was favorable to the doctrine.

4. *Freedom and Grace.* Anselm and Aquinas following Augustine regarded the grace of the Spirit as the sole agency in effecting the conversion of man. In Aquinas' doctrine of grace everything is the result of this divine agency as the prime mover. Grace is described as a certain supernatural gift infused into the soul by God. In practice, however, Aquinas gives room to free will in the preparation for grace. Man is capable of inclining himself to receive the grace of God. In virtue of this, then, he is prepared to do good works. Since the nature of man had simply become weakened through sin, man could by his own strength cooperate in his conversion when supported by grace. A similar view was held by Bonaventura. Peter Lombard and Aquinas adopt the Augustinian distinction between operating grace and cooperating grace, but in reality their teaching tends to Semi-Pelagianism. According to Peter Lombard man needs healing grace, because by original sin "he is wounded as regards natural good, and utterly deprived of these gratuitous gifts which through grace were added to the natural gifts" (*sent.* II. d. 27). Duns Scotus definitely set forth the Semi-Pelagian view. Out of the natural power of his own free will, which original sin has left unimpaired man can merit the grace which renews the heart. Although free will had great virtue in merit, yet without grace it is not sufficient for the salvation of man. Grace does not create the good, it only increases it.

5. *Justification.* In the Scholastic doctrine of justification Semi-Pelagianism and Augustinianism appeared in various shades of con-

flicting differences. The general opinion of the Schoolmen was that faith justifies on the ground of love, and that justification is not a judicial act of God, but a process in man by which he is made righteous. The beginning of the justification of man is marked by the infusion of grace in the soul. Simultaneous with this are the inclination of the free will to God in faith, the turning away of the free will from sin, and the forgiveness of sins. The successive stages of the process, according to Aquinas, are to be regarded as logical, not as chronological, for the divine act of justification is momentary.

Under the Scholastic conception of justification no actual certainty of salvation is attainable. According to Aquinas there are certain signs or indications of a state of grace which however afford no certainty, namely, joy in God, scorn of worldly things, and consciousness that one is not guilty of mortal sin.

6. *Faith, Merit and Good Works.* From the Scholastic conception of justification follows that it is not faith in which the religious life centers, but love and good works, for justification according to the Schoolmen is not a new personal relation of man with God, but the making of man capable of performing good works. Accordingly, the Schoolmen distinguished between *fides informis,* mere faith, and *fides formata caritate,* faith perfected in love. *Fides informis* may be *fides explicita,* explicit faith, i. e., faith with accurate knowledge of the church's doctrine, or *fides implicita,* implicit faith, i. e., readiness to believe whatever the church teaches. But it is only the *fides formata* which is meritorious and brings salvation.

Strictly speaking, merit cannot be predicated of man in relation to God, but according to the pre-arrangement of the divine ordinance there is assured to man the possibility of meritorious conduct. The Schoolmen distinguished a twofold merit. Man can prepare himself to receive grace through the action of his free will by a merit of congruity, *meritum de congruo,* i. e., it seems fitting that God should give recompense to man in response and proportionately to good works performed by him before justification. The *meritum de congruo* proceeds from man's free will. But after the infusion of grace man may merit eternal life by a merit of condignity, *meritum de condigno,* i. e., merit acquired by works performed in the state of grace, which can justly claim the reward of eternal life from God. The *meritum de condigno* originates from grace.

It is also possible for man to earn more merit than he needs for himself to attain salvation. This occurs when he not only obeys all the commandments of the gospel but also observes the so-called evangelical counsels, *consilia evangelica.* Works done according to such counsels, particularly according to the vows of poverty, celibacy and obedience, are called works of supererogation, *opera supererogationis.* Through the supererogatory works of Christ and the saints was created the *thesaurus,* the treasury or fund of superabundant merits. The thesaurus being at the disposal of the pope is managed by the priests (Thom. *suppl.* q. 26, a. 1, 3). From it the church can draw in order to abbreviate the required satisfaction in purgatory. The development of the doctrine of the thesaurus in explicit form was the work of the great Schoolmen, notably Alexander, Albertus Magnus and Thomas Aquinas.

CHAPTER XV

THE SACRAMENTS ACCORDING TO THE SCHOOLMEN

A. SACRAMENTS IN GENERAL.— The ancient church had produced no dogma of the sacraments. This task remained for the Schoolmen who gave the sacramental system their most careful attention. In no other one branch of theology were the Scholastics so productive as in the establishment of the Catholic doctrine of the sacraments. The Schoolmen did for the doctrine of the sacraments what the Church Fathers did for the doctrines of theology and Christology.

1. *Number of Sacraments.* The word *sacramentum* was used, in the early church since Tertullian, for any significant religious rite. Consequently their number was undetermined. Pseudo-Dionysius enumerates six sacraments. Bernard of Clairvaux speaks of many and enumerates ten; Damiani twelve. Peter Lombard, though not the first to enumerate seven sacraments, adhered to the number seven: baptism, Eucharist, confirmation, extreme unction, penance, ordination and marriage. This number was not sanctioned by the church until the council of Florence, in 1439.

2. *Definition and Efficacy of the Sacrament.* The diverse character of the seven sacraments made a clear-cut definition of the sacrament almost impossible. The Schoolmen all started with Augustine's definition of a sacrament as a visible sign of an invisible grace, but went beyond him in the degree of efficacy they ascribed to it. Sacraments are not only visible signs of grace which they denote, but also vehicles of this very grace. Invisible grace is really communicated to the outward sign and through it conferred on the recipient (Thom. III. q. 60, a. 2). Peter Lombard (IV. 1. 2) says that sacraments were instituted not only for the sake of signifying, but for the sake of sanctifying. It is to be noted that the Schoolmen place the divine efficiency in the sacraments, not in the word.

According to Thomas sacraments are necessary (1) because man being surrounded by material things is led up to spiritual things by means of corporeal objects. (2) Through sin man is subject to things material. (3) Man's activity here on earth is through and about corporeal matters. According to Hugo of St. Victor the design of the sacraments is threefold: They were instituted (1) for the sake of humiliation; we must submit to the visible in order to attain to the invisible; (2) for instruction; the visible leads to the invisible; (3)

for spiritual exercise whereby the inner spiritual life of man is strengthened.

Duns Scotus and the later Nominalists defined the sacraments as symbols which signify grace and which, according to a divine covenant, produce in the soul a creative act of God.

The primary effect of the sacraments is to bring justifying grace to man. According to illustrations used by the Schoolmen baptism, the sacrament of regeneration, confers the spiritual life; confirmation strengthens it; the Eucharist nourishes it; penance restores it, if lost by sin; extreme unction heals the soul and, if God sees it to be expedient, restores health to the body; holy orders create the necessary rulers of the church; matrimony brings God's blessing upon the Christian family by which the children of God are multiplied on earth and heaven is filled with his elect.

To the three sacraments, baptism, confirmation and holy orders, there is attributed as a secondary effect the impartation of a certain indestructible mark or character, *character spiritualis,* by later Catholic writers usually designated as *character indelebilis.* The Schoolmen made much of that indelible character, but failed to give a clear definition of its nature. Thomas taught that by the indelible character the recipient is in some special way marked as participating in the priesthood of Christ, which is eternal. Hence the character imprinted upon the human soul is indelible and for this reason these three sacraments cannot be repeated without sacrilege. Duns Scotus and Biel regarded the theory of the indelible character as untenable. Nevertheless Duns Scotus upheld it, but "solely upon the authority of the church." Pope Eugene IV. in the bull Exultate Deo of November 22, 1439, at the council of Florence, made the Scholastic theory of the *character indelebilis* a dogma of the church. Baptism, confirmation and holy orders "imprint indelibly upon the soul a character, that is, a certain spiritual mark distinctive from others. For this reason they are not to be repeated in the same person."

The Schoolmen distinguished in each sacrament the matter and the form. The matter is the sensible element. The form consists of the words used in the rite. But the sensible element becomes a real sacrament only when on the part of the officiating priest there is present an inward intention or will to do what the church does, or at all events what Christ has appointed. Hence Eugene IV. (*1. c.*) mentions matter, form and intention as the three essential constituents of sacrament. The validity of the sacrament, however, does not depend on the personal character of the officiating priest, for the sacraments have power to produce their effects *ex opere operato,* that is, by a virtue inherent in themselves. They are always efficacious when properly administered. But in order to participate in the effects of the sacraments, the recipient must place no *obex* or obstacle to them by bad dispositions, nor be in a state of mortal sin. The effect of the sacrament may be enhanced by the pious disposition of the recipient, *ex opere operantis.* Through his merit and spiritual disposition he may receive as a reward further gifts of grace.

B. THE SEPARATE SACRAMENTS.— 1. *Baptism.* The matter of baptism is water. The mode of baptism was not regarded as essential. Peter Lombard spoke of baptism as immersion. Albert and Thomas preferred immersion but regarded aspersion or affusion as equally valid. Duns spoke only of a visible washing. Durandus recognized both modes. The form of baptism is the use of the words "I baptize thee in the name of the Father, Son and Holy Ghost." Baptism is indispensable to salvation. Hence children who die without baptism cannot be saved. However they do not suffer the pain of fire in hell, but remain in the *limbus puerorum,* the everlasting abode of unbaptized infants, where they are excluded from the beatific vision of God. The Schoolmen admitted of two exceptions. Sacramental baptism may be supplied (1) by the baptism of desire, that is, the earnest desire of receiving the sacrament without the opportunity to be baptized; (2) by the baptism of blood, that is martyrdom for Christ's sake.

The gracious effect of baptism is the impartation of grace which makes the soul acceptable in the sight of God by removing guilt and penalty and making apt for doing good. "The effect of this sacrament is the remission of all original and actual sin, as also of every penalty, which is due for that sin" (Eugene IV., *ut supra*). But although baptism blots out the sins of the past, the sinful impulses remain. We notice here the old conception of concupiscence remaining in the baptized as a tinder, *fomes peccati,* from which at any moment sin may be kindled into flame. According to the Lombard, concupiscence is not destroyed by baptism, but weakened. Finally baptism imparts the indelible character. Faith is required in the recipient to secure the benefits of baptism. In the case of children the faith of the sponsors takes the place of the faith of the children, the sponsors, *patrini,* being under obligation to see to the instruction of the children in the Christian faith. In the case of unbelievers the gracious effect of the sacrament will be theirs only, after they have done penance for their unbelief. Thus baptism justifies the believer and makes him a saint whose past sins, original or actual, are effaced. But by the first grave sin after baptism the sinner loses the life of grace and the friendship of God; only the indelible character remains.

(2) *Confirmation.* Originally, baptism was accompanied with unction symbolizing the communication of the Spirit. In the course of time this was separated from baptism as a particular rite and then came to be viewed as a sacrament, the sacrament of confirmation. It has for its effect the giving of the Holy Spirit and the strengthening of the faith received in baptism. It supplements baptism and imparts like baptism an indelible character. Its matter is an unguent of oil and balsam. Its form consists of the words "I sign thee with the sign of the cross and confirm thee with the chrism of salvation in the name of the Father, Son and Holy Ghost." This sacrament is to be administered by a bishop (Eugene IV., *ut supra*). As in baptism, those to be confirmed must have sponsors. Godparents contract with the child or the candidate a spiritual relationship which constitutes an impediment to marriage. A discussion of these regulations does not come under the scope of the History of Doctrine but belongs to the canon law.

3. *The Eucharist.* The Schoolmen regarded the Eucharist under two different aspects, as a sacrament and as a sacrifice, the latter in their system being by far the more important.

The matter of the sacrament is unleavened wheat bread and wine mixed with water. Its form are the words "this is my body" and "this is the cup of my blood." Its effects are as follows: it increases sanctifying grace in man; it weakens his evil inclinations and gives him both the desire and the power to do good; it cleanses from venial sins.

Toward the middle of the eleventh century Radbertus' theory of transubstantiation had been generally adopted as the orthodox doctrine, and Scholasticism advocated and elaborated the theory. At the fourth Latern council, in 1215, transubstantiation was declared to be an article of faith by pope Innocent III.

Through the words of consecration (Alexander) or by a divine power inherent in the formal words (Thomas) or by an act of divine omnipotence (Bonaventura and Duns Scotus) bread and wine are changed into the body and blood of Christ, only the accidents, or sensible properties of the earthly substance, continue as they are. Christ's body and blood, his soul and deity are not present by way of sacramental change but of natural concomitance, that is, both the body and the blood of the living Christ exist in each element of the Eucharist, so that both are received by communicating in one kind only. It was in accordance with this doc-

trine that the Schoolmen justified the ever-growing custom of withholding the cup from the laity. The council of Constance, which
opened in 1414, finally decreed "that as the body and blood of
Christ were wholly contained under each species the custom . . .
of communicating in one kind should be received as a law which
no one, without the authority of the Church, might reject or alter."
The Schoolmen further taught that the presence of Christ's body
remains in the host as long as the form, *species*, of bread and wine
is retained. Even if a dog or a mouse should swallow the unbroken
host, the body of Christ would remain in it. Since the body and blood
are permanently present in the elements, they can be exhibited
for adoration in the mass and in eucharistic processions. This theory
was expressed in a liturgical form by the institution of the Corpus-
Christi-Day, *festum corporis Christi*, by pope Urban IV., in 1264.

The Schoolmen had no little difficulty in explaining how Christ's
body being locally present in heaven is in its entirety and in its substance present at every celebration of the Eucharist. Alexander and
Thomas held that the celestial body is local in heaven but the sacramental body is substantially, not locally, present in the sacrament.
Over against this view Duns Scotus maintained the presence of
the whole in the whole and entirely in any part whatsoever, and declared that the omnipotent God by a miracle can cause a body to
exist in different places at the same time. Thus Christ's body which
is local in heaven is in its entirety present in its substance at any
number of places where the Eucharist is being celebrated. This
presence of Christ's body in the Eucharist is the result of the direct
operation of God, not of priestly action. This is the so-called consubstantiation theory. But since the church taught a real change of
the bread and wine into the very body of Christ, so that the substance of bread and wine entirely ceases to be, Scotus admitted the
possibility of the cessation of the substances. This view of Scotus
came to dominate the theology of the later Middle Ages. Occam
followed the consubstantiation theory and held that the substance of
bread, not merely the accidents, remains together with the substance of the body of Christ. Occam also held that transubstantiation cannot be defended logically nor proved from Scripture, but
like Duns Scotus and Pierre d'Ailly accepted and defended the
doctrine because of the authority of the church.

Closely connected with the idea of transubstantiation in the
Eucharist was that of the sacrifice. Gregory the Great had already
found the significance of the Eucharist in the sacrifice of the mass,
and since his day it had formed the centre of the Catholic ritual.
The sacrifice of the mass is the same as the sacrifice on the cross,

the former being a constant repetition of the latter. Thus the Eucharist is a real propitiatory sacrifice for the expiation of sins. It is effectual for those present and absent, living and dead. Thomas maintains that this sacrament profits also others than those participating provided they have faith in the sacrament, for "whosoever is not joined to the passion of Christ by faith and love does not attain the benefits."

The sacrifice of the mass redounded to the glory of the priesthood, and the hierarchy celebrated its greatest triumphs in the practice of private masses when only the officiating priest was present.

4. *Penance.* Baptism effaces original sin, the Eucharist cleanses from venial sins. But to free man from mortal sins, penance, the sacrament of confession and absolution has been instituted by Christ. The sacrament of penance is necessary to all who have committed mortal sin after baptism. The effect of the sacrament is the deliverance from the guilt of sin through an infusion of grace and, in the case of mortal sin, deliverance from its eternal punishment; hence also reconciliation with God and justification. Its form consists in the words *ego te absolvo.* The matter, according to Thomas, are the acts of the penitent. According to Duns· Scotus, the absolution as an external ceremony is the matter, and, as possessing significative force, the form. The acts of the penitent are required for the worthy reception of the sacrament. Pope Eugene IV. (Mirbt, *Q.* 236) declared the acts a *quasi materia* and enumerated them as *contritio, confessio* and *satisfactio.* The Scholastic theologians from Peter Lombard down described the sacrament of penance as consisting of the three distinct acts on the sinner's part: *contritio cordis, confessio oris,* and *satisfactio operis.* A distinction was made between *contritio,* a deep sorrow for sin, growing out of love toward God and *attritio,* an imperfect sorrow for sin such as arises from fear of punishment. *Attritio,* insufficient to justify, could nevertheless give the sinner the necessary disposition for receiving the sacrament of confession and absolution which completes *attritio,* transforming it into *contritio.* Practically the same view was held by Duns Scotus, only that he ascribed to *attritio even a meritum de congruo;* the attrite sinner has a claim to a favorable regard of God.

The fourth Lateran council, 1215, had already decreed that every one of either sex after arriving at the age of discretion must make confession at least once a year before his parish priest, or some other priest with the consent of the parish priest, "reverently receiving the sacrament of the Eucharist at least at Easter and faithfully acknowledging in private all his sins" (Mirbt, *Q.* 181). In confessing to his priest the sinner must enumerate all the sins of which he has recollection. The penitent was assured of the secrecy of the priest, for if in any way the priest violated the seal of the confessional he was to be divested of the sacerdotal office and confined for life in a monastery (Fourth Lat. council, *ut supra*). Upon the confession the priest as a skilled physician and a fair judge absolves the sinner from the debt of eternal punishment and binds to the discharge of temporal penalty. Accordingly there still remains the temporal punishment required by divine justice. This requirement must be fulfilled either in this life or in the world to come, that is, in purgatory. Purgatory is, according to the Schoolmen, one of the five abodes in the invisible world: *caelum, purgatorium, limbus patrum, limbus infantum, infernus damnatorum*.

The temporal punishment due to sin, the guilt of which has been forgiven, must be met by the satisfaction of works. Such works enjoined by the priest are chiefly prayer, fasting and almsgiving. The priest may, for consideration, transmute these penances or satisfactions into indulgences transferring to the sinner's account righteousness from the exhaustless treasury of superabundant merits laid up by Christ and the saints. "All the saints intended that whatever they did or suffered for God's sake should be profitable not only to themselves but to the whole church" (Thom. *suppl.* q. 25. a. 2). The Catholic Encyclopedia, 1913, VII, 783, quotes Thomas on the subject: "He who gains indulgences is not thereby released outright from what he owes as penalty, but is provided with the means of paying it" and adds "The church therefore neither leaves the penitent helplessly in debt, nor acquits him of all further accounting; she enables him to meet his obligation." Since the souls in purgatory are yet, because of their sins, before the forum of the church, "they, too, may secure a share in these indulgences on account of some work done by one yet living and applied to them by way of supplication" (Biel, *expos. can. miss., lect.* 57).

Thus, on the one hand, the sacrament of penance brings grace and, on the other hand, it is necessary for the sinner to make reparation for the sins which he has committed. Accordingly, forgiveness of sins is the achievement of divine grace plus man's own effort.

As early as the eighth century it became customary to let private repentance take the place of the public ordinance and to let the absolution follow immediately after the confession and before the penance was performed. Having received the absolution after the confession the penitent was no longer subject to the punishments of hell. But if he failed to perform the works of penance which constituted the temporal punishment due to sin, he had to endure the fire 'of purgatory. It became also customary to shorten the pre-scribed period of penance with due regard to circumstances and especially the penitent's zeal and fervor, or to commute the rigorous penances into other exercises or works of piety, such as prayer, fasting almsgiving and the like. The penitent was even permitted to hire a person and thus perform his penance by proxy (vicarious penance). According to a decree of the council of Clermont, in 1095, those who joined a crusade were freed from all obligation in the matter of penance (plenary indulgence).

Among the Germanic people who were accustomed to the pay-ment of money as a compensation even for the gravest crimes, a money payment was often allowed in lieu of acts of penance (in-dulgence). So much sin was reckoned to involve so much debt; (cf. the German word for penitence, *Busse*, which means a compen-sation or a fine).

From the thirteenth century to the Reformation popes quite frequently granted plenary indulgences *a poena et culpa*, that is remission from penalty and guilt of all sins, and in such cases the papal commissary, instead of the parish priest, may administer the sacrament and absolve the sinner. Whatever Catholic writers may say in defense of the phrase *a poena et culpa* the popular mind cared little about the orthodox definition of indulgence "as the re-mission of temporal punishment due to God, for sins already for-given as to guilt," but accepted the terminology of the Curia *a poena et culpa* and readily inferred that forgiveness of sin was secured by the payment of money.

Indulgence in its primitive form meant the remission of canonical penance. Now it meant deliverance from all penalty and guilt. It was this perversion of the penitential praxis at the close of the Middle Ages that called forth Luther's criticism.

5. *Extreme Unction.* Anointing of the sick was customary in the ancient church. In case a priest was not available, laymen might perform the ceremony. Toward the end of the eighth century anointing of the sick entered upon a definite course of development in that it was brought into relation with remission of sins. After the ninth century it received a sacramental character in connection with penance. The Schoolmen, notably Hugo, Bonaventura and Thomas, gave extreme unction detailed attention. According to the latter it was instituted by Christ and promulgated by his apostles (James 5:14-15). The teachings of the schoolmen concerning this sacra-ment received ecclesiastical sanction at the council of Florence, in 1439, through pope Eugen IV. Its matter is olive oil blessed by a

bishop. This sacrament shall not be given except to a sick person in extreme necessity or immediate danger of death. A priest administers the sacrament and makes with the holy oil the sign of the cross on the eyes, ears, nostrils, lips, hands, feet and loins of the sick person. The form of the sacrament is this: "Through this anointing and his precious mercy may the Lord forgive thee all thy sins of sight . . . and likewise of the other organs." Its effect is the healing of the soul and, if it be to the benefit of the soul, the healing of the body itself.

6. *Ordination or Holy Orders.*— The rite of ordination was used both in the East and in the West as early as the fourth century. The orders in the ancient church were only those of bishop, presbyter and deacon, but no special stress was laid on an exact number of orders, or on a division into major and minor orders. The Schoolmen systematized the matter. Peter Lombard regards the number seven and the division into two classes as settled: *ostiarii, lectores, exorcistae, acoluthi* (minor orders); *subdiaconi, diaconi, presbyteri* (major or holy orders).

The function of the priesthood developed out of the necessity of church life. The enlargement of the penitential system and the sacramental conception of grace made it necessary to assign to the priesthood sacerdotal jurisdiction and authority. The sacrament of ordination, the Schoolmen taught, communicates to the priesthood the power and the grace to perform the priestly functions in a valid and proper manner. The priestly ordination can never be lost, because it imparts an indelible character. To ordain belongs to the bishop. Heretics may, indeed, ordain validly though of course not lawfully. Thomas gave it as his final opinion that sacraments administered by heretics do not bring grace, not that they are in themselves inefficacious, but because of the sin of those who receive the sacraments from them against the prohibition of the church.

The form of the sacrament are the words spoken by the consecrating bishop: "Receive authority for the offering of sacrifice in the church for the living and the dead in the name of the Father . ." As to what constitutes the matter of the sacrament the statements of the Schoolmen are very vacillating. It is usually found in the blessing, the laying on of hands and the anointing, as also the handing over the paten and chalice to the priest.

As to the relation of priests to bishops the question arose whether the bishops are an order distinct from the priests or not. Thomas and Bonaventura affirm that the episcopate is not a distinct order and that consecration to it has not a sacramental character.

Because of the exalted position of the bishops, who alone have the right to ordain, Duns Scotus was inclined to view the consecration of bishops as a special sacrament.

7. *Matrimony.* According to the medieval ascetic ideal a low estimate was placed upon matrimony in comparison with the sanctity of the monastical and priestly states. Nevertheless, matrimony was numbered among the sacraments. According to Thomas Christ raised matrimony to the dignity of a sacrament. It symbolizes Christ's relation to the church, Eph. 5:32 (*mysterion* was rendered *sacramentum* in the Vulgate). The form of the sacrament is not the benediction of the priest, though this is "something sacramental," but the mutual consent of the parties entering upon the marriage relation. Hence the agent in the sacrament or the *minister sacramenti* is he who uses the sacrament, that is, the contracting parties are the agents of this sacrament. In the absence of a visible material element the Scholastics furnish no distinct definition of the matter of the sacrament. The Schoolmen reaffirm the monogamistic character and indissolubility of the marriage union, even where bodily separation may take place. The effects or blessings of matrimony are the mutual inner relation of husband and wife, and the begetting and training of children. As a negative virtue of this sacrament were mentioned the protection against unachastity and the repression of the carnal appetite. This sacrament was forbidden to Holy Orders. Nor were the laity under any necessity of observing it. For matrimony is neither a *sacramentum necessitatis*, as baptism, penance and the Eucharist, nor a *sacramentum dignitatis*, as ordination, but a *sacramentum consilii*.

CHAPTER XVI

HIERARCHICAL CONCEPTION OF THE CHURCH AND EFFORTS AT REFORM

A. HIERARCHICAL CONCEPTION OF THE CHURCH.

1. *The Church.* Although the church had long since ceased to be the communion of believers, Thomas still defines it as "the assembly of the faithful" and "the communion of saints." He means thereby the visible society of all the faithful participating in the sacraments. The church had become a ruling institution consisting of rulers and subjects.

In this institution there is a gradation of rulers. We have noticed already the division into minor and major orders. In addition to these there are gradations of the higher clergy. Bishops by divine institution occupy a higher rank than priests. In regard to the power of the keys the Schoolmen distinguished between the power of the order and the power of jurisdiction and maintained that the latter belongs to the bishop alone and the former to all priests. This means that the bishop alone has plenary power in the dispensing of the sacraments, while all priests are authorized to forgive sins and administer the sacraments except confirmation and holy orders. The key of jurisdiction further denotes the bishop's power of spiritual dominion and jurisdiction in the administration of justice. The bishops have the plenary power together with the pope and in subjection to him. He is "the supreme pontiff" and "the head of the whole church."

2. *Papal claims* and papal rights were ably championed by the great popes of the Scholastic period. Gregory VII. (d. 1085) exerted a powerful influence over the policy of the Roman Church and elaborated and realized the ideal of the papacy as a political power. The Roman bishop is the lord of the church. He is the bishop *universalis.* All other bishops are subject to him. He exercises his power through the bishops and they in turn through the priests. He rules in the church as a king in his kingdom, outside of which their is no salvation and for which he may make or unmake at will laws and articles of faith. He can be judged by no one. He is by the merits of the blessed Peter infallibly made holy. He is also prince (*princeps*) over the kingdoms of the world. The relation of the royal power to that of the apostolic power is like that of the moon to the sun. For, as the moon receives its light from

the sun, so do civil governments and their princes receive power through the pope, who receives it from God. All temporal rulers are of necessity subordinate to the pope and bound to do his bidding or lose their thrones.

Innocent III. (d. 1216) called the pope "the vicar of Christ," and insisted that the Lord left to Peter the governance not of the church only but of the whole world. Boniface VIII. in the bull *Unam sanctam,* in 1302, asserted that the pope is the sole head of the church and that the temporal power of the monarch is borne only at his will and by his permission. The closing sentence of the famous bull reads as follows : "Furthermore, we declare, assert and define that it is altogether necessary to salvation for every human creature to be subject to the Roman pontiff."

B. EFFORTS AT REFORM.— People sighed and groaned and cursed under the yoke of the Roman hierarchy. With this were combined bitter complaints against the corruption and immorality of the clergy, the avarice, injustice and tyranny of the Court of Rome, the traffic in spiritual offices, the sale of indulgences. This widespread discontent called forth severe criticism and demanded "a reformation of the church in head and members."

1. The reformation aimed at was to be one "in head and members," but not in spirit. The *great Reform Councils,* at Pisa, 1409, at Constance, 1414-17, and at Basel, 1431-49, never intended to abolish more than the most grievous oppression and certain gross outward scandals. These councils did not enter upon questions of doctrine and left the Roman interpretation of the dogma untouched.

2. Of the *Scholastics* it was especially *Occam,* who severely criticized the hierarchical system. The conflict of Louis of Bavaria with pope John XXII. and the theological revolt of the Spiritual Franciscans furnished the historical occasion for this criticism. In his writing *Octo quaestiones super potestate et dignitate papali* (1339-42) Occam held and developed the same ideas concerning the church and its relation to the state as set forth by Marsilius of Padua in his *Defensor pacis,* in 1324 (Mirbt, Q. 217 f.). Marsilius supported Louis of Bavaria in his struggle with Rome. Occam proclaimed the principle of distinct separation of church and state, attacking the temporal supremacy of the pope and insisting on the independence of kingly authority. There is no such thing as a necessary dependence of the emperor on the pope. Kingly authority is as much an ordinance of God as spiritual rule. The emperor stands directly under God, and the pope is subject to the emperor in all secular affairs. The papal power extends only to spiritual

things such as doctrine and the administration of the sacraments. And this power has been delegated to the pope upon practical considerations and not at all on Biblical grounds, for the Scripture knows nothing of Christ's appointing Peter as the prince of the apostles. As Christ is the only supreme head of the church, there is no such thing as a divine authority of popes or bishops. "The pope can err." He is fallible as all men are, only "Holy Scripture cannot err." Occam's views on the independence of civil rule were even more decidedly and comprehensively expressed in his *Dialogus inter magistrum et discipulum de imperatorum et pontificum potestate* (1341 and 1343), the second and third part of which are incomplete.

Asserting that not the pope but the Scripture is the infallible authority in the church, Occam had stated in theory the formal principle of the Reformation. Luther calls Occam "my dear master" and was fond of saying "I am of the Occamist faction." And yet, with Occam and the contemporary Schoolmen this was only theory. In practice they made no application of the principle of the divine authority of the Scripture, but submitted to the authority of the Fathers and of the church as being co-equal with, in fact superior to, that of the Scripture.

3. *The Humanists* also, despite their criticism of the church and the Scholastic doctrines, contributed little, very little, to theological and spiritual regeneration. In Italy the renewal of learning was almost entirely literary and artistic, unrestrained by morality and religion. Accordingly, the Italian Humanists had no practical interest in any spiritual or theological reformation. The German and English Humanists were, in the main, men of spiritual earnestness. Cultivating the new learning in a religious spirit they awakened in many minds the love of truth and of liberty. In his humorous and satirical writings Erasmus criticized the clerical follies and abuses. By his edition of the Greek Testament and by translating and publishing the works of the Fathers he rendered great service of a positive character. His aim was to free theology from dogmatism and to bring in a simple, practical, undogmatic Christianity. He would rather be "a pious theologian with Chrysostom than an invincible one with Scotus" (*Ratio verae theol.* opp. V. 137). Erasmus' work, however, was of a pre-reformatory nature only in so far as it set forth certain principles of reform, but "the fatal lack of the 'Erasmian Reformation' was that it failed to offer any tangible method of applying these principles to the existing church system" (*Erasmus* in Schaff-Herzog, Encyclopedia).

4. *The great commotions* which had been raised in the twelfth

and thirteenth centuries by the Cathari and Waldenses had no influence in giving rise to the Protestant movement; on the contrary, the immediate result of their revolt against the organized church "was only a more distinct assertion of the ecclesiastical and sacramental character of Christianity" (Seeberg, *Hist. of Doctr.* II. 95).

5. The so-called *Forerunners of the Reformation,* starting from the Scriptures as the supreme and sole authority, gave utterance to many reformatory thoughts, but in the decisive questions concerning justification and faith their conception was essentially Catholic. In their attempts at reform they were carried so far as to underrate or ignore altogether the value of outward order and organization.

Johann Wessel (d. 1489), one of the Brethren of the Common Life, foreshadowed the German Reformation in his protests against the growing paganizing of the papacy and the superstitious and magical uses of the sacraments. He criticized especially the medieval doctrine of penance. None but God can forgive sins. Repentance is internally complete through the righteousness of Christ and God's free grace, when the sinner truly repents of his sins. The only real satisfaction for sins is a life in God. Accordingly there can be no satisfaction for sins through indulgences or purgatorial fire, although Wessel admitted the necessity of a continuous development of Christian life after death. Luther who published a collection of Wessel's writings in 1521 declared that, had he read Wessel sooner, people would have denounced him for stealing all his ideas from him. The theology of Wessel, however, was essentially medieval. His conception of justification was that of Augustine. He conceived of Christianity on a basis of mysticism. He saw victory over the world in ascotic liberation from the world, or rather in mystic indifference to the world. Ascetic mysticism characterized his practical life.

Wessel's friend, *Johann Ruchrat von Wesel* (d. 1481), likewise held the medieval idea that justification is an habitual grace implanted in men by the gracious act of God. He also criticized the received system and usages of the church, especially abuses connected with indulgences, but held that pilgrimages and alms and the like good works done in love to God are in themselves useful and contribute to the obtaining of eternal life.

John Wycliffe (d. 1384) realized and formulated in his tract *The Truth of Holy Scripture* the formal principle of the Reformation, namely, the supreme and sole authority of the Scriptures for the belief and life of the Christian. Hence it is necessary for all men to know the Bible. Giving the Bible to the people is a holier task than consecrating Christ's body in the mass. In place of the existing hierarchy, which had no warrant in Scripture, Wycliffe put "the poor priests," itinerant preachers, who expounded the Scriptures and spread abroad among the people the teachings of Wycliffe. In the Bible as being divinely inspired and therefore infallible Wycliffe saw "the law of Christ" which is binding on all men. Accordingly, Wycliffe's reform is of the Puritan type. The Bible as the law of Christ is the one authority for believers, and therefore, teachings, tradition, infallibility of the church, transubstantiation, confirmation, ordination, clerical celibacy, extreme unction, compulsory confession, priestly absolution, imposition of penance, supererogatory merits, indulgences, church music, pilgrimages and the like go by the board since they have no ground in Scripture. These ideas are set forth in a comprehensive way in Wycliffe's famous *Trialogus*. In his tract *De eucharistia* he rejected transubstantiation as being contrary to reason and Scripture. Belief in transubstantiation is to Wycliffe worse than pagan superstition. He accepted the Augustinian view of the sacrament as a symbol of an invisible grace. Adopting the predestinarian views of Augustine Wycliffe defines the church as the congregation of all the predestinate. No man's salvation depends on the pope. Papal excommunication can exclude no one from the true church. Wycliffe definitely branded the pope as Antichrist.

One of Wycliffe's fundamental ideas was that the church should be poor as it was in the days of the apostles. But in rejecting all ecclesiastical traditions as mere human inventions he went beyond the limits of evangelical consideration. All his reforms were based on an entirely legalistic conception of Christianity. Wycliffe did not possess the evangelical idea of justification by faith alone. His conception of faith and justification is essentially Catholic. Faith becomes what it should be only through love.

John Huss (d. 1415), the docile pupil of the English reformer, strongly opposed the withholding of the cup from the laity. The essence of Huss' doctrine of the church is contained in his *De ecclesia*, the greater part of which is made up of extracts from Wycliffe's *De ecclesia* and *De potestate papae*. According to it the church is the entire body of those who from eternity have been predestined to salvation. They alone can savingly administer the sacraments. The head of the church cannot be the pope, but Christ alone, since no earthly dignity, no human choice, and no visible sign can confer a membership in it. In all his reformatory efforts Huss was true to the principle, which he firmly declared before the council of Constance, that "he could not possibly do anything to violate his conscience, for which he was responsible to God." But, like Wycliffe, he ignored and rejected all institutions of the church as human inventions. This fundamental error rendered both Wycliffe and Huss incompetent to be reformers of the church.

Reliance on the Scripture as his surest guide, intense moral earnestness and strenuous protests against papal corruption characterize *Girolamo Savonarola* (d. 1489) as a reformer. He aimed at a moral reform and adoption of righteousness in private conduct and in civil government. His government was a theocracy of the Old Testament type. Its new head should be Jesus Christ. But his reformatory efforts did not aim at the restoration of Christianity in its primitive simplicity and purity, or at a radical doctrinal reform. In his *Meditationes* on Psalm 51 and 31, composed during his imprisonment, and which Luther edited with a preface, he teaches justification by faith appealing as a sinner directly to God's mercy. But in his *Il Trionfo della Croce* he accepts the seven sacraments and the other distinctive marks of the medieval church excepting the infallibility of the church and the pope.

The term *Forerunners of the Reformation* or *Reformers before the Reformation* is in fact a misnomer, for all of them lacked more or less the true evangelical Reformation spirit. None of them had grasped that experimental thought of justifying faith as a new relation of man to God, which constituted the basis of the Reformation theology. Dr. Painter in his book *The Reformation Dawn* rightly calls them "Biblical Reformers," since they all regarded the Bible as the basis of their reformatory efforts.

What so many pious, powerful and wise men had tried in vain to accomplish was effected by Martin Luther, who aimed not merely at a correction of abuses of practice, but at a reformation in fundamentals of doctrine.

THIRD PERIOD

DEVELOPMENT AND FIXATION OF DOCTRINE THROUGH THE REFORMATION AND COUNTER REFORMATION

CHAPTER XVII

THE DOCTRINAL VIEWS OF LUTHER AND HIS PLACE IN THE HISTORY OF DOCTRINE

A. The Main Stages of the Development of Luther's Doctrinal Views.—The influence of Luther upon the doctrinal development of the Lutheran Church is so great that no one can understand the doctrines of the Lutheran Church without understanding him. To form a proper estimate of Luther's place and far-reaching influence in the History of Doctrine it is well, first of all, to recall the main stages of development by which God trained and prepared the chief instrument of the Reformation.

1. *When Luther entered the monastery* he had just finished his courses in humanistic studies and especially in philosophy taking the degree of Master of Arts in 1505, which was equivalent to our Doctor of Philosophy and gave him the right publicly to lecture on philosophy. He had received as good and thorough an education as the age afforded and was mentally and intellectually equipped for his great labors.

Luther possessed a deeply religious nature and a particularly delicate and sensitive conscience. His severe training in the home and in the school had made him so conscientious that he often held as a great sin that which was perfectly innocent. Few men have ever had deeper and more oppressive convictions of sinfulness than Luther and that not only after his entrance into the monastery, but before that and after that to the end of his life. Already as a student he felt himself a sinner in the sight of a holy God and he knew that as such he lay under the wrath of an offended judge. Neither did his daily devotions bring peace to his troubled conscience, nor did diligent reading of the Bible, of which he first saw a complete copy in the library of the University of Erfurt, afford him true light, for the Bible was still to him a book veiled by human traditions and notions.

Several fear-inspiring events increased his distress. After experiencing the shock of the death of a friend and shortly afterward being terrified in a violent thunderstorm he determined to give up the world and become a monk. As a faithful son of the medieval church with its doctrines, ceremonies and usages, he held that forgiveness of sins could be had only through the sacrament of penance, and the first part of that sacrament was contrition.

2. *He fled to the monastery* where, so he believed, he could best work out his own salvation by fastings, prayers, penances. Here he discharged all the duties that were required at his hands in deep sincerity. He meditated upon his sins; he made confession; he prayed; he called upon the Virgin Mary and upon all the saints; he watched; he fasted; he mortified his body; he tried hard to merit salvation. "If ever a monk got to heaven by monkery, I would have gotten there," he used to say afterwards. But neither his own works of strictest asceticism, nor the services of the priests and saints brought comfort to his soul. Luther held to the older conception of contrition as sorrow based on the love of God. But the more he prayed and the more he fasted the more he realized the insufficiency of his own contrition, feeling himself no nearer the pardon of God. With increasing power came to him the question, "How may I win a gracious God?" In the depth of his conflict he learned from Staupitz that repentance does not consist in separate acts but in love of righteousness and God. An old cloister brother held up to him the article of the Creed: "I believe in the forgiveness of sins," which means "that each one should believe that just his own sins are forgiven him." Then, amid much prayer and study of the Scriptures a new light, though dimly, began to break in upon his terror-stricken soul. A new understanding of the Scriptures then opened to him. He came to understand that forgiveness was to be won by trusting to God's promises. He saw that all his sins had been laid upon Christ, borne, expiated and blotted out by him. As he was reading Paul's Epistle to the Romans, one day at Wittenberg in 1508 or 1509, he came to the verse 1:17 "the just shall live by faith." After long reflection, he learned to understand in full and living knowledge that the righteousness of God, so often mentioned by Paul, is that which is imputed by God for Christ's sake to faith, that is, an absolutely free gift of God's grace. This central conviction made him as if altogether born anew rejoice in holy joy over the grace of God revealed in Christ. He believed and entered into peace. He knew that he had passed from death into life. This thorough religious experience has been denominated "the Reformation in Luther;" it was indispensable to the Reformation through Luther.

3. *Luther continued his study of theology* devoting himself to

Augustine, Mysticism, the later nominalistic Schoolmen, especially Occam, and above all the Scriptures.

In 1512 he took the Wittenberg doctor's oath "to defend with all his might the faith contained in the Scriptures." In his lectures on the Psalms, delivered 1513-1514, on Romans, 1515-1516, and on Galatians, 1516, Luther set forth and developed his new religious ideas of justifying faith. "With him the centre-point of Christianity was that conviction of justification by faith which he had learned from no teacher, but which was the priceless result of his own spiritual struggles. Whatever else was true or false, that stood fast. It was the key to unlock all mysteries, divine and human; whatever seemed to contradict it, could not rightfully command belief. Naturally Luther finds this principle and its corollaries everywhere in Scripture, not less in the Epistles of Paul, where he first learned it, than in the Psalms, which he proceeds to interpret in accordance with it" (Beard, *Martin Luther and the Reformation*, London, 1896, p. 191).

During this period we notice Luther's *study of the writings of Augustine* and the use which he made of this study. Through Augustine's works he learned that the doctrine of salvation as being entirely dependent on the grace of God, was based on Pauline authority. But following the teaching of Paul, Luther did not accept Augustine's conception of faith as merely a recognition of objective truth or historical fact, but defined it as the trusting of the heart in God's mercy through Christ Jesus.

Another influence that was powerful with Luther at this time, came from the German Mystics. At the end of 1515 or the beginning of 1516 he became acquainted with the sermons of Tauler and the so-called Frankfort Anonymous, the author of an old theological tract, to which Luther gave the name of *German Theology*, when he edited it in 1516, and in a complete form in 1518. In the preface to the German Theology he said that next to the Bible and Augustine he had not met with another book, from which he had learned so much concerning the nature of God, man, Christ, and every thing else. And writing to Spalatin he said that he knew of no sermons, which agreed more faithfully with the gospel than those of Tauler. From this enthusiastic verdict it must not be concluded that Tauler and the Frankfort Anonymous are identical in religious tone with Luther's teaching at every point of its development, or that "German Mysticism is the cradle of the Reformation." In the first place, Luther's doctrinal views were already fixed when he lectured on the Psalms and Romans. In the second place, the theology of the German Mystics was genuinely Catholic. Their piety was that of the medieval church. It consisted chiefly in flight from the world. And their pantheistic speculation, their mystic striving after complete annihilation of self before God because of his sublime superiority to all finite things found no acceptation in Luther's practical mind. We are not, as the Mystics held, to prostrate ourselves before the supreme Being in order to dissolve away into nothingness, but to allow God to humble us, break our old will, give us a new will thus enabling us to walk in the new sphere of life.

What so strongly attracted Luther to those Mystics was their deep religious inwardness over against the cold formulas of the Scholastics and the outward acts and ordinances of the papal system, particularly their deep view of man's spiritual existence, their stern judgment of sinful self-will, their earnest striving and wrestling after direct communion with God, their unconditional surrender to God in unrestricted humility and their absolute dependence on him. "Though they were not the first to teach him what God, Christ, man and all things were, he yet owed to them the clear insight into the apparent tangle of his own development and thereby liberation from the last scruples and doubts about the blessed knowledge that he could and must feel absolutely certain of his God. He did not by any means find this knowledge in a ready and complete form in these two old men of God. He had to arrive at and win it independently, but they indirectly helped him to succeed by making the unfolding of his own religious life clear to him" (Boehmer, *Luther in the Light of Recent Research,* p. 106 f.).

During these years Luther was still unconscious of the fact that there was some real opposition between what he was teaching and the theology of the papal church. Gradually he began to find that his conception of penitence, faith and righteousness was fundamentally different from that of Catholic theology. As early as 1510 he began to form a dislike for the Scholastic theology and Aristotelian philosophy. In 1516 he began to attack Scholasticism and objected to the study of Aristotle, "the destroyer of pious doctrine," "the constructor of words, the deluder of minds." On May 18, 1517, he could write to Johann Lange: "Our theology and St. Augustine flourish, and with God's help rule in our university. Aristotle is gradually descending from his throne, and will soon be overthrown, perhaps forever. The lectures on the Sententiarians are much despised and no one can count on an audience, if he does not lecture on this theology, i. e., on the Bible or Augustine, or some other genuine Father of the Church" (Enders, *Luthers Briefwechsel,* I. 106). On September 4, 1517, Luther published ninety-seven theses

Contra Scholasticam theologiam. From these we quote the following:

It is certain that man, having become an evil tree, can wish and do only that which is evil (4).

It is false to say that free will is able to decide for both sides; rather it must be said not to be a free but a captive will (5).

We do not become righteous by doing what is right, but when we have become righteous then we do what is right (40).

Nearly the whole of Aristotle's Moral Philosophy is in direct opposition to grace (41).

It is an error, that without Aristotle no one becomes a theologian (42).

Much rather, no one becomes a theologian but without Aristotle (44).

4. *Luther at once made practical application of his new idea of faith.* In 1516, in a sermon on indulgences, he assailed certain practical abuses of the church, and in the following year he began his work as a reformer when in his *Ninety-five Theses* he proposed to discuss the true meaning of indulgences. Even now Luther had no thought of breaking with Rome. He uttered no protest against indulgences as satisfaction or penances imposed by the church as outward signs of inward sorrow (see thesis 34). What he assailed were the ecclesiastical abuses of indulgences, of offering, selling and buying spiritual gifts. But a discussion of the true meaning of indulgences necessarily involved a discussion of the sacrament of penance and other doctrines such as purgatory, the office of the keys, the authority of the pope, the church, which made this baneful indulgence-traffic possible. Luther held that indulgence can never remit guilt (76); the pope himself cannot do it (5. 6). He can remit only such penalties as he himself has imposed (20). Repentance is true contrition (2. 3. 4). It has already received pardon from God and does not need indulgence (36. 37). Works of satisfaction are no longer necessary, and the purchase of indulgences is an optional matter and cannot be made obligatory (47). The whole life of believers should be repentance (1). The real and true treasury of merits is the most holy Gospel of the grace and glory of God (62).

In setting forth these views of true repentance Luther practically dissolved the sacrament of penance. True repentance is the penitent disposition of the heart manifesting itself in the daily life of the believer.

5. *The Leipzig-Disputation,* in 1519, led Luther to the conviction that the primacy of the pope is a human appointment and therefore not indispensable, that neither pope nor council are infallible and that the Scripture is the only authority in the church. These views were unfolded and followed to their conclusions in the tract *Of the Papacy at Rome,* 1520. Here, Luther set forth his own

concept of the church. It is the communion of saints. As such it is invisible and needs no bodily head. "The signs by which we can outwardly observe where this church is in the world are baptism, sacrament and the Gospel — not Rome, nor this or that place; for where baptism and the Gospel are, there let no one doubt that there are saints, even though they should be but children in the cradle." The authority of the pope extends only to the outward control of the church. "All bishops are, according to the divine appointment, alike." The Roman bishop is "by human appointment above the others in the external church."

6. During the last half of the year 1520, at a time when he was fully convinced that he had broken forever with Rome Luther published *three monumental works*: (a) In the *Address to the Christian Nobility of the German Nation on the Betterment of the Christian Estate* he scored the corruption of the hierarchical system, rejected the idea of a special priesthood, and committed to the laity, as spiritual priests, the reformation required by God but declined by the pope and the clergy.

(b) In the *Babylonian Captivity of the Church* he attacked the Roman doctrine of the sacraments. Luther meant by that captivity the bondage of the church through the medieval interpretation and multiplication of the sacraments. In the opening paragraph of this dogmatic polemical treatise he recognizes the advance he has made. He had hitherto held that indulgences should not be altogether rejected, "since they were approved by the common opinion of mankind . . . But later . . . I understood that they were nothing but wicked devices of the flatterers of Rome, alike destructive to men's faith and fortunes." In regard to the papacy he had recognized its human, though not its divine right, "but now I know and am sure that the papacy is the kingdom of Babylon and the power of Nimrod the mighty hunter."

Then follow his criticisms of the Roman sacramental system. Strictly speaking, baptism and the Eucharist alone are sacraments as being divinely instituted. Penance, in virtue of the promise attached to it, may be regarded as a sacrament. Private confession may be made to a lay brother. Concerning the Eucharist he rejected transubstantiation, the sacrifice of the mass and the withholding of the cup. *The opus operatum* is rejected, because sacraments without faith are of no benefit. Baptism brings justification only if joined with belief.

(c) The third monumental work was the tract *On the Liberty of a Christian Man*, "a very small book so far as the paper is concerned, but one containing the whole sum of the Christian life," as Luther himself said in his letter to Leo X. which he prefixed to this treatise. The little pamphlet begins with a paradox: "A Christian man is a free lord of all things, and subject to none. A Christian man is a dutiful servant of all things and subject to all." He is free through faith which acquires all that Christ has. He is a servant through love which serves Christ's brethren voluntarily from thankfulness to God. As a servant he does good works. But they are not the ground or the price of his salvation, but the fruit of his faith. "Good works do not make a good man, but a good man does good works." "We conclude, therefore, that a Christian does not live in himself, but in Christ and in his neighbor; in Christ through faith, in his neighbor through love. Through faith he rises above himself to God; through love he descends below himself to his neighbor, and yet remains always in God and in godlike love."

7. The year 1524 witnessed *Luther's break with Erasmus*. The latter had published his *De libero arbitrio*, On Free Will, in which he attacked Luther's Augustinian conception of the inability of the human will. In December, 1526, Luther replied to it with his *De servo arbitrio*, in which he maintained the bondage of the human will and asserted the free, absolute and unconditional will of God.

B. LUTHER'S DOCTRINAL VIEWS PRESENTED IN SYSTEMATIC ORDER.

It is customary to speak of the material and formal principle of the Reformation. By the first is meant Justification by faith alone, by the second, the normative authority of the Scriptures. Strictly speaking there is only one principle on which Luther plants himself, to wit, justifying faith as revealed in the Scriptures.

1. *Rule and Standard of Doctrine.* Regarding the Scriptures as the only infallible authority in matters of faith Luther rejected as unbiblical the Catholic doctrine of the sacraments and denied the infallibility of the pope and the councils and accepted the ancient dogmas, the ecumenical creeds and the decrees of the councils not on account of any authority inherent in themselves, but only because they repeated the old truths of the Scriptures. He regarded the Scriptures as the criterion and touchstone, by which all the teaching of the church must be attested as evangelical truth. "The Word of God shall establish articles of faith, and no one else, not even an angel" (*Smalc. Art.* 476*). The Scriptures are the infallible authority in matters of faith, because they are the testimony of the Holy Spirit. Luther does not present a theory of inspiration, but presupposes everywhere the fact of inspiration, that is to say, that

---

*In quoting from the Lutheran Confessions we use the text of the Concordia Triglotta. Quotations from the Erlangen-Frankfurter Gesamtausgabe of Luther's works are marked (E), those from the Weimar edition (W).

the Scriptures are inspired by the Holy Spirit. The two terms "the Scriptures" and "the Word of God" are, according to Luther, perfectly synonymous. He designates the Scriptures as "the Book given by God, the Holy Spirit, to his church" (E. 26. 100). In the preface to his Commentary on Genesis he calls this writing of Moses "Scripture, Scripture of the Holy Spirit," and in his lectures on Genesis he repeatedly denotes the Holy Spirit as the original author (*Urheber*) of this book. He says (*Smalc. art.* 497) that the Old Testament prophets were holy, "since the Holy Ghost spake through them." Doctrines that no reason can understand are "from heaven, revealed through the Gospel" (*ib.* 491; 477). The Scriptures at large he calls "the Spirit's own writing."

But Luther did not, like Occam and Biel, accept the Scriptures as authoritative and inspired on the authority of the church, but because the testimony of the Holy Spirit in the Scriptures bears testimony to the great truths of our salvation. Faith accepts and verifies them by inner experience. Luther was concerned primarily only with what "brings Christ." "This is the real touchstone by which all books are to be tested, when we see whether they treat of Christ or not, since all Scripture testifies of Christ (Rom. 3:21), and St. Paul will know nothing but Christ (1 Cor. 2:2). That which does not teach Christ, is not apostolic, even though it be taught by St. Peter or St. Paul; on the other hand, whatever preaches Christ would be apostolic, even if Judas, Haman, Pilate and Herod should do it" (E. 63. 157). Hence the different degrees of doctrinal value ascribed to the several books of the Bible, e. g., the Epistle of James is "a veritable epistle of straw" (*ib.* 115) compared with the Gospel of John, the Pauline Epistles, especially Romans, and First Peter, which are "the real kernel and marrow among all the books" (*ib.* 144).

2. *God.* We have noticed already that the pantheistic conception of the Mystics concerning the nature of God and the annihilation of self before the supreme Being has no place in Luther's theology. Nor would he accept any abstract, purely intellectual speculations as to what God is in and of himself, without taking into account his relation to the world and man. Luther was chiefly concerned about God in his relation to the sinner and his salvation. Man does not stand in need of philosophical proofs of God's existence; he carries the direct and certain proof of it within himself, in his own conscience. Accordingly in his teaching Luther starts from the divine and not from the human side of redemption, from God and not from man. From the outset Luther refers us for all our knowledge of God to the revelation of God's love in Christ. Already in the First Exposition of the Psalms he conceives of God as the

Supreme Good. God is good not only when he shows his mercy in preparing salvation for the sinful, but also when he displays his righteousness in acting upon those who are given over to destruction. In his *De servo arbitrio* he maintains that not man but God alone has a free will and that he ordains all things according to the counsel of his will (absolute predestination). Though the lost perish through the unconditioned will of God, this is right, because God wills it. But Luther does not enter upon the question of the origin of sin and evil. God's unsearchable judgments and mysterious ways are a matter of his secret will. It is futile, foolish, presumptuous and wicked to speculate concerning the secret will of God. Man's duty is simply to trust the word and be guided by the will of God as revealed in Christ. Luther emphasized predestination chiefly in combating the Pelagian and Semi-Pelagian doctrine of sin and free will and showed that man is absolutely impotent to choose his own salvation. The good and gracious will of God alone is the cause of our salvation. (*De serv. arb.* W. 18).

Luther regarded God in his relation to believers primarily as *holy love.* "Although the whole world with all diligence has endeavored to ascertain what God is, what He has in mind and does, yet has she never been able to attain to the knowledge and understanding of any of these things. But here (i. e., in our Christian faith) we have everything in richest measure, for here in all three articles He has Himself revealed and opend the deepest abyss of His paternal heart and of His pure unutterable love" (*Large Cat.* 695). According to Luther, love is not an attribute of God but a designation of his essence. To this identity of God and love Luther gives expression in the well-known words (*ad* I John 4:16) "God is himself love and his nature is nothing but pure love; so that if one were to paint God and get his likeness, he must paint such a picture as would be pure love representing the divine nature as the furnace and burning point of that love which fills heaven and earth; and again if one could paint and make a likeness of love he would have to make a picture as would be neither an inanimate work nor human, indeed neither angelic nor heavenly, but God himself" (E. 18. 313).

This concept of God is not based upon reasoning and speculation concerning God's being, for it "surpasses and exceeds the wisdom, mind, and reason of all men," and "we could never attain to the knowledge of the grace and favor of the Father except through the Lord Christ, who is a mirror of the paternal heart, outside of whom we see nothing but an angry and terrible Judge" (*L. C.* 695). Thus Luther conceived of God as almighty love and righteousness *revealed in Christ.* He looked into the heart of Christ and there found the heart of God.

By the revelation of his love God evokes trust in such love and return of love. But where there is no trust in God's love, but indifference and defiance, God cannot but punish persistent opposition to the revelation of his love and finally cut off from it the deliberate contemner, for God is *holy* love. While Luther thus has so much to say in praise of God's love, he likewise bears testimony to the wrath of God which is visited upon the sinner. The wrath of God is thus identical with the divine attribute of *righteousness*, according to which God is Himself righteous and punishes the wicked. "I the Lord, thy God, am a jealous God, visiting the iniquity of the fathers upon the children unto the third and fourth generation of them that hate me" (Ex. 20:5). The same Luther who describes God's love in words of praise and adoration also says that God "commands under penalty of eternal wrath" to honor and worship him as the only true God (*Large Cat.* 585) and that "the Divine Majesty with great earnestness insists upon the commandments, is angry with, and punishes those who despise them" (677) and that "God threatens to punish all that transgress these commandments; therefore we should dread His wrath" (543). The unbeliever remains under the wrath of God. The believer is no longer to think of God as a wrathful judge, for he knows that satisfaction has been rendered to the divine righteousness by the perfect obedience and suffering of Christ who took upon himself this very wrath of God against sin and transformed the wrathful judge into a merciful God (W. 40. 1; 47.21). The believer knows "that as far as we are concerned even God's works of wrath must be nothing but love," for their object is "the subjugation of our foes" and our "testing" (36. 427; 47. 21. 98).

This concept of God, whose holy love must necessarily be reaction against sin in every form, is altogether different from the Scholastic concept of a just and holy God who is supposed to regard a sin under certain circumstances as a venial sin, or to realize the fittingness of giving recompense to the man in response and proportionately to the good works performed by him even in a state of mortal sin.

God's holiness or justice and God's love or mercy are not two different characteristics of God as though he shows love or mercy to some, the elect, and holiness or justice to others, the reprobate (Calvin), but both taken together, *holiness and love* designate God's essence. The union of the supreme love and holiness demands on the part of man a union of the most heartfelt trust and the most reverential submission. Luther expresses this ethical relation to

God in the opening words of his explanation of each of the ten commandments: "We should fear and love (or trust in) God."

Explaining the first commandment Luther says (*Large Cat.* 581) "that it is the intent of this commandment to require true faith and trust of the heart which settles upon the only true God, and clings to him alone." There is, therefore, no room for intermediate advocates with God. To trust and believe in them is nothing but idolatry (*Smalc. Art.* 469). Luther realizing what, in his blindness, he had hitherto been practicing and doing under the papcy says: "If any one had toothache, he fasted and honored St. Appollonia; if he was afraid of fire, he chose St. Lawrence as his helper in need; if he dreaded pestilence, he made a vow to St. Sebastian or Rocchio, and a countless number of such abominations, where everyone selected his own saint, worshipped him and called for help to him in distress (*L. C.* 583).

3. *Christ.* Luther's Christology is briefly and comprehensively stated in his exposition of the second article of the Creed: "Jesus Christ is true God, born of the Father in eternity, and also true man, born of the Virgin Mary." The two natures are united in the person of Christ. This personal union was accomplished in the incarnation in such a way that "when Christ began to be man, He at the same time also began to be God" (E. 7. 185). Luther always insisted upon the inseparable union of the two natures. After the act of incarnation the person is always "God and man,— the inseparable person formed of God and man" (W. 36. 60; 40. 2). In his attempt to define the two natures in the divine-human person of Christ Luther was not guided by mere speculation on the subject. With him the perfect unity of the life of Christ was a matter which deeply concerned his faith in the Redeemer. Says the Formula of Concord quoting Luther: "If I believe this, that only the human nature has suffered for me, then Christ is to me a poor Savior, then He Himself indeed needs a Savior" (1029). "There are not in Christ two separate persons, but only one person; wherever it is, there it is the one undivided person; and wherever you can say, Here is God, there you must also say, Then Christ the man is also here" (1045; see also W. 20. 603; 40. 1; 43. 580). Luther sang:

> He whom the world could not inclose
> Doth in Mary's lap repose,
> He is become an infant small
> Who by His might upholdeth all.

After the controversy with Carlstadt and the Sacramentarians Luther further developed his ideas regarding the mutual relations of the two natures as united in the person of Christ.

4. *The Work of Christ.* Luther did not, like Calvin and the
Reformed theologians, as also the older Lutheran dogmaticians,
arrange the work of Christ under the three offices, priestly, prophetic, kingly. In describing the work of Christ he emphasized
neither Christ's teaching, nor his miracles, nor his example, but he
did emphasize the very heart of the Christian message, to wit: the
sacrifice which Christ made in our place. Christ's subsitutionary,
sacrificial death is the essential element in Luther's ideas of reconciliation, propitiation, redemption and salvation. Luther stresses
particularly the vicarious suffering and death of the innocent for
the guilty. Christ "has redeemed me a lost and condemned creature
with His holy precious blood and with His innocent suffering and
death" (*Sm. Cat.* 545). It was the eternal wrath of God, merited by
our sins, which Christ endured. By rendering satisfaction in our
stead through his fulfillment of the law and through the endurance
of its penalties he effected the sinner's atonement with his offended
God. But Christ's mediatorial work embraces not only his entire
obedience but also his glorious resurrection and ascension. Christ's
resurrection is the divine evidence that his death was the means of
our reconciliation with God. After his going to the Father he
exercises his unlimited power from on high for the salvation of the
world.

The doctrine of vicarious satisfaction does not, as is often
objected, obscure the ethical features of atonement. Just the opposite is true. Christ's redemption has established a new relation
between God and man. It expresses itself first of all in the remission
of sins which man appropriates by faith. Thus the Christ for us
becomes the Christ in us, as Paul says "I live; yet not I ,but Christ
liveth in me; and the life which I now live in the flesh I live by the
faith of the Son of God, who loved me, and gave himself for me"
(*Gal.* 2:20). This change in the heart of man is not the ground but
the result of Christ's redemption. He "has redeemed me with His
precious blood and with His innocent suffering and death, in order
that I may be His own, and live under Him in His kingdom, and
serve Him in everlasting righteousness, innocence and blessedness"
(*Sm. Cat.* 545).

5. *Man.* Concerning the original state of man Luther maintained that God created man in the possession of perfect righteousness and holiness, qualities which together with immortality belonged to his original nature. Original righteousness is therefore
not a superadded gift, as the Scholastics taught, but the natural
perfection of man. In his original state man was positively good
and free. Man's freedom was not a mere formal freedom, a power
of contrary choice, as the Scholastics held, but real freedom, a

determination and inclination to goodness. Man had the right will, entirely pure morally, and entirely devoted to love of God and fellowmen, as Luther shows in his *Exposition of Genesis,* 1:26, 27. Man's freedom, however, was concreated and therefore relative, a freedom of endowment and not yet one of attainment by self-determination. Hence Luther calls man's innocence a "childish innocence" (*ib.* 2:17). Whether Adam should become absolutely free, like God and the holy angels, depended upon the use, which he should make of his freedom during the period of probation (*ib.* 1:26).

Adam's fall resulted in the loss of his original righteousness, and the corruption of human nature which is propagated in the race. "Sin originated and entered the world from one man Adam, by whose disobedience all men were made sinners and subject to death and the devil. This is called original or capital sin" (*Smalc. Art.* 477). Original sin is, therefore, not merely a lack of original righteousness, as the Schoolmen defined it, but the inward alienation of the entire man from God, the corruption of the will, so that man refuses to trust the mercy of God, does not fear him, but setting aside His word and will, obeys the impulses of the flesh; it is the tendency of the will toward self and away from, or against, God. Its essence consists above all in unbelief as the real chief sin, and cause of all sin and crime. Original sin is the root of all actual sins; it is "so deep and horrible a corruption of nature that no reason can understand it, but it must be learned and believed from the revelation of Scriptures" (*Smalc. Art.* 477).

Since original sin involves the total corruption of human nature and the spiritual death of the natural man, it follows that nothing but sin can proceed from the total corruption of the natural man and that the natural man has no power to will, or to work out his own salvation, as Luther says in his explanation of the third article of the Creed: "I believe that I cannot by my own reason or strength believe in Jesus Christ, my Lord, or come to Him; but the Holy Ghost has called me by the Gospel, enlightened me with His gifts, sanctified and kept me in the faith." Not even the power of choice can be conceded the unregenerate man, for then he would have a free will capable of inclining to good or evil, as he may elect. This impotence of the natural will, usually styled "the bondage of the will," is the consequence of the natural depravity of man; hence free will can never be predicated of man, i. e., of the unregenerate man and only in his relation to God and spiritual things (W. 2. 247, 370; 7. 146). Human cooperation in salvation, or synergism, is therefore wholly excluded. Man has, as Luther put it, only *capacitas passiva.* But though merely the passive subject of conversion man has not lost his identity as a rational being. The Formula of Concord (915) explains what Luther means by *capacitas passiva*: "When Luther says that with respect to his conversion man is purely passive, that is, does nothing whatever toward it, but only suffers what God works in him, his meaning is not that conversion takes place without the preaching and hearing of God's Word; nor is this his meaning that in conversion no new emotion whatever is awakened in us by the Holy Ghost and no spiritual operation begun; but he means that man of himself, or from his natural powers, cannot do anything or help towards his conversion, and that conversion is not only in part, but altogether an operation, gift and present, and work of the Holy Ghost alone".

6. *Justification effected by Faith.* The fundamental question with Luther was, How do I find a gracious God? Upon what rests my confidence that I am righteous before him, that is, pleasing and acceptable to him? Luther and the Lutheran Confessions answer with one accord: Nothing whatever in man but only God's grace in Christ Jesus is the true ground of our salvation (45; 53; 461; 795; 927). Luther derived his concept of justification immediately from the Scriptures, but defined it at first in the sense and words of Augustine and Scholastic tradition. He distinguished between the infusion of grace, *iustificatio,* and the forgiveness of sin and imputation of Christ's righteousness to the believer, *imputatio* (*Comm. ad Gal.* 1. 14, 16; E. 3. 435). The infusion of grace is not a momentary act but a process of purification for the extirpation of concupiscence, a making over of the sinful man to a righteous one. In his later theology, the Christ working effectually in us takes the place of the infused grace (E. 19. 109; 12. 285). Luther no longer understands by grace a "quality" introduced into the soul of man, as the Scholastics taught, but God's "clemency or favor which he bears towards us." It is through grace that our sins are forgiven and Christ's righteousness imputed. Thus Luther places the righteous-making in the forgiveness and imputation. For Christ's sake God regards the sinner as righteous (*Comm. in Gal.* 1. 195). "God will and does account us entirely righteous and holy for the sake of Christ, our Mediator. And although sin in the flesh has not yet been altogether removed or become dead, yet He will not punish or remember it" (*Smalc. Art.* 499). With this righteousness salvation and every blessing are imparted to the believer, "for where there is forgiveness of sins, there is also life and salvation" (*Small Cat.* 557).

This justification is God's work; it is a justification "without us." It comes to pass through faith alone wrought by the Holy Spirit in that he reveals to man God's love in Christ (E. 7. 164). Faith receives and accepts the righteousness which God gives. Faith is a "certain sure confidence of the heart and firm assent, by which Christ is apprehended" (*in Gal.* 1.191). Wherever faith lays hold upon Christ, the believer becomes one with him. On account of the union of the believer with Christ, God imputes to the believer the righteousness which Christ has secured for him. This righteousness is, properly speaking, not to be obtained through our faith in itself, but because Christ constitutes the substance and power of our faith. "It is not our righteousness, but Christ's — in fact, this righteousness is Christ himself, and yet becomes my righteousness if I believe" (E. 3. 435; 7. 178). This righteousness apprehended by faith — and not a feeling or experience of divine grace — is the sure foundation upon which rest the consolation of the believing conscience and the certainty of salvation.

The doctrine of justification is the *articulus stantis et cadentis ecclesiae,* the article by which the church stands or falls, "of which nothing can be yielded or surrendered," for "upon this article all things depend which we teach and practice in opposition to the Pope, the devil and the whole world" (*Smalc. Art.* 461 f.).

Justifying faith is a new relation of man to God. "By faith we acquire a new and clean heart" (*ib.* 499). It is living faith and gives real life and constancy to moral earnestness and joyousness. The living energy of faith manifests itself in good works. Says Luther in the Preface to St. Paul's Epistle to the Romans: "Faith is a divine work in us, that changes us and regenerates us of God, and puts to death the old Adam, makes us entirely different men in heart, spirit, mind, and all powers, and brings with it the Holy Ghost. Oh, it is a living, busy, active, powerful thing that we have in faith, so that it is impossible for it not to do good without ceasing. Nor does it ask whether good works are to be done; but before the question is asked, it has wrought them, and is always engaged in doing them . . . man becomes ready and cheerful, without coercion, to do good to every one, to serve every one, and to suffer everything for love and praise to God, who has conferred this grace on him, so that it is impossible to separate works from faith, yea, just as impossible as it is for heat and light to be separated from fire" (quoted from *Form. of Conc.* 941). "Such faith, renewal, and forgiveness of sins is followed by good works. And what there is still sinful or imperfect also in them shall not be accounted as sin or defect, even for Christ's sake; but the entire man, both as to his person and his works is to be called and to be righteous and holy from pure grace and mercy, shed upon us and spread over us in

Christ" (*Smalc. Art.* 499). A regenerate man does not become such by his good works, but being born again in Christ, he brings forth the fruits of goodness. Accordingly only the works that proceed from true and living faith are good works. Moreover, only such works are good as God has commanded in his word and law. Says Luther in the Conclusion of the Ten Commandments (L. Cat. 669 f.): "Thus we have the Ten Commandments, a compend of divine doctrine, as to what we are to do in order that our whole life may be pleasing to God, and the true fountain and channel from and in which everything must arise and flow that is to be a good work, so that outside of the Ten Commandments no work or thing can be good or pleasing to God, however great or precious it be in the eyes of the world."

In contrast with the self-chosen holiness and worship, self-imposed imaginary duties and false monastic ideals of Rome Luther stressed the value of life's vocation in family, state and human society. The works of the believer are truly good in any secular calling ordered of God (Smalc. Art. 501). The Table of Duties in Luther's Small Catechism (561) points in the same direction. It consists of certain passages of Scripture for "various holy orders and stations" and the various holy orders and stations are, besides bishops, pastors and teachers, "civil government, husbands and wives, parents and children, servants, masters and mistresses, young persons and widows."

In the present life regeneration and renewal are not complete, but only begun. Perfection is the ideal after which the believer must aim though its perfect attainment is not possible in the earthly life. In opposition to the Catholic error that the righteous can perfectly keep the commandments of God and fulfill them, Luther maintained that there is no complete instantaneous perfection and ceasing from sin in this life. (E. 14. 52; 27. 188).

7. The Holy Spirit works justifying faith in man through *the means of grace*, for only through the Word and sacrament does the Spirit come to us (E. 29. 208; 9. 210). The Schoolmen following Augustine located the divine efficacy not in the Word but in the sacraments; justifying grace is brought to man through the sacraments. Luther emphasized especially the Word as the vehicle of grace. Over against the "Schwarmer" or Enthusiasts, such as the Zwickau Prophets, Carlstadt, Muenzer and others, who rejected the objective reality of the means of grace and believed that through mystic contemplation and asceticism they were able to enter into direct communion with the Holy Spirit, Luther upheld the objective nature of the Word and sacrament and maintained that the Holy

Spirit speaks only through the Word of God. "In those things which concern the spoken, outward Word, we must firmly hold that God grants His Spirit or grace to no one, except through or with the preceding outward Word, in order that we may thus be protected against the enthusiasts, i. e., spirits who boast that they have the Spirit without and before the Word, and accordingly judge Scripture or the spoken Word, and explain and stretch it at their pleasure, as Muenzer did, and many still do at the present day who wish to be' acute judges between the spirit and the letter, and yet know not what they say or declare" (*Smalc. Art.* 495).

The *Word as a means of grace* produces repentance or conversion. To repentance are ascribed two parts, namely, contrition, sorrow or terror on account of sin, and faith that sins are forgiven and grace is obtained through Christ. The Word as commanding what man should do and leave undone, giving knowledge of sin, threatening temporal and eternal punishment and leading him to contrition is designated as *Law*. Everything that reproves sin is, and belongs to, the preaching of the Law (*ib.*, 479). Even the suffering and death of Christ is a terrible declaration of God's wrath against sin (E. 13. 116).

Contrition is not sufficient for true and salutary conversion to God if faith in Christ be not added. Contrition alone leads into despair. "Therefore, to a true and salutary repentance the preaching of the Law is not sufficient but the Gospel should be added thereto" (E. 12. 372). The Word as offering the grace of God in Christ Jesus is designated as *Gospel*. "The consolatory promise of grace through the Gospel must be believed, as Christ declares, Mark 1:15: Repent and believe the Gospel, i. e., become different and do otherwise, and believe my promise" (*Smalc. Art.* 481).

Through the entire life the converted sinner needs the preaching of both the Law and the Gospel. "In Christians this repentance continues until death, because through the entire life it contends with sin remaining in the flesh" (*ib.* 489). Both Law and Gospel must always be preached in the church, but both must also be retained unmixed. "As Dr. Luther has urged this distinction, with special diligence in nearly all his writings, and has properly shown that the knowledge of God derived from the Gospel is far different from that which is taught and learned from the Law" (*Form. of Conc.* 959). "The doctrine of the Law makes no Christian, for the wrath and displeasure of God abide upon us still, because we cannot keep what God demands of us; but . . . the doctrine of faith brings pure grace, and makes us godly and acceptable to God, because here we see that God gives Himself entire to us, with all that he has and is able to do" (*L. Cat.* 697). The Law is that which shows what we must do; the Gospel, where we are to get the power to do it. The Law indicates the disease, the Gospel the remedy. In his Commentary on Galatians Luther says that whoever can properly distinguish from each other the Law and the Gospel deserves to be called a theologian.

In defining the nature of a *sacrament* Luther adopted the Augustinian formula that a sacrament is a visible form of invisible grace. Sacraments are therefore not merely marks of profession (Zwingli), but vehicles of grace which they figure to the senses (Augustine). In other words, the sacraments bring to the believer that which they outwardly signify. At a later period Luther held that through the sacrament also the unbeliever receives something. The power and efficacy of the sacraments depend solely upon God's appointment and promise. Neither unbelief in the recipient, nor unworthiness in the administrant can make the sacraments inoperative. The saving effect of the sacraments, however, is conditioned upon the faith of him who receives them.

8. *Baptism,* instituted by Christ himself, is necessary to salvation, Mark 16:16 (*ib.* 579). "Baptism is no trifle, but instituted by God Himself, . . . it is most solemnly commanded that we must be baptized or we cannot be saved" (*L. Cat.* 733). The sacramental union of the water with the Word makes baptism a means of grace. Luther called baptism as comprehended in God's command and connected with God's Word "a divine water;" "not that the water in itself is nobler than other water, but that God's Word and command are added" (735). Baptism is God's means by which we are received "into the kingdom of Christ, . . . the Sacrament by which we are first received into the Christian Church" (749).

Baptism works forgiveness of sins, i. e., it removes the guilt of all sin, actual and original, although the material of original sin, that is, concupiscence, remains (W. 2. 728). Together with the forgiveness of sins man receives through baptism the Holy Spirit who begins the sanctifying work in man (*ib.* 730). Thus baptism creates a relation of fellowship of God with man. This new relation is designated as the new birth, or regeneration; hence baptism is called "the washing of regeneration and renewing of the Holy Ghost," Tit. 3:5 (*Small Cat.* 551).

Baptism is truly a means of grace whether man believes or not. For man's faith does not make a sacrament nor does his unbelief unmake it. "My faith does not make baptism but receives it" (*L. Cat.* 745). The beneficial effect of baptism, however, is dependent upon faith which appropriates baptismal grace. "Faith alone makes the person worthy to receive profitably the saving, divine water" (741). "Without faith it profits nothing, notwithstanding it is in itself a divine superabundant treasure" (739).

Baptism seals the covenant relation which God establishes with us, and God's covenant remains forever; it remains even if a person receives baptism without faith, or if after baptism he falls from faith, "for God's ordinance and Word cannot be made variable or be altered by men" (747), "for gold is not the less gold though a harlot wear it in sin and shame" (*ib.*). If such a one comes to faith he is not to be baptized again, but he simply returns in true repentance to the covenant relation once and forever established in baptism. "Our baptism abides forever; even though some one should fall from it and sin, nevertheless we always have access thereto, that we may again subdue the old man. But we need not again be sprinkled with water" (751).

The effect of baptism must last throughout the entire life. The effect is twofold: baptism is a never-failing fountain (1) of power and encouragement for the daily conflict with sin, and (2) of consolation and strength for the daily renewal of the spiritual life. Answering the question: What does such baptizing with water signify? Luther says in his Small Catechism: "The old Adam in us should, by daily contrition and repentance, be drowned and die with all sins and evil lusts, and again a new man daily come forth and arise, who shall live before God in righteousness and purity forever" (551); and in the Large Catechism: "These two parts, to be sunk under the water and drawn out again, signify the power and operation of Baptism, which is nothing else than putting to death the old Adam, and after that the resurrection of the new man, both of which must take place in us all our lives, so that a truly Christian life is nothing else than a daily baptism, once begun and ever to be continued" (749).

Repentance, therefore, is not a new sacrament, a second plank grasped by a shipwrecked man after the ship of baptism is broken, as the Schoolmen taught, "for the ship never breaks, because it is the ordinance of God, and not a work of ours; but it happens, indeed, that we slip and fall out of the ship. Yet if any one fall out, let him see to it that he swim up and cling to it till he again come into it and live in it, as he had formerly begun" (751). "Here you see that Baptism, both in its power and signification, comprehends also the third Sacrament, which has been called repentance, as it is really nothing else than Baptism. For what else is repentance but an earnest attack upon the old man and entering upon a new life? Therefore, if you live in repentance, you walk in Baptism, which not only signifies such a new life, but also produces, begins and exercises it" (*ib.*).

In opposition to the Anabaptists who laid the emphasis in the sacrament upon their own act as against the act of God and saw in baptism nothing but a sign that the new birth has already taken place, and consequently rejected infant baptism, Luther maintained the right and necessity of infant baptism. Children are to be baptized as well as adults, for baptism is necessary to salvation. The promise of salvation belongs not alone to the old, but also to little children, "for they belong to the promised redemption made through Christ, and the Church should administer it [Baptism and the announcement of that promise] to them" (*Smalc. Art.* 493).

As to the question, Can little children believe? Luther advises the simple to dismiss this question from their minds and refer it to the learned. If, however, one wishes to answer, one should point to the fact that infant baptism is pleasing to God, because he has given the Holy Ghost to many who were baptized in infancy. To deny this is to maintain that the Christian church, the communion of saints, has ceased to exist (*L. Cat.* 743). Luther ascribed to the infant a receptivity or faith of its own, which faith the Holy Spirit effects in response to the prayers of the sponsors and parents. But the necessity of infant baptism is not dependent on the faith of the infant but solely upon the command of God. "We bring the child in the conviction and hope that it believes, and we pray that God may grant it faith; but we do not baptize it upon that, but solely upon the command of God" (747).

9. *Lord's Supper.* Like baptism, the Lord's Supper is a sacrament only on account of the words by which Christ has instituted it (753). "Upon these words rest all our foundation, protection and defense against all errors and deception that have ever come or may yet come" (757). "It is the Word which makes and distinguishes this Sacrament, so that it is not mere bread and wine, but is, and is called, the body and blood of Christ" (755).

From the beginning of his activity to the end of his life, Luther held to the *real presence* of Christ's body and blood in the Supper and regarded its denial as a Hussite heresy (W. 6. 80). In his *Sermon von dem hochwuerdigen Sakrament,* 1519, he describes the real presence of the body of Christ in the bread in terms of transubstantiation: "The bread is changed into his true natural body, and the wine into his natural true blood" (W. 2. 749). But since 1520 he rejected transubstantiation and adopted the view of the later Scholastics, particularly Occam, that the substance of the elements remains and with them the body and blood of Christ are at the same time given. "In the Sacrament it is not necessary to the presence of the real body and real blood that the bread and wine should be transubstantiated,. so that Christ may be contained beneath the accidents; but while both bread and wine continue there, it can be said with truth 'this bread is my body; this wine is my blood,' and conversely" (*de capt. Babyl.* W. 6. 508 f.). Nor does the real presence consist in a local or physical inclusion in the elements as though the body and blood of Christ were locally enclosed in the bread and wine, or combined in their essence, or mingled together (impanation, subpanation, or consubstantiation). It is true, in describing the real presence Luther uses in the Small Catechism the phrase "under the bread and wine" (555); in the Large Catechism, "in and under" (755); Melanchthon, in the Apology, says "with" (247); the Formula of Concord uses all three prepositions together (983). But thereby Luther and the Lutheran Confessions do not imply a local conjunction or presence, or commingling of Christ's body with the elements into one substance, but designate an intimate sacramental union of the body and blood of Christ with the visible elements, i. e., an illocal, supernatural union, and confined to sacramental action or actual use, the heavenly gift and the earthly element each retaining its own substance.

In the controversy upon the Lord's Supper Luther explained the ubiquity on the ground of the personal union of the two natures. The two natures are one single person. Wherever Christ is there he is entire. Luther also distinguished between a ubiquitous and sacramental presence. Christ is everywhere, but we can really find and apprehend him where he by his words binds himself to the bread for the reception of the communicant (E. 29. 338; 30. 67 f.).

In order to receive the blessing, which the body and blood of Christ bring, the spiritual eating must accompany the bodily eating; for it is faith alone that apprehends life and salvation in the present body of Christ (*L. Cat.* 761). Believers receive the body and blood of Christ as a pledge and assurance that their sins are surely forgiven. "What is the benefit of such eating and drinking? That is shown us in these words: Given, and shed for you, for the remission of sins; namely, that in the Sacrament forgiveness of sins, life and salvation are given us through these words. For where there is forgiveness of sins, there is also life and salvation" (*Sm. Cat.* 557). Therefore Luther calls this sacrament "a food of souls which nourishes and strengthens the new man," as distinguished from "Baptism by which we are first borne anew" (757).

10. *The Church.* The Word of God is proclaimed and the sacraments are administered only in the church. Hence Luther said:

"Whoever would find Christ, must first of all find the church; . . . for outside of the Christian church is no truth, no Christ, no salvation" (*L. Cat.* 693). This church is not an outward organization, but "a congregation of saints," or "an assemblage of all Christian believers on earth." There has always been and always will be a true church, a communion of saints (*ib.* 691), so called as sanctified by the Holy Spirit in the Word of God and true faith. For the same reason the church is called holy. The saints, one in faith, and they only, are the one true church, spread throughout the Christendom of all times and ages. The church in this sense is an object of faith, and the term "church" used in this sense has no plural form. "I believe that there is upon earth a little holy group and congregation of pure saints, under one head, even Christ, called together by the Holy Ghost in one faith, one mind and understanding, with manifold gifts, yet agreeing in love, without sects or schisms" (*ib.*). Since this one true church embraces all believers everywhere it is called catholic. In order to express the universality of the church Luther retained the term, already used before his time, "Christian" church instead of "catholic," for "throughout the whole world where there are Christians there is the church" (E. 23. 281).

11. *The Ministry.* Since the preaching of the Word and the administration of the sacraments are absolutely essential for the existence of the church, a ministry of the gospel is necessary. Therefore the church must appoint and ordain suitable persons to this office (*Smalc. Art.* 497; 523). To the church itself, and to no class in the church, is given the peculiar power and authority to preach the gospel, remit and retain sins, and administer the sacraments. Hence the church itself calls and ordains those who shall exercise this ministry for it (*Smalc. Art.* 511). In case of necessity, as in the absence of a regularly called minister, "even a layman absolves, and becomes the minister and pastor of another," for he is part of the true church which has the authority to administer the Gospel (522).

The ministry, then, is an office, *ministerium ecclesiasticum*, and not a divinely privileged rank or order of men according to which the bishops of today are the direct successors of the apostles. There is parity of all ministers of the Gospel. According to the needs and circumstances there are diversities of ministration, but all distinctions of rank among the ministers of the Gospel are of human origin. Even the pope who "claims for himself that by divine right he is supreme above all bishops and pastors in all Christendom" (503), "is only the bishop and pastor of the Church at Rome" (471). The papacy was not instituted by God; it is "a human figment, . . . it exercises no Christian office, and therefore it is necessary for the Church to continue and to exist without the Pope" (473).

In the Smalcald Articles both Luther (*Art. IV. Of the Papacy*) and Melanchthon in his Tract (*Of the Power and Primacy of the Pope*) oppose and denounce the pope as "the Antichrist, who has exalted himself above, and opposed himself against Christ, because he will not permit Christians to be saved without his power, . . and condemns, murders, and tortures all Christians who do not exalt and honor these abominations of the Pope above all things" (475).

12. *Ecclesiastical Rites and Usages.* The spirit of historic conservatism is a marked characteristic of Luther's reformatory work as distinguished from that of the Swiss Reformers. It is particularly noticeable in Luther's liturgical reforms. He retained, to a large extent, the eccleisastical year with its set lessons and festivals. The festivals of the saints, of course, suffered some eclipse and gradually disappeared. "For when advantage and assistance, both bodily and spiritual, are no more to be expected, the worship of the saints will soon vanish" (469). In reconstructing the ancient liturgy for use in the church Luther rejected only what he deemed false and barren in the mother church, and adopted and developed what was true, fruitful and edifying, and molded it into forms which in style were already familiar to the people. His appreciation of the value of the set forms and ceremonies led him to retain many of the prayers and hymns of the medieval church along with new provisions of his own. It was not new forms but a new spirit which Luther gave to his church. The conception and spirit of the Roman liturgy excluded the people from active participation in the service, the sacrifice of the mass being performed for the people, but not through the people, nor even necessarily in their presence. According to Luther the service is constituted through the activity of the believing subject. The congregational *Confiteor* and *Credo*, and congregational singing as introduced by Luther, both symbolize and realize the principle of the direct access of the believer to God. That these acts of worship together with the preaching of the Word should be in the vernacular was a matter of course. In the *German Mass and Order of Divine Service*, 1526, Luther set forth the principles of Lutheran worship which furnished the model for Lutheran communities. There is, however, no authoritative form of liturgy for the whole church. The forms and expressions of worship are not essential. The one thing essential is living faith, and the forms of worship have their value only in defining, inculcating and directing this faith.

What is true concerning the observance of rites and usages in general is true in regard to the observance of the Lord's Day in particular. Luther maintained that the Mosaic Law is a permanent requirement valid for all times in so far as it coincides with inborn natural right. Since the Sabbath has no natural law, being appointed by Moses beyond the natural law, it is done away with and therefore not a law binding on Christians. In the Small Catechism Luther does not speak of a prescribed day at all, giving the third commandment in this form, literally translated: "Thou shalt sanctify the day of rest" or "holy day" (*Feiertag*), and according to his own interpretation, the essential thing in this commandment is not a special day of the week, but only the hearing of the Word of God (541).

From the fact that Luther teaches that the Jewish Sabbath is abolished it must not be inferred that the third commandment is done away with. Says he in his Large Catechism: "To grasp a Christian meaning for the simple as to what God requires in this commandment, note that we keep holy days not for the sake of intelligent and learned Christians (for they have no need of it), but first of all for bodily causes and necessities which nature teaches and requires, for the common people, man-servants, and maid-servants, who have been attending to their work and trade the whole week, that for a day they may retire in order to rest and be refreshed. Secondly, and most especially, that on such day of rest (since we can get no other opportunity) freedom and time to be taken to attend divine service, so that we come together to hear and treat of God's Word, and then to praise God, to sing and pray. However, this, I say, is not so restricted to any time, as with the Jews, that it must be just on this or that day; for in itself no one day is better than another; but this should indeed be done daily; however, since the masses cannot give such attendance, there must be at least one day in the week set apart. But since from of old Sunday (the Lord's Day) has been appointed for this purpose, we also should continue the same in order that everything be done in harmonious order and no one create disorder by unnecessary innovations" (693f.).

13. *Relation of Civil Government to the Church.* The "secular power" or "civil government" exists in accordance with the divine ordinance (E. 22. 63). Accordingly obedience to civil authority and to the laws of the land is a religious duty (*Von weltl. Obrigkeit,* W. 11. 245-281). The laws of the secular power do not extend over the souls of men, but only over the body and property and that which is outward in the world (E. 22. 82. 83. 86). Hence it lies not within the province of civil government to exercise any compulsion in matters of faith. It is the office of the bishops to

guard against false doctrine and heresy (*ib.* 90). The civil authorities, however, are to allow and secure in their countries and cities the free preaching of the Word (*ib.* 49; 39. 244, 250). The prince should tolerate in his realm only the One Church of the pure Word (23.5 ff.; 26. 103). Effective measures should be taken against false teachers (39. 250 ff.; 43. 313), yet Luther nowhere sanctioned the use of the sword against heretics. When he advised the use of the sword against the Anabaptist insurrectionists he did so not because of their false teaching, but because of their open and active opposition to civil authority (E. 16. 259 f.; 26. 256).

14. *Eschatology.* There was little occasion for Luther to treat in detail of the last things, that is, the state after death, the completion and perfection of the kingdom of God. He plainly states the Biblical teaching of Christ's return, the resurrection of all the dead, eternal life for the godly in heaven, and eternal punishment for the wicked in hell. He rejected therefore the doctrine of the Anabaptistic chiliasts as to an earthly kingdom which Christ is to establish with his saints before the day of judgment, and likewise their error of the restoration of all things (E. 11. 85; 45. 110 ff.). He also expressly rejected the Roman error of purgatory, "for it conflicts with the chief article which teaches that only Christ, and not the works of men, art to help set free souls" (*Smalc. Art.* 465). The application *ex opere operato* of the mass on behalf of the dead, prayer for the dead, "all this may be safely omitted, even if it were no error and idolatry" since nothing has been divinely commanded or enjoined upon us concerning the dead (*ib.*).

CHAPTER XVIII

ZWINGLI'S REFORMATORY IDEAS AND HIS PLACE IN THE HISTORY OF DOCTRINE

A. ZWINGLI'S REFORMATORY IDEAS.— Almost contemporaneous with, but rather independent of, the Lutheran movement in Germany was the Zwinglian reformation in Switzerland. In his reformatory work Luther went on from one degree of clearness to another. When Zwingli began the reformation, his religious consciousness had come to definite results in every direction.

Without passing through any such deep religious experiences and spiritual struggles as Luther, Zwingli (1484-1531) came forth from his humanistic culture and scientific study of the Scriptures and entered upon his reformatory work. From Erasmus he had learned that the source of doctrine is the Bible and not the church. In his teaching and reformatory efforts he laid the emphasis upon the authority and sufficiency of the Bible. It is the revelation of God's will to us (I. 54)*. "It is perfect in itself, and revealed for the welfare of man" (68). Through it the Holy Spirit teaches us "all that we should know of God" (176).

Was Zwingli dependent on Luther? Zwingli boasts that he had started the reformation in Switzerland independently of Luther. Says Dr. Seeberg: "Zwingli's dependence upon Luther may without hesitation be asserted as a settled historical fact . . . the study of the Scriptures was and remained for him the source of his doctrinal views; and he found Luther's ideas in the Scriptures — after he had learned them from Luther" (*Hist. of Doctr.* II. 308).

Zwingli agreed with Luther that in *the state of integrity* man was in the possession of perfect righteousness and holiness, but differed from Luther in that he maintained that we were "made in the image of God in our minds and souls, not in our bodies, whence it would follow that God must also have a body" which would mean that "God is a compound and that the parts might be separated, all of which is opposed to the immutability of the divine nature" (I. 56). We also notice the low estimate which Zwingli places upon man's physical body. In man there are conjoined two completely diverse natures: "the soul was deposited into the clay

---

* We quote from Zwingli's Werke, ed. Schuler u. Schulthess, VIII vols., 1828-1842.

of the body; the body was prepared out of clay to be the dwelling place of the soul. But neither part can deny its nature. The spirit loves truth and worships the Godhead; the body likewise is drawn toward its origin, the clay and the flesh, and follows their nature." He also assumed the possibility of sinning among the endowments of man's moral nature in his primitive state (IV. 138 ff.). *Original sin*, Zwingli held, is the infirmity and defect which one derives from birth without his own fault, and therefore involves no guilt. Infants without exception, dying before they have committed actual sin, are admitted to the kingdom of heaven (II. 287; III. 203 f.). From original sin grows actual sin which is disobedience toward God. Sin has so "shattered" man's nature that he is unable to free himself from sin and guilt (I. 184).

Christ is our deliverer. By his innocent suffering Christ made payment to the divine justice for all our sins both original and actual, became a sacrifice for us and thus delivered us, bought us and reconciled us with God. Consequently there is no need of the sacrifice of the mass, or of any human mediators, such as priests or saints. Christ is our teacher. He revealed to us the will of God. We are to follow him, for he is our leader and exemplar. Christ is our head. We are the members, who came to God by faith through the righteousness of the head.

Faith is confidence in God's grace. It is wrought by the Holy Spirit who is directly operating and makes man's heart feel the Word of God to be true (I. 79, 81). "Christian faith is something which is felt in the soul of the believer, as health in the body" (III. 198). Faith is followed by good works. Since the Holy Spirit works them in the believer the standard of good works is not the law but the example of Christ (I. 212-214). Thus Zwingli makes the gospel a new law. The presence of faith is a proof of election, for the Holy Spirit works faith only in the elect. Salvation depends only upon the eternal election of God. This excludes at once free will and all merit on the part of man (I. 176; IV. 116-121). The elect are not confined to the number of those who attain faith before they die, but unbaptized children and even pious heathen are among the elect and accordingly will be saved. Everything — good and evil, the first sin as well as all others — is based upon the will of God. God did not merely foresee the fall of man but caused it (IV. 112-115). This act was not revolting to God's ethical being, for God is above law.

Luther conceived of God as almighty love and righteousness revealed in Christ; he looked into the heart of Christ and there found the heart of God. According to Zwingli God is to be known before Christ. He is the infinite unchangeable power of all things, absolute causality. Zwingli designated God's absolute rule in the world as the divine providence and defined it as "the perpetual and immutable government and administration of the affairs of the universe" (IV. 84). Zwingli's theory of election is often regarded as a consequence of his "speculative and *a priori* idea of God." He himself testifies that he was led to the peculiar doctrine, which he taught, by the Scriptures. He developed his theory of election in opposition to the Catholic doctrine of good works and merits.

The totality of the elect constitutes the true invisible *church.* In his earlier theology Zwingli taught that the church is the communion of all believers in Christ. Later his idea of election led him to define the church as the elect of all ages and places (VI. 337, 447).

Church and state are not separated and independent, each in its sphere; on the contrary, Christianity is a matter of the state. The state is a theocracy after the Old Testament patterns. The discipline of the church is to be carried out by governmental agencies. The duty of the government is laid down by God in the Bible. A government which sets itself against God and the Bible is to be abrogated (I. 42. 524).

Zwingli *minimized the significance of the Word* in that he severed the influence of the Spirit from the "instrument" of the Word. He held that the Holy Spirit operates immediately upon man's heart. He distinguished sharply between the external and internal word; only the latter, he said, is efficacious. For the same reason very little significance is attached to the *sacraments,* which are mere symbols. *Baptism* is an introductory symbol of obligatory character; hence infant baptism is necessary. At first, Zwingli was not in favor of infant baptism. But when the Anabaptists began to establish churches of the regenerates and made pedo-baptism a prominent object of their assaults, he insisted upon baptism as an obligatory symbol, the rite of initiation of the new dispensation as circumcision was of the old. The *Lord's supper* is not the repetition of the sacrifice of Christ, but the faithful remembrance that "that sacrifice had been made once for all" (III. 147 ff.). His theory of the Lord's Supper involved Zwingli in a long and acrimonious dispute with Luther.

B. THE CONTROVERSY UPON THE LORD'S SUPPER.— In Zwingli's mind the sacraments were rites which rather imposed obligations on the recipient than conferred benefits. Accordingly, he considered the Lord's Supper (1) as a memorial celebration reminding us of our redemption through the death of Christ, and (2) as a feast of confession and thanksgiving. In 1523 Zwingli became acquainted with Honius' interpretation of the word *est* in the words of institution. Honius or Hoen, a Dutch Protestant Advocate, had come to the conclusion that *est* here means *significat*. He acquainted Luther and Zwingli also with this view. Luther rejected it. Zwingli was so well pleased with it that he published the writing of Honius without mentioning the author. Honius' view brought Zwingli's idea concerning the Lord's Supper to a definite conclusion. Bread and wine signify the body and blood offered up in sacrifice for us. There is only a spiritual eating in the Supper. Faith in the sacrifice of Christ which is confessed by the congregation is really the eating of Christ's body. This is said to be in keeping with John 6:63 f., "the flesh profiteth nothing." The real body of Christ being in heaven cannot be in a number of different places on earth (II. 2, 71, 72, 81). Starting from the proposition *finitum non est capax infiniti*, the finite cannot take up the infinite, Zwingli carefully discriminated Christ's two natures in the state of humiliation as well as in the state of exaltation. The one nature does not participate in the life and experience of the other. If the Scripture attributes properties of one nature to the other or to the entire person this must be explained by way of *Alloeosis*, i. e., a rhetorical exchange of one part for another (II. 2, 68 f.). Explaining John 12:32 "And I, if I be lifted up from the earth, will draw all men unto me," Zwingli refers the first clause of this passage to the human nature, the second, to the divine nature of Christ.

Over against (1) the theory of Zwingli who explained the "is" of the words of institution as "symbolizes," (2) the misinterpretation of the word "this" by Carlstadt who held that Jesus on uttering this word by a gesture pointed to his own body, and (3) the view of Oecolampadius, who explained the word "body" as a sign of the body, Luther adhered to the plain and simple words of the institution rejecting any metaphorical interpretation. From the outset Luther believed in the real presence of the body of Christ in the Lord's Supper. He now had to answer the question as to the possibility of the bodily presence in many places at the same time. He explained the ubiquity of the body of Christ on the ground of the personal union of the two natures. There is a communication of properties (*communicatio idiomatum*) of one nature to the other, or to the whole person. The two natures are one single person. Wherever Christ is there he is entire. If Christ is present in the Lord's Supper he is there according to his divine and human natures. "The sitting at the right hand of God" does not designate a "circumscriptive or local existence," such as Christ's body had during his earthly life; nor a "definitive existence" or multipresence, such as is attributed to angels and demons, and to Christ's body which passed through the sealed tombstone and afterward through the locked doors and as it also is in the host; but a "repletive" or supernatural existence, as Christ's humanity in virtue of its personal union with God and exaltation to his right hand is at the same time in all places yet measured and limited by no place. As God is the all-permeating and all-moving will, it follows that his "right hand" is everywhere. As Christ's body is at the right hand of God it follows that it is absolutely omnipresent. Here Luther distinguished between a ubiquitous and sacramental presence. Christ is everywhere, but we can really find and apprehend him where he by his word binds himself to the bread for the reception of the communicant.

There can be no question that Luther, in the use of the Scholastic material by which he sought to establish this theory, followed Occam who had taught the actual repletive presence of God and the definitive presence in many places of the body of Christ in the host. Occam, however, held to the local presence of the body of Christ in heaven, although he admits the possibility of the ubiquity of this body in the universe.

In establishing his theory of the ubiquity of Christ's body Luther was not guided by dialectic or speculative interests but by a profound religious motive. What he contended for, especially in opposition to Zwingli, was that the veritable body of Christ, which was born of the Virgin, the same Christ who has redeemed us, is present in the Lord's Supper in order to assure us of his redeeming act. We do therefore really eat the body of Christ (*manducatio oralis*), and pope Nicholas II. was justified in requiring this confession from Berengar. Unbelievers, too, receive the body, (*manducatio infidelium*, though to their own hurt. But in order to receive the blessing which the body brings the spiritual eating must accompany the bodily eating; for it is faith alone that apprehends life and salvation in the present body of Christ.

The controversy on the Lord's Supper had already in 1526 assumed considerable dimensions. Various efforts at harmony were made yet without result. The Colloquy at Marburg, in 1529, made the difference in the conceptions of Luther and Zwingli still more apparent, and at the end of it nothing had been accomplished.

C. Zwingli's Influence on Doctrinal Development. — Zwingli's theological views are set forth in his *Sixty Seven Articles of Belief*, published at Zurich in 1523. His disciples gave them confessional expression with important modifications, owing to the influence of Bucer's irenic efforts, in the *Tetrapolitana* presented by the four cities of Strassburg, Constanz, Memminger and Lindau to the Diet of Augsburg, 1530; the *Basileensis prior,* 1534, which occupies an intermediate position between Luther and Zwingli; and the *Helvetica prior,* 1536. In these confessions predestination is not discussed, Zwingli's characteristic view regarding the influence of the Holy Spirit separate from the means of grace is accepted, justification by faith alone and the sole authority of the Scriptures are maintained.

Zwingli died in 1531. The direct influence of his theology was short-lived, except that through his energetic opposition the Lutheran view on the Lord's Supper remained the controverted point among the Swiss theologians. Even men like Bullinger, Zwingli's successor in Zuerich, accepted his doctrinal views in a modified form. Calvinism triumphed over Zwinglianism in Switzerland.

After the Marburg Colloquy the theologians of Southwestern Germany, where Zwingli's influence had been strongly felt — notably *Martin Bucer* (d. 151) — regarded with less disfavor Luther's doctrinal views. Bucer and Luther agreed on the doctrines of sin, grace, justification and sanctification. As far as the doctrine of the Lord's Supper was concerned the Colloquy at Marburg and the study of Luther's works upon the Lord's Supper had led Bucer to a deeper appreciation of Luther's view upon the subject. His formula was "that the true body and the true blood of Christ are truly present in the Lord's Supper and are offered with the words of the Lord in the sacrament." An attempt at least was made to find a middle ground between the views of Luther and Zwingli. The outcome of it was the Wittenberg Concord which gave clear expression to Luther's view that "with the bread and wine the body and blood of Christ are truly and substantially present, offered and received" and that, of course, transubstantiation or any local inclusion is to be rejected, that, however, by virtue of the sacramental union the bread is the body, and that the body and blood of Christ are truly offered also to the unworthy and received by them. On May 25, 1536, the Wittenberg Concord was signed by all, but it proved to be only a temporary truce between the Saxons and the Upper German cities.

CHAPTER XIX

LUTHER'S VIEWS AS EXPRESSED IN THE AUGUSTANA AND ITS APOLOGY

A. Augsburg Confession.— Luther's theological views received confessional expression through Luther himself and his co-laborers, notably Melanchthon, in the earlier Lutheran Symbols: the two Catechisms by Luther, 1529, and the Smalcald Articles, composed by Luther and adopted by the theologians at Smalcald, in 1537, with a view to their presentation to a general council to be held under the auspices of pope Paul III. Through Melanchthon the new dogma of the church received its symbolical form in the Augsburg Confession, 1530, and its Apology, 1531.

On January 21, 1530, Emperor Charles V. proclaimed a diet to convene at Augsburg for the purpose of deliberating upon the war with the Turks and upon matters of religion. John the Constant, Elector of Saxony, as soon as he had received the writ, directed Luther, Melanchthon, Bugenhagen and Jonas to meet at Torgau in order to prepare a summary of the Protestant faith to be presented to the diet if called for. This summary prepared by these theologians was called the *Torgau Articles*. On the basis of these and the so-called *Schwabach Articles* and *Marburg Articles* of 1529, in the preparation of which Luther had taken a leading part, Melanchthon, on his journey to Augsburg, prepared an "Apology"— as the Augsburg Confession at first was called. This document was revised into the Augsburg Confession. It met with the full approval of Luther who had been left at Coburg because he was still under sentence of excommunication and proscription. On June 25, in order to exclude the people, the diet met in the small chapel of the Episcopal Palace where the Augsburg Confession was read, against the wish of the Emperor, in the German language. The reading being over, a German and a Latin copy of the document were handed to the Emperor who gave the German copy to the Elector of Mayance, and took the Latin copy along. No trace of either has been found. For the standard text of the Confession we depend entirely upon Melanchthon's *editio princeps* of the Augsburg Confession issued by him in Latin and German, in 1531.

The aim of the Reformers in the Augsburg Confession was not to found a new church, nor introduce and establish a new dogma, but (1) to prove that their doctrine being based upon the Word of

God stands in perfect harmony with the church universal in the early centuries, and (2) to discard certain abuses in doctrine and ceremonies which had been introduced in open opposition to the Word of God.

Though the Augsburg Confession does not present an outline of a dogmatical system it is, nevertheless, constructed on a definite plan: The centre of all doctrines lies in the fourth article, to wit, the doctrine of justification by faith alone. The first three articles contain the theological (I. Of God), the anthropological (II. Of sin), the Christological and soteriological (III. Of the Son of God) presuppositions of justification by faith. All the other articles, not only those pertaining to doctrine, but also those relating to abuses (XXII-XXVIII), depend upon the chief and fundamental article of justification by faith and receive their light from it.

B. The Doctrinal Statements.— The Lutheran Church has in common with the Catholic Church an assent to the doctrines of the Trinity and the incarnation. The Augsburg Confession, Apology and Smalcald Articles begin with repeating the doctrines of the ancient church as these are given in the Apostles, Nicene and Athanasian Creeds. "Concerning these articles there is no contention or dispute, since we on both sides confess them" (*Smalc. Art.* 461). Based upon the theology of the Ecumenical Creeds Article I sets forth the *unity of the divine essence* and the *trinity of persons of the same essence.*

Original sin (Art. II) is sin received with the origin of our being. It consists, negatively, in the absence of true fear of God and trust in him; positively, in concupiscence which is not merely an evil, a malady, or a defect, but truly sin. Against the Scholastic teaching that in the baptized concupiscence is no sin, the second part of Art. II of the Apology states that baptism removes the imputation of sin, although the material of sin, i. e., concupiscence remains (107 ff.). To deny that original sin is truly sin means "to obscure the glory of Christ's merits and benefits" (*Augsb. C.* II. 45). That the doctrine of original sin stands in closest relation to that of justification by faith is seen in the rejection of the Pelagian view "that man can be justified before God by his own strength and reason" (*ib.*).

In asserting that "all men begotten in the natural way are born with sin" Art. II exempts the humanity of Christ from this statement and implies the falseness of the Scholastic figment in regard to the sinlessness of the mother of Jesus.

Art. III restates the Christology of the Chalcedonian Creed:

"the divine and human inseparably conjoined in one person." The object of *Christ's work* is to reconcile the Father to us and to become a sacrifice for our sins, but also for all other sins. This was stated to reject the Catholic doctrine of the sacrifice of the mass by which daily sins are blotted out. Nor does Christ cease to be our Mediator. He was raised again to reign, and to justify and sanctify all those who believe in him, by sending the Holy Spirit into their hearts. There are *no human mediators* or intercessors, for Christ is the only Mediator, High Priest and Intercessor; his work cannot be supplemented by saints (*A. C.* and *Apol.* XXI) nor by the sacrifice of the mass (*ib.* XXIV), nor by the works of the justified. "This foundation shall stand forever, namely, that for Christ's sake we are accepted with God, and justified by faith, not on account of our love and works. This we shall make so plain and certain that anybody may grasp it. As long as the heart is not at peace with God, it cannot be righteous; for it flees from the wrath of God, despairs, and would have God not to judge it. Therefore the heart cannot be righteous and accepted with God while it is not at peace with God. Now, faith alone makes the heart to be content, and obtains peace and life (Rom. 5:1), because it confidently and frankly relies on the promise of God for Christ's sake" (167).

The specific points in the confessional statement of Art. IV. are: Justification consists of two parts: *non-imputation* or forgiveness of sins and the *imputation* of the righteousness of Christ. They are not two separate acts of God, but actually two sides of one and the same act. Justification is thus a forensic act by which God freely, *gratis*, forgives a sinner his sins and imputes to him the righteousness of Christ. The sinner's justification was made possible only through Christ and the merit of his most perfect obedience in life, sufferings and death. Hence we are justified *propter Christum*. The instrumental cause of justification, that is, the means for its attainment is faith alone. Hence it is said that we are justified *per fidem* or *fide*. Faith apprehends Christ who by his obedience is righteousness for us before God. *Docent quod . . . gratis justificentur propter Christum perfidem.* "Faith justifies and saves not on the ground that it is a work in itself worthy, but only because it receives the promised mercy" (137). It is the only appropriate organ which lays hold on and appropriates Christ's righteousness. Accordingly it can be said that "faith is the very righteousness by which we are accounted righteous before God" (147). "This God imputes for righteousness before Him" (45).

This conception of faith as the receiving of God's grace in Christ excludes the whole Scholastic system of justification as a process in man by which holiness is infused into him and by which he is gradually transformed from a sinner into a righteous man. It excludes faith as the intellectual acceptance of the doctrines of the church, faith which must receive an inward content, i. e., must be perfected by love. It excludes all human merit. Justification, then, is not a moral transformation but a judicial change, a new relation between man and God on terms which God approves.

Melanchthon `in the Apology expresses the same views on justifying faith as Luther held:. By faith alone we obtain the remission of sins for Christ's sake and by faith alone we are justified, i. e., of unrighteous men made righteous, or regenerated (143). Faith, on the one hand, receives the imputed righteousness of Christ. On the other hand, it is the beginning of a new life of the process of making man actually righteous. With God's forensic declaration that the believer in Christ is righteous is given at once the new life of the believer.

From faith spring forth *good works* as the *fruits of faith* (Art. VI, *Of New Obedience*). Only the work that proceeds from a true and living faith is a good work. "For without faith human nature can in no wise do the works of the First or of the Second Commandment. Without faith it does not call upon God, nor expect anything from God, nor bear the cross, but seeks, and trusts in, man's help" (57).

Although in external, temporal and civil affairs fallen man has a free will to choose good and evil, in eternal, inner and spiritual things he possesses no ability to choose the good and therefore cannot without the Holy Spirit who is given through the Word of God become pleasing to God (Art. XVIII, *Of Free Will*).

Good works are *necessary,* not as the ground of our salvation, for there is no proportion between the two, but as proof of our faith (Art. VI). Only such works are good as God has commanded in his Word and Law, and not such as have been devised and commanded by the church (Art. XXVII, *Of Monastic Vows*).

God works in us justifying and saving faith through *Word and Sacraments* as the divinely appointed instrumentalities, generally called means of grace. "That we may obtain this faith the ministry of teaching the Gospel and administering the sacraments was instituted" (Art. V, *Of the Ministry*).

It has often been said that the Augsburg Confession, Art. V, teaches absolute predestination in the much discussed passage ... "the Holy Ghost ... who worketh faith where and when it pleases God." This is, however, an erroneous opinion. It was over against the Enthusiasts, such as Anabaptists, Zwickau Prophets, Muenzer, Carlstadt and others, who with their so-called inner light, inner word, and immediate inspiration and revelation despised the divinely appointed instrumentalities, that Melanchthon emphasized that the receiving of the Holy Spirit is not a matter of man's power, but "through the Word and Sacraments, as through instruments, the Holy Ghost is given, who works faith where and when it pleases God." God has appointed the means through which the Holy Spirit imparts himself and therefore "works faith"— not where and when it pleases man, but "where and when it pleases God in those who hear the Gospel."

The sacraments are not merely marks of profession (Zwingli) but signs and evidences of the divine will toward us for the purpose of quickening and strengthening our faith (Art. XIII, *Of the Use of the Sacraments*). The sacraments of themselves are means of grace and actually contain and offer the grace of God by virtue of the word and will of Christ. "Sacraments and Word are effectual by reason of the institution and commandment of Christ, notwithstanding they be administered by evil men" (Art. VIII, *What the Church is*). But their saving effect is conditioned upon the faith of him who receives them. The Apology expressly rejects the Scholastic doctrine of the *ex opere operato,* according to which the sacraments are effectual already by the mere performance of the outward acts (387).

Baptism is necessary to salvation (Art. IX, *Of Baptism*). It is God's means of grace. Through it also children are brought to God and made partakers of his grace. The Lutheran Confessions are silent as to the mode of baptism.

The real presence of the body and blood of Christ in the *Lord's Supper* is so explicitly stated in Art. X that the Confutators interpreted it in the sense of transubstantiation, "the body and blood of Christ are truly present, and are distributed to those who eat in the Supper of the Lord."

The Augsburg Confession, in placing Art. XIII (*Of the Use of the Sacraments*) after the discussion of baptism, the Lord's Supper and repentance, indicates that there are three sacraments. Melanchthon says in the Apology: "If we call Sacraments rites which have the command of God and to which the promise of grace has been added it is easy to decide what are properly Sacraments . . . Therefore Baptism, the Lord's Supper and Absolution, which is the Sacrament of Repentance, are truly Sacraments" (309). Later, Luther demanded three constituents as essential to a sacrament, namely, divine institution, earthly element and heavenly gift, and so he enumerated in the Smalcald Articles two sacraments, and also in the two Catechisms.

The Augsburg Confession recognizes *private absolution* (Art. XI, *Of Confession*), but rejects auricular confession with a special enumeration of all and each of our sins, which is impossible. A person may sin or fall again after baptism. As God pardons such fallen ones when they truly repent, the church must also grant them absolution (Art. XII, *Of Repentance*). Repentance consists of two parts: *contrition,* sorrow or terror on account of sin, and *faith* born of the Gospel, or *absolution,* that is, faith that sins are forgiven and grace is obtained through Christ. Good works and reformation of life must follow as fruits of genuine repentance.

The *church* proper is not an outward organization but "the congregation of saints, in which the Gospel is rightly taught and the Sacraments are rightly administered" (Art. VII, *Of the Church*). But since the true church exists in a visible, earthly form, it can never exist without commixture of hypocrites and ungodly men (Art. VIII, *What the Church is*).

The church in its empirical, earthly form has need of some sort of *human ordinances* in which to clothe the administration of the means of grace, the preaching of the Word, and public worship, but these must prove their legitimacy by the Gospel (Art. XXVI, *Of the Distinction of Meats* and XXVIII, *Of Ecclesiastical Power*), and cannot claim divine sanction or unconditioned obligation (Art. VII, *Of the Church* and XV, *Of Ecclesiastical Usages*). "Of this kind is the observance of the Lord's Day, Easter, Pentecost, and like holy-days and rites. For those who judge that by the authority of the Church the observance of the Lord's Day instead of the Sabbath day was ordained as a thing necessary, do greatly err. Scripture has abrogated the Sabbath day; for it teaches that, since the Gospel has been revealed, all the ceremonies of Moses can be omitted" (Art. XXVIII, 91).

Since the peculiar power and authority to preach the Gospel, remit sins, and administer the sacraments, is given to the church, the church alone, and no one else, designates those who shall exercise this ministry for it, and therefore ". . . no one should publicly teach in the church or administer the Sacraments unless he be regularly called," *nisi rite vocatus* (Art. XIV, *Of Ecclesiastical Order*).

The Lutheran Confessions stand for the *complete separation of church and state.* Church and state are two distinct independent domains. The former is concerned about man's relation to God; the latter, about the citizen's place in the commonwealth and his relation to the government. While the church has the power of the keys it does not have the power of the sword. The power of the keys is "exercised only by teaching or preaching the Gospel and administering the sacraments" (Art. XXVIII, *Of Ecclesiastical Power*). While civil government has to "defend bodies and bodily things against manifest injuries, and restrain men with the sword and bodily punishments in order to preserve civil justice and peace" (*ib.*), it has no jurisdiction over man's relation to God, his conscience and his spiritual interests. The civil government exercises its power and regulates its affairs by human law. It has the authority to make, apply and enforce laws, Rom. 13:1; Tit. 3:1).

Church and state are wholly diverse and therefore they cannot conflict, provided neither encroaches upon the other within its rightful sphere. "Since the power of the Church grants eternal things, and is exercised only by the ministry of the Word, it does not interfere with civil government. For civil government deals with other things than does the Gospel . . . Therefore the power of the Church and the civil power must not be confounded. The power of the Church has its own commission, to teach the Gospel and to administer the Sacraments. Let it not break into the office of another; let it not transfer the kingdoms of this world; let it not abrogate the laws of civil rulers; let it not abolish lawful obedience; let it not interfere with judgments concerning civil ordinances or contracts; let it not prescribe laws to civil rulers concerning the form of the Commonwealth. As Christ says, John 18:36: My kingdom is not of this world; also Luke 12:14: Who made me a judge or a divider over you? Paul also says, Phil. 3: 20: Our citizenship is in heaven; 2 Cor. 10:4: The weapons of our warfare are not carnal, but mighty through God to the casting down of imaginations. After this manner our teachers discriminate between the duties of both these powers, and command that both be honored and acknowledged as gifts and blessings of God (Art. XXVIII, 85). From this it follows "that lawful civil ordinances are good works of God, and that it is right for Christians to bear civil office, to sit as judges, to judge matters by the Imperial and other existing laws, to award just punishments, to engage in just wars, to serve as soldiers, to make legal contracts, to hold property, to make oaths when required by the magistrates, to marry a wife, to be given in marriage" (Art. XVI, 51). It further follows that obedience to magistrates and to the laws of the land is a religious duty. "Christians are necessarily bound to obey their own magistrates and laws, save only when commanded to sin; for then they ought to obey God rather than men, Acts 5:29" (*ib.*).

It is interesting to note how this conception of church and state involved a fundamental change concerning the formal basis of the accepted dogma. Since the time of Gregory VII. the church was a so-called spiritual universal state, a ruling power which to a large extent also ruled the state. The proclamation of the pope, the decisions of the council, the doctrines of the church formulated by official teachers of the infallible church received as such dogmatic authority in the church. According to the Reformers the right of passing judgment upon doctrine belongs to the congregation of believers. But how do the teachings of evangelical truth receive dogmatic authority in the church?

The new Christian community needed an outward organization. The Reformers did not recognize the necessity for an ecclesiastical organization distinct from that of the state. The simplest arrangement was to entrust the care of the church to the existing secular authorities. The Reformers believed it the duty of the secular authorities to protect religion and the church. The princes and magistrates were therefore at once recognized as the official representatives of the new church. The Treaty of Augsburg, 1555, gave authoritative recognition to the princes as the official representatives of the church in their country. It was not for them to interpret the Bible or to formulate faith; this was the task of the theologians. But Biblical doctrine formulated by the theologians attained a legal character only when officially adopted by the secular government in the name of the church.

CHAPTER XX

MELANCHTHON'S DOCTRINAL VIEWS AND HIS PLACE IN THE HISTORY OF DOCTRINE

A. MELANCHTHON'S SIGNIFICANCE FOR THE HISTORY OF DOCTRINE lies in the fact that he collected, defended and systematized Luther's doctrinal views. His universal culture, his many-sidedness and calmness, his clear thought and elegant style fitted him to become "the scribe of the Reformation." His famous *Loci communes*, 1521, were the first systematized presentation of the theology of the Reformation. In the first edition Melanchthon presented the leading ideas of Luther concerning salvation. The later editions approached more and more the plan of a textbook of dogma. At first sight the Loci seem to be in the form of isolated paragraphs, but by closer study of them we notice two definite constantly recurring ideas around which he groups all the results of his theological research, namely, the church of the pure doctrine and justification by grace.

B. BRIEF SUMMARY OF MELANCHTHON'S RELIGIOUS IDEAS.— The sources and standards of the Christian truth are the Scriptures. The church bears testimony to the prophetic and apostolic doctrine of the Scriptures in the Three Ecumenical Creeds. This genuine true doctrine was brought to light and set forth by Luther (*C. R.* XI. 728)[*].

1. Biblical revelation and human reason, though two different realms of knowledge, are not opposites. Theology requires every branch of science as a prerequisite and support (XI. 281. 394). Thus *the church* assumes more the character of a school. It consists of teachers and taught who confess the pure evangelical doctrine. Melanchthon considered the church *visible* on the ground of its self-expression in the preaching of the word and the administration of the sacraments (*ib.* 273). According to Luther the church is the communion of believers. According to Melanchthon the church is the communion of those who adhere to the true belief. There can be no doubt that in Melanchthon's conception of the church "are to be found the germs of the errors of the orthodoxy of the seventeenth century" (Seeberg *Hist. of Doctr.* II. 356). And Dr. Wiegand (*DG.* II. 128) says: "The era of orthodoxy has its roots in Melanchthon's, not in Luther's, conception of the church."

---

[*] Melanchon's Works in *Corpus Reformatorum* (C. R.) I-XXVIII, 1834-1860.

In the Apology Melanchthon explains what is meant by "the pure doctrine of the Gospel," namely, "the foundation, i. e., the true knowledge of Christ and faith." Upon this foundation the church is built. There are also those "who build upon the foundation stubble that will perish, i. e., certain unprofitable opinions, . . . which, nevertheless, because they do not overthrow the foundation, are both forgiven them and also corrected." But there are such doctrines which overthrow the foundation as when the Romish Church condemns the article that remission of sins is received by faith, or teaches that men merit the remission of sins by love to God, prior to grace, and that the Sacraments justify *ex opere operato* (233). The papacy, therefore, defending such errors, is no longer a member of the true church but thereby "establishes the Kingdom of Antichrist. For the kingdom of Antichrist is a new service of God, devised by human authority rejecting Christ, just as the kingdom of Mahommet . . . " (319).

2. With Melanchthon's intellectual conception of the church corresponds his idea of faith and justification. *Justification by faith* is the centre of pure doctrine and the chief article of faith. Since man, because of original sin, is subject to condemnation and even the regenerate cannot actually please God, the effect of the law is to terrify and to produce contrition (C. R. XXI. 692. 876. 883 f.). While Luther made faith itself the principle of justification and sanctification, Melanchthon laid more stress on the law in regard to the relation of grace to repentance and good works. Inseparably connected with the preaching of the law is the promise of grace, consisting in remission of sins and assuring of reconciliation. God's grace is founded in Christ as the Mediator and Propitiator (XII. 605). In this connection Melanchthon reproduces Anselm's theory of satisfaction. (*ib.* XII, 605 ff.).

Justification is a forensic act of God and therefore distinctly separated from sanctification, the believer's life, which necessarily follows justification. Faith apprehends justification or the forgivenes of sins (XXI. 742). Melanchthon's conception of faith as merely the organ which apprehends the forgiveness of sins lacks the depth of Luther's confession of faith as an ethical principle and life-giving power. Moreover, by distinguishing three elements in faith, namely, knowledge, assent and confidence (*ib.* 795) Melanchthon prepared the way for the mechanical view of the later dogmaticians who regarded knowledge and assent as preliminary steps to confidence.

Justification is at once accompanied by the impartation of the Holy Spirit (XXVI. 364), who renews man and prompts him to do good works (XXI. 429. 762. 775 f.). Though Melanchthon distinguishes only logically and not chronologically between justification and renovation, nevertheless, in the Loci he does not, as he does in the Augsburg Confession and Apology clearly set forth the relation between the origin of faith and the impartation of the Holy Spirit. There the Spirit works faith through the word; here the Spirit is given as a consequence of justification which faith apprehends.

3. In his later theology Melanchthon came consciously to *differ from Luther* on two doctrines, *man's free will* and *the Lord's Supper*. At first, Melanchthon had uncompromisingly insisted on the necessity of every event. But gradually, especially under Erasmus' influence, he gave up his original deterministic position, until in the Loci of 1535 he named three concurrent causes in conversion: *the will*, the consenting cause, cooperates with *the word*, the instrumental cause, and *the Holy Spirit*, the creative cause (XXI. 332. 376 f.). Finally in the Loci of 1543 he explains the difference of final destiny among men by the different methods of treating grace, i. e., by man's decision for or against God (*ib.* 659 f.; 652).

Regarding the Lord's Supper, Melanchthon always held to the real presence of Christ in the Supper, but gradually, especially in view of the testimonies of the Church Fathers, he came to differ from Luther's conception of that presence. He rejected the doctrine of the ubiquity of the body of Christ and held to a spiritual presence of Christ. He regarded Bucer's formula with favor. His own view is indicated in the tenth Article of the Augustana of 1540 where Melanchthon changed the words "that the body and blood of Christ are truly present" into "that with the bread and wine the body and blood of Christ are truly offered to those that participate in the Lord's Supper," also omitting the clause "and they reject those that teach otherwise." This altered edition of 1540 is known as the *Variata* or *Altered Augsburg Confession* as distinguished from the *Invariata* or *Unaltered* of 1530 or 1531. The change attracted little attention and was felt to be an improved modification and correct interpretation of the Invariata till after the death of Melanchthon, when dogmatic controversies widened the chasm between the orthodox Lutherans and the Philippists, it gave offence to the former, who insisted upon strict adherence to the Invariata, while the latter adhered to the Variata as their party-symbol. The Book of Concord (1580) gives the text of the Invariata as the proper historical Confession of Augsburg, and since then down to the present day the Invariata, and not the Variata, has been the confessional basis of the Lutheran Church.

CHAPTER XXI

CONTROVERSIES IN THE LUTHERAN CHURCH AFTER LUTHER'S DEATH SETTLED BY THE FORMULA OF CONCORD

A. GENERAL SURVEY OF DOCTRINAL DEVELOPMENT TO THE ADOPTION OF THE FORMULA OF CONCORD.— Melanchthon's departure from Luther's doctrine gave rise to dissensions which began to distract the Lutheran Church soon after the death of Luther. There soon arose *two opposite parties* within the Lutheran Church. Both of them fell into extremes and exaggerations. The *first party* embraced the adherents of Melanchthon. They were therefore called Melanchthonians or Philippists. They were also known as Synergists and Crypto-Calvinists. They had their stronghold in the Universities of Wittenberg and Leipzig. The *second party* embraced the genuine adherents of Luther, the so-called Gnesio-Lutherans, such as Amsdorf and Flacius. Their headquarters were Magdeburg and the University of Jena. Between these two opposite extremes there stood a *centre party* embracing loyal Luthrans such as Brenz, Andreae, Chemnitz and others who rejected all extreme positions of either the Gnesio-Lutherans or the Philippists and played an important part in the great work of unification.

The conflict raged over a large field of dogma. Among questions in dispute were the Interim and the matter of adiaphora; the Osiandristic controversy concerning justification; the Majoristic controversy concerning the necessity of good works; the antinomistic and synergistic controversies; the controversies on the Lord's Supper, Christology and predestination.

The seriousness of the situation was keenly felt when at the Religious Colloquy at Worms, 1557, the Gnesio-Lutherans questioned the right of their Philippist opponents to appeal to the Augsburg Confession. Various vain efforts at unification were made. To the Frankfort Recess, 1558, the Gnesio-Lutherans responded in the Weimar Confutation, 1559, condemning the Philippists. At the Diet of Naumburg, in 1561, the controversy on the Lord's Supper was in the foreground. The difference between the Invariata and Variata was noted and the insufficiency of the Augsburg Confession as a confessional basis was realized. Some progress toward unification was made by the introduction of *corpora doctrinae* in different parts of the country. These bodies of doctrine usually comprised, besides the Ecumenical Creeds, Augsburg Confession and Apology, writings of Luther, chiefly his Catechisms and the Smalcald Articles. The next step was to establish a *common corpus doctrinae* for the whole Lutheran Church of Germany. This was finally done in the Formula of Concord, in two parts, the briefer *Epitome,* a summary of the Torgau Book prepared by Andreae and revised in the cloister of Bergen, near Magdeburg, in 1577, and the larger *Solida Declaratio* or *Comprehensive Summary* which is identical with the Bergen Book, each divided into twelve articles as follows : I,*Original Sin;* II, *Free Will;* III, *Righteousness of Faith;* IV, *Good Works;* V, *Law and Gospel;* VI, *Third Use of the Law;* VII, *Lord's Supper;* VIII, *Person of Christ;* IX, *Christ's Descent into Hell;* X, *Church* Usages and Ceremonies,*called Adiaphora;* XI, *God's Eternal Election;* XII, *Other Factions and Sects.* The Epitome treats more briefly, the Solida Declaratio more fully, all contested doctrines.

The task of the Formula of Concord was to bring reconciliation and peace to the Lutheran churches and to solve the questions in debate. Accordingly, the Formula establishes first a body of doctrine which should find acceptance with all Lutherans in that it states the summary content, rule and standard according to which all dogmas should be judged, and all controversies which have arisen should be set forth and settled in a Christian way, to wit: The Holy Scriptures, the Apostles', Nicene, and Athanasian Creeds, the Unaltered Augsburg Confession, the Apology, the Smalcald Articles, the Small and Large Catechism. It then, in twelve Articles (*ut supra*), formulates the existing consensus of belief with regard to the controversies within the Lutheran Church after the death of Luther.

The significance of the Formula of Concord lies in the fact that it cut off the extremes of both Philippism and Gnesio-Lutheranism, recorded the conception of the Lutheran doctrine and established peace within the Lutheran Church. Thus the Formula marks the completion of doctrinal construction in the Lutheran Church of the sixteenth century. It became the basis for the development of Lutheran theology.

B. SEPARATE CONTROVERSIES SETTLED BY THE FORMULA OF CONCORD.— It remains briefly to delineate the doctrinal development of the separate controversies and show how they were settled by the first eleven articles of the Formula of Concord.

1. THE INTERIMISTIC OR ADIAPHORISTIC CONTROVERSY.— On the ground that church rites are non-essential, *adiaphora,* and hence concessions to the Romanists permissible, provided the essential

matter, pure doctrine, be preserved, Melanchthon and the Wittenberg theologians defended the Leipzig Interim (1548), which sanctioned jurisdiction of Catholic bishops and the observance of almost all Roman Catholic ceremonies. Passionate opposition was led by Flacius who declared that nothing is adiaphoron in case of confession and offense. *Nihil est adiaphoron in statu confessionis et scandali.* Melanchthon subsequently confessed that he yielded too much in the interests of peace, but the strife was kept up between the Philippists and the strict Lutherans until the Formula of Concord in Article X decided the matter in the sense of Flacius and against the Philippists.

2. *The Majoristic Controversy.* Melanchthon maintained the necessity of good works as the necessary outcome of faith. Defending Melanchthon's view George Major and Justus Menius declared that good works are necessary to salvation. They are, as Major explained, not necessary to gain salvation, but to retain it.

Major and Menius were opposed by Amsdorf and Flacius. Amsdorf, however, who had held as early as 1554 that good works are not necessary to salvation, now went so far as to declare that good works are detrimental to salvation.

The statements of both Major and Amsdorf are rejected in Article IV. "After man has been justified by faith, then a true living faith worketh by love, Gal. 5:6, so that thus good works always follow justifying faith, and are surely found with it, if it be true and living; for it never is alone, but always has with it love and hope" (795). It can be as little without good works as fire can be without light and warmth (941). Good works are to be wholly excluded from the article of justification and salvation. They are the sure fruits of true faith. It is therefore correct to say that good works are necessary, not as the ground of salvation (Major's error), for there is no proportion between the two, but as proof of our salvation. Hence "those who are born again and renewed by the Holy Ghost, are bound to do good works." Not that the regenerate render new obedience "from coercion or the driving of the Law, but from a voluntary spirit." Nor do good works "maintain faith and salvation in us, but the Spirit of God alone, through faith, of whose presence and indwelling good works are evidences" (799).

3. *The Antinomistic Controversy.* (a) Melanchthon had asserted that the law leads to repentance and the knowledge of sin (second use of the law). Repentance is the antecedent of faith. Without repentance the preaching of the gospel is unintelligible. John Agricola maintained that repentance, consciousness of sin and

the fear of God are to be based upon the gospel and not upon the law. This view, though in a modified form, was later on held by the Wittenberg Philippists.

This controversy, which regarded the second use of the law and the special significance of the gospel, was settled by Article V, which sharply distinguishes between law and gospel. The former teaches what is just and pleasing in the sight of God, refutes whatever is opposed to the divine will and threatens temporal and eternal punishment of sin. The latter is the preaching of the grace of God in Christ Jesus. Both law and gospel must always be preached in the church, but both must also be retained unmixed. "The mere preaching of the Law either makes *presumptuous* men, who imagine that they can fulfill the Law by outward works, or forces them utterly to despair" (955). The mere preaching of the Gospel makes *secure* men. It offers its comfort only "to penitent sinners who are terrified by the preaching of the Law . . . And lest repentance or the terrors of the Law turn into despair, the preaching of the Gospel must be added that it may be a repentance unto salvation," 2 Cor. 7:10 (*ib.*).

(b) In connection with the Majoristic controversy over the necessity of good works, Andreas Poach of Erfurt maintained that the gospel alone leads to the doing of good, and that it is the office of the law only to accuse and condemn, and Anton Otto denied that the law had any significance whatever for believers. Thus arose the dispute concerning the third use of the law.

The question as to the significance of the law for the regenerate was decided by Article VI which denotes three uses of the law: (1) to maintain outward discipline, (2) to lead men to the knowledge of their sin, (3) to regulate and direct the whole life of the regenerate. The Formula of Concord maintains the third use of the law for the regenerate. "Although men truly believing in Christ and truly converted to God have been freed and exempted from the curse and coercion of the Law, they nevertheless are not on this account without Law, but have been redeemed by the Son of God in order that they should . . . constantly exercise themselves in its observance, Ps. 1:2; Ps. 119. For even our first parents before the Fall did not live without Law, who had the Law of God written also in their hearts, because they were created in the image of God" (805). In the present life regeneration and renewal are not complete, but only begun. It is needful that the law of the Lord always shine before the believers in order that they do not fall into a self-chosen holiness and worship and establish a human standard of righteousness (807). "As regards the distinction between the works of the Law and the fruits of the Spirit, we believe, teach and confess that the works which are done according to the Law are and are called works of the Law as long as they are only extorted from man by urging the punishment and threatening of God's wrath. Fruits of the Spirit, however, are the works which the Spirit of God who dwells in believers works through the regenerate, and which are done by believers so far as they are regenerate, as though they knew of no command, threat, or reward; for in this manner the children of God live in the Law and walk according to the Law of God, which mode of living St. Paul in his epistles calls the Law of Christ and the Law of the mind," Rom. 7:25; 8:7; Rom. 8:2; Gal. 6:2 (807).

4. *The Osiandristic and Stancarian Controversy.*— Andreas Osiander, one of the Reformers at Nuremberg, afterwards professor at Koenigsberg, objected (about 1550) to the forensic doctrine of justification as an imputation, and interpreted it as an infusion of the essential righteousness or divine nature of Christ. The prerequisite of justification is redemption. It was effected in that Christ fulfilled the law for us. Thus reconciled and forgiven we are not yet justified. We become righteous only through the indwelling of Christ. Not the Christ f o r us, but the Christ w i t h i n us, is the ground of our justification. Accordingly, justification is not a forensic act but a making righteous.

Justification as taught by Osiander is not the Roman Catholic infusion of grace based upon the merit of good works. Through the word Christ enters man's heart and, embraced by faith, begets in him a new life.

Both, Gnesio-Lutherans and Philippists opposed Osiander, because he separated forgiveness of sin from justification, regarded the renewal the ground instead of the result of jutsification, and one-sidedly emphasized the divine nature of Christ.

In opposition to Osiander, Francesco Stancaro, an Italian ex-priest, who also became professor in Koenigsberg, asserted that Christ is our righteousness only according to his human nature, thus reviving an opinion proposed by Peter Lombard (see p. xxx) and other Scholastics.

The controversy was settled by Article III which affirms that Christ is our righteousness according to both natures by his absolute obedience manifested in doing and suffering. "His obedience, not only in suffering and dying, but also in this that He in our stead was voluntarily made under the Law and fulfilled it by His obedience, is imputed to us for righteousness, so that on account of His complete obedience, which He rendered His heavenly Father for us, by doing and suffering, in living and dying, God forgives our sins. . . and eternally saves us" (919). His righteousness is imputed and not infused (937). Faith preceded by true repentance apprehends justification. The Holy Spirit works faith as well as the renewal and sanctification (929).

5. *The Synergistic Controversy.*—Pfeffinger in Leipzig had in 1555, following Melanchthon, taught that man is not "purely passive," but by his own natural powers co-operates to a certain extent in his conversion. A similar view was held by Victorin Strigel who taught that sin had not destroyed will but depraved it and, although bound, wounded and weakly, it enters into coordinate action with the inception of conversion.

In opposition to Pfeffinger and Strigel, Flacius asserted that man is by nature wholly dead and his heart petrified. He is worse than a log or stone inasmuch as he is not only passive, but resisting and hostile toward the work of God before, in, and after conversion (789). The Formula of Concord decided and settled the controversy by Article II rejecting the Melanchthonian synergism, and asserting: (1) *The entire bondage of the will to sin before regeneration.* The heart of the unregenerate man is compared "to a hard stone, which does not yield to the one who touches it, but resists, and to a rough block, and to a wild unmanageable beast, etc." (889). (2) *The conversion of man without his co-operation.* ". . . in conversion God, through the drawing of the Holy Ghost, makes out of stubborn and unwilling men willing ones" (791). The Holy Ghost, however, does not effect conversion without means. "By this means, and in no other way, namely through His holy Word . . . and the holy Sacraments . . . God desires to call men to eternal salvation, draw them to Himself, and convert, regenerate and sanctify them" (901). This Word man can externally hear and read, even though he is not converted to God and regenerate, "for in these external things . . . man even since the Fall has to a certain extent a free will, so that he can go to church and hear or not hear the sermon" (*ib.*). Man's inability to work out his own salvation does not do away with man's responsibility. Man is responsible for the attitude which he assumes toward the will of God. While the Holy Ghost alone converts man, yet man is always free to resist the Holy Ghost and reject the offered grace. "When such a person despises the instrument of the Holy Ghost, and will not hear, no injustice is done to him if the Holy Ghost does not enlighten him, but allows him to remain in darkness of his unbelief and to perish; Matt. 23:37. And in this respect it may well be said that man is not a stone or block. For a stone or block does not resist the person who moves it, nor does it understand and is sensible of what is being done with it, as man with his will so long resists God the Lord until he is converted" (903). God does not force man to become godly, but "draws him in such a way that his darkened understanding is turned into an enlightened one and his perverse will into an obedient one. And this is what the Scriptures call creating a new heart, Ps. 51:10" (*ib.*). (3) *The co-operation of the renewed will of man in the work of renewal after conversion.* "For after the Holy Ghost has wrought and accomplished this, and man's will has been changed and renewed by His divine power and working alone, then the new will of man is an instrument and organ of God the Holy Ghost, so that he not only accepts grace, but also cooperates with the Holy Ghost in the works which follow" (791).

6. *The Flacian Controversy.*— In combating Strigel, Flacius had gone so far as to maintain that original sin is not an accident or attribute but the very substance or essence of fallen man who ceased to be in any sense the image of God and became the very image of Satan.

The Formula of Concord, in Article I, rejects Flacius' theory, which identifies original sin with substance, as a Manichean error, defines original sin not as a physical defect but as a moral depravity, and sharply distinguishes between human nature and the corruption of human nature, between substance and accident. "Although original sin, like a spiritual poison and leprosy (as Luther says), has poisoned and corrupted the whole human nature, so that we cannot show and point out to the eye the nature apart by itself, and original sin apart by itself, nevertheless the *corrupt nature*, or essence of the corrupt man, body and soul, . . . and *original sin*, which dwells in man's nature or essence, and corrupts it, are not one thing" (869). Moreover, God is not the author of sin but of nature. "God even since the Fall is the Creator of man, and creates his body and soul. Therefore corrupt man cannot, without any distinction be sin itself, otherwise God would be a creator of sin" (871). And finally, "the devil can create no substance, but can only in an accidental way, God permitting, corrupt the substance created by God" (785).

7. *The Crypto - Calvinistic Controversy.* (a) In 1552, Joachim Westphal of Hamburg raised his voice against those who denied the presence of Christ's body in the Lord's Supper. He pointed out to the adherents of Luther the alarming progress which Calvin's doctrine of the Lord's Supper had made, and accused Melanchthon and his adherents of agreement with Calvin. From this time the Philippists rested under the suspicion of Crypto-Cal-

vinism. Several well-meant attempts at pacification on the part of the Lutheran princes were unsuccessful.

In the last year of Melanchthon's life there occurred the most passionate outbreak. Melanchthon himself refused to take sides in the controversy. After his death (1560) wild conflicts raged throughout Germany. The Philippists who were very strong in Electoral Saxony attempted to gain ascendency over the entire German Evangelical Church, but met their downfall first in Electoral Saxony. The *Exegesis perspicua et ferme integra de sacra coena* written by Joachim Curaeus and published in 1574 was meant to deal a final blow to Lutheranism and banish it forever from Saxony. The Exegesis controverted the Lutheran conception of ubiquity, the *communicatio idiomatum,* the *manducatio oralis* and the *manducatio infidelium.* The appearance of the Exegesis, however, caused the rejection of Calvin's doctrine of the Lord's Supper and the condemnation of the Saxon Crypto-Calvinism, and the Torgau Confession of 1574 completed the downfall of the Philippists.

This phase of the controversy was settled by Article VII, *Of the Holy Supper.* The Formula rejects the opinions of Zwingli and Calvin who maintained only a spiritual presence of Christ's divine nature. " . . . over against this it is taught in the Augsburg Confession from God's Word concerning the Lord's Supper: That the true body and blood of Christ are truly present in the Holy Supper under the form of bread and wine, and are dispensed and received, and the contrary doctrine is rejected (namely that of the Sacramentarians) that the body of Christ, because he ascended to heaven, is not truly and essentially present there upon earth in the Sacrament" (975).

Following in the main the thoughts of Luther and confirming the expressions of the other Lutheran Confessions the Formula of Concord asserts that on account of the sacramental union the bread and wine are truly the body and blood of Christ (811). The bodily presence of Christ in the Lord's Supper is not ascribed to the consecration but alone to the almighty power of Jesus Christ and is based upon Christ's words of the institution. "Not the word or work of any man produces the true presence of the body and blood of Christ in the Supper, whether it be the merit or recitation of the minister, or the eating and drinking or faith of the communicants; but all this should be ascribed alone to the power of Almighty God and the word, institution, and ordination of our Lord Jesus Christ" (999).

From the bodily presence it follows that the body and blood of Christ are taken with the bread and wine not only spiritually by faith, but also orally by mouth, yet not Capernaitically but in a supernatural heavenly mode because of the sacramental union (955). " . . . just as in Christ two distinct unchanged natures are inseparably united, so in the Holy Supper the two substances, the natural bread and the true natural body of Christ are present to-,gether here upon earth in the appointed administration of the Sacrament . . . this union of the body and blood of Christ with the bread and wine is not a personal union, as that of the two natures of Christ, but as Dr. Luther and our theologians call it, a sacramental union" (985). It also follows that not only true believers but also the unworthy and unbelievers receive the true body and blood of Christ, not for life and consolation, but for judgment and condemnation. "The body of Christ is not only received spiritually by faith, which occurs also outside of the use of the Sacrament, but also orally, not only by believing and godly, but also by unworthy, unbelieving, false and wicked Christians" (997; 983). The Formula of Concord mentions as the beneficial effect of receiving Christ's body and blood particularly that we "in all troubles and temptations firmly rely, with sure confidence and trust, and abide in the consolation that we have a gracious God, and eternal salvation on account of the Lord Jesus Christ" (995).

The Lord's Supper is a sacrament only if the institution of Christ is observed as he appointed it. "Where his institution is observed and His words are spoken over the bread and wine, and the consecrated bread and wine are distributed, Christ Himself, through the spoken words, is still efficacious by virtue of the first institution, through His word which He wishes to be there repeated" (999). The consecration alone makes no sacrament; it must be followed by distribution and reception. "This blessing or the recitation of the words of the institution of Christ alone does not make a sacrament if the entire action of the Supper, as it was instituted by Christ, is not observed (as when the consecrated bread is not distributed, received or partaken of, but is enclosed, sacrificed, or carried about)" (1001). This was directed against the Roman Catholic abuse and perversion of the sacrament, namely, the withdrawal of the cup from the laity, the sacrifice of the mass and exhibition of the host for adoration in the mass and in eucharistic processions. "Nothing has the nature of a sacrament apart from the use instituted by Christ" (*ib.*).

(b) The controversy upon the Lord's Supper involved also a dispute concerning the Lutheran *Christology*. The Heidelberg theologians denied the absolute omnipresence (ubiquitas) of Christ and the *communicatio idiomatum*. Against this the Wurtemberg theologians, Jacob Andreae and especially Brenz, defended the Lutheran Christology. The latter carried Luther's conception of the personal union of both natures to its logical conclusion and maintained that the absolute omnipresence of Christ did not begin with the exaltation but with the first moment of his incarnation. Wherever the deity is, there is also the humanity of Christ. Christ was omnipotent and omniscient while he lay in the manger. During his earthly life he exercised these divine attributes, although secretly. While he hung on the cross in humiliation, he darkened the sun in his majesty. While he lay dead in the sepulchre, he at the same time was filling and ruling heaven and earth.

Brenz's theory does not clearly distinguish between the two states and makes incarnation not only the assumption of the human nature but also a deification of it and the subsequent exaltation merely the manifestation of what actually existed.

The Saxon Crypto-Calvinists also rejected the *communicatio idiomatum*. Against them Martin Chemnitz, in 1571, published his famous book *De duabus naturis in Christo*. The humanity of Christ receives by virtue of the personal union the divine attributes. It is permeated with deity, after analogy of heat in the iron. This interpenetration is termed *perichoresis*. The humanity is the organ of the will of the Logos. Hence the ubiquity is to be understood not as an absolute but as a relative ubiquity, a multivolipresence, depending altogether on the will of Christ. The God-man determines to be bodily present where and when he pleases to be or has promised to be.

The decision of the Formula of Concord was chiefly influenced by the Christology of Chemnitz, especially by his detailed exposition of the *communicatio idiomatum*. According to Article VIII, *Of the Person of Christ*, neither nature exists apart from the other. The two natures are one single person, the God-man, so that where the one is the other must also be. ". . . in this one undivided person of Christ there are two distinct natures, the divine which is from eternity, and the human, which in time was assumed into the unity of the person of the Son of God; which two natures in the person of Christ are never either separated from, or mingled with, one another, or changed the one into the other, but each abides in its nature and essence in the person of Christ to all eternity" (1017).

The communion of natures in personal unity involves a real mutual *communicatio idiomatum*, or interchange of properties. "From this basis of the personal union, that is, from the manner in which the divine and the human nature in the person of Christ, are united with one another, namely, that they have not only the names in common, but have also in deed and truth communion with one another, without any commingling or equalizing of the same in their essence, flows also the doctrine *de communicatione idiomatum*, that is, concerning the true communion of the properties of the natures" (1025).

(1) According to Article VIII of the *Solida Declaratio* the properties of one nature are transferred and applied to the whole person. This is technically called *the idiomatic genus.* "Since in Christ two distinct natures exist and remain unchanged and unconfused in their natural essence and properties, and yet of both natures there is only one person, hence, that which is, indeed, an attribute of only one nature is ascribed not to that nature alone, as separate, but to the entire person, which is at the same time God and man" (1027). "The person, i. e., Christ suffers and dies. Now the person is true God; therefore it is rightly said: The Son of God suffers. For although the one part (to speak thus), namely, the divinity, does not suffer, yet the person which is God, suffers in the other part, namely, in His humanity. . . . For in His nature God cannot die; but now that God and man are united in one person, it is correctly called God's death, when the man dies who is one thing or one person with God" (1029).

(2) The redemptory functions and actions which belong to the whole person are predicated only of one or the other nature. This is called the *apotelesmatic genus.* The person, neither God nor man alone but the God-man, effects salvation according to both natures. He shed His blood according to the human nature, but the divine nature gave infinite and divine efficacy and merit to the human satisfaction. The Greek word *apotelesma* designates an official act, more specifically Christ's redemptory work. Hence the name apotelesmatic genus designates the method of communication of attributes applied with special reference to the redemptory work of the God-man. "As to the execution of the office of Christ, the person does not act and work in, with, through, or according to only one nature, but in, according to, with and through both natures, or, as the Council of Chalcedon expresses it, one nature operates in communion with the other what is a property of each. Therefore, Christ is our Mediator, Redeemer, King, High Priest, Head, Shepherd, etc., not according to one nature only, whether it be the divine or human, but according to both natures" (1031).

(3) The human nature is clothed and magnified by the divine nature, which imparts to the human nature its attributes, that is, omnipotence, omnipresence and omniscience (1021). The divine attributes do not become the attributes of the human nature as if

the human nature were transformed into the divine. Both natures remain separate and distinct. But the human nature shares in the attributes of the divine nature, whence it follows that "also according to His assumed human nature and with the same, He can be, and also is present, where He will; . . . the entire person of Christ is present, to which both natures belong, the divine and the human. . . Even as He has instituted His Holy Supper for the certain assurance and confirmation of this, that also according to that nature according to which He has flesh and blood He will be with us, and dwell, work and be efficacious in us" (1043). This is called the *magestic genus*. The divine nature, however, has received no accession or detraction from the incarnation, for a communication of the properties of the human nature to the divine nature would be inconsistent with the unchangeableness of the divine nature (1031).

In the *humiliation* the divine nature, though never wholly quiescent, refrained to a certain extent from the exercise and revelation of its full glory. After the resurrection from the dead, the human nature also "has its *exaltation* above all creatures in heaven and on earth; which is nothing else than that He entirely laid aside the form of a servant, and yet did not lay aside His human nature, but retains it to eternity, and is put in the full possession and use of the divine majesty according to His assumed human nature" (1023).

The Formula of Concord presents here a loose and incongruous combination of the views of Luther and Brenz and those of Chemnitz. The real gain from the controversy is the separation of the two states which now took an important place in Christology.

8. *The Controversy upon the Descensus ad Inferos.*— Johann Aepinus, Superintendent of Hamburg, in 1544, considered the *descensus* the final act of Christ's humiliation and taught that Christ descended into Hades to suffer the pains of hell for the salvation of men. He explained I Pet. 3:18 as referring to a proclamation made by Christ in his divine nature before the incarnation. Garcaeus of Hamburg opposed him. The controversy, though a bitter one, was of a local nature only.

The Formula of Concord in Article XI implies that the descent belongs to the state of exaltation, and asserts that "the entire person, God and Man, after the burial descended into hell, conquered the devil, destroyed the power of hell and took from the devil all his might. We should not, however, trouble ourselves with high and acute thoughts as to how this occurred . . . but believe it and adhere to the Word. Thus we retain the substance and consolation that neither hell nor the devil can take captive or injure us and all who believe in Christ" (1051).

9. *The Controversy upon Predestination.—* In 1560 Hesshusen assailed the Calvinistic view of predestination. Soon after, Johann Marbach, a Lutheran pastor of Strassburg, combated Hieronymus Zanchius, Reformed professor at Strassburg who taught that the elect by virtue of the gift of preserverance cannot lose faith. This controversy was settled by the adoption of a mediating formula.

The Formula of Concord, however, in order . . . "to prevent disagreement and separation in the future among our successors, as well as among us," stated the common faith of the Lutheran Church concerning the doctrine of predestination in Article XI.

Over against the Calvinistic view of predestination the Formula states that God desires that all should be saved. He calls all sinners, and in his word he promises to give them salvation. God's grace extends its operation equally to all; it is truly *universal;* and God's call is *serious and efficacious* in all. "Christ calls to himself all sinners and promises them rest and He is in earnest that all men should come to Him and suffer themselves to be helped, to whom He offers Himself in His Word, and wishes them to hear it and not to stop their ears or despise the Word" (833). "As the preaching of repentance, so also the promise of the Gospel is *universalis*, that is, it pertains to all men" (1071). Consequently, it is not God's foreknowledge or his election which is responsible that many are lost, but the human will which does not accept the free grace of God. God's call can be resisted and therefore it is not always effectual. "That many are called and few chosen, Matt. 22: 14, does not mean that God is not willing to save everybody; but the reason is that they either do not at all hear God's Word, but wilfully despise it . . . or, when they have heard it, make light of it again and do not heed it, for which not God or His election, but their wickedness is responsible" (835).

We must accurately distinguish between God's *foreknowledge* and *predestination* or eternal election. Foreknowledge extends to all creatures and things both evil and good, but it is not the cause of evil or sin. Predestination extends to God's children and all good things; it is the cause of their salvation (831; 1063).

The gracious will of God is based upon the merit of Christ, not upon our works or anything in us. It is therefore out of God's pure, free mercy in Christ that we are saved (*sola gratia*). "It is false and wrong [conflicts with the Word of God] when it is taught that not alone the mercy of God and the most holy merit of Christ, but that also in us there is a cause of God's election, on account of which God has chosen us to eternal life. For not only before we had done anything good, but also before we were born, yea even before the foundations of the world were laid, He elected us in Christ" (1093). "By this doctrine and explanation of the eternal and saving choice (predestination) of the elect children of God, His own glory is entirely and fully given to God, that in Christ He saves us out of pure and free mercy, without any merits or good works of ours, according to the purpose of His will, Eph. 1:5 f." (1091).

God in His eternal divine counsel determined that he would save no one except those who truly believe on Christ (835). "For this has been decided by the Father, from eternity, that whom He would save He would save through Christ" (1085).

This gracious election of God in Christ is revealed in the Scriptures and sealed in the sacraments. "He has not only promised this gracious election with mere words, but has also certified it with an oath and sealed it with the holy Sacraments" (835).

The Formula of Concord reproduces Luther's distinction between the secret and the revealed will and states that it is for us to avoid speculation on the hidden will of God and to confine our attention to his revealed and gracious will. The earnestness of the universal promise admits of no hidden will of God at variance with his revealed will, even though there are many things still secret to us (1075; 1079).

Those who believe in Christ know themselves as elect. Their partaking of salvation is founded upon God's eternal purpose which cannot fail nor be overthrown. Therefore God's eternal election engenders assurance of our salvation, for it rests alone in the hands of God. Hence the Formula of Concord calls the doctrine of predestination a very useful, salutary consolatory doctrine, "for it establishes very effectually the article that we are justified and saved without all works and merits of ours, purely out of grace alone, for Christ's sake" (1077).

The elect, however, are not to be idle but "should use the greatest diligence to live according to the will of God" (835) and "make their calling and election sure, in order that they may doubt the less concerning it the more they experience the power and strength of the Spirit within them. For the Spirit bears witness to the elect that they are God's children, Rom. 8:16. . . . And since our salvation to eternal life is founded not upon our godliness or virtue, but alone upon the merit of Christ and the gracious will of His Father, who cannot deny Himself, because He is unchangeable in will and essence, therefore, when His children depart from obedience and stumble, He has them called again to repentance through the Word, and the Holy Ghost wishes thereby to be efficacious in them for conversion; and when they turn to Him again in true repentance by a right faith, He will always manifest the old paternal heart to all those who tremble at His Word and from their heart turn again to Him, as it is written, Jer. 3:1" (1087).

To sum up: The Formula of Concord maintains that whoever is saved is saved by grace alone, and whoever is lost is lost through his own fault alone. The Formula of Concord acknowledges, but does not attempt to solve, the mystery why some are saved and some are lost. Later the Lutheran dogmaticians attempted to offer a solution by teaching that God determined to save all those *whom he foresaw* would believe. But the dogmatical phrase that predestination takes place "in foresight of faith," *intuitu fidei*, does not solve the mystery, since faith, according to the Scripture, is a free gift of grace and can therefore never be the cause of election. But the Formula of Concord, true to its character of a confession, simply bears testimony to two great truths taught in the Bible and does not attempt to solve the problems involved and therefore "remains on the right safe way." For where "God has concealed much concerning this mystery" we are not to "harmonize, inquire or draw conclusions," but to believe, defend and faithfully "to adhere to the revealed Word of God" (1078 f.).

The Formula of Concord attempted to ward off error from without and from within and establish permanent peace and harmony within the Lutheran Church. This was the purpose of the first eleven Articles. Article XII treats of *Other Factions and Sects* and recounts the errors of the Anabaptists, the Schwenkfeldians and the "new Antitrinitarians." As the first eleven Articles present the already fixed results of doctrinal development, so the twelfth Article simply puts on record the complete severance of the Lutheran Church from the sects, which had long been a historical fact. "The Formula of Concord was to leave no doubt regarding the fact that the Lutheran Church offers a united front in every direction: against the Romanists, the Calvinists, the errorists that had risen in their own midst, and self-evidently also against the sects and fanatics, old and modern, with whom the Romanists slanderously identified them" (Concordia Triglotta, on Art. XII, p. 228 f.).

The Formula of Concord received symbolical recognition when the princes and magistrates as the legal and official representatives of the respective communities adopted the Formula by attaching their signature. It was published at Dresden, June 25, 1580, on the fiftieth anniversary of the Augsburg Confession and issued in one volume with the previous Lutheran Symbols as the *Book of Concord*.

CHAPTER XXII

SECTS OF THE SIXTEENTH CENTURY IN OPPOSITION TO THE CHURCH'S DOCTRINE

A. The strict adherence of the reformers to the objective means of grace, the Word of God and the sacraments, provoked *dissent in the form of mysticism* or subjectivism in the apprehension of the Christian religion. Likewise their spirit of historical conservatism toward civil and ecclesiastical institutions axcited a *revolution against the existing order* of things in church and state. Radical leaders, such as Carlstadt and Muenzer, insisted that Luther should go faster and further in his reforms.

During the sojourn of Luther at the Wartburg, Andreas Bodenstein, better known as Carlstadt, abolished all existing forms which he deemed inconsistent with the new doctrine, and introduced sweeping changes in the rites of worship. The trouble was increased by the arrival of certain fanatics from Zwickau, "celestial prophets" as they boldly styled themselves, who claimed to be directly inspired by the Holy Ghost. On the ground of the alleged instigation of the Spirit these "prophets" insisted on the immediate abolition of the existing church order.

Realizing the importance of the crisis Luther returned to Wittenberg, in March, 1522, and contended resolutely and successfully against this species of subjectivism. He rejected the claim of the enthusiasts to the "inner light" as the supreme tribunal of truth and maintained that the Holy Ghost speaks only through the Word of God. There must be no violent abolition of church rites and usages. Ecclesiastical changes must come about naturally. The inward power of the Word must accomplish the work. As a result of Luther's interference the commotion was subdued. Carlstadt and the Zwickau prophets were expelled from Wittenberg and order was restored. The wild and destructive fanaticism, however, did not cease to exist, but spread rapidly through Germany combining itself with the political radicalism of the peasants' insurrection.

Thomas Muenzer, a prominent Zwickau prophet and zealous preacher of ecclesiastical revolution, acquainted with the works of Suso, Tauler and other Mystics, had been a disciple of Luther. But he soon became dissatisfied with the moderate and conservative character of the Lutheran Reformation and attempted to bring to pass revolutionary changes of a social, ecclesiastical and political nature.

He also pronounced infant baptism unscriptural. Wherever he went he announced his spiritual gospel by pointing to the near advent of the Antichrist. Following the "inner light" to kill the godless and establish a kingdom of the saints here on earth he became involved in the Peasants' War, was defeated and beheaded by the magistrates in 1525.

His adherents, like their leader, were hostile to infant baptism as being inefficacious and having no Scripture warrant. They were therefore known as Antipedobaptists. As they insisted on rebaptism in case of those who had been baptized in their infancy, they were known as Anabaptists or Rebaptizers. They held that the church must be composed only of the saints, that is, of those who are truly regenerate, being baptized on confession of faith. They repudiated any union of church and state or any interference of the civil power with ecclesiastical affairs. They also maintained that no believer should hold the office of magistrate. The party was everywhere persecuted.

Anabaptist opinions of a more moderate and conservative nature spread in Switzerland. Zwingli with his novel doctrine of the sacraments as outward testimonies of the grace already present in the individual was not able to beat the Antipedobaptists in argument and had to resort to ridicule and persecution, forcing from his former friend Balthasar Huebmaier on pain of death a humiliating and false confession. Huebmaier represented the simple, conservative Anabaptist doctrine. The Anabaptist leaders, however, were under suspicion of sympathizing with fanatical schemes of sedition. As their movement spread from Switzerland into Moravia, Tyrol, Salzburg and the two Austrias, a systematic persecution began. Huebmaier was executed at Vienna, in 1527.

In Holland, as early as 1537, Menno Simons had gathered and organized into regular congregations those Anabaptist fanatics who under the leadership of Muenzer, Storch and others had caused general confusion for a number of years in Germany and other states of Europe, and in 1533, in the city of Muenster in Westphalia, established a "millennium" with communism and polygamy, and a reign of terror and licentiousness. Menno Simons, a former Catholic priest, severed his connection with the Roman Catholic Church, in 1536, affiliated himself with the more conservative Anabaptists, was rebaptized and ordained an elder at Groningen, in 1537, with imposition of hands by Obbe Philips who is regarded as the actual founder of the Mennonite body. Simons was an Anabaptist of the pacific type. After his death, in 1559, his followers were called

Mennonites. They separated already during the lifetime of Menno into a stricter and a more lenient party, but they have in common the following beliefs and practices: Regeneration is effected solely by the Holy Spirit without external means such as the Word or the sacraments. The two sacraments are signs or symbols. Baptism is a public testimony of faith ... Partaking of the Lord's Supper expresses a common union with one another and a fellowship of love for, and faith in, Christ. Infant baptism is rejected as unscriptural. Baptism of believers is, as a rule, administered by affusion. Feet washing, though not a sacrament, is an ordinance instituted, and its proper observance commanded, by Christ. Only true believers and regenerate persons constitute the church. Civil government is a divine appointment; therefore a Christian obeys the magistrate wherever it does not conflict with the Word of God or interfere with the dictates of conscience. On the ground of Matt. 5:37 and James 5:12 oaths are to be rejected. Likewise war is to be rejected, since Christ has forbidden his followers the use of carnal force in resisting evil. Civil government, while a divine appointment, is not an institution of Christ's kingdom, and therefore secular office-holding is inconsistent with true Christian character.

Menno Simons held a peculiar view as to Christ's incarnation. He maintained that Christ did not assume his flesh and blood of the Virgin Mary, but that "the whole Christ, God and man, man and God, is God's Son and is in heaven." If the man Christ were of the flesh and blood of Mary, he would be a created being and could not be God's Son. The peculiar doctrine was also held by the Obbenites, followers of Obbe Philips, before Menno identified himself with them. The Formula of Concord takes note of this erroneous view under "Erroneous Articles of the Anabaptists" (C. Trigl. 1097 f.).

In 1606, John Smyth, who had been a clergyman of the Church of England, fled, with a small body of Separatists, from England to Holland to escape persecution. Here he came in contact with Mennonites and followers of Arminius. This led the erratic though able man to the adoption of many new opinions. He became convinced that infant baptism has no Scripture ground and therefore baptized himself, hence called the Se-Baptist. He set forth his radical views on infant baptism in his publication *The Character of the Beast*, 1609, on account of which he was excommunicated from the English Separatist Church at Amsterdam. Several of his followers joined him and the first English Baptist Church was organized at Amsterdam, practicing the baptism of believers only. Smyth's se-baptism was probably an affusion. Puritans, Separatists and Mennonites practiced both affusion and immersion at this time. In 1611, Thomas Helwys, who succeeded Smyth in the leadership, returned with his followers to London, where they established the first Baptist Church in England.

Quite different in spirit from Muenzer and other religious radicals of the sixteenth century was the Silesian mystic Caspar Schwenkfeld. A disciple of Luther he helped, as early as 1519, to spread the principles of the Reformation in Silesia. In 1522 he made personal acquaintance with the Wittenberg divines with whom he worked at first in harmony. Soon, however, he developed certain lines of belief which were not acceptable to the Lutheran reformers. He became so dissatisfied with Lutheranism that he declared he would rather join the Papists than the Lutherans. Both Catholics and Lutherans urged the Duke of Liegnitz, in whose court service Schwenkfeld was employed, to dismiss him and suppress his teaching. In 1528 he was banished from his native country. Southern Germany became now the chief scene of his labors. In the face of constant opposition on the part of the German and Swiss reformers he sought quietly to carry on a reformation according to his own views. He was unable to stay in any place for more than a short time. He died at Ulm, in 1561, leaving behind a small company of adherents. They were found chiefly in South Germany, Tyrol and Silesia. In the last named region of Germany they formed a distinct sect which has lasted until the present time.

Schwenkfeld denied the Lutheran conception of the Word of God and the sacraments as means of grace. He called Luther's insisting upon the unconditional authority of the Word of God a bondage to the letter, and gave to the inner word of God's Spirit in man a place superior to the outward Word of God in Scripture. The baptism of adults is as unavailing as that of infants. A service of prayer and exhortation over newly born infants, as they are presented at church for the first time, takes the place of infant baptism. In the Lord's Supper the bread is a symbol of the true bread of the soul, which is Christ himself. With Schwenkfeld the essential thing in the salvation of man is not faith in Christ's death and atonement but the mystic union with the deified and glorified Christ. Schwenkfeld confounded justification with sanctification and, similarly with Osiander, declared it to be a work within the believer, an incarnation of Christ in him, permeating him with the Spirit of Christ until he becomes one with Christ. The Formula of Concord, in Article XII, condemns seven erroneous articles of the Schwenkfeldians.

B. About the middle of the sixteenth century there arose and spread a far-reaching radical movement in the form of a *rationalism* which attacked even the ecumenical basis of the church. This rationalism had its roots in the Renaissance culture. The movement was in the direction of *Unitarianism.*

Anti-Trinitarian views were held by Anabaptists, such as Denk, Hetzer, Melchior Hofmann and others. The chief exponents of Unitarianism in this period were Italians imbued with the spirit of the Italian Renaissance, such as Gentilis, Blandrata, Gribaldi, Faustus Socinus and his uncle Laelius. The Spanish physician and classical scholar Michael Servetus obtained a special prominence among the earlier representatives of this movement by reason of his tragic fate. In his *Christianismi Restitutio* he denies the tripersonality of the Godhead and the eternity of the Son. He also rejects infant baptism. The *Restitutio* aroused the antagonism of Catholics and Protestants alike. After he had escaped the Catholic inquisition, he was arrested while passing through Geneva, and with the full consent of Calvin, condemned as heretic and burned alive, in 1553, though Calvin preferred for him the milder execution by the sword.

The heretical sect of the Socinians represents in this period the organized opposition to the doctrine of the Trinity. They were the followers of Faustus Socinus, an Italian free-thinker and anti-Trinitarian (b. at Siena, 1539, d. near Crakow, 1604), who originated his doctrine on the basis of hints and suggestions found in the papers left by his uncle, Laelius Socinus (d. 1562). They rejected official creeds altogether. Their deviations from universal Christian faith are exhibited in the Racovian Catechism, published in 1605, a year after the death of Faustus. The Racovian Catechism became the chief symbol of the Socinians.

The Socinians adhered to the authority of the Scripture as a sufficient source of divine revelation, and rejected traditions "which were not only established and invented without any reason or just necessity but are also most detrimental to Christian faith." Faustus admitted that the sacred writers both of the Old and New Testament were inspired in respect to the content of religious truth, and that in secondary matters even the apostles might err. The Catechism does not expressly speak of the inspiration of the Scripture but merely maintains the trustworthiness and certainty of Holy Writ. Scripture is not to be interpreted and judged by Scripture but in accordance with reason, and moral significance and utility. Accordingly the Old Testament, though inspired, is practically superfluous and of only historical and not at all dogmatic value.

The New Testament is the only source of Christian knowledge, but only in so far as it is doctrine, i. e., a new divine legislation.

The doctrine of the Trinity as being opposed to reason is rejected. "Plurality of persons in one divine essence is impossible" (Faustus). God is an individual; he is neither omnipresent, for Scripture says, he is in heaven; nor is he omniscient, for his foreknowledge is limited to the necessary and does not apply to the possible. If he foreknew the free acts of men, there would be no human freedom. Accordingly predestination is rejected. God being inscrutable in himself has revealed himself through Christ who was a man miraculously conceived by the Virgin Mary, but who did not exist before he was born of Mary. He is the Son of God by adoption. Before entering upon his office as a teacher he was caught up into heaven for a season (John 3:13, 31; 6:38, 62) like Paul. There he was empowered to show men the way to God through his teaching and life. Christ's suffering and death are in no sense a vicarious atonement. His death and resurrection merely testify to the truth of his teaching. The Catechism expressly teaches that the New Testament denies to Christ the divine nature. After his resurrection God rewarded his obedience by delegating divine power to him as to a viceroy; therefore he may be worshipped. Only since his ascension has Christ an immortal body. This doctrine was in its essence a revival of Dynamic Monarchianism, taught in the third century by Paul of Samosata : Christ becomes Son of God by the infusion of a divine character into a human person.

Creation out of nothing is denied. Got created the world out of pre-existing matter. Man is created mortal. God's image in man denotes man's dominion over all the creatures upon earth. By the exercise of his own free will man attains to faith, i. e., he accepts Christ's teaching and by following Christ's example he obtains eternal life. There is no such thing as native total depravity. Human sin is merely the imitation of Adam's sin, as salvation is the imitation and adoption of Christ's virtue.

The Holy Spirit is not a divine person but a power of influence exerted by God. Baptism and Communion are not means of grace, but useful, though not necessary, ceremonies. Baptism was instituted for the first still sensual Christians among Jews and Gentiles. It may be applied to more recent proselytes, but it is unessential for those born of Christian parents. Immersion is essential; baptism was not commanded or designed for infants; yet the sprinkling of infants may, in Christian love, be tolerated. The Lord's Supper is a memorial of Christ's death. Great emphasis is laid upon the symbolic idea of the breaking of the bread.

The true church is essentially a school of the true knowledge of God — "the company of those who hold and profess sound doctrine." Any one without being properly called may teach in the church. Active obedience to the civil power is due only where there is no conflict with God's word. Faustus strongly emphasized the unlawfulness not only of war but of the taking of human life in any circumstances. Holding magisterial office is in conflict with the law of Christ. There is no resurrection of the body nor eternal punishment of the wicked; the ungodly together with the devil and his angels will be finally annihilated.

Socinianism flourished especially in Poland where it triumphed over the Church of Rome in these lines:

> *Tota ruit Babylon; destruxit tecta Lutherus,*
> *Calvinus muros, sed fundamenta Socinus.*

The triumph, however, was short-lived. Upon the instigation of the Jesuits the Socinians were expelled from Poland in 1658. Since then only scattered Socinian congregations have existed, except in Transylvania where they maintain themselves to the present day numbering ca. 60,000.

CHAPTER XXIII

CALVIN'S THEOLOGY AND HIS PLACE IN THE
HISTORY OF DOCTRINE

John Calvin (b. 1509, d. 1564) belonged to the second generation of reformers. Having received his reformatory ideas in an
essentially complete form his task was to unfold these ideas. His
well-trained, logical mind, disciplined by legal studies, a clear and
beautiful style, the religious depth of thought, and a genius for
organization fitted him for his task and made him preeminently the
theologian of the new era.

Calvin built his theology on the foundation laid by Luther and
Bucer. His theology far more approximated that of Luther than
that of Zwingli. Though highly esteemed by Luther Calvin never
stood in any close personal relation with him, but was intimate with
Melanchthon and exerted some influence over him. Later a number
of Melanchthonians definitely identified their cause with Calvinism.
In Upper Germany Bucer's compromising theology passed over into
Calvinism, and in Switzerland Calvinism triumphed everywhere
over Zwinglianism.

Calvin's system of theology is laid down in his *Institutio re-
ligionis christianae,* first published in Latin in 1536, then in French,
and much enlarged in subsequent editions. The Institutes have
remained ever since the standard of orthodox Protestant belief in all
the Reformed Churches.

A. The dominant thought in Calvin's doctrinal system is the
infinite and transcendent SOVEREIGNTY OF GOD. God is the Lord
who rules omnipotently (Inst. I. 163, 8)[*]. He is the author and
director of all things. The will of God is the cause of all events.
Even the actions of the wicked must be referred to the determination of the divine will (I. 18). According to Calvin God is the
omnipotent will ruling the universe. According to Luther God is
the omnipotent will manifesting his love in Christ Jesus. Calvin's
concept of the sovereignty of God, and Luther's concept of God's
love in Christ Jesus, are vitally related to the practical life of the
believer. "In the one case, we have acts of compulsion even in the
heart, subjection, law, service; in the other, inward conquest by the

---

[*] We use the Sixth American Edition of the Institutes, transl. from the
original Latin, and collated with Calvin's last edition in French, publ. by
Presbyt. Board of Publication, Philadelphia.

power of love, free self-surrender, filial love without compulsion. The one does not necessarily exclude the other; but the tone and emphasis give rise to the differences which undeniably exist. From the practical energies of the Reformed ideals — with which praxis has not always been able to keep pace — the Lutheran Church may learn a valuable lesson. But when in any age of evangelical Christianity, faith grows dim, and love grows cold, and it seems as though the gospel were no longer sufficient to satisfy the advanced spirit of the 'modern' world, then will deliverance be found, not in the views of Calvin, but in return to the Gospel and faith of Luther. Evangelical Christianity has yet much to learn from her Luther" (Seeberg, *Hist. of Doctr.* II. 416 f.).

In Protestant thought and life of today we note a deplorable lack of Calvin's reverence for the majestic and sovereign God. "It would do much of Protestant thinking and preaching some good if that attribute of the divine character received more emphasis. There is such a thing as bringing God so close to the human level as to lose all reverence for Him. We have heard of sermons and prayers that were shockingly familiar and irreverent. Calvin would rise from his grave if he were in a position to know how little the majesty and sovereignty of God count in the teaching and preaching of today. He would be shocked to find how the love of God is exalted to the virtual denial of His holiness and justice" (*The Lutheran*, July 28, 1927, p. 14).

All things minister to the glory of God (I. 16-18). Even the *election* of some and the *reprobation* of others redound to the glory of God. "The great and only object of our election is, that we should be to the praise of divine grace" (III. 22, 3); the reprobate are raised up for this purpose, that the glory of God may be displayed by their means" (*ib.* 11). All things being ordained for the manifestation of his glory "God determined the fall of the first man only because he foresaw it would tend to the just illustration of the glory of his name" (III. 23, 8).

Calvin maintains that God's providence according to which he ordains, rules and governs the minutest detail does nevertheless not destroy the freedom and responsibility of man. But if all things happen because God wills and ordains them, is there any room for man's liberty and responsibility? Calvin attempts to explain the difficulty by distinguishing between necessity which is "in some measure voluntary," and external coercion. "Man having been corrupted by his fall, sins voluntarily . . . with the strongest propensity of disposition, not with violent coercion; with the bias of his own passions, and not with external compulsion. . . . Thus the soul, in a certain strange and evil manner, under this kind of voluntary and free yet pernicious necessity, is both enslaved and free; enslaved by necessity, free by its will; and what is more wonderful and more miserable, it is guilty, because free" (II.3, 5).

It is further maintained that although God uses the agency of the impious, and inclines their minds to execute his judgments, he does so without the least stain upon his purity (I. 18). Calvin, however, opposes the idea that God merely permits the reprobate to be blinded by Satan and maintains that God's providence "not only exerts its power in the elect, who are influenced by the Holy Spirit, but also compels the compliance of the reprobate" (I. 18, 2; also II. 4, 3). God even determined the fall of the first man (III. 23, 8). "Man falls according to the appointment of Divine Providence," says Calvin; but in order not to represent God as compelling a reluctant person to commit sin, he adds immediately "but he falls by his own fault" (*ib.*). This is the so-called supra-lapsarian view (from *supra* – above, and *lapsus* – the fall). The supralapsarians place the degree of predestination above or before that of the fall, that is, the objects of predestination are viewed as not yet fallen, while the infralapsarians (from *infra* – below, and *lapsus* – the fall) place the decree of predestination below or after that of the fall, that is, the objects of predestination are viewed as *fallen*.

Providence in its relation to the eternal destiny of mankind is known as *predestination*. Calvin defines it as a twofold decree, a decree of election and a decree of reprobation. "Predestination we call the eternal decree of God, by which he has determined in himself, what he would have to become of every individual of mankind. For they are not all created with a similar destiny; but eternal life is foreordained for some, and eternal damnation for others" (III. 21, 5). The ground of election is not the foreseen faith of the persons elected, but the sovereign good pleasure of God. The ground of reprobation is not the forseen sin in the reprobate, but the just, but unknown, will of God. "We affirm that this counsel, as far as concerns the elect, is founded on his gratuitous mercy, totally irrespective of human merits; but that to those whom he devotes to condemnation, the gate of life is closed by a just and irreprehensible, but incomprehensible judgment" (*ib.* 7).

The controlling idea of the Calvinistic system, that of the sovereignty of God, leaves *no room for mediators* whom God himself has not chosen or ordained. To worship them is to deprive God of his honor and glory which belongs to him alone (I. 14, 10). The same is true of image worship. It is held that Ex. 20: 4, 5, Deut. 4:15 not only forbid the worship of images, but also the imaging of God

(I. 11, 2). Calvin objects to Gregory's view that "images are the books of the illiterate" and maintains "that whatever men learn respecting God from images is equally frivolous and false" (*ib.* 5).

B. God is made known to man by the SCRIPTURES (I. 6). Because God is sovereign his Word is the supreme law. The Scripture being the divine rule of everything in matters of faith and practice demands unconditional obedience on our part. The Bible is preeminently a divine law code each paragraph of which is equally binding on all men everywhere and at all times. It is, therefore, "not now left to faithful ministers to frame any new doctrine, but it behooves them simply to adhere to the doctrine to which God has made all subject, without any exception" (IV. 8, 9). Accordingly fanatics or enthusiasts, who discard the Scripture under the pretence of resorting to immediate revelations, are to be rejected (I. 9). Since it is our duty to embrace "with gentle docility and without any exception all that is delivered in the sacred Scriptures" (I. 18, 4), it follows that one cannot ascribe to the several books of the Bible nor even to the two testaments different degrees of doctrinal values (see Luther's view p. xxx). Each book is part and parcel of the one infallible rule of faith and practice. Calvin describes the meaning and significance of the old covenant as being exactly the same as that of the new. ". . . all those persons from the beginning of the world whom God has adopted into the society of his people, have been federally connected with him by the same law and the same doctrine which are in force among us. . . . The people of God have never had any other rule of religion and piety" (II. 10, 1). "The covenant of all the fathers is so far from differing substantially from ours, that it is the very same; it only varies in the administration" (*ib.* 2).

The Scriptures are the oracles of God, for their writers being "under the guidance and dictation of the Holy Spirit" were his sure and authentic amanuenses (IV. 8, 8). How do we know that the Holy Spirit is the author of the Scripture? On what grounds do we accept the Scripture as divinely inspired? Certainly not on the authority of an infallible church. Calvin had broken with this ancient authoritative system. There was for him no way to escape the necessity of restating some new basis of authority. The conviction that the Scripture was dictated and inspired by the Holy Spirit, says Calvin, is confirmed by the internal testimony of the Holy Spirit (I. 7, 5). Although the Scripture is the work of the Holy Spirit we cannot know and recognize it as such, unless the Holy Spirit persuades us of the divinity of the Scripture (I. 9, 3). The testimony of the Spirit is therefore necessary to confirm the

Scripture in order to the complete establishment of its authority. Thus combining the later Scholastic view of inspiration with Luther's conception of it Calvin was the first to propound the inspiration theory of the later orthodox theology, namely, that the same Spirit, who inspired the sacred writers, also testifies to the believer that the Scriptures are the Word of God. After the certainty of the divine origin of the Scripture has been established in our minds, *rational proofs* to confirm our belief of the Scripture have their proper place and are of great value (I. 8. 1).

C. ANTHROPOLOGY.

1. *Man.* Luther and Calvin agree in their opposition to the Scholastic doctrine of man's original state and their emphasis on man's concreated holiness and righteousness, but differ among themselves, in two points, in their definition of the compass of man's primitive perfection.

(1) In the anthropology of Calvin there is to be noted a decidedly low estimate which he places upon man's physical body. "Let it be understood that by his being made of earth and clay, a restraint was laid upon pride; since nothing is more absurd than to glory in their excellence, who not only inhabit a cottage of clay, but who are themselves composed partly of dust and ashes" (I. 15, 1). The body is "but a prison;" we are "kept in bondage by the fetters of the body" (III. 9, 4). "We are absent from God as long as we dwell in the body, . . but when absent from the body we are present with the Lord." The soul's "liberation from the prison of the body" is the "introduction into complete liberty;" hence it should be understood that this mortal life is "of itself nothing but misery," and that therefore the terrestrial life as compared with the celestial "should undoubtedly be despised and accounted of no value" (I. 15, 2). Luther's conception of man as a harmonious unity is foreign to Calvin's anthropology. Calvin admits that the glory of God is displayed in man's external form, yet he thinks that "extending the image of God promiscuously to the body as well as to the soul confounds heaven and earth together" (*ib.* 3). This Platonizing and spiritualistic tendency which resembles very much the dualism as we find it in the Scholastic anthropology is still more apparent in Zwingli's anthropology (see p. xxx).

(2) Calvin, like Luther, emphasized man's concreated holiness and righteousness. But here we notice the second point of difference between Lutheran and Calvinistic anthropology. Luther saw in the free will of man in his original state the *right direction* of the natural will, so that nothing in man or outside man could hinder him from being what he was, holy and righteous; the possibility of

sinning being merely a possibility of giving up his God-given freedom. Calvin saw in man's original freedom a *mere formal freedom,* a power of contrary choice. Leaving aside "the question respecting the secret predestination of God . . . what was the real nature of man? Adam could have stood if he would, since he fell merely by his own will; but because his will was flexible to either side, and he was not endued with constancy to persevere, therefore he so easily fell" (I. 15, 8). This conception of man's will in his original state as being "flexible to either side" and not being "endued with constancy to persevere," comes very near the Scholastic idea of the superadded gift of grace which man needed to prevent an inner moral contradiction. The following much discussed passage seems to be proof of the assertion made. "And, indeed, I much approve of that common observation, which has been borrowed from Augustine, that the natural talents in man have been corrupted by sin, but that of the supernatural ones he has been wholly deprived" (II. 2, 12).

For reasons sufficient unto himself God sovereignly decreed to permit Adam to fall from the state of integrity and holiness (III. 23, 8). Adam's sin consisted in disobedience, "revolting from the government of the Creator" (II. 1, 4). His fall involved the whole human race. "By his fall he drew all his posterity with him into destruction" (*ib.*). The question, how is Adam's sin transmitted to all his posterity? is answered by Calvin "because it was ordained by God, that the gifts which he conferred on the first man should by him be preserved or lost both for himself and for all his posterity" (II. 1, 7). Original sin, i. e., the hereditary depravity and corruption of our nature attaches to all men and pervades the entire being of man (*ib.* 8). It first makes man an object of God's wrath and then manifests itself in the works of the flesh (*ib.*). It is truly sin and, like actual sin, brings guilt upon the sinner (*ib.* 9, 10, 11). Zwingli's theory of original sin as a defect, which one derives from birth without his own fault, and which therefore involves no sin, was not adopted by Calvin.

2. *Man's Conversion.* Fallen man has lost all ability of the will to any spiritual good (III. 14, 1) but he commits evil by free will and not from coercion (II. 2, 7). But man destitute of saving knowledge and dead in sin is called to salvation by the preaching of the gospel. However, only the elect are called effectually (*irresistible grace*) (III. 24). And whosoever is called effctually, "not only can come, but also actually comes" (*ib.* 1). Calvin sharply distinguishes between the *external calling* taking place only through the word as an outward means, and the *internal calling* being effected by the Spirit accompanying the word. The external calling

very often takes place without the inner calling, but the latter always presupposes the former. "There is a universal call, by which God, in the external preaching of the word, invites all, . . . and a special call, . . . when by the inward illumination of his Spirit, he causes the word preached to sink into their hearts" (III. 24, 8). Explaining John 6:45, "Every one that hath heard and learned of the Father cometh unto me," Calvin says, "when the Father is heard within he takes away the heart of stone and gives a heart of flesh" (*ib.* 1). This special call "favors only believers, i. e., the elect," while the external call is intended to be "a savour of death, and an occasion of heavier condemnation" to the reprobate (*ib.* 8).

The first act of inward calling is *faith* which the Holy Spirit works in us. Calvin, like Luther, maintains that faith is a free gift of God, but lays more stress than Luther upon the intellectual element of faith. "Faith consists in a knowledge of God in Christ" (III. 2, 2, 3). "Faith is a knowledge of the will of God respecting us . . . And the foundation of this is a previous persuasion of the divine veracity" (*ib.* 6).

From faith proceeds *repentance* which extends through the whole life of the believer. It consists in the mortification of the flesh together with the crucifying of the old man within us and a and a vivification by the Spirit. In contradistinction to Luther's teaching that contrition or repentance wrought by the law precedes faith, Calvin maintains that repentence follows faith. "Repentance not only immediately follows faith, but is produced by it" (III. 3. 1). By repentance Calvin means the renewal of life which follows faith. He admits "that many are overcome or led to obedience by terrors of conscience before they have imbibed a knowledge of grace" (III. 3, 2), but this he would not call repentance. Nor is it necessary according to Calvin that a person pass through this "initial fear," these terrors of conscience, for Christ has many ways to draw us to himself.

Luther certainly did not want to dictate a certain method of conversion, but he did strictly hold to, and insist upon, the only safe and certain, because Biblical, method of conversion, according to which the Holy Spirit, through the law, working recognition of guilt and remorse for sin, leads man to repentance so that he cries out "What must I do to be saved?" and, through the gospel, revealing to the repentent sinner God's love in Christ works faith which receives and accepts the righteousness which God gives.

Calvin apparently felt that his arrangement of faith and repentance was not quite in harmony with Scripture, as when Christ and the Baptist "first exhort the people to repentance, and afterwards adds that the kingdom of heaven is at hand" (*ib.*). But even in these texts Calvin sees nothing but proofs of his idea of faith and repentance and says of those who do not see this that "they superstitiously attend to the connection of syllables and disregard the sense and coherence of the words" (*ib.*).— Yet leaving aside "superstitiously attending to the connection of syllables" and merely regarding "the sense and coherence" of these words: "The time is fulfilled and the kingdom of heaven is at hand: repent ye, and believe the gospel," Mark 1:15, we cannot but say that repentance must precede faith.

D. CHRIST.— To redeem man from his state of guilt God decreed that his Son should become man.

1. *Christ's Person.* In agreement with the ancient Creeds, particularly the Chalcedonian, Calvin states (II. 14) that in Christ there is but one person and this one person has two natures. "Each nature retains its properties entire, and yet both together constitute one Christ" (*ib.* 1) "To confound the two natures in Christ, and to separate them, are equally wrong" (*ib.* 4).

We have noticed (p. xxx) that there was disagreement between Luther and the Swiss Reformer as to the mutual relation of the two natures in Christ. Calvin's Christology does not essentially differ from that of Zwingli. He repudiates the idea that "the Word of God was confined within the narrow prison of an earthly body," and goes even so far as to say, "the Son of God miraculously descended from heaven, yet in such a manner that he never left heaven" (II. 13. 4). Speaking of Christ's agony in Gethsemane Calvin says, "We see that what was contrary to his will as man, was agreeable to his will as God" (*ib.* 16, 12). Properly speaking it was not Christ who suffered and died for us, but his human nature. In opposition to Luther's view of a real communion of the two natures, Calvin as well as Zwingli held that God is so infinitely exalted above the creature, and so essentially different from it, that the finite cannot take up the infinite.

2. *Christ's Work.* The incarnate Christ took upon him the office of prophet, priest and king. As prophet he revealed the Father (II. 15, 1, 2). As priest he made atonement through his sacrifice (II. 12, 3; 15, 6). By his obedience he fulfilled the law in our stead (II. 16, 5). By his suffering unto death he endured the wrath of God including eternal death and condemnation. By his resurrection and ascension to heaven he perfected his work and restored man to righteousness. The ascended Lord is our advocate and interecessor in heaven (II. 16, 13; 16). As king he exercises spiritual and eternal dominion over the church and through the Spirit bestows grace

upon man (*ib.*). The distinctive Calvinistic teaching is chiefly apparent regarding the priestly office of Christ. On the one hand, Calvin lays great emphasis on the objective necessity of Christ's redemptive work. "Christ by his obedience has really procured and merited grace from the Father for us. . Christ has satisfied for our sins. We have been purified by his blood, and his death was an expiation for sins" (II. 17, 3, 4). On the other hand, in viewing Christ's atoning sacrifice Calvin is influenced by his conception of God's sovereignty and predestination. God has chosen the elect before the foundation of the world. He is sovereign. Therefore there can be with him no necessity of Christ's work for the salvation of the elect. "When we speak of the merit of Christ, therefore, we do not consider him as the origin of it, but we ascend to the ordination of God which is the first cause; . . . Christ could merit nothing except by the good pleasure of God, by which he had been predestinated to appease the divine wrath by his sacrifice" (*ib.* 1). From the fact that God has purposed that only the elect should be saved, and others left to the just consequences of their sins, it follows that Christ did not die for the whole world and, consequently, the atonement is particular and not general. The vicarious satisfaction of Christ is said to be inseparably connected with election, the former being possible only through the latter. (II. 17, 1).

Concerning the states of Christ there is a difference between Calvin's and Luther's teaching. According to Luther, Christ's descent into Hades is the first stage of his exaltation. According to Calvin it is the last stage of his humiliation. The Formula of Concord, following Luther, states that Christ, the entire person, God and man, after the burial descended into hell to triumph over the power of darkness. Calvin taught that Christ on the cross when he felt himself forsaken of God, experienced in his own soul the pains of the lost. This is, according to Calvin, the meaning of Christ's descent into Hades. "If his soul had experienced no punishment, he would have been only a Redeemer for the body" (II. 16, 12). "He suffered in his soul the dreadful torments of a person condemned and irretrievably lost" (*ib.* 10). "The order of things in the Apostles' Creed, according to which the descent is subsequent to the burial, which really preceded it" is to be explained not chronologically but logically. "For the relation of those sufferings of Christ, which were visible to men, is very properly followed by that invisible and incomprehensible vengeance which he suffered from the hand of God" (*ib.*)

E. JUSTIFICATION AND SANCTIFICATION.— The believer united to Christ by faith or "grafted into him" receives a *duplex gratia*, a twofold grace, namely, justification and regeneration or sanctification.

1. *Justification.* In full accord with Luther Calvin asserts that justification consists in the forgiveness of sin and in the imputation of Christ's righteousness. God justifies "by absolving and pardoning us; we are justified by gratuitous imputation . . . Sinners being invested with the righteousness of Christ . . . are accounted righteous . . . Justification is opposed to accusation; which antithesis clearly demonstrates, that the form of expression is borrowed from the practice of courts" (III. 11, 11). "Man is justified by faith alone" (*ib.* 19). Not that "faith were to justify of itself, or by an intrinsic efficacy"; it is only "a vessel," "the instrument by which righteousness is received" (*ib.* 7). Justification as a forensic act must not be confounded with the renewal of life. "It is one thing to be justified, and another thing to be made new creatures." Osiander in confusing the two "erroneously made of two good parts one corrupt whole . . . in justification there is no regard paid to works" (*ib.* 6).

This clear-cut presentation of this doctrine, however, suffers some eclipse from Calvin's theory of predestination. Although he states that "Christ is apprehended and possessed by us by faith and we, being by his innocence reconciled to God, have a propitious father instead of a judge" (*ib.* 1), he also maintains "those, whom God has chosen, he designates as his children, and determines himself to be their Father" (III. 24. 1). God, then, does not first justify the sinner who by faith apprehends Christ's righteousness; God has from eternity determined to look up him as being righteous in his sight. By faith the sinner merely realizes that he is justified and in virtue of this realization has peace with God through Jesus Christ. "Though by choosing his people, the Lord has adopted them as his children, yet we see that they enter not on the possession of so great a blessing till they are called; on the other hand, as soon as they are called, they immediately enjoy some communication of his election" (*ib.*).

2. *Regeneration or Sanctification.* The word regeneration is here not used in its narrower sense meaning the procreation of a true and saving faith, but in its broader sense designating the moral renewing of man, or sanctification. Calvin uses the term in this wider sense and calls it also repentance. "No one can embrace the grace of the gospel, but he must depart from the error of his former life, enter into the right way, and devote all his attention to the exercise of repentance" (III. 3. 1). Sanctification comes to the believer from Christ no less than justification. But the two are not to be confounded, neither are they to be separated. "You must first possess Christ; but you cannot possess him without becoming a partaker of his sanctification; for he cannot be divided . . . Union

with Christ, by which we are justified, contains sanctification as well as righteousness" (III. 16, 1). This way of regarding the matter is said "to maintain the glory of God unimpaired and undiminished and to assure rest and peace to us" (*ib.* 13. 1).

Since Calvin presents God as working effectually in the predestinated to the end of the sanctification of man, it cannot be said that his theory of predestination leads to moral indifference; on the contrary, "Paul declares the end of our election to be, that we may lead a holy and blameless life. If the object of election be holiness of life, it should rather awaken and stimulate us to a cheerful practice of it, than be used as a pretext for slothfulness" (*ib.* 23, 12).

It should be noticed that Calvin concludes the discussion of man's salvation with a presentation of the doctrine of predestination. He does that in order to make predestination a support for the certainty of salvation. The assurance which the believer has of salvation rests on the divine choice of the man to salvation. The soteriological significance of Calvin's doctrine of predestination lies in the absolute exclusion of any kind of synergism "that the pure grace of God may be magnified." The certainty of salvation is but increased by the fact that God "adopts not all promiscuously to the hope of salvation, but gives to some what he refuses to others" (*ib.* 21. 1). "They who know not themselves to be God's peculiar people will be tortured with continual anxiety." On the other hand, there is not "any other basis for solid confidence" but God's eternal predestination "even according to the authority of Christ . . . who promises to preserve in safety all whom the Father has committed to his care" (*ib.*). They alone receive the gift of perseverance and continue in faith and holiness unto the end (III. 2, 11).

Calvin's theory of the certainty of salvation either makes men self-confident and secure or drives them to despair. Calvin himself admits that believers, "in recogniznig the grace of God towards them, are not only disturbed with inquietude which frequently befalls them, but sometimes also tremble with the most distressing terrors" (*ib.* 17).

Good works also are to assure the elect of his faith and increase the certainty of his salvation (III. 15,7,8). While there is general agreement between Luther and Calvin concerning the relation of good works to justification there are differences in their conception (1) of the source, (2) the standard and (3) the purpose of good works.

(1) Calvin does not show that faith is the propelling cause of the believer's life. He is fond of attributing man's sanctification to the influence of the Holy Spirit (III. 3, 8 f.). In fact he lays the

emphasis not on faith but on the *Holy Spirit as the source of good works*. The believers cannot "perform any other obedience to him, than that which he has given them" (III. 8, 4). Luther lays the emphasis on justifying faith as the spontaneous source of God-pleasing actions. Out of the same faith that apprehends Christ's righteousness spring the motives of holy living. Faith is a living active thing; and the living energy of faith manifests itself in good works.

(2) As far as the *standard* of good works is concerned both Luther and Calvin agree that the law of God is the rule of life and conduct, but Calvin emphasizes the significance of the law for the believer in such a way that a marked legalism characterizes his theology. "It is the duty of believers to present their bodies a living sacrifice, holy and acceptable unto God" (III. 7, 1). Speaking of the significance of the law for the regenerate Calvin calls "the third use of the law the 'principal one'— and which is more nearly connected with the proper end of it." He compares the relation of the believer to the law to that of a "servant" to his "master." "By frequent meditation on the law the servant of God will be excited to obedience . . . To the flesh the law serves as a whip, urging it, like a dull and tardy animal, forward to its work; and even to the spiritual man, who is not yet delivered from the burden of the flesh, it will be a perpetual spur, that will not permit him to loiter" (II. 7, 12). Commandment, law, duty, servant, obedience — these frequently recurring terms are expressive of the rigorous legalism which characterizes Calvin's conception of Christianity. Luther teaches that the regenerate is ever "ready and cheerful, without coercion, to do good to every one, to serve every one, and to suffer everything for love and praise to God."

(3) Nor does Luther emphasize the glory of God as being the object and end of good works. The relation of the believer to God is, according to Luther, not that of a servant to his master, nor that of a subject to his sovereign, but that of a son to his father; it manifests itself in love. This love needs not be told what its *end and purpose* should be. Its motive power is the love of God in Christ Jesus. Its end and object is to love God and the neighbor, (1 John 4:11, 19).

F. The Church.— Like Zwingli, Calvin conceives of the church as the totality of the elect of all ages and places. As such it is invisible and an object of faith (IV. 1, 2, 7). The elect, however, are found in an empirical communion, the visible church, i. e., the multitude of professed believers, which includes also hypocrites among its members (*ib.*). We are to believe in the invisible church which is known to God alone. We are commanded to honor the visible church and to maintain communion with it (*ib.*). Of this visible organized church Calvin predicates all those properties which belong to the church as the communion of believers. Thus he maintains that the third article of the Creed "relates in some measure" to the external church (*ib.*). Of the visible church he says, "there is no other way of entrance into life, unless we are conceived by her, born of her, nourished at her breast, and continually preserved under her care and government, . . out of her bosom there can be no hope of remission of sins or any salvation" (*ib.* 4). Withdrawal from the visible church is therefore also a denial of God and Christ (*ib.*)

The preaching of the word and the administration of the sacraments are the marks of the true visible church. In keeping with his concept of God Calvin maintains that the power of God is not confined to external means (IV. 1, 5). To many "he has given the true knowledge of himself in an internal manner, by the illumination of his Spirit, without the intervention of any preaching" (IV. 16, 19). But while God is not confined to external means, "yet he has confined us to the ordinary manner of teaching . . . . though he could easily make his people perfect in a single moment, yet it was not his will that they should grow to mature age, but under the education of the church" (IV. 1, 5).

According to Luther's view the church is the communion of believers where the pure Word of God is preached and the sacraments are administered in accord with Christ's institution. The task of the church, therefore, is to see to it that the pure Word of God is preached and the sacraments are rightly administered. According to Calvin's view the church is the instituted visible church, under the care and government of which we are preserved "till we are divested of this mortal flesh and become like angels" (*ib.* 4). The task of the church, therefore, is to see to it that there be the right kind of church organization and church government and that church discipline be properly exercised.

At first sight it seems that Calvin does not share Zwingli's view of the relation of church and state. Like Luther, he distinguishes two kinds of government, "one, which is situated in the soul, or the inner man, and relates to eternal life," and "the other, which relates to civil justice, and the regulation of external conduct" (IV. 20, 1). But since, on the one hand, he makes "the regulation of external conduct" a task of the church, and on the other hand, demands that civil government see to it "that idolatry, sacrileges against the name of God, blasphemies against his truth, and other offences against religion, may not openly appear and be dissemi-

nated among the people" (*ib.* 3), he actually abandons the separation of the church and state and lets the one encroach upon the
territory of the other. What should be the attitude of the Christian
to a government that refuses to cooperate with the church? Zwingli
held that a government which sets itself against God and the Bible
is to be abrogated. Calvin has not adopted this view of Zwingli;
on the contrary, he enjoins the duty upon the people to respect and
obey the magistrates "whatever their characters may be," for "they
have their government only from God" (*ib.* 20, 25). "But in the
obedience due to the authority of governors, it is always necessary
to make one exception: that it do not seduce us from obedience to
him, to whose will the desires of all kings ought to be subject"
(*ib.* 32).

Calvin, like Zwingli, aimed at a theocracy after the Old Testament pattern. Church and state though separate in organization
cooperate closely to support each other. The church's authority
is absolute in matters of doctrine. The discipline of the church is
to be carried out by governmental agencies. "No government can
be happily constituted, unless its first object be the promotion of
piety;" therefore Christian princes and magistrates "should employ
their utmost efforts in asserting and defending the honor of him,
whose vice-gerents they are and by whose favor they govern . . .
Their office extends to both tables of the law" (*ib.* 9). The end in
view in this theocracy is to produce a people of God by governmental
agencies. God is the Lord whose will rules all. It is the duty of
the church and state to carry out his will. Hence civil authority, in
its service to God, is under obligation to exercise Christian
discipline.

Calvin's Biblicism determined also his position in regard to
church rites and ceremonies. Usages, customs, festivals that have
been observed in the church for centuries but cannot be substan-
tiated by express scriptural command are to be abandoned. Since
the New Testament mentions neither the observance of festivals in
commemoration of the great events of the life of Christ, nor of
saints' days, we are bound to observe only Sunday as the Lord's
Day. Calvin made exceptions in the case of the Swiss of Bern,
who desired to keep the gospel festivals, but his Puritan followers
rejected the Christian year with its festivals insisting only on strict
Sabbath observance in a spirit of Jewish legalism. Calvin, like
Luther, saw in the Sabbath law a part of the ceremonial law of the
Jews and not a part of the moral law which is binding on all men
in all times and therefore he asserted the abrogation of the Jewish
Sabbath, but he departed from Luther's view by maintaining that

the Lord's Day was substituted in the room of the Sabbath (II. 8, 1, 34). This latter view of the substitution of the Sunday for the Sabbath soon became the dominant one in the Reformed Church and the perpetual moral obligation to observe the first day of the week as a day of rest and worship was emphatically maintained.

G. THE MEANS OF GRACE are the Word of God and the Sacraments.

1. *The Word of God.* According to Zwingli the Word of God is not a means of grace. He severed the influence of the Holy Spirit from "the instrument" of the Word and held that the Holy Spirit operates immediately upon man's heart. Calvin goes further than Zwingli in that, in the case of the elect, he holds to a real divine energy connected with the Word. He says that "our ignorance, slothfulness, and the vanity of our minds require external aids, in order to the production of faith in our hearts, and its increase;" and "God has provided such aids in compassion to our infirmity" (IV. 1, 1). But from this it must not be concluded that this "prescribes a perpetual rule for God, precluding his employment of any other method; which he has certainly employed in the calling of many" (IV. 16, 19). In the same way "infants are regenerated by the power of God which is as easy to him as it is wonderful and mysterious to us" (*ib*. 18).

2. *The Sacraments.* Zwingli attaches very little significance to the sacraments; they are mere symbols. According to Calvin a sacrament is something more than a mere sign. He defines it as an outward sign, by which God seals the promises of his grace to our consciences and we in turn testify our piety toward him (IV. 14, 1). But "the sacraments produce the effect, which they represent, in the elect alone;" for the unbelieving they are merely signs without contents (*ib*. 15). In order to be efficacious the Spirit, "this inner teacher who inwardly opens, moves, and enlightens the heart," must follow the sacraments (*ib*. 7).

While Zwingli saw in *baptism* merely an introductory symbol of obligatory character, Calvin regarded it as a seal of a covenant "like some sealed diploma." It *signifies* for the elect the beginning of the development of the "new life" in the church. It *testifies* to us forgiveness of sin, not only for the past alone, but also for the future. It serves both for the *confirmation of faith* and a *confession before men* (IV. 15, 1 - 6). It *signifies, testifies;* but nowhere does Calvin say: baptism *bestows,* or *gives* the new life, or forgiveness of sin.

Baptism is necessary for all Christians because commanded by Christ, but it is not necessary for salvation. Unbaptized children are not "deprived of the grace of regeneration." Hence even in case of necessity "it is not right for private persons to take upon themselves the administration of baptism . . . this is a part of the public ministry of the church" (*ib.* 20.). The doctrine that "baptism is necessary to salvation" is styled by Calvin as an ill-stated notion from which resulted mischievous consequences" (*ib.*). Children of believers are said to be born in covenant relation. "The sacrament is afterwards added as a seal, not to give efficacy to the promise of God, as if it wanted validity in itself, but only to confirm it to us" (*ib.* 22).

The mode of baptism, whether immersion, or sprinkling, or pouring, "is of no importance; churches ought to be left at liberty, in this respect, according to the difference of countries," although "it is certain that immersion was the practice of the ancient church" (IV. 15, 19).

Calvin maintained a real presence of Christ in the *Lord's Supper*. He was opposed to Zwingli's view that eating the flesh of Christ and drinking his blood means only that Christ is received by faith. (IV. 17, 5 ff.). He calls the object received in the Lord's Supper the substance of the sacrament. "What I call the matter or substance, is Christ, with his death and resurrection . . . If it be true that the visible sign is given to us to seal the donation of the invisible substance we ought to entertain a confident assurance, that in receiving the symbol of this body, we at the same time truly receive the body itself" (*ib.* 10). "In the mystery of the Supper, under the symbols of bread and wine, Christ is truly exhibited to us, even his body and blood, in which he has fulfilled all obedience to procure our justification. And the design of this exhibition is, first, that we may be united into one body with him, and, secondly, that being made partakers of his substance we may experience his power in the communication of all blessings" (*ib.* 11). In his conception of the Lord's Supper Calvin stands nearer to Luther than to Zwingli, and yet his view differs widely from that of Luther. Luther held to a real bodily presence. Calvin styles that a "preposterous error." "Christ's body is finite, according to the invariable condition of a human body, and is contained in heaven, where it was once received, till it shall return to judgment; so we esteem it utterly unlawful to bring it back under these corruptible elements, or to imagine it to be present everywhere" (*ib.* 12).

What, then, does Calvin mean when he says that "we at the same time truly receive the body itself," or "that we may enjoy a real participation of him"? (*ib.* 10, 11). He does not mean the body but all the blessings which Christ offers in his body. Calvin denied any bodily presence of Christ and maintained only Christ's spiritual influence, his power and efficacy as Redeemer. Accordingly the body and blood of Christ are taken with the bread and wine *not orally by mouth,* as Luther held, but *spiritually by faith.* Bread and wine are signs, which "represent to us the invisible nourishment which we receive from the body and blood of Christ . . . And because this mystery of the secret union of Christ with believers is incomprehensible by nature, he exhibits a figure and image of it in visible signs . . and . . by giving tokens and pledges, renders it equally as certain to us as if we beheld it with our eyes" (*ib.* 1). Explaining 1 Cor. 10:16 Calvin says that "a communication" is one thing and "the body" quite another; *koinonia* only designates the medium whereby we obtain communion with the body of Christ.

Calvin also held that only the believer, that is, the elect, through faith receives spiritually the body and blood in the Supper, while the unbeliever receives mere bread and wine. Consequently Calvin rejected Luther's doctrine of the *manducatio indignorum,* i. e., that also the unworthy and unbelievers receive the true body and blood of Christ. Calvin says that "this sacred bread of the Lord's Supper" which is "to be spiritual food . . . to the sincere worshippers of God, . . . is changed into a most obnoxious poison to all whose faith it does not nourish" (*ib.* 40).

But if Christ's body is "contained in heaven" how is "the union of Christ with the believer in the Lord's Supper possible?" Calvin answers: "Not by the exhibition of a vain or uneffectual sign, but by the exertion of the energy of his Spirit" (*ib.* 10). "He feeds them with his own body, of which he gives them a participation by the influence of the Spirit" (*ib.* 18). Christ being at the right hand of God in heaven, does not descend to earth, but believers by the power of the Holy Spirit are raised to communion with him in heaven (*ib.* 36), or Christ by the power of his Spirit and the outward symbol descends to us (*ib.* 24). In Calvin's Liturgy (see his *La maniere de celebrer la cene*) the ancient *Sursum corda* is paraphrased: "Let us lift up our hearts and minds thither where Jesus Christ is in the glory of his Father." This spiritual union of Christ with the believer is, of course, not confined to the Lord's Supper, but takes place whenever faith is exercised.

H. CALVIN'S PLACE IN THE HISTORY OF DOCTRINE.— Luther and Calvin have more in common than in distinction. Both agree in the rejection of Roman hierarchism and Pelagianism as well as in the recognition of the dogma of the ancient church. There was no essential difference in their conception of the doctrine of sin and grace, faith and works, atonement, justification and sanctification.

Calvin differed essentially from Luther in his conception of the *sacraments* and *predestination* as also in his aim and method of *practical reform.*

In the sphere of Calvin's doctrinal and practical activity we frequently notice a *relationship with medieval ideas and movements.* Calvin's determinism and concept of God are related to the ideas of Augustine and Gottschalk, Aquinas and Scotus. In his concept of the sacraments we notice the influence of Scotus and the later Nominalists. Calvin's conception of the Lord's Supper calls to mind Berengar's position in the eleventh century. Calvin's rejection of "the prodigious ubiquity" in the Supper, based upon his interpretation of the right hand of God, reminds us of Augustine and the Scholastics with their local concept of the right hand of God. Likewise in his practical reformatory activity in the church Calvin betrays his dependence upon medieval ideas (cp. Savonarola's programme of reform).

The importance of Calvin's theology in the history of doctrinal development becomes at once apparent when we remember that not the Zwinglian but the Calvinistic type became the dominant one in the Reformed Church. It is true, the Reformed theology had its origin in the reformatory movement begun in Switzerland under the leadership of Zwingli, but its fundamental principles received their ultimate form and systematic exposition through Calvin. His theology in its essential points became the adopted doctrine of the Reformed Church.

CHAPTER XXIV

CALVINISM, THE ACCEPTED DOCTRINE OF THE REFORMED CHURCH

A. Calvin's doctrinal views received symbolical expression in almost all of the LATER REFORMED CONFESSIONS.

1. The *Zuerich Consensus* or *Consensus Tigurinus,* 1549, embodies the United views of Calvin and Bullinger on the Lord's Supper. The Zwinglian type is here combined with the Calvinistic. The words of the institution are to be taken figuratively, and yet the Lord's Supper is not a mere empty symbol, but with the symbol the believer receives Christ with all spiritual gifts.

2. The *Confessio Gallicana,* which was drawn up under the influence of Calvin, 1559, exactly presents Calvin's conception of the Lord's Supper. "Thus all who bring pure faith, like a vessel, to the sacred table of Christ, receive truly that of which it is a sign; for the body and blood of Jesus Christ give food and drink to the soul, no less than bread and wine nourish the body" (Article 37).

3. The *Westminster Shorter Catechism* defines the Lord's Supper as "a sacrament, wherein, by giving and receiving bread and wine, according to Christ's appointment, his death is showed forth, and the worthy receivers are, not after a corporal and carnal manner, but by faith, made paratakers of his body and blood, with all his benefits, to their spiritual nourishment and growth in grace" (q. 96).

4. The *Heidelberg Catechism* presents a milder type of Calvinism than the other Reformed Confessions. It says nothing of limited atonement, of a double predestination or eternal decree of reprobation. It seems to approach the Lutheran view when it says (q. 79) that "Christ by his visible sign and pledge" wants "to assure us that we are as really partakers of his true body and blood," but it makes it at once clear that it does not present Luther's but Calvin's view when it adds: "through the working of the Holy Ghost, as we receive by the mouth of the body these holy tokens in remembrance of him."

5. The *Confessio Helvetica Posterior* harmonizes the German and the French Swiss, the Zuerich and the Genevan theology, but with all its elasticity it expresses the peculiarly Reformed conception of Christianity.

6. Calvin's doctrine of predestination was attacked, in 1543, by Albertus Pighius, a Dutch Roman Catholic controverialist, who taught the freedom of the will in the Semipelagian sense and predestination conditioned by foreknowledge, and, in 1551, by Jerome

Bolsec, formerly a Carmelite monk, then Protestant and physician near Geneva, who objected to Calvin's doctrine of predestination as unscriptural and blasphemous. In consequence of these attacks Calvin composed the *Consensus Genevensis,* in which he defended and more distinctly set forth his doctrine of predestination.

7. The *Confessio Hungarica* or *Czengerina* was drawn up and adopted by a Hungarian Reformed synod held at Czenger in 1558, but not printed till 1570. It was occasioned by the anti-Trinitarian controversies and the controversy on the Lord's Supper. Accordingly it rejects the anti-Trinitarian and Socinian teaching and strongly opposes the Roman Catholic transubstantiation and the Lutheran "sarcophagia: "it is silent about Calvin's double predestination.

B. The influence of Calvin's theology is also to be noticed in the rise and development of PROTESTANTISM IN ENGLAND. The British Reformation, which began with the refusal of king Henry VIII (1509-1547) to own further allegiance to the pope, and the resultant declaration of his own supremacy in his realm, did not interrupt the historic continuity of the English people. The breach with Rome was a mere political expedient to which the despotic and licentious monarch resorted to accomplish and justify his divorce from Catherine of Aragon and his marriage with Anne Boleyn. He remained a Catholic in his belief and sentiment and would not allow any deviation in essentials from the religion of Catholic Europe.

1. Under Edward VI (1547-1553) Cranmer and the reform party were left free to carry out their ideas. German reformers came to England and gained influence over Cranmer. The First Prayer Book of Edward, the communion office of which was Lutheran in character — the formula of administration containing only the first clause of that now in use — was authorized by an Act of Uniformity in 1549, and in 1552 the Second Prayer Book, with a marked Swiss influence in the communion service — the formula of administration containing the second clause now in use. In the *Prayer Book of Elizabeth* (1559) the two clauses are combined: "The body of our Lord Jesus Christ, which was given for thee, preserve thy body and soul, unto everlasting life. Take and eat this in remembrance that Christ died for thee, and feed on him in thy heart by faith with thanksgiving."

2. The Anglican Confession or the *Thirty-nine Articles* of the Church of England were a gradual formation. In the reign of Edward VI Cranmer with the aid of Ridley had drawn up the Forty-two Articles of Religion for the English Reformed Church. They were revised by other bishops and laid before the synod of

London in 1552 and published in 1553. It is, however, doubtful whether they ever received the official sanction of convocation. During the Catholic reaction under Mary the Bloody (1553-1558) the Articles were set aside, but under Elizabeth (1558-1603) they were revised in 1562 and reduced to thirty-nine articles. They were adopted by two convocations in 1571, and the clergy were required to subscribe to them. Since then they have been the doctrinal symbol of the Church of England. It is a moderately Calvinistic creed. Art. 17, of Predestination and Election, says nothing of the decree of reprobation and speaks exclusively on predestination to life. Concerning the sacraments (Art. 15, 17, 18, 19) the creed follows the Swiss reformers, Bullinger and Calvin.

The polity of the creed is that of a national episcopal church, the reigning sovereign being the supreme governor of the Church of England. The episcopal organization and the ritual of the Anglican Church were largely retained from the Roman Catholic Church. In 1628 a declaration issued by Charles I, in concert with archbishop Laud, known as "His Majesty's Declaration," was prefixed to the Thirty-nine Articles prohibiting all controversies and dissensions (between Calvinists and Arminians, Puritans and High-Churchmen) restricting theological opinions to "the literal and grammatical sense" of the Articles and threatening to visit all offenders with severe penalties.

3. The *Lambeth Articles,* nine in number, drawn up by Whitaker, the Regius Professor of Divinity, and signed by Archbishop Whitgift, Bishop Fletcher of London, Bishop Vaughan of Bangor and other learned divines at a conference in Lambeth Palace in London, in 1595, state in the most explicit terms the Calvinistic Doctrine of predestination. They were adopted with a view to supplement the Thirty-nine Articles, but met with serious opposition and were never approved by a regular synod of the church and therefore have no symbolical authority. But they are of historical interest. They show the ascendancy of Calvinism in the Church of England at the close of the sixteenth and the beginning of the seventeenth century. They also throw some light on the question whether Art. XVII of the Anglican Confession (of Predestination and Election) is to be understood in a Calvinistic sense. "If that were the case the Lambeth Articles would have been unnecessary; and if they formed merely an exposition of the teaching of the seventeenth article, there could have been no serious opposition to their adoption" (Clark, *The Angl. Reformation,* p. 345).

C. ARMINIANISM VERSUS CALVINISM.— Calvin's adherents, notably his successor Beza, advocated the doctrine of predestination in its most extreme supralapsarian form, so that even the fall of the human race appears to them essential to the divine plan of the world. This strict view of predestination, which was also held and defended by Francis Gomarus, professor at Leyden, repelled his colleague, Jacobus Arminius (d. at Leyden 1609) and his followers, notably Episcopius and Uytenbogaart, from Calvinism and led them to formulate their doctrine and set it forth in *The Five Articles of the Remonstrantia,* in 1610, addressed to the States of Holland and West Friesland: (1) Divine predestination is conditioned upon a divine foreknowledge of man's faith and perseverance. (2) Christ died for all men, on condition of their repentance and faith. (3) Man is unable to attain saving faith without regeneration through the Holy Spirit. (4) Grace is indispensable at every step of the spiritual life, but it does not work irresistibly. (5) The regenerate are able through the assistance of grace to overcome all temptations.

The view of the Remonstrants was at once sharply condemned in a *Contra-Remonstrantia.* As the dissensions led to disturbances it was decided to settle the dispute by a synod. It met at Dort (Dortrecht), November 13, 1618, and adjourned May 9, 1619. Foreign countries had been invited to participate, and delegates were present from the Palatinate, Nassau, Hesse, East Friesland, Bremen, Emden, German Switzerland, Geneva, England and Scotland. It was the largest and, next to the Westminster Assembly, the most imposing of all synods of the Reformed Churches. The Counter-Remonstrants were in the majority. The Arminians though invited were not permitted to sit as members.

The Synod of Dort condemned the Five Articles of the Remonstrance, decided for the infralapsarian view (against Gomarus) and expressed its final decision in the form of canons, which were adopted and signed by all at the 136th session. *The Canons of Dort* define the Five Points of Calvinism over against Aminianism: (1) absolute predestination, (2) limited atonement, (3) total depravity and absolute inability of man, (4) irresistible grace, and (5) perseverance of the saints.

The decision of the Synod of Dort was established by law as the official doctrine of the State Church of the Netherlands. The Canons were also officially indorsed by the Reformed Church of France and received with respectful consideration — though not adopted — in Switzerland, the Palatinate and by the Puritans. The English Episcopal Church, however, rejected them. The Reformed Dutch Church in America recognizes them as a public standard of doctrine.

"The Canons of Dort, both in spirit and letter, present Calvinism not in its extreme, yet in its unadulterated form" (Fisher, *Hist. of*

Doctr. p. 339). This is correct in so far as the Canons decided against supralapsarianism. But the decrees of Dort give predestination a prominence such as was not given it by Calvin in his doctrinal system. Predestination is not the fundamental principle of Calvin's theology. He treats of predestination in connection with a discussion of salvation and makes predestination a support for the certainty of salvation. According to the Canons predestination is made the starting point, the fundamental idea; predestination is the cause of salvation.

After their condemnation by the Synod of Dort the Arminians formed a proscribed sect until in 1630 religious freedom was declared in the Netherlands which now became a place of refuge to the persecuted of nearly every form of Christian belief. The Arminians do not form a distinct church, yet Arminian views have entered widely into the thought of the church, both in England and America, especially in the Methodist Church.

The doctrinal position of the Arminians is charactized in the following words of the Confession: "We believe that all those churches which abide in the faith and in the confession of the necessary truth, are to be regarded as true churches even though in many another point they may be of different opinion and in other things deviate widely from the truth" (XXII, 4). Thus making allowance for all kinds of deviation from the truth Arminianism in its later development departed more and more from the traditional interpretation of Christianity and became allied with Socinianism, Rationalism and Universalism.

D. The School of Saumur versus strict Calvinism.—Calvin's theory of inspiration as a verbal dictation by the Holy Spirit was pushed to its extreme consequences by the Buxtorfs, father and son, at Basle, who asserted the inspiration of even the Hebrew vowels, and by Gisbert Voet at Utrecht, who made the same claim for the punctuation. Louis Cappel (d. 1652), professor in the theological academy at Saumur, opposed the mechanical theory of inspiration and disproved the traditional view of the literal integrity and sacredness of the Massoretic text by showing that the Hebrew system of vocalization was of late origin, dating from the Jewish grammarians after the completion of the Babylonian Talmud in the fifth century A. D. The *Formula Consensus Helvetica* of 1674, however, affirmed the literal inspiration of the Scriptures and the integrity of the traditional Hebrew text of the Old Testament, including the vowels as well as the consonants (Art. 1, 2, 3).

Moses Amyraldus or Moise Amyraut in Saumur (d. 1664), in his teaching on grace and predestination, seemed to go beyond that of the Synod of Dort by adding a conditional universal grace to the unconditional. His theory has been called *hypothetical unversalism*. God wills all men to be saved, on condition that they repent and believe; and if all should repent and believe no purpose of God would stand in the way of their salvation. But owing to inherited corruption, they stubbornly reject, so that this universal will for salvation actually saves none. Salvation depends upon the divine election. The elect will be saved as inevitably as others will be damned. Amyraldus published his ideas in his *Traite de la predestination*, which immediately aroused strong opposition. Two national synods, however, acquitted him as orthodox and the controversy would soon have died out had not the Swiss theologians kept up the agitation. The matter was settled by the *Formula Consensus Helvetica* which states clearly the difference between strict Calvinism and the School of Saumur. It rejects Amyraldus' view, condemns universal atonement and the doctrine that God desires the salvation of all, and teaches the strictest particularism in the election.

The Helvetic Consensus was introduced everywhere in the Reformed Church of Switzerland and officially adopted by several of the Cantons. Its authority, however, was confined to Switzerland. Calvin's theory of predestination in its strict form was thus officially accepted as the doctrine of the Reformed Church of Switzerland.

The rigor of Calvinistic teaching, which had made everything rest on the divine decrees, was softened by the introduction of the Federal Theology or the Scheme of Covenants. The Federal Theology was based upon the conception that (1) before the fall Adam, the federal head of the human race, was under a "covenant of works", wherein God promised him eternal blessedness, if he perfectly kept the law. When Adam ate of the forbidden fruit he was not only our ancestor but at the same time our representative covenanthead, acting in our place and on our behalf. The "covenant of works" is said to offer an explanation for the imputation of Adam's sin and guilt to all his descendants, as if they all personally had eaten of the fruit of the tree. (2) Since the fall man is under a "covenant of grace" wherein eternal life is to be obtained as a free gift of God's grace by all who believe in Christ, the federal head of the church. The Dutch theologian Cocceius (d. 1669), professor at Franeker and then at Leyden, was one of the leading expounders of the Federal Theology. The doctrine of the Covenants received dogmatic formulation and symbolic sanction at a comparatively late period; hence the earlier confessional standards do not mention it, but it is clearly set forth in the Westminster Confession, ch. VII, *Of God's Covenant with Man*.

CHAPTER XXV

SCHOLASTIC THEOLOGY EXALTED TO THE POSITION OF ECCLESIASTICAL DOGMA BY THE COUNCIL OF TRENT

A. PURPOSE AND SIGNIFICANCE OF THE COUNCIL OF TRENT.— Confronted by the Protestant Reformation, which by the middle of the sixteenth century had made astonishing progress, the Catholics found themselves compelled to examine the state of their own church. On the one hand, the ecclesiastical life stood in urgent need of reform. On the other hand, it became necessary in opposition to the Protestant doctrine to defend and define the doctrine of the Catholic Church. The desire from many quarters was expressed that a general council should undertake the task of condemning the principles and doctrines of Protestantism, defining the doctrine of the Roman Catholic Church on all disputed points, and reforming ecclesiastical abuses. After long delays Paul III. convened such a council in the Austrian city of Trent on the 13th of December, 1545. With long intermissions (first period 1545-49 — second period 1551 - 52 — third period 1562 - 63) it held twenty-five public sessions up to the 4th of December, 1563. The council claimed to be ecumenical, though neither the Greek nor the Protestant Church was represented. The numbering of the ecumenical councils is not fixed, but the council of Trent is now generally acknowledged as the eighteenth ecumenical council throughout the Roman Catholic Church, although it did not immediately acquire equal authority in all Roman Catholic countries. The papal bull of Pius IV., *Benedictus Deus,* issued on January 26, 1564, solemnly confirmed the decisions of the council, reserving to the pope the exclusive right of explanation of the more obscure points of doctrine contained in the decrees.

The decisions of the council regard dogma and discipline. The disciplinary ordinances bear the title *decretum de reformatione.* The doctrinal decisions are divided into *decreta* and *canones.* The decrees state at length the Catholic doctrine. The canons, in the form of short propositions, condemn the opposite views of the Protestant Church ending always with *anathema sit,* "let him be accursed."

From the discussions of the council it is evident that, owing to the opposition of the Thomist and Scotist theories, marked differences of opinion existed within it even on most important subjects. It was the policy of the council to condemn the Protestant doctrine

251

without offending the leading parties of the Catholic Church, hence the constant recourse to reticence, equivocation and compromising formulae. "The contradictory principles of the opposing schools came into prominence in the discussion of nearly every question. It was possible to preserve an outward unity only by the employment of the most studied diplomatic arts. The points of controversy were either avoided altogether or carefully veiled. Thus, to the student familiar with the history of the formation of the doctrinal definitions of the council, the latter but too often appear as the deliberate productions of church politics and diplomatic refinements. The decrees do not present to us a vigorous and joyous confession of sincere faith, but formulas of compromise artfully welded together, bent to this side or that with great labor and pains, and then finally filed into proper dimensions" (Seeberg, *Hist. of Doctr.* II, 431).

The significance of the council of Trent in the History of Doctrine is threefold: (1) It fixed the results of Scholastic theology and gleaned from it all that could be of service to the church. (2) It elaborated the Catholic creed by defining certain doctrinal points till then undecided. (3) In branding the Protestant teaching as heresy and furnishing a definite statement of orthodox faith it gave to its own members the practical lead which they needed in their resistance to advancing Protestantism.

B. THE DOGMATIC DECISIONS OF THE COUNCIL.— The concern of the History of Doctrine is not to give an account of the reformatory enactments of the council touching on numerous phases of ecclesiastical life, but to trace the historical development of the dogma to its final formulation.

The doctrinal decisions of the council which concern our discipline may be summed up as follows: Session III states the purpose of the council . . . "the extirpating of heresies, and the reforming of manners, for the sake of which it is chiefly assembled," and accepts the Nicaeno-Constantinopolitan Creed "as being that principle wherein all who profess the faith of Christ necessarily agree." Session IV points out the authoritative sources of the ecclesiastical dogma: the canonical Scriptures, Apocrypha, tradition of the church and the Vulgate translation. After protracting and equivocating debates between the Thomists and the Scotists Session V reached its conclusions on original sin. No less than 61 general congregations and 44 other congregations were held until Session VI accepted the decree and canons on justification. The following Sessions chiefly re-state in their decrees the Scholastic doctrines: VII, on the sacraments; XIII, on the Eucharist; XIV, on the sacraments of penance and extreme unction; XXI, on communion under both kinds, and of little children; XXII, on the sacrifice of the mass; XXIII, on the sacrament of order; XXIV, on the sacrament of matrimony; XXV, on purgatory, invocation, veneration and relics of saints, sacred images, indulgences.

1. Turning now to the separate dogmatic decisions of the council we first notice *the complete coordination of Scripture and tradition as the two authentic sources of the Church's teaching* (*Sess.* IV). "The synod following the example of the orthodox Fathers, receives and venerates with an equal affection of piety and reverence, all the books both of the Old and of the New Testament . . . as also the said traditions." The Holy Scriptures are the Word of God, for they have "God for their author." Traditions are divinely revealed truths or precepts otherwise than by Holy Writ, "having been dictated, either by Christ's own word of mouth, or by the Holy Ghost."[*] In fact, the Scriptures are to be interpreted by tradition, i. e., according "to that sense which holy mother Church. . . . hath held and doth hold." But while Scripture and tradition are acknowledged as the authentic sources of dogma, yet there is a supreme authority other than Scripture and tradition, namely, "holy mother Church, whose it is to judge of the true sense and interpretation of the holy Scriptures."

In determining the *canon* of the Scriptures the council of Trent followed, not without the influence of doctrinal bias, the long prevalent custom in the Latin Church of using the canonical books and the Apocrypha of the Old Testament (Tobias, Judith, Wisdom, Ecclesiasticus, Baruch, 1 and 2 Maccabees) promiscuously. The Tridentine decree enumerates fourteen epistles of Paul, thus assigning Hebrews to Paul. The Pauline authorship of that epistle became therefore an article of faith, and "if any one shall not receive as sacred and canonical the books of Holy Scripture entire with all their parts, as the holy synod of Trent has enumerated them, . . . let him be anathema."

The council also declared the *Vulgate* translation to be authoritative for the text of the Scripture,—"that the said old and Vulgate edition, which by the lengthened usage of so many ages, has been approved of in the Church, be, in public lectures, disputations, sermons, and expositions held as authentic, and that no one is to dare, or presume to reject it, under any pretext whatever." In the first Index, 1559, under the title of *Biblia prohibita*, pope Paul IV. prohibited the publication and possession of translations of the Bible in German, French, Spanish, Italian, English or Dutch, without the permission of the Holy Office or the Congregation of the

---

[*] We quote from the text in Schaff, *Creeds*, vol. II.

Inquisition, and Pius IV, in the constitution *Dominici gregis custodiae* of March 24, 1564, expressly condemned all versions of the Scriptures by heretical authors.

2. In the discussion concerning *original sin* (Sess. V) the Thomists and Scotists at once collided in their views as to the relation of the Virgin Mary to original sin. The council of Trent left the doctrine of the immaculate conception unsettled and merely declared that in its decree on the subject of original sin it did not include "the blessed and immaculate Virgin Mary, Mother of God" (V, 5).

The Scotists defined original sin as something negative, as the *lack of original righteousness*. The spiritual equilibrium was lost and to that extent man was weakened and no longer inclined toward the good. The Thomists, however, saw in original sin not only a negation, the lack of original righteousness, but also something positive, consisting essentially in *concupiscence*. In order to satisfy the contending parties the council of Trent avoided or rather carefully veiled the point of controversy and stated that Adam through his own fault lost the holiness and righteousness wherein he had been "constituted"— the ambiguous word *constitutus* was substituted for *creatus* — thereby the whole Adam was changed for the worse (V, 1).

Adam's sin and guilt are transmitted by propagation, not by imitation, to posterity (V. 3). As the children of Adam were really corrupted by original sin they could not of themselves arise from their fall (*ib.*). There is no other remedy to release from the bonds of sin, death and devil but the grace of Christ conferred in baptism upon infants as well as adults (V, 3, 4). Through baptism original sin is remitted, but concupiscence remains. Concupiscence is defined as *fomes peccati*, "the tinder of evil," or an incentive to sin, but not as in itself *peccatum*, "sin." It proceeds from sin and inclines to sin, but in the regenerate it is not truly and properly sin (V, 5).

The customary distinction between *mortal* and *venial sins* was accepted by the council of Trent (VI, 15 and XIV, 5) and thereby received dogmatic sanction. The Tridentine decree does not give a precise definition of mortal and venial sins. It maintains (VI, 15) that by every mortal sin "the grace of justification is lost, . . . though faith be not lost," and according to 1 Cor. 6:9, 10 enumerates those who are guilty of mortal sin, but makes the enumeration at once indefinite by adding "and all others who commit deadly sins."

3. The council of Trent discussed and formulated the dogma of *justification* with reference to the "heretics" of the sixteenth

century. In defining the doctrine of justification the council was confronted with great difficulties. The decree which was finally accepted by the council (*Sess.* VI) treats (1) of the preparation for justification, (2) of justification itself, and (3) of the fruit of justification or the merit of good works.

(1) *Preparation for Justification.* Infants are cleansed from the stain of original sin in baptism without any preparation on their part, but adults must pass through a moral preparation (VI, 5). The council, combining the two conflicting theories of the Scotists and Thomists on the subject, states that man consenting to the work of God and working with him *prepares himself* for justification (Scotist view). At the same time the process of justification receives its first impulse, *independent of man's merit,* from the *gratia praeveniens,* the supernatural grace of vocation (Thomist view). By consenting to prevenient grace man exercises *faith.* It marks the beginning, the preparation for justification. But faith is not the only disposition required for justification. Faith produces in the soul a *fear* of God's avenging justice, and then through contemplation of God's mercy awakens the *hope* of forgiveness for Christ's sake which is soon followed by the first beginning of *charity* (VI, 6). Then follows

(2) *Justification itself.* The council of Trent rejects the evangelical doctrine that men are justified by the remission of sins and the imputation of Christ's righteousness (VI, *canon* 11), and states (VI, 7) that justification comprises not remission of sins merely, but also the sanctification and renewal of the inner man by means of the voluntary acceptance of sanctifying grace and other supernatural gifts. Justification is not a *forensic act, by which God declares a man,* who believes in Christ, *free from the guilt of sin and as righteous in his sight,* that is, as though he had no sin, but a *process within man by which God makes the sinner just and holy.* Hence sin is not, as the Reformers maintained, no longer imputed, but is really destroyed; it is not merely covered, but actually blotted out.

The council condemned in four canons (9, 12, 13, 14) the Biblical doctrine of justification by faith alone. "If any one saith, that by faith alone the impious is justified, in such wise as to mean, that nothing else is required to cooperate in order to the obtaining the grace of justification, and that it is not in any way necessary, that he be prepared and disposed by the movement of his own will: let him be anathema" (c. 9). In the light of this canon must be explained canon 1, in which the Tridentine Fathers seem to approach to the evangelical view: "If any one saith, that man may be justified before God by his own works, whether done through the teaching of human nature, or that of the law, without the grace of God through Jesus Christ: let him be anathema." This canon merely says that man is justified not by works *alone*, but also through God's grace. Accordingly, two things are necessary for conversion: (a) a certain disposition on the part of the sinner in order to be fit — or "not unworthy"— to obtain grace, and (b) the necessary help of divine grace.

The council implicitly accepts the Scholastic distinction between *fides informis*, mere faith, and *fides formata caritate*, faith perfected in love, the latter only being meritorious and bringing justification. The council quotes Paul (Gal. 5:6) "In Christ Jesus neither circumcision availeth any thing nor uncircumcision, but faith which worked by charity" (VI, 7), as though the apostle had in mind *fides informis* which must be perfected in love! Whenever the apostle speaks of justifying faith he means living faith, a new relation of man to God, and this faith is never without love. The Tridentine Fathers best illustrated their unbiblical conception of faith by canon 28. Here they admit that sanctifying grace can be lost, but at the same time maintain that this does not always entail loss of faith. "If any one saith, that . . . the faith which remains, though it be not lively faith, is not a true faith; or that he who hath faith without charity is not a Christian: let him be anathema." Here we learn that faith which is not a lively faith, or, in plain English, *dead* faith, is nevertheless *true* faith, and that he, whose faith is dead and without love, is nevertheless a Christian.

Over against "the Protestant heresy" the council maintained the *uncertainty* of justification. No one can be absolutely certain of his or her salvation unless by special revelation (VI, 9). According to Luther Christ's righteousness apprehended by faith is the sure foundation upon which rest the consolation of the believing conscience and the certainty of salvation. According to the Tridentine decree salvation is man's own achievement; it rests upon his own preparatory dispositions and is preserved and increased by his own good works. He can never know whether or not he has done enough. Hence the council of Trent advises the faithful "to work out their own salvation with fear and trembling, in labors, in watchings, in almsdeeds, in prayers and oblations, in fastings and chastity: for, knowing that they are born again unto a hope of glory, but not as yet unto glory, they ought to fear for the combat which yet remains," etc. (VI, 13). Against *Calvin* who maintained that the predestined cannot lose their justification, and against *Luther* who made the loss of justification depend solely on unbelief, the council asserts the amissibility of justification not only through unbelief, but by any mortal sin (VI, 15; *canon* 15, 16, 17, 27). Those who have committed mortal sin may be restored to justification through the sacrament of penance (VI, 14).

Sanctifying grace originally received can be increased by the performance of:

3. *Good Works.* The council of Trent (*canon* 24) condemns the evangelical doctrine that good works are the fruits and signs of justification and asserts that good works preserve and increase inward sanctity. Good works are truly meritorious (*canon* 32). The Tridentine decree (VI, 14) distinctly asserts that "the justified .... have, by those very works which have been done in God, fully satisfied the divine law according to the state of this life, and ... have truly merited eternal life." Canon 33 claims that the Catholic doctrine of justification does not in any way derogate from the glory of God or the merits of Christ, but rather renders the truth of faith and the glory of God and Jesus Christ more illustrious.

The standard of good works are not only the commandments of God, but also the commandments of the Church which are binding upon all Christians. "If any one saith, that the man who is justified .... is not bound to observe the commandments of God and of the Church ... let him be anathema" (*canon* 20).

4. *The Sacraments.* Following the Schoolmen the council of Trent placed the divine efficacy in the sacraments, not in the word,— "the most holy Sacraments of the Church, through which all true justice either begins, or being begun is increased, or being lost is repaired" (*Sess.* VII); hence the enormous significance of the sacraments in the Catholic Church. The council confirmed the general positions developed by the Schoolmen. Canon 1 affirms the sacramental character of the seven sacraments. As to the matter and form of the sacrament, the intention of the officiating priest, the *ex opere operato* effect of the sacrament, and the right disposition of the recipient, the council merely reaffirms (*canon* 6, 7, 8, 11) the Scholastic teaching. The council did not decide the question whether the sign includes in itself grace (Thomist view), or whether God accompanies the sign with his own energy (Scotist view). Canon 9 claims for the three sacraments, baptism, confirmation and order, the *character indelebilis*. Only the bishop can confirm and ordain validly (VII, canon 3; XXIII, *canon* 7).

(1) *Baptism* is indispensable to salvation (VII, *canon* 5). Once validly conferred "with the intention of doing what the Church doth" baptism can never be repeated (c. 4, 11). It cleanses from

original sin and all other sins, remits all temporal and eternal punishment due to sin, infuses sanctifying grace, supernatural gifts and virtues, and imprints in our soul an indelible mark. The calling to mind one's baptism does not free one from sins committed after it. Sins committed after baptism are imputed to the baptized person even if he has faith (c. 9. 10).

(2) *Confirmation* is not a vain ceremony but a true and proper sacrament (c. 1). The "ordinary minister of holy confirmation" is the bishop alone and not any simple priest (c. 3).

(3) *The Eucharist* surpasses all the other sacraments in dignity and excellence (XIII, 3). It is a sacrament in which by means of the consecration the bread and wine are converted into the body and blood of Christ (*ib.*). The matter of this sacrament is unleavened wheat bread and genuine wine of the grape mixed with water, "because it is believed that Christ the Lord did this, as also because from his side there came out blood and water, the memory of which mystery is renewed by this commixture; and, whereas in the apocalypss of blessed John the peoples are called 'waters,' the union of that faithful people with Christ their head is thereby represented" (XXII, 7).

By the words: "Do this for a commemoration of me," Jesus gave his apostles the power to change bread and wine into his body and blood. From the apostles this power has passed to their successors in the priesthood, the bishops and the priests (XXII, *canon* 2). They, and they only have the power to consecrate the body and blood of Christ. "By the consecration of the bread and of the wine, a conversion is made of the whole substance of the bread into the substance of the body of Christ our Lord, and of the whole substance of the wine into the substance of his blood; which conversion is, by the holy Catholic Church, suitably and properly called Transubstantiation" (XIII, 4). Under each appearance or species Christ is present wholly and undivided, with body and soul, with flesh and blood, with his divinity and humanity "by the force of that natural connection and concomitancy whereby the parts of Christ our Lord, who hath now risen from the dead, to die no more, are united together" (XIII, 3). The entire Christ is present in the Eucharist after, as well as before, the distribution (*ib.* c. 4). "For the apostles had not as yet received the Eucharist from the hand of the Lord, when nevertheless himself affirmed with truth that to be his own body which he presented to them" (XIII, 4). And "if any one saith, . . . that in the hosts, or consecrated particles, which are reserved or which remain after communion, the true body of the Lord remaineth not: let him be anathema" (*canon* 4).

The council of Trent condemned the Reformed view that Christ is present in the sacrament "as in a sign, or figure, or virtue" (c. 1), and the Lutheran view of the real presence of Christ's body and blood with in and under the bread and wine (c. 4).

Since Christ is permanently present in the elements, they can be exhibited in the mass and in eucharistic processions. The council urges the faithful to "render in veneration the worship of *latria*, which is true to the true God, to this most holy sacrament" (XIII, 5). The council further declared that "this sublime and venerable sacrament be, with special veneration and solemnity, celebrated every year, on a certain day, and that a festival; and that it be borne reverently and with honor in processions through the streets and public places" (*ib.*). In all this gorgeous display of Catholic propaganda the council of Trent sees nothing less than a "triumph over falsehood and heresy, that thus her adversaries at the sight of so much splendor, and in the midst of so great joy of the universal Church, may either pine away weakened and broken; or touched with shame and confounded, at length repent" (*ib.*).

The Schoolmen had already justified the ever growing custom of *withholding the cup from the laity*. The council of Trent declared it to be a practice commanded by the Church from of old for good and sufficient reasons (*Sess.* XXI). The priests, however, when employed in their sacred function, receive both species, for the command of Christ: "Do this for a commemoration for me" is said to apply solely to the priesthood (XXII, c. 2). The Tridentine Fathers apparently were not concerned about the fact that Paul writes in 1 Cor. 11:28, : let a man examine himself, and so let him eat of that bread and drink of that cup." The addressees of Paul's epistle were not priests but members of the church at Corinth. Not only the clear teaching of the Scriptures but even the testimony of popes militate against the Roman practice of the withdrawal of the cup. Pope Leo I. (440-461) — apparently speaking *ex cathedra* — made it obligatory on all to receive communion under both kinds when the Manichaeans "at all times declined to drink the blood of our redemption" (*Serm.* 42; *De Quadrag.* IV). Pope Gelasius I., also speaking *ex cathedra*, demanded that persons who "abstain from the chalice of the sacred blood should either partake of the entire sacraments, or should be excluded from the entire sacraments — *aut integra sacramenta percipiant, aut ab integris arceantur* — because the division of one and the same mystery cannot be without a great sacrilege" (see Berington and Kirk, *The Faith of Catholics*, vol. II, p. 382 f.). The council of Trent, however, has removed all difficulties by declaring "that this power has ever been in the

Church, that in the dispensation of the sacraments . . . it may ordain or change what things ever it may judge most expedient, for the profit of those who receive, or for the veneration of the said sacraments, according to the difference of circumstances, times and places" (XXI, 2).

The *effects* of the Eucharist are as follows: It increases sanctifying grace in man; it weakens his evil inclinations and gives him both the desire and the power to do good; it cleanses from venial sins, preserves from mortal sin and is a pledge of our glorious resurrection and everlasting happiness (XIII, 2).

All persons who have attained to the use of reason and are sufficiently instructed in "this holy mystery" are bound to receive this sacrament "at least once a year," and that at Easter-time (canon 9). "Little children, before they have arrived at years of discretion," are not admitted to the sacrament (XXI, c. 4).

The council of Trent also declared the Eucharist to be a veritable *propitiatory sacrifice* (XXII, 1; c. 1). Here the council reproduced and adopted the Scholastic views on the sacrifice of the mass which is said to have been foretold in the Old Testament already, Mal. 1:10, 11 (XXI, 1). The sacrifice of the mass is identical with the sacrifice of the cross. The only difference is that on the cross Christ offered himself "in a bloody manner," while in the mass the priest offers to God the body and blood of Christ in an "unbloody manner" (XXII, 2).

The mass is offered always for certain persons : for those present and for those absent, for the living and the dead (see Canon of the Mass). "Not only for the sins, punishments, satisfactions, and other necessities of the faithful who are living, but also for those who are departed in Christ, and who are not as yet fully purified, is it rightly offered, agreeably to a tradition of the apostles" (XXII, 2).

Throughout the greater part of the world the Catholic Church uses Latin as the language of the mass. Canon 9 of Sess. XXII condemns every one who says "that the mass ought to be celebrated in the vulgar tongue only." The council also prescribes (*ib.*) that "a part of the canon and the words of consecration are" to be "pronounced in a low tone."

(4) *The sacrament of penance* is said to be necessary for salvation to all, who have committed mortal sin after baptism. Baptism effaces original sin, the Eucharist cleanses from venial sins; but, to free man from mortal sins, penance, the sacrament of confession and absolution, has been instituted. If "those whom Christ our Lord has once, by the laver of baptism, made the members of his

own body, . . . should afterwards have defiled themselves by any crime, he would no longer have them cleansed by a repetition of baptism — that being nowise lawful in the Catholic Church — but be placed as criminals before this tribunal; that by the sentence of the priest, they might be freed, not once, but as often as, being penitent, they should, from their sins committed, flee thereunto" (XIV, 2). The full and entire remission of all sins, which we obtained in baptism without labor, "we are no ways able to arrive at by the sacrament of penance, without many tears and great labors on our parts, the divine justice demanding this;" hence the Fathers justly called penance "a laborious kind of baptism," *laboriosus quidam baptismus*. Just as baptism is the means of obtaining forgiveness of original sin, and of actual sins committed before baptism, so repentance is a means instituted for the forgiveness of sins committed after baptism (*ib.*); "therefore penance is rightly called a second plank after ship-wreck" (*secunda post naufragium tabula*) (*ib.* c. 2).

Christ is said to have instituted this sacrament when he communicated to the apostles and their lawful successors the power of forgiving and retaining sins: "Receive ye the Holy Ghost; whose sins you shall forgive, they are forgiven them; and whose sins you shall retain, they are retained" (John 20, 22-23) (*Sess.* XIV, 1).

The council defined the Church's doctrine on penance against the Reformers of the sixteenth century. "If any one shall deny that sacramental confession was instituted, or is necessary to salvation, of divine right . . ; or saith, that the manner of confessing secretly to a priest alone, . . . is alien from the institution and command of Christ, and is a human invention: let him be anathema" (c. 6).

The *form* of this sacrament consists in the words: *Ego te absolvo*, etc.," which the priest always pronounces in Latin (*ib.* 3). For want of a visible element it is difficult to define the *matter* of this sacrament. The council of Trent (*ib.*) declared the acts of the penitent himself, contrition, confession, and satisfaction, as the *quasi materia* of this sacrament. The *effect* of the sacrament depends in no wise on the worthiness of the priest; "even priests who are in mortal sin, exercise, through the virtue of the Holy Ghost which was bestowed in ordination, the office of forgiving sins; . . . . it is erroneous" to "contend that this power exists not in bad priests" (*ib.* 6). The effect of the sacrament of penance is deliverance from guilt of sin through an infusion of grace and, in the case of mortal sin, deliverance from its eternal punishment, hence also reconciliation with God and justification (*ib.* 1. 3. 4).

The sacrament of penance embraces three distinct acts on the

sinner's part — contrition, confession, and satisfaction (*ib*. 3, and
c. 4). The council of Trent defines *contrition* as "a sorrow of mind,
and a detestation for sin committed, with the purpose of not sinning
for the future" (*ib*. 4). A distinction is made between perfect contrition, *contritio caritate perfecta* — a deep sorrow for sin, growing
out of love toward God, and imperfect contrition, *attritio*,— a sorrow
for sin such as arises from fear of punishment. Perfect contrition
is not necessary for the valid reception of this sacrament, for perfect
contrition is sufficient of itself for the remission of sin. A person
with perfect contrition does, in reality, not need the sacrament of
penance (*ib*.). And yet the Church demands "that the precept of
confession should be complied with, at least once a year, by all and
each, when they have attained to years of discretion" (*ib*. 5; and
c. 8). Why should one who is already as he ought to be, namely,
"made righteous," receive the sacrament of penance? He is bound
to receive it, nevertheless, according to the sophistry of the Tridentine Fathers who declared "that, although it sometimes happens
that this contrition is perfect through charity, and reconciles man
with God before this sacrament be actually received, the said reconciliation, nevertheless, is not to be ascribed to that contrition,
independently of the desire of the sacrament which is included
therein" (*ib*. 4). Attrition or imperfect contrition, i. e., the sorrow
we feel chiefly because of the punishment which by our sins we
have merited, is sufficient for a worthy reception of the sacrament
of penance. Of this imperfect contrition the council of Trent (*ib*.)
says that "it does not only not make a man a hypocrite and a greater
sinner, but it is even a gift of God, and an impulse of the Holy
Ghost"; it assists the penitent and disposes him toward the sacrament of penance by which it is completed, the sacrament effecting
this by its own inherent power.

Confession is to be made before the parish priest. Hence the
council of Trent (*ib*.) 7 declared "that the absolution which the
priest pronounces upon one over whom he has not either an ordinary or a delegated jurisdiction, ought to be of no weight whatever."
In the same chapter it is stated that the power of absolving from
"certain more grievous cases of crimes" is often reserved to the
bishop or to the pope; such cases are known as *casus reservati*,
reserved cases. In danger of death, however, "all priests may
absolve all penitents whatsoever from every kind of sins and censure
whatever."

All mortal sins which one can remember whether secret or
public must be confessed not only in general (*in genere*) but in all
their particulars (*in specie*). "For it is manifest that priests could

not have exercised this judgment without knowledge of the cause;
neither indeed could they have observed equity in enjoining punishments, if the said faithful should have declared their sins in general
only, and not rather specifically, and one by one, ... for if the
sick be ashamed to show his wound to the physician, his medical art
cures not that which it knows not of . . . Those circumstances which
change the species of the sin are also to be explained in confession,
because that, without them, the sins themselves are niether entirely
set forth by the penitents nor are they known clearly to the judges;
and it cannot be that they can estimate rightly the grievousness of
the crimes and impose on the penitents the punishment which
ought to be inflicted on account of them" (*ib.* 5).

According to the Word of God it is impossible to make a confession such as Rome demands. Who can discern his errors?
Ps. 19:12. But the Tridentine Fathers not only maintained that it
is "impious to assert that confession, enjoined to be made in this
manner, is impossible," but also made the impossible thing possible
by declaring that "other sins, which do not occur to the penitent
after diligent thought, are understood to be included as a whole in
that same confession" (*ib.*). Here is an apparent inconsistency in
Rome's teaching. On the one hand, the faithful are told that certain
sins, of which the priest knows nothing, are understood and included
in that same confession and consequently must be forgiven. On
the other hand, the Church teaches that only those sins, which are
made known to the priest, can be forgiven.

Those who think that confession is a difficult and intolerable
practice or regard "the shame of making known one's sins" as "a
grievous thing" are encouraged to look to the "great advantages and
consolations, which are most assuredly bestowed by absolution
upon all who worthily approach to this sacrament" (*ib.*). As to
venial sins the Tridentine decree states (*ib.*) that it is not necessary
to confess them, but it is well and advisable to do so.

The absolution given by a priest to a penitent who confesses his
sins with the proper dispositions remits both the guilt and the eternal
punishment of mortal sin, but the temporal punishments which the
penitent must suffer here or in purgatory are remitted by works of
satisfaction, commonly called penance (*Sess.* VI, 14; XIV, 8). "It
beseems the divine clemency that sins be not in such wise pardoned
us without any satisfaction" (XIV, 8). The works of penance enjoined by the priest are fastings, prayers, almsdeeds and the like
(*ib.* c. 13). These penitential works or "punishments"— (note that
prayer is here regarded as a punishment!) — are to be "imposed

at the discretion of the priest according to the measure of our delinquency" (*ib*. 9). "The priests . . . ought, as far as the Spirit and prudence shall suggest, to enjoin salutary and suitable satisfactions, according to the quality of the crimes and the ability of the penitent" (*ib*. 8). The council of Trent urges the faithful to strive to satisfy the divine justice not only by the penalties imposed by the priest, but also by other voluntary works of penance by patience in suffering (*ib*. 9). From the council's assertion that it is necessary for the sinner to confess his sins to the priest and make reparation for the sins which he has committed, a Protestant cannot but conclude that the forgiveness of sins is the achievement of man's own effort crowned by priestly mediation. Yet the council maintains that "no Catholic ever thought, that, by this kind of satisfaction on our part, the efficacy of the merit and of the satisfaction of our Lord Jesus Christ is either obscured or in any way lessened"; on the contrary, the atoning efficacy of our satisfaction is "derived from the satisfaction rendered by Christ" (*ib*. 8).

The priest may transmute the penances or satisfactions of the penitent into *indulgences*. By an indulgence Catholics mean, not the forgiveness of a sin, or a permission to commit sin, but the remission in whole or in part of the temporal punishment due to sin after sacramental absolution. Concerning indulgences the council of Trent decreed that, since the power of granting indulgences has been given to the Church by Christ and since the Church from the earliest time has made use of this divinely given power, "the use of indulgences, for the Christian people most salutary, and approved of by the authority of sacred councils, is to be retained in the Church" (*Sess*. XXV). To gain an indulgence one must strictly perform the works which the Church prescribes, such as fastings, pilgrimages, almsgiving, confession, hearing mass and the like. In granting indulgences, however, the council desired "that, in accordance with the ancient and approved custom in the Church, moderation be observed; lest by excessive facility, ecclesiastical discipline be enervated; . . that the abuses which have crept therein, . . be amended and corrected." The council laid upon each bishop the duty of finding out such abuses as exist in his own diocese, of bringing them before the next provincial synod, and of reporting them, with the assent of the other bishops, to the Roman pontiff, "by whose authority and prudence that which may be expedient for the universal Church will be ordained; that thus the gift of holy indulgences may be dispensed to all the faithful, piously, holily, and incorruptly."

In the same session (XXV) the doctrines of purgatory, the invocation, and relics of saints, and sacred images were reaffirmed. There is a *purgatory* (XXV), and the souls there detained, because they have not yet fully atoned for the temporal punishments due to their sins (VI. c. 30), "are helped by the suffrages of the faithful, but principally by the acceptable sacrifice of the altar" (XXV). The council maintains that the doctrine of purgatory is set forth in "the Sacred Writings and the ancient tradition of the Fathers," and commands all bishops diligently to teach "the sound doctrine concerning purgatory, transmitted by the holy Fathers and sacred councils," but bids them exclude from popular addresses all "the more difficult and subtle questions which tend not to edification."

Likewise "all bishops and others who sustain the office and charge of teaching are to instruct the faithful diligently and these in turn are bound to believe that the *saints* reigning with Christ are to be honored and invoked, that they offer prayers to God for men and that their relics are to be held in veneration" (*ib.*). It is claimed that the Roman Catholic Church in distinction from the Greek Church commands the invocation of saints not as a religious duty, but as good and wholesome —"it is good and wholesome suppliantly to invoke them" (*ib.*), but the Tridentine decree immediately adds: "that they think impiously who deny that the saints are to be invoked." The council further declared that due honor and veneration are to be given the images of Christ, Mary and the other saints "because the honor which is shown them is referred to the prototype which those images represent; in such wise that by the images which we kiss, and before which we uncover the head, and prostrate ourselves, we adore Christ; and we venerate the saints, whose similitude they bear" (*ib.*).

(5) The council of Trent declared (*Sess.* XXIII, 1) that *Holy Orders* is a sacrament instituted by Christ at the last supper and that "to the apostles" whom he then constituted priests of the New Testament "and to their successors in the priesthood, was the power delivered of consecrating, offering and administering his body and blood, as also of forgiving and retaining sins." Accordingly the chief powers conferred upon the priesthood are (1) to offer the sacrifice of the mass, (2) to forgive and retain sins, and (3) to administer the sacraments of baptism, penance, Eucharist and extreme unction, and to unite in matrimony. Only bishops can ordain validly and administer the sacrament of confirmation. "They are superior to priests; administer the sacrament of confirmation; ordain the ministers of the Church; and they can perform very many other things; over which functions others of an inferior order have no power ... they are placed ... by the Holy Ghost to rule the Church

of God" (XXIII, 4). Accordingly the hierarchical government of the Church is a divine institution (XXIII, 1. c. 6).

It should be noted that the *priesthood* and not the *prophetic* function is the essential thing in the Catholic ministry. The council of Trent rejected in unmistakable terms the evangelical doctrine of the universal priesthood of believers. "If any one affirm, that all Christians indiscriminately are priests of the New Testament, or that they are all mutually endowed with an equal spiritual power, he clearly does nothing but confound the ecclesiastical hierarchy, which is an army set in array" (XXIII, 4). Besides the priesthood there are other major and minor orders, by which as it were by steps the candidate arises to the priesthood (c. 2). They are in ascending gradation acolyth, exorcist, lector, and doorkeeper (*ib.* 2). These are known as the four minor orders and are sometimes conferred all at one time, sometimes at two or more ordinations. The three major or higher orders are those of subdeacons and deacons, together with those of priests and bishops (*ib.* 2. 4). The minor orders are given only to those who have previously received the tonsure (*ib.* 2). The Catholic Church claims to have "weighty reasons" for enforcing the celibacy of the clergy. The council of Trent simply declared the state of virginity or celibacy to be better and holier than that of marriage (XXIV, c. 10), and asserted that God gives the gift of chastity to those who ask for it rightly and that he does not suffer us to be tempted above that which we are able (*ib.* c. 9).

In order to turn aside every attack on the papal power the dispute between the *episcopal and curial theories* — whether the seat of authority is in the council or in the pope, or in both united; or whether, in the introductory clause of the decrees, to the words: *Sacrosancta oecumenica et generalis Tridentina synodus* should be added the words: *universalem ecclesiam repraesentans* — was left undecided. For the same reason the much disputed question whether bishops have apostolic power by divine right immediately from Christ, as has the pope, or, only by human right, deriving their apostolic succession through the pope, was skillfully avoided. The *Catechismus Romanus* (1566), designed as a homiletical and catechetical handbook for the clergy, was more favorable to the papal supremacy. It made the pope the visible head of the Church as Christ is its invisible head (I. 10, 10).

(6) *Marriage* was discussed (Sess. XXIV) in a general way. The council mentions neither form nor matter of this sacrament. The same council which manifestly regards marriage as a sort of necessary evil, which the more advanced in holiness must avoid,

maintains that matrimony is a sacrament, "a great sacrament" according to Eph. 5:32, through which great and special grace is received (XXIV, and c. 1). Thus the Catholic Church holds that Christ raised matrimony to the dignity of a sacrament, and yet anathematizes any one who says "that it is not better and more blessed to remain in virginity, or in celibacy, than to be united in matrimony" (c. 10). The council further maintains that "matrimony, in the evangelical law, excels in grace, through Christ, the ancient marriages," for he has "merited for us by his passion the grace which might perfect that natural love, and confirm that indissoluble union and sanctify the married." A marriage validly contracted and confirmed by the conjugal act *can never be dissolved* except by death. Even in case of adultery there can be no divorce as in such case the marriage bond is not broken, and neither party can marry again during the lifetime of the other (c. 7). But "for many causes, a separation may take place between husband and wife, *quoad thorum seu quoad cohabitationem*, in regard of bed, or in regard of cohabitation, for a determinate or for an indeterminate period" (c. 8), but if a person thus separated marries again, whilst the other party is still living, he or she lives in adultery (c. 7).

(7) *Extreme unction* is said to have been "instituted by Christ our Lord, as truly and properly a sacrament of the New Law, insinuated indeed in Mark, but recommended and promulgated to the faithful by James the Apostle, and brother of the Lord" (XIV, 1). The *matter* of this sacrament is oil blessed by a bishop (*ib.*). The *form* are the words: "By this holy unction and his bountiful mercy may God pardon thee whatever thou hast sinned by sight, hearing," etc. A priest alone can administer extreme unction. The council of Trent (*ib.* 3, and c. 4) maintained that "the elders of the church" (James 5:14) are "not the elders by age, or the foremost in dignity amongst the people, but either bishops, or priests by bishops rightly ordained by the imposition of the hands of the priesthood." Regarding the *effect* of this sacrament the Tridentine decree says that "the unction very aptly represents the grace of the Holy Ghost, with which the soul of the sick person is invisibly anointed (XIV, 1). The anointing with the Holy Ghost "cleanses away sins, ... and raises up and strengthens the soul of the sick person" (*ib.* 2). If health is profitable for the sick person's salvation, this sacrament contributes to its restoration (*ib*).

C. THE TRIDENTINE PROFESSION AND THE CATECHISMS.— The council of Trent gave formal sanction to those Scholastic theories and ecclesiastical practices against which the Reformers protested, but the decrees of the council contain no profession of faith. In Sessions XXIV and XXV, however, the council declared the necessity of an obligatory formula of faith. Such a formula, consisting of twelve articles, was drawn up by a commission of cardinals under the direction of Pius IV., and published in 1564. Article I contains the N. C. Creed. Articles II - XII are a short conspectus of the articles of faith as settled by the council. Later, two articles, one on the immaculate conception of the Virgin Mary and one on the infallibility of the pope, were added. The Profession, known as *Professio Fidei Tridentinae*, must be subscribed or sworn to by all priests and public teachers of the Church and also by Protestant converts; hence it is also called the *Profession of Converts*.

As to the relation of Scripture and tradition the Tridentine Profession goes beyond the declaration of the council. While the Tridentine decree completely coordinates Scripture and tradition, articles II and III of the Tridentine Profession assign the former a place second to the latter: "I most steadfastly admit and embrace apostolic and ecclesiastic traditions, and all other observances and constitutions of the same Church" (II). "I also admit the holy Scriptures" etc. (III). The Profession also contains clauses concerning subjects which were deliberately left untouched by the council, such as the Church and the position of the pope within the Church: ". . . I promise and swear true obedience to the Bishop of Rome, successor to St. Peter, Prince of the Apostles, and Vicar of Jesus Christ" (X). "I do . . . freely profess and truly hold this true Catholic faith, without which no one can be saved" (XII).

The council of Trent, in Session XXIV, had proposed a new *catechism* for the purpose of religious instruction in harmony with the decisions of the council. Several catechisms had appeared before and during the council, among them the catechism of the Jesuits composed by Peter Canisius, but none of them gave perfect satisfaction. Even the outline of the proposed catechism, which was laid before the council, was rejected. The council in its last session left to the pope, Pius IV., the preparation of a catechism. He selected for this task four distinguished theologians who under the advice of Carlo Borromeo composed the catechism which after careful revision was published by order of Pius V. in 1566 under the title *Catechismus Romanus ex decreto concilii Tridentini ad parochos*. It was, as the title indicates, designed merely as a manual for pastors in the ministry and not for pupils. The Roman Catechism is divided into four parts: *de symbolo apostolico, de sacramentis, de decalogo, de oratione dominica*.

Since this catechism was composed under Thomist influence it met with the opposition of the Jesuits. It never received a formal universal sanction of the Church, yet, occasioned by the council of Trent, coinciding with the decrees of the council, it was published by papal authority and hence must be regarded as one of the witnesses of genuine Catholicism.

The *Catechismus Romanus* was far surpassed in popularity by the triple *Catechism of Peter Canisius* — the larger one of 1555, a dogmatic manual for clergymen; then the short outline of instruction for children and youth, 1556; and then his catechism for students of the lower and middle grades, *Parvus Catechismus,* also known as *Catechismus Catholicus;* it is an extract from the larger Catechism, written in the winter of 1557 - 58. Even the *Catechism of Bellarmine,* published in 1603 and authorized by pope Clement VIII., as a true exposition of the Roman Catechism, could not compete with the catechisms of Canisius.

CHAPTER XXVI

TRIUMPH OF JESUIT THEOLOGY OVER AUGUSTINIANISM AND THOMISM, AND COMPLETION OF THE DOGMA OF THE ROMAN CATHOLIC CHURCH

After the council of Trent the Jesuits, who devoted themselves to preaching, hearing confessions, and the education of the young, made the defense and propagation of modern Romanism, theoretically and practically, the task of their lives.

A. JESUITISM VERSUS AUGUSTINIANISM.— Next to the Pauline epistles the writings of Augustine had chiefly determined the belief of both Luther and Calvin. Accordingly the Counter Reformation assumed an attitude of practical, though veiled, hostility toward the evangelical teachings of Augustine. Already at the council of Trent, in the discussions of the doctrines of sin and grace, the Thomist theologians had opposed the Scotist tendency toward Pelagianism. The Franciscans and Jesuits became now the chief supporters of the Scotist theory which in the main triumphed over the Thomist theology.

Against the growing Pelagianism there occurred a revival of Augustinianism. Michael Bajus, professor at the university of Louvain, upheld the Augustinian doctrine of grace. The Franciscans obtained from pope Pius V, in the bull *Ex omnibus afflictionibus*, 1567, the condemnation of 79 points of his teaching — all thoroughly Augustinian. Gregory XIII confirmed the decisions of his predecessor in the bull *Provisionis nostrae*, 1579.

The Spanish Jesuit Luis Molina endeavored to blend Augustinianism with popular Roman Catholic synergism. He developed and applied the theory of *scientia media* — the doctrine that God foresaw what each one would do of his own free will. God saves or condemns men according as he foreknows which men would cooperate with grace and which of them would remain obdurate. Through the cooperation of grace men can accomplish some moral good. Grace elevates the soul and makes it capable of supernatural works; but the free will is unceasingly active even with the gift and growth of grace, and it is in human power to render the help of God effective or non-effective.

The bold synergism as taught by Molina was attacked even by a few Jesuits, but especially by the Dominicans. In order to settle the dispute between the two orders, Clement VIII. convoked a

Congregatio de auxiliis gratiae, in 1597; it came to an end in 1607 with no result. Unwilling to offend the Jesuits the popes would not render a decision against them.

A new reformatory movement in the seventeenth century proceeding on Augustinianism and combating the Pelagian theology and lax moral principles of the Jesuits, was *Jansenism.* Cornelius Jansen (d. 1638), bishop of Ypres, laid down the results of his studies of Augustine in his comprehensive work *Augustinus,* published at Louvain, in 1640, after his death. As the genuine teachings of Augustine were herein set forth the Jesuits violently assailed the work, and under their influence pope Urban VIII., in the bull *In eminenti,* 1641, reproached Jansen, who had been dead for four years, for the renewal of the theory of Bajus.

Jansen's ideas spread from the Netherlands into France where they were popularized by his friend Duvergier. They gained a powerful centre and support in the cloister of *Port Royal.* The leaders of the Jansenist party, especially Antoine Arnauld, Blaise Pascal and Pierre Nicole, who were devoted Catholics, attacked the theology and ethics of the Jesuits. At the same time the Jesuits were eagerly at work to effect the condemnation of the Jansenist principles. Pope Innocent X. was induced to condemn, in the bull *Cum occasione,* 1663, as false and heretical five theses extracted from Jansen's *Augustinus* without explaining the meaning. They are as follows: Some commandments of God cannot be fulfilled by the just though they be willing and striving according to those powers which are theirs; they also lack the grace which would make fulfillment possible. (2) In the state of fallen nature resistance is never offered to inward grace. (3) In the fallen state merit and demerit do not depend on freedom from necessity, but freedom from coercion suffices. (4) The Semipelagians admitted the necessity of an inward prevenient grace for the performance of single acts, even for the beginning of faith, and they were heretics, because they asserted that this grace was of such a nature that the will of man was able either to resist or to obey it. (5) It is Semipelagian to say that Christ died, or shed his blood, for all men without exception. The Jansenists admitted that these sentences, torn as they were from their context, were heretical, but they did not admit that Jansen had held these propositions in their heretical sense. Arnauld insisting on the distinction between *question du fait* and *question du droit* maintained that *in fact* Jansen had not taught these theses which the pope had *rightly* condemned. Nevertheless, in 1657, pope Alexander VII. anathematized all those who should say that the five theses are not in Jansenius, and, in 1664, required all clergy to accept by a new signature the papal pronouncements against Jansenius.

Port Royal was destroyed in 1710, but Jansenism was not exterminated. The strife was revived by the publication of Paquier Quesnel's work *Le Nouveau Testament en francois avec des reflexions morales sur chaque verset* (4 vols., Paris, 1692-94; Engl. transl., *The New Testament, with Moral Reflections upon Every Verse*, by R. Russel, 4 vols., London, 1919-25). This Biblical commentary represented the Jansenist doctrine, both dogmatic and practical. The Jesuits obtained, through pope Clement IX., in the notorious bull *Unigenitus* (Sept. 8, 1713), a condemnation of no less than 101 theses of the work. Among these, however, were not only some almost literally Augustinian propositions, but even some substantially identical with the teachings of the Holy Scriptures, e. g., "the grace of Jesus Christ is necessary for every good work; without it nothing truly good can be done (2). No grace is imparted except through faith (26). Faith is the primal grace and the source of all others (27). Outside of the church no grace is granted (29). Faith justifies when it is operative, but it is operative only through love (51). Faith, the exercise, increase and reward of faith, are entirely a gift of God's pure favor (69). The reading of the holy Scripture is for all (80). The obscurity of the sacred Word of God is no reason for the laity to dispense themselves from its reading (81).

The bull *Unigenitus* thus marks the complete severance of Augustinian doctrine from the official teaching of the Roman Catholic Church. Fenelon, who gave unconditional support to the bull, admits that public opinion credited the bull with "condemning St. Augustine, St. Paul and even Jesus Christ." It caused a violent uproar. Several bishops appealed from the pope and his bull to a general council and were therefore styled *Appellants* in distinction from the *Acceptants* who accepted the bull. Louis XV. opposed the Appellants in every way. In 1730 the bull became part and parcel of the law of the kingdom. Pope Benedict XIV. manifested considerably more caution in regard to the bull *Unigenitus* by refusing the ministrations of the Church only to those Appellants who had publicly condemned the bull. Nevertheless, he confirmed it as legally valid (Encyclical of Oct. 16, 1756).

B. Dogma of The Immaculate Conception.— The council of Trent left the doctrine of the immaculate conception unsettled. The Jesuits, however, in a general assembly, in 1593, formally adopted the doctrine of the immaculate conception and became its unyielding champions against the Jansenists and all other opponents. It was the zealous activity of the Jesuits and their influence which effected the triumph of the Scotist view and brought about the final papal definition of this already popular doctrine. The Jesuits, who were also zealous supporters of papal infallibility, maintained that the pope has the right to decide authoritatively without the concurrence of any council a question of doctrine.

In his encyclical of Febr. 2, 1849, pope Pius IX. invited the opinion of the bishops as to whether the apostolic see should define the doctrine. A large majority answered in favor of the definition. A commission, in which Peronne and his fellow Jesuit Passaglia were the leading members, was appointed to consider the question. The commission reported in accord with the pope's inclination and declared that no evidence from the Scripture was needed, but tradition alone sufficed.

In the bull *Ineffabilis Deus, of Dec.* 8, 1854, pope Pius IX. proclaimed "that the doctrine which holds the Blessed Virgin Mary to have been, from the first instant of her conception, by a singular grace and privilege of Almighty God, in view of the merits of Christ Jesus the Savior of mankind, preserved free from all stain of original sin, was revealed by God, and is, therefore, to be firmly and constantly believed by all the faithful" (Schaff, *Creeds,* II, 211 f.).

C. DEFINITION OF PAPAL POWER AND INFALLIBILITY.— The council of Trent did not venture to make an outspoken decision between the curial and episcopal theories (see p. xxx). Episcopalism had still many advocates in France and Germany. According to the episcopal system in France the bishops with the pope represented the Church in general councils. Pontifical definitions in matters of faith required the consent of the whole church before they could be considered irreformable. *The Declaration of the Clergy of France,* 1682, aimed at national independence and placed the Church above its head. This document lays down: (1) that St. Peter and his successors have power in things spiritual but not in things temporal and civil: (2) that a general council is above the pope; (3) that the ancient rules, customs and institutions received by the kingdom and the Church of France remain likewise inviolable; (4) that the infallible teaching authority of the Church belongs to pope and bishops jointly.

In Germany, Johann Nikolaus von Hontheim, suffragan bishop of Treves, in his book *De statu ecclesiae et legitima potestate Romani pontificis,* published under the pseudonym of *Justinus Febronius,* 1763, advocated the reduction of papal authority to a simple primacy. The book stirred up a great deal of excitement and controversy at the time. It gave an impulse to the Congress of Ems, 1786, a meeting of representatives of the archbishops of Mayence, Treves, Cologne and Salzburg, who prepared the *Ems Agreement,* known as the *Punctation of Ems.* The papal nunciatures in the form in which they then existed chiefly occasioned the Punctation. In twenty-three articles the document gives definite expression to the prevalent desire of the higher clergy in Germany to shake off their depressing dependence on the Curia.

In his answer to the archbishops, which finally came to them, dated Nov. 14, 1789, pope Pius VI. denied the justness of any of the articles and rejected as folly the theory that all bishops have the same share as the pope in the government of the Church. Hontheim's book had been placed on the Index already in 1764. He himself retracted in 1778 then nearly fourscore years old. The archbishops had to acquiesce. Under the pressure of the revolutionary trend of the time, which proceeded from France, the interest in the movement declined. In France, the old Gallican spirit was gradually decaying. The downfall of the old regime allowed the pope to acquire a degree of power which he had never before possessed. In opposition to Gallicanism there arose a new party, the *Ultramontanists,* who were zealous advocates of papal sovereignty and infallibility. The designation *Ultramontanism* is here applied to a tendency representing a definite form of Catholicism within the Roman Catholic Church. We do not attempt to offer a definition of Ultramontanism by a concise formula, but merely point out the varied character of its manifestations. On this point we will hear two Catholic authorities: Franz Xaver Kraus, professor of church history (d. 1890), classes as Ultramontane (1) Whoever sets the concept of the Church above that of religion; (2) whoever confounds the pope with the Church; (3) whoever believes the kingdom of God is of this world, and maintains, with medieval Catholicism, that the power of the keys includes temporal jurisdiction over princes and nations; (4) whoever holds that religious conviction can be imposed by material power, or may legitimately be crushed by it; (5) whoever is always ready to sacrifice a clear command of his own conscience to the claims of an alien authority (E. Hauviller, *F. X. Kraus,* 1904, p. 100). The Catholic church historian Ignaz von Doellinger (d. 1890) sums up the Ultramontane view in the following proposition: "The pope is the supreme, the infallible, and consequently the sole authority in everything that concerns religion, the Church, and morality, and each of his utterances on these topics demands unconditional submission—internal no less than external" (Doellinger-Reusch, *Kleinere Schriften,* 1890, p. 221). And was not Doellinger right?

Not only did the Vatican Council bear him out on this statement which Doellinger had made in 1865. The *Syllabus* likewise is ample proof for Doellinger's assertion that the Ultramontane view embraces "not merely religion and the Church, but science and the state, politics, morals and the social order — in a word, the whole intellectual life of men and nations" (*ib.*). On December 8, 1864, Pius IX. issued an encyclical letter, known as the *Syllabus*, denouncing eighty errors of the age. It is, as the official title says, "a collection (*syllabus*) containing the principal errors of our times as noted in the Allocutions, Encyclicals and other Apostolic Letters of our Holy Father Pope Pius IX." The errors condemned in the Syllabus are grouped under ten heads as follows : 1. Pantheism, naturalism, and absolute rationalism; 2. moderate rationalism; 3. indifferentism and latitudinarianism; 4. socialism, communism, secret societies, Bible societies, clerico-liberal societies; 5. errors regarding the Church and her rights; 6. errors regarding civil society, both in itself and in its relation to the Church; 7. errors regarding Christian and natural ethics; 8. errors regarding Christian marriage; 9. errors regarding the temporal power of the pope; 10. errors regarding modern liberalism. In spite of the opposition, which the Syllabus, particularly paragraphs 5, 6 and 10, aroused, it is nevertheless an official document and an integral part of the Roman Catholic Dogma.

An important factor in the advancement of curialism in the nineteenth century were *the Jesuits*. Pope Pius VII. had re-established the Jesuit Order in the bull *Sollicitudo omnium,* August 7, 1814. With renewed zest the Jesuits advocated papal absolutism in politics and religion. They succeeded at least in asserting the old claims of the Curia everywhere to unlimited spiritual power, though the glory of its worldly power was waning. In all countries the Catholic Church became more and more dependent immediately on the pope as her lord, while the position of bishops was more and more reduced to that of papal delegates, and all important matters were referred to the pope or settled by his nuncios. The entire development of post-Reformation Catholicism was on the side of the Roman Curia.

The Vatican Council which was opened on the festival of the Immaculate Conception of the Virgin Mary, December 8, 1869, in the Basilica of the Vatican, gave dogmatic form to the Ultramontane view and proclaimed in its fourth public session, chapter IV, the decree "concerning the infallible teaching of the Roman Pontiff." At first the dogma of papal infallibility was resisted for a long time in the council by a considerable number of eminent prelates, and the infallibilists were confronted with no slight task in their endeavor to establish their theory by Scripture and tradition, and to defend it against the argument of history. But when on July 18, 1870, after many of the opponents of the definition had preferred to leave Rome, the final vote was taken, all the 535 dignitaries present voted for the dogma except two who changed their votes before the close of the session, so that the decision was legally unanimous. After the vote, Pius IX. read the decree of his own infallibility as defined in the *Constitutio Vaticana,* the bull *Pastor Aeternus.*

The first definition of the Constitution deals with the *relation of the episcopal authority to the papal.* It entirely revolutionized the position of the pope within the Church in that it made him the universal bishop in all the Church, conceding to him "complete and supreme jurisdictional authority over the whole the Church, not merely in matters pertaining to faith and morals but also in those touching the discipline and government of the Church; and this authority is a regular and immediate authority extending over all churches collectively and each church individually — *sive in omnes ac singulas ecclesias* — and over all pastors and believers collectively and each pastor and believer individually — *sive in omnes et singulos pastores et fideles*" (*Sess.* IV, 3; Mirbt, *Q.* 464; Schaff, *Creeds,* II. 265).

The second definition presents the doctrine of *papal infallibility* and makes the recognition of that doctrine incumbent on all Catholic Christians : "We, the sacred council approving, teach, and so define as a dogma divinely revealed : That the Roman Pontiff, when he speaks *ex cathedra* — that is to say, when in the discharge of the office of pastor and teacher of all Christians, by virtue of his supreme apostolic authority, he defines a doctrine regarding faith and morals to be held by the universal Church — is, through the divine assistance promised to the blessed Peter himself, possessed of that infallibility with which the divine Redeemer willed that his Church should be endowed for defining doctrine concerning faith and morals; and that therefore such definitions of the Roman pontiff are of themselves and not from the consent of the Church unalterable, *irreformabiles.* But if any one shall venture, which may God avert, to contradict our definition, let him be accursed" (*Sess.* IV, 4; Mirbt, *Q.* 465 f. Schaff, *Creeds,* II. 270 f.).

The second definition involved a *fundamental alteration in the status of the ecumenical councils.* They no longer constitute, in conjunction with the pope, the representation of the Church. Their function of defining the doctrine of the Church is now, since the quality of infallibility is ascribed to the pope alone, reduced to that of an advisory organ of the Church : "We, the sacred council approving, teach and define . . ." In the future, ecumenical councils may still be convened and drawn into requisition, but their independent authority is a thing of the past.

Concerning *the limitations of the infallibility* of the pope — when *ex cathedra*, as the pastor and teacher of all Christians he defines a doctrine of faith and morals to be held by the whole Church — no criterion is assigned by which it can be ascertained, in a concrete instance, whether the infallible decision is present; nor has the papal see ever given an authentic interpretation of the *ex cathedra*.

The *Vatican decrees* belong to the sphere of *revealed truths of faith* and consequently *are to be accepted as final.* When the new dogma was published excitement and controversy concerning it rapidly subsided. Many of those who resisted the decree of papal infallibility as inopportune, unhistorical or uncanonical formulated their loyal adhesion to the promulgated dogma. Those who refused to accept the degree retired or were excommunicated. Thus the Church of Rome gained one of her most brilliant triumphs.

D. In Germany, the excommunicated priests, faithful to their leader Johann Joseph Ignaz von Doellinger, formed a separate ecclesiastical organization on the episcopal model, the OLD CATH-OLIC CHURCH. At a congress at Munich, Sept. 22-24, 1871, with J. F. von Schulte (prof. of canon law in Prague, later in the University of Bonn) presiding, a program of the movement was adopted. The Jansenist bishops of Holland threw in their lot with the Old Catholics and transferred to them their Latin episcopal succession by consecrating Joseph Hubert Reinkens, professor of Theology at Breslau, who had been chosen first bishop of the Old Catholic Church.

The *doctrinal position* of the Old Catholics was at first that of Tridentine Romanism. Soon, however, they attempted to get into close relations with the Evangelical, the Anglican and Greek Churches. To this end a union conference was held at Bonn, 1874, which recognized besides the Scriptures and the doctrine of the church based upon it, the binding authority of the ancient undivided church. The doctrinal consensus of the Old Catholics, Oriental, and Anglo-Catholics was formulated in the *Fourteen Theses* of the Old Catholic Union Conference at Bonn, 1874, and the *Old Catholic Agreement* on the *Filioque Controversy*, 1875. (see Schaff, *Creeds*, II, 545-554). The Old Catholic Church has two official catechisms, adopted by the Old Catholic Conference at Bonn, 1874, and a manual of instruction: *Leitfaden fuer den kath. Religionsunterricht in hoeheren Schulen*, publ. by the Old Catholic Conference at Bonn, 1877.

The Old Catholics reject besides the dogma of papal infallibility also that of the immaculate conception. They did away with the abuses arising from penance and and removed the compulsory celibacy of the priesthood. They encourage Bible reading and use the vernacular in their worship. But they retain all the other distinctive doctrines of the Roman Catholic Church. The Old Catholic movement, therefore, does not represent "an approach to Evangelical faith, but genuine Catholicism, which, however, has rid itself of the disfigurements and disguises of modern Ultramontanism and Jesuitism" (Graul, *Distinctive Doctrines*, 121).

The Greek or Eastern Church, accepting only the decrees of the first seven ecumenical councils, declines the peculiar tenets of the Roman Catholic Church. The Roman Catholic Church is the continuing Church of the Middle Ages, for the Council of Trent exalted the scholastic theology of the Middle Ages to the position of the ecclesiastical dogma. Protestantism embraces the Churches that sprang from the Reformation. Professing the scriptural principle these churches have issued a number of confessional writings or symbols with the purpose of declaring publicly against error and false teaching the faith which purported to be drawn from the Scriptures. Of the numerous confessions issued by the different branches of the Reformed Church E. F. Karl Mueller in *Die Bekenntnissschriften der ref. Kirche*, Leipzig, 1903, counts no less than 58. None of them is so universally accepted as, for example, the Augsburg Confession in the Lutheran Church. Nor did any of the Reformed symbols become such a dynamic factor in German religious thought and life as can be claimed for the Lutheran confessions. "The Lutheran Church differs from all other churches in being essentially the Church of the pure Word and unadulterated Sacraments. Not the great number of her adherents, not her organizations, not her charitable and other institutions, not her beautiful customs and liturgical forms, etc., but the precious truths confessed by her symbols in perfect agreement with the Holy Scriptures constitute the true beauty and rich treasures of our Church, as well as the never-failing source of her vitality and power" (Preface, Conc. Triglotta, p. IV).

The faith drawn from the Scriptures and stated in the confessions needed to be given order and arrangement. That was the task of the dogmaticians of the seventeenth century. Like the Scholastics of the Middle Ages whose task was to support the traditional dogma by the evidences of reason or philosophy and present the whole mass of dogma in a schematic and harmonious unity, so these modern "scholastics" made it their business to elaborate a

system of doctrine which was to give a scientific form to the substance of evangelical truth and thus bring it within the full comprehension of the church. The period of the "new Scholasticism" or
orthodoxy lasted still longer in the Lutheran Church than in the
Reformed Church, or till about the year 1700. This scholastic
orthodoxy has imparted to Lutheran theology a fulness and wealth,
a precision and consistency of structure as can not be found in any
other church communion. Prominent among the champions of
Lutheran orthodoxy were Chemnitz, Johann Gerhard, Hutter,
Hollaz, Quenstedt, Carpzov, Calovius. The period of orthodoxy is
often spoken of as that of "dead orthodoxy" and dogmatic Lutheranism of the seventeenth century has been branded as a carica-
ture of evangelical Christianity. This criticism ignores altogether
the great achievements of orthodoxy. It also is blind to the fact
that in the period of "dead orthodoxy" there is to be noticed in the
German church more true piety and spiritual life than in the period
of Pietism which most decried the dead formalism of Lutheran
orthodoxy. Whatever may be said as to the charge raised by Pietism against dogmatic Lutheranism of the period, the fact remains
and cannot be gainsaid that, the position held by the old Lutheran
theologians was in strict conformity with the fundamental principles
of the Church of the Reformation. It must, however, be admitted
that the development of a system of theological doctrine is fraught
with the danger of treating saving truth chiefly as dogma. The old
dogmaticians, it is charged, did not altogether escape this danger.

Among those who directly or indirectly opposed the "new
Scholasticism" were mystics like the Lutheran pastor Valentin
Weigel (d. 1588) and the famous shoemaker Jacob Bohme (d.
1624), "the prince of modern theosophists," with whom Weigel
shared some elements of theosophic speculation. Over against the
discursive reasoning of the theologians, theosophic mysticism
stressed the inward illumination. The soul gains true insight when
touched by the immediate presence of God. A healthier type of
mysticism was that of John Arndt (d. 1621), the profoundly spiritual author of the four books on True Christianity, translated into
almost all European languages and still a classic of Lutheran devotional literature. Arndt's mysticism is in the main that of the
medieval writers like Tauler and Thomas a Kempis. Formally, he
held fast to the doctrine of the Lutheran Church. In his theology
the dogmatic and polemic elements are thoroughly subordinate to
the devout and spiritual. It is quite natural that in a disputatious
age in which everything that is not cast in the established dogmatic
mold is taboo, a man like Arndt exposed himself to much criticism.

In stressing inward piety over against pure doctrine, Arndt became the forerunner of the Pietistic movement which found its culmination in Spener and Francke in the eighteenth century.

The at times one-sided dogmaticism of Lutheran theology occasioned *constant controversy.* The tendency to carry theological principles to their extreme logical conclusions brought *orthodoxy into conflict with itself.* In the early part of the seventeenth century there arose a controversy between the Lutheran divines of the universities of Giessen and Tubingen over the question whether Christ in the state of humiliation refrained from the use of his divine attributes, or whether he used them, though in a hidden way. Both schools were agreed as to the possession of the divine attributes by Christ in the state of humiliation. But while the Giessen divines, Mentzer and Feuerborn, pronounced the state of humiliation an actual kenoosis chreseoos (a non-use) i. e., a complete though free surrender of the divine attributes, the Tuebingen divines Lucas Osiander, M. Nicolai and others maintained a krophis chreseoos (a concealed use), i. e. full possession but concealed use of the divine attributes. The controversy known as the Cryptist Kenotist Controversy broke out in 1619 but subsided during the turbulent time of the Thirty Years' War without leading to any positive result.

A very strong reaction against the dogmaticism of Lutheran theology arose in connection with the efforts of George Calixtus for the reconciliation of Lutheran and Reformed theology. The disputes to which these efforts gave rise, known as the Syncretistic controversy, lasted during the whole lifetime of Calixtus who died in 1656. After studying philology, philosophy and theology at Helmstaedt and other German universities he visited France, Holland and England, broadening his mind and sympathies as he became acquainted with the conditions of the Reformed and Catholic Churches. On his return in 1614 he was appointed professor of theology at Helmstaedt where he remained until his death. Convinced that genuine Christians are to be found in all Christian communions he labored for forty-three years to promote union between the separated churches, particularly the Lutheran and the Reformed. In fact he entertained the hope of reconciling divided Christendom by removing all unimportant differences. As a basis of union he suggested the Holy Scriptures and the consensus of the first five Christian centuries, from the Apostolicum to the creed of Chalcedon. Roman Catholics saw in the scheme of Calixtus nothing but an apostasy from the faith of their fathers. Lutheran theologians pronounced it a religious medley or syncretism. On account of his irenic attitude toward the Reformed and Romanists alike Calixtus was accused sometimes of being a crypto-Calvinist, and sometimes of being a crypto-Catholic. After the conference of Thorn held in 1645 to prevent religious strife between Catholics, Lutherans and Reformed, his efforts were more generally assailed and his liberalism looked upon as a base apostasy from the true faith. A most furious controversy arose and distracted the Lutheran Church. On the one side were Calixtus and the theologians of Helmstaedt and Koenigsberg, on the other the theologians of Electoral Saxony with Abraham Calovius in Wittenberg, at their head. Calovius contended for purity of doctrine as an ecclesiastical norm, drawn from Scripture and therefore complete and beyond improvement. According to Calixtus the prime object of theology is Christian life, and orthodoxy can never be made the test of Christian character. Pure doctrine is also of varying degrees of value within itself, giving room for a broader unity on essentials. In 1655 the Wittenberg theologians drew up a plan for a new confessional document and prepared the *Consensus repetitus fidei vere Lutheranae,* in which among other things the syncretism of Calixtus and his school was rejected. But in spite of the eminent efforts of Calovius who produced in the same year several stately volumes of controversial literature referring to the heresies of Calixtus as "the excrements of Satan," the desired acceptance of the confession could not be secured. The Consensus was never legally ratified.

After the death of Calixtus his son and successor Friedrich Ulrich, inferior to his father in mind and moderation, continued the syncretistic controversy, but met with no approval among the Lutherans. The union project of Calixtus only stirred to a fiercer zeal the uncompromising spirit of dogmatism which it opposed. The attempt to heal present differences by a mere return to the unanimous teaching of the first five centuries minimized the significance of that which was of real religious importance. The loyal Lutherans saw in this tendency a surrender of the faith of the Reformation. In order to maintain the religious content of the Reformation, and that not from mere combativeness, they took a definite and uncompromising stand against the syncretistic tendency of the age. With respect to the relation to Catholics the teaching of Calixtus that those doctrines which alone are necessary to salvation are to be found also in the Roman Catholic Church favored the secession to that church of a considerable number of persons of note. The syncretistic controversy subsided after the death of Calovius, 1686 without having contributed anything important to the theology of that period.

In opposition to formalism, both in doctrine and life, there arose about the middle of the seventeenth century everywhere, in Catholic and Protestant communions, mystic pietistic movements which laid stress upon Christianity as the renewal of the heart and life of man. In post-tridentine Catholicism we notice this tendency in France in the revival of Augustinianism in opposition to Jesuitism and the worldliness of the external Church. In the Lutheran Church in Germany we find it in the Pietism of Spener and Francke which arose in opposition to the then prevalent orthodoxy. The name of Pietists was at first disparagingly used as a term of reproach and ridicule, like that of Methodists later in England. Long before the time of Spener a reaction had begun against the ruling tendencies in the church and in theology. Long before Spener's movement there were found sects both in England and Holland which were indifferent to questions of dogma as such, and practiced strict holiness and discipline, "precision" even in mode of life. Gisbert Voet (d. 1676), one of the leading Dutch theologians of this period, spoke of the "puritanism" exercised in the conventicles of the regenerate as "the exact and perfect agreement of human actions with the law prescribed by God, accepted by real believers and followed with zeal." It must also be remembered that behind the mystic-pietistic tendencies of the age there was a rich devotional literature, e. g., John Bunyan's *Pilgrim's Progress,* Richard Baxter's *Saints' Everlasting Rest,* John Arndt's *True Christianity,* and especially *Practice of Piety* by Lewis Bayly, Bishop of Bangor. Spener is known to have been greatly influenced by the work of Arndt, Baxter and Bishop Bayly. But even though certain influences of Dutch and English Pietism may have reached Germany, Lutheran Pietism was not a product of foreign Calvinism; it was essentially a German movement.

Philip Jacob Spener (1635-1705) the founder of the movement "united in himself the influence of the reformed tendency to a vigorous and almost ascetic Christian life, and the Lutheran tendency to the purely scriptural doctrine of the Bible" (Sohm). He was heartily attached to the Lutheran Church and loyal to the principles of Protestantism. But while he correctly taught justification by faith, he laid the emphasis upon its fruit in sanctification. To Spener religion was not knowledge, but practice, *a habitus practicus.* During his pastorate at Frankfort (1666-1686) his plan of church reform was worked out and made known to the world. Against the merely intellectual attachment to pure doctrine and the formalism of church-life Spener insisted on an effectual application of the truths of the Bible and a demonstration of it in personal renovation and holiness. To bring about the desired transformation of the

lives of the people he devoted himself to the preaching of the Word
in a simple and practical way. To train the younger members in
religion he used the method of catechisation, thus laying the foundation for the present system in the Lutheran Church of catechetical
instruction of catechumens. His catechism and catechetical sermons were the fruit of these endeavors. He also introduced the
collegia pietatis, private gatherings under the direction of a pastor
for the furtherance of true piety. In his noted work *Pia desideria*
(publ. 1675) he depicted the Christianity of his period which left
much to be desired, and set forth six proposals for improvement.
They were as follows: (1) A wider circulation and study of the
Word of God. (2) The establishment and maintenance of the
spiritual priesthood, employing pious and capable laymen as
preachers. (3) The principle that mere knowledge is not sufficient
in Christianity; practice and experience must be added to theory.
(4) Gentleness and love rather than argument in dealing with
theological opponents. (5) The training of the clergy must stress
personal piety as well as intellectual knowledge. (6) Change of
the method of preaching which should aim at conversion and
edification, with less emphasis on rhetorical art and homiletic erudi-
tion. At first the orthodox received the proposals of Spener
with favor. But when the Pietists put these proposals into practice
thus disturbing the accustomed mode of life, the orthodox rose up
in passionate reaction against these "innovations." They regarded
and treated the Pietists as a new sect, accusing them of contempt
of regular worship and theological science, and of promoting
separatism. Condemned and excluded from the orthodox universities of Leipzig and Wittenberg, the Pietists found a refuge at the
newly founded University of Halle (1694) with August Hermann
Francke at its head. But the controversy continued and soon
involved the whole German Church in a passionate strife, in which,
on both sides, indiscretions were committed. The chief opponent
of Spener was Carpzov (d. 1657) professor at Leipzig. Among
the later champions of sound Lutheran doctrine Loescher, (d. 1749)
superintendent of Dresden, was the most estimable and able.

The outward course of the controversy does not come within
the scope of our discussion. Pietism was of a practical rather than
theological nature; yet it did not preclude points of contact with
scientific theology. The chief points of controversy centered around
the doctrines of regeneration, justification, sanctification, church,
and millennium. The orthodox affirmed that regeneration is an
act of God, taking place in baptism, the effect of which must last
throughout the entire life. For baptism is a never failing fountain

of power and encouragement for the daily conflict with sin and of consolation and strength for the daily renewal of the spiritual life. The Pietists identified awakening or conversion with regeneration, which only begins in baptism and in subsequent life is to be consummated or "sealed" by actual experience or subjective feeling of God's grace. Hence they regarded confirmation as a renewal, on the part of God and man, of the baptismal covenant. On the basis of such actual experience of conversion or regeneration the catechumens vowed henceforth to be Christ's own. In a similar way the Pietists confused justification with sanctification. The orthodox regarded justification as God's act, in which good works have no place, and sanctification as the believer's life in which good works have their very important place. The Pietists held that only a living faith which gives evidence of a pious life and active Christianity attains justification. Thus in their striving after sanctification, they lost sight of the meaning of justification. Sanctification, as viewed by the Pietists, demanded as a proof of assured salvation also the renunciation of the world. The world dances, plays cards, goes to the theatre, uses tobacco, etc., therefore a Christian must abstain from these things. The orthodox placed these things among the *adiaphora*. Although the Pietists did not form a new church, their conception of the church tended toward separatism. According to the orthodox the objective means of grace constitute the basis and foundation of the church. They beget, nourish and foster believers. According to the Pietists the true believers and their faith constitute, preserve and renew the church; hence their practice of fostering little associations of "truly awakened", *ecclesiolae in ecclesia*, which cut themselves off from the "great masses" and thus weakened the power and significance of church organization. The orthodox held that the power and efficacy of the means of grace depend solely upon God's appointment and promise, and not on the worthiness of the administrant. The Pietists maintained that the saving effect of the means of grace resides in the person of the preacher and his faith, and that Word and sacraments have no saving power, if administered by an unconverted person. Therefore the Pietists insisted that no one is qualified to teach theology unless he is a model of piety, thus exalting a pious life and active Christianity above learning and intellect or subscription to creeds. Spener also stood for a mild form of chiliasm. He held that after the conversion of the Jews and the fall of the papacy there would begin here on earth a period of the most glorious and undisturbed development of the church of Christ, "an ante-sabbath of the eternal sabbath". This moderate millennial view held by Spener called forth severe criticism on the part of his opponents, especially since it led to exaggeration and fanaticism among many of his adherents less distinguished than himself for wisdom and moderation.

Pietism, no doubt, had its faults. Yet it contributed largely to the revival of Biblical studies in Germany. It also called to the remembrance of clergy and laity alike that the idea of the universal spiritual priesthood of Christians involves both a privilege and an obligation. It gives them not only a right to the throne of grace without the mediation of an earthly priest, but lays upon them the duty and obligation to teach the Word to others. Pietism insisted that each Christian has a part in God's plan for the salvation of men. Pietism as a distinct movement had run its course by the middle of the eighteenth century, but as an influence it has come down to the present day. It was carried into the Moravian Church by Nicolaus Ludwig Zinzendorf (1700-1760) godson of Spener brought up under pietistic influences and trained at the Paedagogium in Halle where the pietistic strain in his character was encouraged and established. In connection with the Moravian settlement on his estate in Upper Lusatia, Saxony, he consecrated himself wholly to the service of God and was ordained a bishop. He had before been received into the Lutheran ministry. His idea was to carry out into practice the Pietist ideas of Spener. He did not mean to form a new church but rather to reform the established church by special associations, within the church, of the preeminently religious. His doctrinal position coincides with that of the Moravian Church. "Though the Moravians are in general agreement with evangelical Christianity, yet a certain one-sidedness characterizes their doctrinal views. A strongly Christ-centered tendency of their teaching prevades all official statements, the liturgy and the characteristic preaching of the Moravian Brethren. The emphasis is almost exclusively laid on the work of the Son in man's salvation." ". . . . . the great theme of our preaching is Jesus Christ, in whom we have the grace of the Lord, the love of the Father and the communion of the Holy Ghost" (Syn. Results, 1869). In the work of the Son again they are content with emphasizing just one point of doctrine, namely, the "bloody merit of Christ." "We regard it as the main calling of the Brethren Church to proclaim the Lord's Death" (*ib.*). The Moravian Brethren are fond of regarding Christ's death as a divine love-sacrifice and consequently preach almost exclusively the gospel of God's love ignoring the significance of the law either as a mirror of sin or as a rule of virtue. Their preaching is especially adapted to arouse pious feeling. This is in keeping with their tendency to make Christianity preeminently a matter of feeling. Their liturgy, their emotional hymns, their sweet music, their love-feasts which they celebrate in imitation of the agapae of apostolic times, all tend in the same direction.

"There was a period in the history of the Moravian Church 1743-1750, when this subjectivism degenerated into a sickly sentimentalism and fanatical excrescences for which Zinzendorf furnished occasion by the composition of sensuous hymns in which he fancifully expressed the believer's joy and love to Christ, or portrayed the Trinity in a grossly offending way, the Father being called Papa, Grandfather, or Father-in- law; Jesus, the Lamb of God and Brother of the Christian; the Holy Spirit, Mama, and the eternal Spouse of God the Father." Extravagances of this kind incurred the censure of such true Christian scholars in the Lutheran Church as Bengel, who certainly were not chargeable with a want of the true spirit of devotion. "When Zinzendorf and his colaborers began to realize into what wild and dangerous excesses people had been led they earnestly labored to bring them back from this aberration to the sober faith and reverent love taught by the Scriptures. It was particularly Bishop Spangenberg, Zinzendorf's successor, who purged the Moravian Church from these extravagant and fanatic tendencies."

CHAPTER XXVII

THEOLOGY IN GREAT BRITAIN
During The Seventeenth And Eighteenth Century

In England in the post-reformation period we do not notice any successive scientific development of theology. During the sixteenth and seventeenth centuries England can boast of many names of note among her theologians. Yet they have contributed little to the history of dogmatic theology. After the fundamental doctrines of the Reformation had been received from the continent and established in the country, the development took place in the sphere of practice rather than in the sphere of thought. The relation between church and state attained to supreme importance. As a consequence we meet in this period with grave disturbances in the history of the church and virulent controversies concerning the constitution of the church, its government and worship, and the entire political, social and moral life. In continental Protestantism these matters were disputed and settled in different ways by different schools of theological thought. Different schools or tendencies of the continent became in England different church parties or sects.

We have seen in a former chapter that the Anglican Confession, as adopted in 1571, is a moderately Calvinistic creed. Its polity, however, is that of a national episcopal church, the reigning sovereign being the supreme governor of the Church of England. The episcopal organization and the ritual of the Anglican Church were largely retained from the Roman Catholic Church. In opposition to this the Puritans introduced a presbyterial constitution. "Puritan", originally a term of reproach, denoted one who stood for "pure", i. e. Calvinistic doctrine, a simple ritual and a severe church discipline. Says Dr. Neal the great historian of Puritanism, "A Puritan was a man of severe morals, a Calvinist in doctrine, and a non-conformist to the ceremonies and discipline of the church". On the other hand, the word "prelacy", meaning no more originally than the office and dignity of a prelate, was applied by the Puritans in a derogatory sense to the episcopacy titled by and associated with civil authority. Episcopacy was ultimately resisted by Presbyterians and Independents as an expression and instrument of arbitrary government, "Prelacy" being confounded with "Popery" in a common condemnation. "The real presbyterial idea was worked out by Calvin whose teachings also form the basis of the doctrinal standards of nearly all Presbyterian bodies; hence the words "Calvinistic" and "Presbyterian" are to a large extent synonymous." It is interesting to note that both parties, the Puritans and the Prelatist, regarded church government as essential to the true and procreative church. The Puritans, finding in the Scripture a divine law, argued that the ordinary offices of pastors, teachers, elders and deacons were instituted to be of perpetual duration and therefore this form of church government is the only correct one in every age. The chief supporter in this period for a *jure divino* Presbyterianism was Thomas Cartwright (d. 1603), professor at Cambridge, who was compelled, at the instance of John Whitgift, to live in exile on the continent. The Prelatists, not only finding their form of church government prescribed in the Scripture but also appealing to Christian antiquity, asserted that the orders of bishops, priests and deacons had been in the church from the apostles' time and that these orders are to be continued. Archbishop Bancroft of Canterbury (d. 1610), opposing Cartwright, is said to have been the first of the English prelates to assert the *jure divino* episcopacy, while men like Cranmer, Hooker and even Whitgift hesitated to consider episcopacy to be of divine right.

At the end of the sixteenth century another church party arose called the Brownists. Later the Separatists repudiated the name and became known as Independents or Congregationalists. "Congregationalism as a distinct denomination can be traced back to the latter part of the sixteenth century, the first organization being formed in 1580 at Norwich by Rev. Robert Browne, an English Puritan, who had become dissatisfied with the Established Church as being an anti-Christian institution. He urged a reformation "without tarrying for any"— a complete separation of church and state. Every church community, Browne held, is complete and independent in itself. His adherents were nicknamed Brownists by their enemies. Later Browne became an apostate from his principles, abandoned the work of reform and reentered the state church. Congregationalism, however, had other and more worthy representatives, such as the martyrs Henry Barrowe, John Greenwood and John Penry, and Francis Johnson, who was banished from the kingdom for life, and especially John Robinson who may be considered as the founder of Independency as a developed and organized system."

The earliest leaders of Congregationalism were chiefly concerned with the problems of ecclesiastical polity and not with doctrinal belief. Their principle was the independence of each congregation in regard both to doctrine and practice. On doctrinal grounds they were in essential agreement with the Presbyterians, but differed from them by maintaining the autonomy of each local church as independent of the legislative and judicial authority of presbyters and synods. Later, as their denomination spread, they formed a union of churches. Thus Congregationalism developed into that system of faith and practice common to those evangelical churches which recognize the absolute independence of each local church, and maintain the principle and duty of cooperative fellowship among such independent churches. The coordinate principle of independence and fellowship excludes alike prelacy and Presbyterianism. It is clamied that this form of ecclesiastical polity was exactly that of the apostolic churches until after the middle of the second century. "On the one hand, each congregation, being independent of all other churches, has the right to adopt, supplement or alter its own creed, and, as a consequence, there are numerous Congregational creeds, with purely local authority. On the other hand, the local creed must be in harmony with the common faith of the church body, else can there be no cooperative fellowship among the churches." One of the earliest creedal statements of the Presbyterian churches was the Westminster Confession. The principles of Congregationalism, however, "were clearly set forth in the distinctive and fundamental Congregational confession, i. e., The Savoy Declaration or Confession of Faith and Order, adopted by the English Congregationalists at a meeting in the Savoy palace, London, in 1658. It differs little from the Westminster Confession except that it discards the Presbyterianism in polity and denies the authority of magistrates in ecclesiastical matters. It contains three parts, (1) a lengthy Preface with a quite liberal view as to the authority of public confessions and the toleration of other creeds; (2) the Declaration of Faith, following the order of the Westminster Confession which has 33 chapters, restates in 32 chapters the Westminster creed with modifications pertaining to matters of church government and discipline; (3) "the institution of Churches and the Order appointed in them by Jesus Christ" set forth the distinctive Congregational platform of discipline".

Oppression and persecution by the government compelled the Independents to seek shelter first in Holland and then in America. But despite these severities, Independency in England continued to increase. The same is true as to Puritanism. Violent suppression by the government only increased its opposition. It is

an acknowledged fact that a persecution which does not extermi-
nate a religious party never fails to strengthen it.

Another stage of opposition to the state church was reached
when many English Puritans and Brownists became Baptists, as
they preferred to be called, rather than Anabaptists. They agreed
with the Brownists in (1) rejecting all authority of the civil
magistrate in matters of religion, (2) upholding the necessity
of separating from the Church of England, and (3) maintaining
the independence of each local congregation. They differed
from the Brownists on two points: (1) as to the mode in which
baptism ought to be administered, and (2) as to the persons who
are qualified for the reception of the rite. Since errors in religion
were to be punished as crimes against the state, the Anabaptists
as well as all other dissenters were soon to know by experience
that the Protestant Church could here and there rival the
intolerance of Rome.

For the outward course of the strife which agitated the church
in England and Scotland in the sixteenth and seventeenth centuries we must presume upon a thorough knowledge of church
history on the part of the reader. Independency played an
important part in English history in the time of Oliver Cromwell
(1653-58). Presbyterianism was at the summit of its pride and
power, with the Church of England at its feet, in 1650.

On July 1, 1643, there met in Westminster Abbey, by act of
Parliament, a synod consisting chiefly of divines, hence called
Assembly of Divines, "with the purpose of settling the government, liturgy and doctrine of the Church of England. It held
1163 regular sessions ending February 22, 1649. The Westminster Assembly began with a revision of the Thirty-nine Articles,
but the work was suspended by an order of Parliament, October
12, 1643, requiring the Assembly 'to confer and treat' of church
government and discipline. There at once serious differences
arose among the members of the Assembly which contained
representatives of the Presbyterian, the Episcopalian and Independent parties. The Episcopalians soon ceased to attend the Assembly.
The Independents were few in number. The Presbyterians were
preponderant and gained in strength. The Confession of Faith constructed by the Assembly is strictly Calvinistic in Doctrine and anti-
episcopal in government. It emphasizes the sole authority of the
Scriptures, the sovereignty of God, the rights of conscience, and
the sole jurisdiction of the church within its own domain", assigning
to civil authority the right and duty to provide for the unity and
tranquillity of the church, for the preservation of pure doctrine, for

the suppression of blasphemy and heresy, for the removal of all corruptions and abuses and for the right administration of all divinely established institutions. "For the better effecting whereof he hath power to call synods, to be present at them, and to provide that whatsoever is transacted in them be according to the mind of God" (Ch. XXIII. 3). Herein the Westminster Confession goes beyond the principle and practice of Calvinists generally. In maintaining the perpetual obligation of the Sabbath as a moral institution the Westminster Confession goes beyond the view of Calvin who, like Luther, asserted the abrogation of the Jewish Sabbath (See p. 342). Nevertheless Calvin held that the Lord's Day was substituted in the room of the Sabbath. Out of his view of the substitution of Sunday for the Sabbath grew the Puritan theory of the Christian Sabbath which received its first symbolical indorsement in the Irish Articles. "The first day of the week, which is the Lord's Day, is wholly to be dedicated unto the service of God; and therefore we are bound therein to rest from our common and daily business and to bestow that leisure upon holy exercises, both public and private" (Art. LVI). "The Puritan view is stated still more distinctly by the Westminster Confession, ch. XXI, "As it is of the law of nature, that, in general, a due proportion of time be set apart for the worship of God; so, in his Word, by a positive, moral, and perpetual commandment, binding all men in all ages, he has particularly appointed one day in seven for a Sabbath, to be kept holy unto him: which, from the beginning of the world to the resurrection of Christ, was changed into the first day of the week, which in Scripture is called the Lord's Day, and is to be continued to the end of the world, as the Christian Sabbath (7). This Sabbath is then kept holy unto the Lord, when men, after a due preparing of their hearts, and ordering of their common affairs beforehand, do not only observe an holy rest all the day from their own works, words, and thoughts, about their worldly employments and recreations; but also are taken up the whole time in the public and private exercises of his worship, and in the duties of necessity and mercy (8)". "The Westminster Confession of Faith was adopted by the Scottish Parliament in 1649, while the English Parliament adopted it with some changes, in 1648. In Scotland, where it took the place of the Confessio Scoticana, its influence has lasted to the present day. In England it was modified under Cromwell, and the Book of Common Prayer and the Thirty-nine Articles were restored. The Presbyterian Church of England, organized in 1876, has, of course, no historical relation to the Westminster Assembly."

Perhaps the greatest single name in the history of English Puritanism is that of Richard Baxter. Though without a university education, and always sickly, he acquired exceptional learning. Both by temperament and conviction he was essentially a moderate, conservative, mediating man. In politics and in church matters he occupied a middle position. So also in theology he took up a mediating position between the Calvinists and the Arminians. He was one of the most voluminous of English writers; he left 168 treatises. He is now chiefly known as the author of the *Reformed Pastor, A Call to the Unconverted,* and *The Saints' Everlasting Rest.* His type of theology may be described as moderate Calvinism. It is most elaborately set forth in his *Catholic Theology* and his *Methodus theologiae Christianae.* The sufferings of Christ are not the literal penalty due to the sinner. Christ died for sin, not for persons. Hence Christ did not suffer the *identical,* but the *equivalent* punishment to that deserved by mankind because of offended law. The benefits of vicarious atonement are accessible and available to all men for their salvation, but in the divine appointment they have a special reference to the subjects of personal election. God's eternal decree contemplates no reprobation, but rather redemption of all who will accept Christ as their Savior. Nevertheless election is absolute. God elects a certain portion of mankind without any reference to their faith as the ground of their election. In the work of justification it is not Christ's righteousness that is imputed to the sinner, but the faith of the sinner himself in the righteousness of Christ. In his theory of atonement Baxter leaned very distinctly toward the doctrine of Grotius, known as the governmental theory of atonement. Concerning election he held essentially the same theory as Amyraut. Baxter's theology became known as Baxterianism, or the New Theology, and so passed over to America as New School Theology. Baxter died in London on the 8th of December 1691 surrounded by attached friends and reverenced by the religious world. His funeral was attended by churchmen and non-conformists. A similar tribute of general esteem was paid to him nearly two centuries later when at Kidderminster, where his continued labors as a pastor had been signally successful, a statue in honor of him was erected, bearing the inscription: "Between the years 1641 and 1660 this town was the scene of the labors of Richard Baxter, renowned equally for his Christian learning and his pastoral fidelity. In a stormy and divided age he advocated unity and comprehension, pointing the way to everlasting rest".

In an age of externalized religion, when the minds of men are agitated with questions as to the right form of church government and worship, and a mechanically interpreted Scripture is made the external authority in matters of faith and practice, it should occasion no surprise that men take refuge in the mystical view of religion, as we witness it in the sect called Quakers. The Religious Society of Friends as they called themselves or Quakers as they were called originally in derision, originated in England during the intense religious excitement of the middle of the seventeenth century. "Dissatisfied with the teachings and practices of the day and longing for a higher and more spiritual life" Fox, an unlettered youth, a shoemaker by trade, came forward in 1648 and emphasized the importance of repentance and personal striving after the truth. Many were attracted by his disconnected but fervent preaching and soon joined him in professing the same faith in the spirituality of true religion. His followers first called themselves "Children of Truth," or "Children of Light," and finally adopted the name "Religious Society of Friends."

"The Quakers were strictly opposed to all outward authority in religion and utterly broke with historical Christianity. They even avoided the use of technical theological phraseology. As a consequence they have no formal creed or confession of binding authority, although they have set forth their tenets in a number of confessions, or "apologies," in defence of their views. The most important and authoritative expressions of their belief are the Apology of Robert Barclay, written in 1675, and his Catechism, 1673. The writings of George Fox and of the celebrated William Penn are also regarded as authoritative.

"Fox and his followers did not aim at an outward organization, but gradually a form of church government came into being. It is modelled somewhat on the Presbyterian system. The separate congregations or "particular meetings" are grouped into superior meetings, known as monthly, quarterly, and yearly; these act as the executive of the society including in their supervision matters both of spiritual discipline and secular policy. The yearly meeting is the body of final authority." In England the Quakers have enjoyed religious liberty since 1689, when by the Toleration Act freedom of worship was granted to all Protestant Dissenters.

We treat here of mysticism in the sense in which it is productive of error in the sphere of Christian doctrine, as the endeavor of the human mind to obtain knowledge of God and spiritual things exceeding the limits of the written revelation. Such was the mysticism of George Fox and his adherents, who placed the direct illumination of the Spirit, the inner light, above the divine Word in Scripture. Such was also the mysticism of Emanuel Swedenborg (1688-1772), who claimed that there were vouchsafed to him special revelations according to which he was to interpret the Word in Scripture. Swedenborg "was already a distinguished scientist when in 1743 he began to devote himself to theosophical speculations." He often fell into ecstatic states, in which, sometimes transposed to heaven, sometimes to hell, he was in communion with spirits; in fact, he believed himself to be a dweller within the spiritual world. In this way — he tells us — God revealed to him the true relation between the material and the spiritual world and commissioned him to reform degenerate Christianity to a Church of the New Jerusalem as the completion of all churchdom. In text-books it is usually stated that Swedenborg received his revelations through angels, but he himself claims for his mission direct revelation from God. "That the Lord manifested Himself before me His servant, and sent me to this office, that He afterward opened the eyes of my spirit and thus introduced me into the spiritual world and granted me to see the heavens and the hells, and to talk with angels and spirits, and this now continuously for several years, I affirm in truth; as also that from the first day of that call I have not received anything whatever pertaining to the doctrines of that church from any angel, but from the Lord alone while I have read the Word" (True Chr. Rel. 779).

Swedenborg's works, both scientific and theosophical, are numerous. With his scientific writings we are not concerned at present. His principle theosophical writings are: The Divine Love and Wisdom, which presents Swedenborg's system most briefly and comprehensively; The Divine Providence; Conjugial Love — Swedenborg uses "conjugial" instead of "conjugal" to denote his own conception of marriage as a spiritual union corresponding to that of Christ and the Church; Arcana Coelestia, an exposition of the spiritiual sense of Genesis and Exodus, in eight volumes; The Apocalypse Revealed; The Apocalypse Explained; The New Jerusalem and Its Heavenly Doctrines; The True Christian Religion, Containing the Universal Theology of the New Church; Heaven and Hell; The Last Judgment.

Swedenborg died in London, March 29, 1772. He was buried in the Swedish Church of the city. In 1908 his remains were removed at the request of the Swedish government to the cathedral at Upsala, where they lie in a monument erected two years later to his memory by the Swedish Parliament.

In the middle of the seventeenth century there arose in the Church of England a class of divines who held a middle position between the High Churchmen and the fanatical Puritans. They differed widely in their theological opinions, but agreed in a spirit of toleration toward dissenters and in emphasizing only the funda-

mentals of religion. Representatives of this movement were John
Hales of Eton (d. 1656) and William Chillingworth. Hales was a
man of notable tolerance and the foe of religious disputation. In
1619 he accompanied the English ambassador to the Hague who
dispatched him to Dort to report upon the proceedings of the synod
then sitting. There he inclined toward Episcopius and "bade John
Calvin good night." He returned to Eton and spent his time among
his books and in the company of literary men. In his irenical tract
Schism and Schismatics (1636) he distinguished between theological and religious differences and insisted that mere points of dogma
about which men love to dispute have no place in any liturgy.
William Chillingworth (d. 1644) was of a kindred spirit. In his
youth he became disgusted with the theological controversies of
his Church and took refuge in Catholicism. But the apparently
firmer foundation offered by the Church of Rome proved delusive.
He retraced his steps and then settled upon Scripture interpreted
by reason. His main work the *Religion of Protestants* exercised an
enormous and long continued influence. He maintained that the
Bible, not the confessions of Protestantism, but "the Bible only is
the religion of Protestants". He argued strongly for free inquiry
and denied that any church is infallible. According to these men
Christianity is preeminently a religion of peace and tolerance. The
general basis of Christian communion is the Bible interpreted by
reason. The Apostles' Creed is sufficient test for church membership. The national worship should be so ordered as to exclude
none who hold this belief. Even those articles of faith which are
to be regarded as fundamental should be left in that breadth and
generality in which the Bible states them.

The movement begun by these men passed on into a higher
and broader stream of thought with the so called Cambridge Platonists, a group of thinkers who exerted far reaching influences on
English theology and thought in general. Unlike the group of
divines before considered, these were Puritans in origin and training. The leaders among them, with the exception of More, all
belonged to the famous Puritan college *Emmanuel*. Yet they were
not Puritans in any sense. The Puritans were Calvinists, the new
school were low Arminians. Episcopius, the Arminian professor,
was one of their favorite authors. They professed indifference to
what they considered small matters in dispute between the Puritans
and the Prelatist and showed a spirit of tolerance toward dissenters.
Combining theology with philosophy they gave human reason a
prominent place and function in matters of religion. Their intellectual efforts have therefore been styled "the first elaborate
attempt, from the Protestant side, to wed Christianity and philos-

ophy". In philosophy they followed in general Bacon and Descartes, but their chief authorities in this field were Plato and especially the Neo-platonists, hence Coleridge said they might be called Plotinists rather than Platonists — Plotinus being the chief exponent of Neo-platonism. From these sources they attempted to evolve a philosophy of religion which would win the adhesion of sceptics and inquirers and promote peace among Christian believers. From the position thus gained they also reacted against the principles of Hobbes and very ably opposed the atheistic and materialistic tendency of his philosophy. The Cambridge Platonists were characterized also by the mystical spirit, especially in the case of Henry More (d. 1687), tending always to the contemplation of things transcendental. "They were called 'men of latitude', and upon this, men of narrow thoughts fastened upon them the name of *latitudinarians*", says Bishop Burnet, himself of the Latitudinarian school. The most important of these were Benjamin Whichcote, Ralph Cudworth and Henry More. In the society of these men were trained all the influential English divines of the next generation, Tillotson, Patrick, Lloyd and Stillingfleet, the latter a man of unrivalled and varied learning, and an all-round controversialist. In 1661 Stillingfleet published his *Irenicum, A Weapon Salve for the Church's Wound,* an attempt at a compromise between the Anglican and the Presbyterian communions in England. The liberal position he held is clearly stated in his own words as follows : "What possible reason can be assigned or given why such things should not be sufficient for communion with a Church which are sufficient for eternal salvation? And certainly those things are sufficient for that which are laid down as the necessary duties of Christianity by our Lord and Saviour in His Word. What ground can there be why Christians should not stand upon the same terms now which they did in the time of Christ and His apostles?". The latitudinarians were Christian philosophers rather than divines. This became most apparent in their way of preaching. Their discourses in the pulpit seldom interfered with matters of Christian doctrine. They generally deal with conventional morality, based as much on reason and philosophy as on the law of God.

The influence which the Cambridge scholars exerted on their age and the contribution which they made to modern thought can scarcely be overrated. They helped to prepare the way for a broad, comprehensive church. The Latitudinarian school has found its modern representatives in the Broad Church party, a term applied to members of the Church of England or its daughter churches, who hold liberal views as to doctrine and fellowship. But the Latitudinarians failed in their efforts actually to establish the desired Christian communion. It is also claimed that they were "the purifiers of popular theology". This statement needs modification. The Cambridge School was predominantly rational and ethical. Inquiring into the reasonableness, rather than the scriptural warrant, of the truths, and divorcing Christian practice from evangelical doctrine, it became subversive of the traditional Protestant theology. The English church historian Perry attributes the spiritual apathy of the eighteenth century to the. influence of the Latitudinarians (Hist. of the English Church, II, 514ff.). And J. B. Marsden in his *History of Christian Churches and Sects,* I, 286, describes the attempts and failures of the Latitudinarian divines as follows: "They attempted a divorce between evangelical doctrine and Christian practice. The former they at first neglected, and at length lost out of sight; the latter they displayed with admirable clearness, and if any other principles than those of the gospel could possibly have enforced it, they would not have so completely failed. But the founders of the school made no deep impression in the days of Charles II.; and their still more gifted pupils saw religion, in the Church of England, almost expiring in spite of all their efforts; and learned how vain it was for men without warmth and fervour to recall a nation to holiness, and how impossible to effect a second reformation without the aid of those inspiring doctrines which had quickened England into new life under Latimer and the first reformers".

The spirit of the Cambridge School became the dominant spirit of the Established Church in England. In their theology the Latitudinarians were Arminians. But Arminian influence was found not only in the Established Church, but in the communions of the Dissenters as well. Many of their students for the ministry who had studied in Holland inclined to Arminianism and the Arminians were infested with Socinianism. These men carried their liberal ideas back to England with them, and gradually English theological life became saturated with the new theology.

John Biddle (d. 1662), usually called the father of English Unitarianism, published a number of writings in which he expressed opinions which were very much after the Socinian order. He was therefore often arrested, put on trial, committed to prison, and finally died in prison. His adherents were called Biddellians, or Socinians, or Unitarians.

Against the Roman Catholic Petavius and two Arminian writers who held Socinian views Bishop Bull wrote his great work *Defensio Fidei Nicaenae* (1685). He tried to show that the doctrine of the Trinity was held by the ante-Nicene fathers of the church. But in his own view the Son, even in respect to his divinity, is in a degree subordinate to the Father, inasmuch as he is from him. The Arian controversy properly so called began with the publication in 1712 of Dr. Samuel Clarke's far-reaching work named *Scripture Doctrine of the Trinity*, which exposed him to the charge of Arianism and involved him in a prolonged controversy. He emphasized the subordination of the Son to the Father, saying that the Son derives his being and attributes from the Father, but that the Scripture is silent as to when the Son had his origin and whether from the will of the Father or not. "The nature of his views on the Trinity was adequately tested by a Roman Catholic named Dr. Hawarden, who was invited to meet Clarke by Queen Caroline. Clarke unfolded his theory, endeavouring to defend it as scriptural and orthodox. Hawarden listened patiently, and then said that he had just one question to ask, and would the reply be given in a monesyllable? Clarke agreed; 'Then I ask', said Hawarden, 'can God the Father annihilate the Son and the Holy Ghost? Answer me, "Yes or No".' Clarke continued for some time in deep thought, and then said it was a question which he had never considered. The conference then ended." Benjamin Hoadly, Bishop of Bangor, was in entire accord with Clarke's refined Arianism. He was one of the leaders of the rational clergy of the age and the extreme Latitudinarian party in church and state, and consequently became obnoxious to both the orthodox clergy and the high church party. He advocated what has since been called low church principles, against spiritual tyranny. In 1717, in a sermon on the text, "My kingdom is not of this world", he attacked the divine authority of kings and especially that of the clergy and ridiculed the value of any tests of orthodoxy. There is no such thing as a visible church of Christ, he said. The kingdoms of this world could not suggest proper views of that government which ought to prevail, in a visible and sensible manner, in Christ's kingdom. No one, not even a Christian of the highest rank, has the right to make new laws for Christ's people, or to interpret or enforce new laws, in matters relating purely to conscience, since Christ is the only authoritative lawgiver. This sermon, which the king, George I., who heard it, ordered to be printed, precipitated a war of pamphlets known as the Bangorian Controversy, which lasted for several years. The ideas set forth in this sermon and other writings of Hoadly were controverted, with the asperity common to a disputatious age, by a host of writers, of whom Sherlock, dean of Chichester, and William Law may be mentioned as the chief. The controversial writings and theological essays of Hoadly have little merit, but in their day they did excellent service for the cause of civil and religious liberty.

"In England advocates of Arian and Socinian views were at first either executed or saved by recantation; later they were excluded from the benefits of the Toleration Act of 1689, and threatened by the act of 1698 with loss of civil rights and imprisonment. Nevertheless Unitarian views found increasing favor both in the Church of England and among the dissenters until the latter part of the 18th. century a distinct Unitarian denomination was formed. Among the leaders of the movement were Theophilus Lindsey, Thomas Belsham and Joseph Priestly; the latter removed to the United States in 1794 and settled at Northumberland, Pa. In 1779 the Toleration Act was amended, belief 'in Scripture' being substituted for belief 'in the Anglican Articles'."

During the sixteenth and seventeenth centuries the Copernican Discovery, together with the physical doctrines of Descartes and Newton, and the new philosophical theories of Hobbes and Locke, had prepared the way for a new philosophy of life, commonly known as English Deism. Besides these, other impulses contributed to the rise and development of deistic thought. There was already a school of distinctively latitudinarian thought in the Church of England. Arminianism had revived the rational side of theological method. Arian and Unitarian ideas had encouraged departure from the historic faith of the church. Time-honored beliefs were shaken in the minds of many and men were ready to welcome a new religious philosophy not grounded in the faith of the church, but in what is made known through human reason. In religious matters the deists rejected all authority of the Bible and supernatural revelation, and declared reason and nature to be the only reliable sources of religious truth. They were therefore occasionally called "rationalists". The name "free thinkers" which was adopted by the deists expresses perhaps best the real tendency of deism. Because they acknowledged only a natural instead of a revealed religion, their opponents designated them as "Naturalists", a name generally used of such as recognized no god but nature. The term "deism" denotes the general belief in a deity, though wholly distinct from the universe and purely mechanically operating on it. The English deists, unlike the Naturalists, did not deny altogether the providence and immanence of the deity.

Deism was not a Christian movement, although the deists repeatedly laid claim to the name Christians or Christian deists. As such, deism does not belong to the history of Christian doctrine. It will be treated here only in so far as it is a defiance of the accepted theology. The chief names among the deists are those of Lord Herbert (1583-1648), Charles Blount (1654-1693), died by suicide, Matthew Tindal (1657-1733), Thomas Woolston (1669-1733), John Toland (1670-1722), the third earl of Shaftesbury (1671-1713), Viscount Bolingbroke (1678-1751), Anthony Collins (1676-1729) and Thomas Chubb (1679-1747). Deism is not a system of doctrine, nor is it the outcome of any one line of philosophical thought. The deists held diverse opinions, some inclining to a rationalistic Christianity, some to materialistic infidelity; but they were agreed in a common effort to construct a religion of nature with the human reason as the sole authority. Lord Herbert of Cherbury, "the Father of Deism", in his two works *De Veritate* and *De Religione Gentilium,* laid down the main line of that religious philosophy which in various forms continued to contain the fundamentals of their theology. At the foundation of all religions he finds five truths : (1) that there is one supreme god, (2) that he is to be worshipped, (3) that piety and virtue are the principal part of his worship, (4) that man should repent of sin and abandon it, and (5) that there are rewards for the good and punishments for the evil, partly in this life and partly in a future state. These five fundamentals, the so-called "Five Articles" of the English deists, constitute the nucleus of that one universal religion which Lord Herbert maintains is adequate to meet all the religious wants of mankind. Accepting this list of essential religious truths the deists would naturally reject the doctrines of the trinity, the deity and incarnation of the Son, the fall of man, redemption, and endless rewards and punishments. By his rationalistic treatment of religious doctrine the philosopher Thomas Hobbes (d. 1679) helped much to lay the foundations of English Deism, he is therefore sometimes called the second deist. In his principal work *The Leviathan, or the Matter, Form, and Power of a Commonwealth, Ecclesiastical and Civil,* he set forth his political philosophy that the highest form of civil government is an absolute monarchy with despotic control over everything relating to law, morals and religion. Hobbes absolutely separates religion from philosophy. God cannot be an object of speculative thought, for we do not know any more of him than that he exists. Religion as an outward exercise is a matter of the state. Christianity is of importance only as a support of absolute royalty and as an antidote against revolution. The state of nature is a state of war. To put an end to the war of all against all is the office and function of the sovereign ruler, whose power is in no sense original or divine, but merely delegated to him. The individual, indeed, may believe what he chooses, but he is in duty bound wholly to submit to such government even in religious professions and in all the externals of worship. There is no good or evil in itself, but what the authority of the commonwealth declares to be for the good of all is good and what is bad is evil. The precepts of Scripture which as such are only counsel and advice, become obligatory laws by the authority of the commonwealth. "In epistemology and psychology Hobbes was a sensualist, in metaphysics almost a materialist, and in ethics a hedonist. The only source of knowledge, he maintains, is sensation, the only objects of knowledge are bodies, either natural or political, and the only end of action is self-interest" (Schaff-Herzog Encyclop. V, 302). From Hobbes downward deism grows more and more· materialistic and sensual. Lord Herbert had indulged in but little criticism of the Christian revelation either as a whole or in its details. Hobbes went a step further entering upon the field of Biblical criticism. He denied that Moses was the author of the Pentateuch, but he accepted as genuine what the Pentateuch itself claims was written by Moses. Blount not only adopted Hobbes' argument against the Mosaic authorship of the Pentateuch, but asserted the total inconsistency of the Mosaic Hexaemeron with the Copernican theory of the heavens and designated all miracles as pure priestly frauds. Shaftesbury, in his *Characteristics of Men, Manners, Opinions and, Times* (1711), points out the pernicious influence upon mankind of a belief in the doctrine of a future life and of future rewards and punishments. "Fanaticism", i. e., orthodox belief, is best encountered by "raillery" and "good humor". As to the certainty and philosophical demonstrability of the immortality of the soul the deists were not agreed. They have therefore sometimes been grouped into "mortal" and "immortal" deists.

A conspicuous part in the deistic controversy, on the anti-deistic side, was taken by John Locke (1632-1704) who carried his rational principles into the realms of religion by writing the *Reasonableness of Christianity* (1695), in which he advocates acceptance of the truths of primitive Christianity in order to end all religious strife of the present day. These truths Locke derived from the Gospels and the Acts, as distinguished from the Epistles. He admitted the truth of the biblical history, of miracles, of the Messiahship of Christ, of the kingdom of God, and of Christ as the ruler of that kingdom. But since Locke holds to a revelation which reveals only the reasonable and the universally cognizable, he actually reduces Christianity to the low level of a sound human understanding. Locke did not believe in the deity of Christ, nor did he accept the doctrine of the satisfaction of Christ, but regarded the principal office of Christ to be that of a ruler and teacher. Toland, in his *Christianity not Mysterious* (1696), went beyond the statement of Hobbes and Locke that there is nothing in Christianity contrary to

reason, and maintained that there is nothing in it *above* reason.
Revelation neither contradicts nor transcends the dictates of reason.
Revelation can never be made the basis of truth; it is merely a
means of information, and our beliefs in revelation must be thoroughly consistent with reason. In his *Amyntor* (1699) and Naza-
renus (1718) Toland also advanced the theory of the departure
from primitive Christianity in the early church resulting in two
schools each possessing its "own gospel", the school of the Judaizing
Christians and the more liberal school of Paul. Toland thus anticipated that theory which was later elaborated by the Tuebingen
School. Other deists of note in this period were Tindal, Bolingbroke, Collins, and Chubb. Tindal's *Christianity as old as the
Creation* was an attempt to prove that natural religion is absolutely
valid and cannot be dispensed with, but that the gospel is only a
republication of the law of nature, and that Christianity is therefore
as old as creation. Collins, one of the ablest of the deists, in his
Discourse of Free-thinking insisted on the value and necessity of
unprejudiced inquiry. Setting out from Locke's proposition that
revelation was truth sanctioned by reason he asserted that what is
contrary to reason is not revelation, hence prophecy and miracles
are to be rejected. Chubb, the least learnedly educated of the
deists, but a very popular compiler, in his attempt to reconstruct
ture Christianity reduced Christianity to Deism. Bolingbroke, a
high civil officer, profligate in his habits and unprincipled, assumed
that monotheism was the primitive religion. All other religions are
the products of enthusiasm, fraud, and superstition.

As an opponent to positive Christianity David Hume (d. 1776),
celebrated historian and skeptic, may yet be added to the deists.
In Hume deistic rationalism led to complete skepticism. Hume's
chief works are *Dialogues Concerning Natural Religion,* written
in 1751, but not published till 1779, after his death, and *Natural
History of Religion* (1757). He denied the possibility of attaining
a knowledge of deity through the reason. Belief is founded on
experience. We have no experience of a miracle, but we do have
experience of the falsehood of testimony. Accordingly no amount
of testimony will suffice to prove an alleged miracle. Belief in
deity arises from the misconception or arbitrary misinterpretation
of experience. In the latter part of the eighteenth century about
300 English clergy and laymen formed the Feathers' Tavern Association, so named from the fact that the members held their meetings in the Feathers Tavern in the Strand, London. The society
agitated for a revision of the English liturgy. In 1771 a petition to
parliament was drawn up the gist of which was that the anathemas

be stricken from the Athanasian Creed and subscription to doctrinal articles be abolished. The petition signed by Deists, Arians and Socinians was opposed in a strong speech by Edmund Burke and rejected by Parliament by a vote of 217 to 71. The Association was short lived and accomplished nothing.

In reply to English Deism there arose a flood of apologetic literature. Chief among the apologists were Baxter, the two Cambridge Platonists, More and Cudworth, Richard Bentley, Samuel Clarke, John Conybeare, Joseph Butler, George Berkeley and William Paley. The polemical power of their refutations however was considerably weakened because of their more or less latitudinarian spirit. Their answer to deism was itself essentially rationalistic. In order to save the fundamentals of the faith they showed that Christianity is not a religion of unreason and superstition, but in perfect accord with the mandates of reason and conscience. English deistic unbelief met with sympathy chiefly among educated and prominent worldlings. The clergy in general adhered formally to positive religion, while the common people became more and more indifferent to all religion. About the middle of the eighteenth century deism had outlived itself. The English statesman and political writer Edmund Burke, in his *Reflections on the Revolution in France, and on the proceedings in certain societies in London relative to that event,* 1790, penned these words which have since become a stock piece in books of recitations, "Who born within the last forty years, has read one word of Collins and Toland and Tindal and Chubb and Morgan and that whole race who called themselves Free-thinkers?". Having done its disintegrating work in England deism entered continental Europe. In the stream of English writings by Hobbes, Herbert, Shaftesbury, Bolingbroke and Hume it came into the French literature of the Encyclopedists, Rousseau and Voltaire, and through them it was imported into Germany. In France English deism gave place to skepticism and atheism; whereas in Germany it passed over into Rationalism.

Toward the middle of the eighteenth century in England we find nonconformity infested with unitarianism, and episcopacy vitiated by dead formalism of both orthodoxy and worship. In the higher classes we notice an almost universal skepticism, and in all classes a profound indifference toward everything serious or sacred. It was the golden age of English Deism of which Bishop Butler (1692-1752) said that Christianity was regarded "not so much as a subject of inquiry; but that it is now, at length, discovered to be fictitious". When in 1747 the primacy was offered to Butler, he declined it on the ground that "it was too late for him

to try to support a falling church". Yet, the dawn of a brighter
day began with the evangelical revival, for which William Law
had, in a large measure, prepared the way. His *Practical Treatise
on Christian Perfection* (1726) and his *Serious Call to a Devout
and Holy Life* (1729) did much to promote a spiritual awakening
and deeply influenced the leaders of the evangelical movement.
The rise of the movement as given in the words of its founders
John and Charles Wesley was as follows: "In 1729 two young men
in England, reading the Bible, saw they could not be saved without
holiness, followed after it, and incited others so to do. In 1737
they saw, likewise, that men are justified before they are sanctified;
but still holiness was their object. God then thrust them out to
raise a holy people . . . ". Notwithstanding its one-sidedness and
extravagances the general effect of the Evangelical Revival upon
Anglicanism and Dissent was a great quickening of spiritual life.
Among the Anglican leaders, who had caught something of Wesley's
spirit, were John Newton, John Fletcher, Samuel Walker, Thomas
Scott and Henry Venn. These men were as eager as himself for the
conversion of sinners, but they remained in their own communion.
Before the close of the century they came to be known as "Evangelicals", while the name "Methodist" became restricted to those
who left the Established Church. "While Wesley looked upon the
world as his parish, these Evangelicals looked upon their parish as
their world" (Pullan, Religion since the Reformation. p. 147).

CHAPTER XXVIII

THE ERA OF THE ENLIGHTENMENT IN GERMANY

By the middle of the eighteenth century relationalism had crept into the Protestant theology of Germany. Gottfried Wilhelm Lieb-nitz (d. 1716) and Christian Wolff (d. 1754) had prepared the way for it. Leibnitz' principal religious work is his *Theodicee* (a term originated by Leibnitz himself), which is an attempt to demonstrate the agreement of reason with faith. Starting from the proposition that the world as it is is the best possible world, he endeavors to show that the presence of evil in the world is a necessary condition of the presence of the greatest moral good, for evil is the natural result of the necessary limitation of every thing created. Evil is therefore not something moral nor physical, but metaphysical. The philosophy of Leibnitz began to exercise its influence upon theology in the following period when Wolff presented it in a modified form. The Leibnitz-Wolffian school attempted to establish a system of natural religion independently of, though not necessarily in opposition to, revelation. But when Wolff in the department of natural philosophy and science asserted the fundamental principle of the modern philosophy, that *clearness is the standard of truth*, applying it not only to the sciences, but to mental cultivation in general, he came into conflict with the Pietists of Halle, who succeeded in obtaining from Frederick William I a government order by which Wolff was compelled to leave Halle within forty-eight hours under penalty of the halter (1723). Their victory, which was in fact a moral defeat, was short-lived. One of the first acts by which Frederick the Great signalized his reign was to recall (1740) the philosopher to Halle. Wolff's teaching was was propagated in other universities. It ruled the schools of Germany for nearly a century. On it the pious and learned Baumgarten laid the foundations of a science of aesthetics. The Pietists were unable to stem the tide of rationalism. English deism had already been introduced into Germany by the English deist John Toland and by English deistic books. Freemasonry, also an outcome of English deism and latitudinarianism, had been transplanted in the thirties from England into Germany where it was soon adopted in radical, rationalistic circles. Frederick the Great who had joined the Freemasons in 1738 and energetically labored for the spread of masonry was made grand master of the grand lodge "zu den drei Weltkugeln" in Berlin in 1744. French naturalism was welcomed at the court of the Prussian king. The arrival of Voltaire in Berlin late in 1751 marks the real beginning of that movement styled by the Germans the period of "Aufklaerung". At the head of the movement stood the universities of Halle and Berlin. From these places there proceeded a flood of popular or vulgar enlightenment based upon the Wolffian philosophy and spread among the people. A universal German library, the "Allgemeine Deutsche Biblothek" (106 Vols. 1765-92), published by the bookseller Nicolai in Berlin, assumed the position of an inquisitorial tribunal assailing all faith in revelation. German rationalism, unlike English and French deism, sheltered itself within the organization of a Christian Church, but in its tendencies it proved just as destructive as that of England and France. German rationalism centered upon the Bible. In England the Bible was flung aside by the deists. In France it became an object of coarse jesting. In Germany it was made a subject of critical study. German rationalism began by accepting the testimony of Scripture and only insisted on rendering its authority more secure by establishing on grounds of reason what had been received by revelation. It soon found that human reason is inadequate to unveil the mysteries of God. But in order to make the impossible possible it was conjectured that the Bible being an ancient book might contain errors of doctrinal statement, accommodations to the age in which it was written, myths and legends whose origin we cannot trace. Rationalism made human reason the supreme judge of revealed religion. A doctrine that cannot be measured by human reason must henceforth be eliminated from the sacred record. This course once chosen ultimately led to the complete annihilation of all belief whatsoever.

The four principal Lutheran theologians, who prepared the way for the admission of rationalism into theology, were Ernesti of Leipzig in New Testament exegesis (d. 1781), Michaelis of Goettingen in Old Testament exegesis (d. 1791), Semler of Halle in Biblical and historical criticism (d. 1791), Toellner of Frankfurt-on-the-Oder in dogmatic theology (d. 1774). Semler, the ablest of the four, is known as the father of modern Biblical criticism; he is also called "the father of German rationalism". Trained in pietism Semler possessed a kind of religion of habit, which he called his private religion. He insisted upon the distinction between religion i. e., the particular Christian's religious convictions, and theology recognized by the church. By this distinction he created free course for his criticism. Hence as a professor of Christian theology he felt it to be his task freely to criticize the Bible; to contest the genuineness of Biblical books; to show that the canon of the Old Testament, like that of the New, grew up by degrees, and hence may not pass for "inspired" in the traditional sense; to explain miracles and prophecies as deceptions or accommodations to prevailing ideas of time and surroundings, and therefore to establish the fact that the New Testament doctrine contains, besides a kernel of truth, a mass of superstitious notions which were of significance only for the superstitious contemporaries of Christ and his apostles. It is in keeping with his theological views that Semler treats the history of Christian doctrine as a series of aberrations showing that the religion of Christ had been all along mistaken by the world. Such is the creed of Semler. With it falls to the ground the last trace of dogmatic Christianity for which Semler proposed to substitute practical morality. At the end Semler realized the destructive influence of rationalism. He had sown the wind and he lived to reap the storm, but unable to resist the storm, he died broken-hearted. The enlightenment was at its height. Gotthold Ephraim Lessing (1729-1781), the great classical writer and critic, mingled in the religious controversies of the time. Though criticizing the current rationalistic theology as shallow and hopelessly inconsistent, he became one of the greatest promoters of extreme rationalism. When he was librarian at Wolfenbuettel he published the so-called *Wolfenbuetteler Fragmente* (1774-1778), purporting to be from a manuscript of an unknown author; in reality they were a series of deistic tracts written by Hermann Samuel Reimarus (d. 1768), professor of oriental languages in Hamburg. The tracts attributed the introduction of Christianity to bold deception. The publication of the Fragments created profound excitement among orthodox theologians. Lessing was bitterly condemned for having published writings of so dangerous a tendency. He explained that he did it in the interest of free and fearless criticism, of which he was a life-long champion. Like the deists, he held that revealed truth is attainable only by reason. Unlike the deists, he saw in revealed religions preparatory stages to the truths of natural religion. Only so much of Christianity as adapts itself to the wants of human nature, is essential in it. Christianity was a life-giving power before the New Testament canon in its present form was recognized by the church; hence the Scripture is not necessary to a belief in Christianity. In his *Nathan der Weise*, which was to some extent the outcome of his theological controversies, he sets forth the idea that in positive religions, Judaism, Christianity, Mohammedanism, that alone is true which can be harmonized with nature and reason and that one's creed is of little moment, provided there is a spirit of charity and tolerance toward those who maintain wholly different doctrines.

Rationalism did its destructive work first in the schools of learning where one fundamental Christian doctrine after the other went by the board, but it soon affected the current preaching, where its influence was disastrous. Rationalistic leaders in the church boldly advocated the limitation of pulpit discussion to the teaching of practical morality, and the exclusion of all doctrinal questions as of little utility to the common man. As a consequence we find in this period that ill-famed preaching of a Christianity which dispensed with Christ, but instead discussed all sorts of generally useful matters of science, trade and farming. But even here degeneracy soon appeared. In pushing the theory of practical utility in preaching some of the rationalistic preachers of this period stooped to such themes as The Preference of Stall-feeding for Cattle over Grazing or the Unspeakable Blessing of Potato Culture. According to its principle that nothing exists which has not its ground in human reason, rationalism did away with dogmatic Christianity and substituted for it practical morality, and morality having its ground not in man's conscience but in human reason soon became identical with utility or happiness. Virtue is founded in utility. Whatever is profitable is good; whatever is harmful is wrong. Or, virtue is only good because it tends to promote happiness; vice is only bad because it tends to produce misery. Utilitarianism and eudemonism are but the legitimate outcome of the fundamental principle of Rationalism.

The chief of the eighteenth century rationalists was the philosopher Immanuel Kant (1724-1804) professor at the University of Koenigsberg. He is the founder of the Critical System of Philosophy, so called because it is presented in the form of three Critiques, that of Pure Reason (1781); of the Practical Reason (1788); of the Judgment (1790), the latter supplementing the first. His philosophy marks both the completion and self-destruction of eighteenth century rationalism. In his *Critique of the Pure Reason* (1781) which is of a critical, destructive nature, Kant attempts to prove that all efforts of reason to explain the mystery of the universe had been in vain, for the transcendent world, the existence of God and the immortality of the soul are unknowable to pure reason. Here, reason was shown its limits. Here, the previous course of rational theology stood fundamentally condemned. In his Critique of the Practical Reason (1788) which has a constructive purpose, he shows the utter indispensableness of a belief in God, liberty and immortality as the requisites for the moral life. With Kant the ideas of God, liberty and immortality are unprovable postulates of the moral or practical reason. They cannot be derived through deductions from nature, but they are present in us apart from all sense experience. These postulates which · are inherent in us belong to a realm into which reason limited by sense cannot penetrate. They admit, therefore, of no further proof. They are to be accepted as practical requirements. Kant insists upon the autonomy and absoluteness of the moral consciousness. In opposition to the naturalism and eudemonism of his time Kant maintains the grandeur of the moral law which demands absolute obedience, regardless of any possible advantage or pleasure. This is Kant's "categorical imperative" stated by him as follows "Act so that the maxim of thy will may at any time be adopted as a universal law". At the age of sixty-nine Kant published his book *On Religion within its Limits of Reason alone* which treats in a rather rationalizing style of the peculiarities of Christianity. Morality, according to Kant, is the essence of religion. He defined religion as "the recognition of our duties as divine commands". Since religion can be based on morality alone, it follows that the Bible cannot be the judge of a moral code, but must of itself be judged by its value for morality. Miracles cannot prove a religion since we can never quite rely on the testimony which supports them; neither can belief in miracles be helpful in the performance of duty. The Confessions of the church have value only in so far as they further the moral development of the race. The real church is a community of the people for mutual help in the practice of virtue. The historical Christ is the ideal of a perfect man. Saving faith is the belief in that ideal. When our minds have formed that ideal which is represented in Christ, the historical Christ may cease to be an object of veneration. The true Christ, then, is the inward idea of a perfect man. Kant accepts the biblical account of the fall and admits that man is not good by nature, but insists that he is to become good by the discipline of the free will. The formation of a holy character is man's own achievement, although Kant does not exclude divine assistance from the work of regeneration, but divine influences on the soul can neither be proved nor denied.

Kant's philosophy in so far as it refers to religion has its great and lasting merits. It has destroyed the vaunting claims of human reason by demonstrating its incompetence to explain the mysteries of the universe or to disprove the main truths of theism. It has declared eudemonism unmoral by giving such a prominence to the authority of conscience, that morality must henceforth shine by its own light. It has invested the conception of the word law with inviolable majesty and holiness. Yet Kant's philosophy is in essential agreement with the ideas of the Enlightenment. Far from building up what he had successfully destroyed he established a type of rationalism which made mere morality the aim and end of religion. "He gave the word religion a new meaning and one essentially opposed to Christianity" (Pullan, Religion since the Reformation, 172-173). "Kant razed to earth those walls of Rationalism which had sought to enclose the light of heaven, but it was not given to him to rear a temple in their room; he extinguished the artificial lamp of reason, but he could not say to the natural darkness, 'Let there be light'" (Matheson, Aids to the Study of German Theology, p. 32).

There arose in the last half of the eighteenth century a movement which especially affected literature, art, religion and theology. It is known as the romantic movement. Rationalism with its one-sided stress upon reason, its individualistic and social utilitarianism, its denial of personal freedom and its elimination of mystery and paved the way for it. In its scope romanticism, like rationalism, was an international movement. In the present discussion we are chiefly concerned about German Romanticism. The beginning of the movement was marked by an interest in the religious and social institutions and art of the Middle Ages. Thus romanticism became instinctively opposed to rationalism. Since the medieval view of the world was decidedly Christian, rationalistic opponents stamped even the expression "romantic" as a term of abuse for Jesuitism and obscurantism of all kinds. Three distinguished leaders of the movement, Stolberg, poet and translator, Schlegel, historian and art critic, and Werner, dramatist and preacher, became convinced that medieval Christianity can be combined with modern learning and modern liberty and joined the membership of the Roman Catholic Church. Their liberalism, however, was rejected by Rome. The romantic movement was more than a literary and artistic revival. Gradually it became a religious movement. Schiller (d. 1805) enthusiastic for everything that was noble, beautiful and good, by his poetic interpretations of Kant's rationalism and Kant's ethics advertised Christianity as "the only aesthetic religion". Goethe (d. 1832), who in his early youth had some sympathy for the Moravians, and in his later years believed that he himself did not need Christianity, was nevertheless convinced that Christianity is "the highest principle of feeling and action" and "far above all philosophy". Klopstock (d. 1803) in his Messiah presented lofty old German ideals through Christian poetry. He emphasized the immediacy of feeling. So did Herder (d. 1803), court preacher at Weimar and stimulating writer on historical and theological topics. In his book on the "Spirit of Hebrew Poetry" he awakened a deep and appreciative interest in the Scriptures. In his "Philosophy of the History of Mankind" he found the soul of humanity expressed in the Christian religion. But Christianity, according to Herder, is mere morality. The romantic writings are all more or less tinged with pantheism and mysticism, but they manifest a great religious inwardness over against the abstract superficial intellectualism of the illumination.

In opposition to the frigid rationalism of the Kantian school Jacobi (d. 1819) propounded a philosophy which was characterized by poetic fancy and religious sentiment rather than by logical necessity. He maintained that the ground of certitude is not understanding, but instinctive faith founded in a necessity of feeling. He defined religion as faith founded on feeling of the reality of the ideal, but at the same time termed instinctive faith an act of reason.

Both Herder and Jacobi sought to rest religion upon heart-perception. In this way they became the forerunners of Schleier-macher (1768-1834), theologian, philosopher and author, who exercised an enormous influence not only over the theology in Germany, but over the religious life of modern Europe itself. In him is represented the whole class of thinkers who identified religious belief with religious feeling. Schleiermacher was the son of a Prussian army chaplain of the Reformed confession. Diverse influences contributed to his education and thought — his early training in Moravian Pietism, his intercourse with the leaders of the romantic movement in Berlin, the faith-philosophy of Jacobi no less than the critical philosophy of Kant and the Pantheistic philosophy of Spinoza. A brief outline of the essential features of his system will enable us to notice these diverse influences. Schleiermacher's works were published in three sections: (1) Theological, 11 vols.; (2) Sermons, 15 vols.; (3) Philosophical and Miscellaneous, 9 vols. Of special interest for a study of the fundamental religious philosophy of Schleiermacher are his "Reden", Discourses for "the cultured despisers of religion", (1799) and "Der christliche Glaube", Doctrine of Faith according to the Principles of the Evangelical Church (1821). The "Reden" were directed against the Illuminati of his day who had departed not merely from Christianity but from religion in general. To them Schleiermacher declared that religion is no mere summary of abstract ideas, such as God, duty, immortality, nor a code of morals, but a life native to the human soul and independent of the dictates of any philosophy. Man cannot, therefore, attain the idea of "the absolute unity" (God) by either cognition or volition, but finds it in the inner depths of his own personality, in immediate self-consciousness or — which is the same in Schleiermacher's terminology — feeling.

That feeling is the seat of all religion is also the fundamental

thought of his great dogmatic work *Der christliche Glaube.* But
religious feeling is not merely sense and taste for the infinite, but
the immediate consciousness of absolute dependence upon God,
who is the highest causality, the unknown unity in which all things
are included manifesting himself in his attributes of omnipotence,
eternity, omnipresence, and omniscience. But the attributes of God
are nothing more than views of him from different human stand-
points. God in himself is an unchangeable unity. His personality
is also only an attribute. God becomes personal in man, but
whether he is personality in himself cannot be known nor demonstrated. Here we observe the close resemblance of the God of
Schleiermacher and the God of Kant, God is unknowable. In
Schleiermacher's conception of an impersonal God immanent within
man contemporaries discovered surviving traces of Spinoza's pantheism. On the other hand, Schleiermacher assigns to this impersonal God such actions as only a person could perform. We notice
here an inconsistency in Schleiermacher's theological system. Man
was created with two natures, the lower or earthly and the higher
or heavenly, but either of them good in itself. The two, however,
meet and must needs conflict with one another since the lower
carnal nature does not yield to the higher spiritual. From this
inevitable conflict evil arises. There was no fall from original
righteousness or concreated holiness. Man was so constituted that
he could not but fall. On this point Schleiermacher's view coincides with Calvin's supralapsarian view. The sin by which man
fell was not the sin of an individual, but of the whole race. Original
sin is therefore the natural condition of all men from the beginning.
Adam's fall and the universal corruption, i. e., enslavement by the
sensual consciousness, resulting from it, necessitate the redemption
of mankind which depends entirely upon the person of Christ.
Christ brings redemption in that he liberates the God-consciousness
of the human race. He is the archetype of humanity, the original
pattern after whose image and likeness the human race was fash-
ioned. In him resided the consciousness of God in absolute power.
Schleiermacher admits, perhaps, that Christ could not have come
into the world by a natural process, but he nowhere regards him as
"God revealed in the flesh". Not only Christ's supernatural birth,
but also his resurrection, ascension, second advent and miracles are
regarded by Schleiermacher as of little moment. Christ is the ideal
man, perfectly sinless. His sinlessness constitutes his divinity. He
came into the world and by taking a human form united himself
to all humanity and lifted it up to his own level, not by doing
anything for it but by simply living in it. Christ became what we
are that we might become what he is. The idea of an effect of

Christ's work on God has no place in Schleiermacher's system. He recognizes only a working of Christ on man which he describes as redemption and atonement. The redemptive agency of Christ consists in the communication of the power of his consciousness of God to the believer. The atoning work of Christ consists in the communication of the blessedness of such consciousness. The result of Christ's redemptive and atoning work in man is regeneration which marks the beginning of the process of evolution toward goodness, or sanctification. Viewed from the side of regeneration this is termed justification, from the side of man, conversion. Sin becomes in the believer a vanishing element, and physical evil, which sin brings in its train, is no longer felt as penalty. Christ, the representative of the human race, suffered the punishment of the sins of all humanity. His suffering was vicarious. It was by no means a mark of God's anger, but of Christ's sympathetic compassion for men as sinners. But not only to Christ but to every believer, in whom Christ lives, suffering is vicarious. To the believer it is no longer punishment of his own sin, but something which must be borne as a natural concomitant of our fallen condition. Out of the communion with Christ's life there grow up the new personality of the individual Christian as well as the community of believers, the church, for Christ becomes a mysterious divine essence, uncomprehended and incomprehensible, in the hearts of all his people. As the Fall of man is foreordained so is also the salvation of the entire human race the object of God's election. All will ultimately be saved. But, though conversion is exclusively due to God's agency, its occurrence in each case is at a particular time.

As Schleiermacher is silent on Christ's pre-existence, so is he also silent on a personal risen Redeemer. By the assertion that Christ lives again in his church Schleiermacher means that mysterious influence, that inward consciousness of fellowship with God which supplies the place of a personal risen Savior. Likewise the Holy Spirit is not a person, but an influence, the spirit prevading the whole community founded by Christ. Reception into fellowship with Christ is identical with reception of the Holy Spirit. Schleiermacher's theory of the Trinity is closely akin to Sabellianism.

Notwithstanding the inconsistencies and errors in his theological system, Schleiermacher was "a prince among theologians", a devout worshipper, an earnest preacher, and a lover of souls. By placing religion in the consciousness of man and his dependence on God, he made the heart an organ of science and shattered the rationalism of the Kantians who had almost expelled feeling from religion.

By giving Christ the central place and making his consciousness of God the final standard he combated with respect to the ideal, the person, the power of Christ, the destructive forces of criticism and philosophy. But Schleiermacher did not teach Biblical Christianity. Seeking to gather the antithetic conceptions of other thinkers into his own philosophy and to find in Christianity the unity of all facts he proved to be monist and dualist, idealist and realist, rationalist and mystic, naturalist and supranaturalist, theist and pantheist. Kurtz calls him an Origen of the nineteenth century because in him, as once in Origen, almost all distinctive and constructive tendencies which have since then been unfolded were originally comprehended. There is in Schleiermacher's system of theology not a single feature that is distinctively new. Gathering its material from all parts, Schleiermacher's theology extended its influence to each separate school of theological belief, and of theological unbelief too. By teaching that religion is primarily the self-consciousness of absolute dependence on God, he prepared the way for the modern grounding of religion in experience. Neander saw in Schleiermacher's theology the return to evangelical truth. When he heard of the death of his teacher and colleague at Berlin, he remarked that from Schleiermacher a new epoch in theological thinking would date. One cannot but conclude that Christian theology must have been at a very low ebb when a man of his inconsistent theories and apparent heresies could render it such a service as entitled him to be called "the renewer and prince of theological science".

Nor was Schleiermacher's theology in keeping with confessional Protestantism. Convinced that the church proceeds from Christ he hoped for a new unity of even the visible church. This led him to ignore altogether the ancient creeds and definitions of the faith as witnesses of the church to Christ. Regarding dogmatic decisions in no wise binding upon Protestants he gave undivided support to the favorite scheme of King Frederick William III to unite the Lutherans and the Calvinists in one national Church, with both the Augsburg Confession and the Heidelberg Catechism, and a new liturgy. On October 31, 1817, the three hundredth anniversary of the posting up of Luther's theses, the king announced the reunion as in conformity with "the great purposes of Christianity, the original intentions of the Reformers, and the spirit of Protestantism". To render Protestant worship more attractive the king himself prepared for this United Evangelical Church a liturgy which in an abridged and improved form, approved by Schleiermacher, was made legally binding on the church in 1830. The union was gradually effected in other German states, the Palatinate and Baden.

It encountered, however, vehement opposition. Those who retained "the Lutheran consciousness" and rejected this artificial church union were harshly persecuted, some of the leaders being fined and imprisoned. Many genuine Lutherans, who left the church, migrated to America and Australia. Those who remained in Germany formed an exclusively religious party. In 1845 they were recognized as the church of the "Separated old-Lutherans". The Christian world was thus left with a very impressive warning against a reunion which ignores spiritual renovation. Even many today have yet to learn the lesson that there can be no true union where there is no unity of faith.

Fichte (1762-1814) determined to begin where Kant had ended. Kant had demonstrated that no testimony derived from outward experience is of any value. Fichte made his starting point the non-existence of an outward world and prolaims the absoluteness of the ego. Only the ego appears as real. The Non-ego attains reality through the Ego. Thus all reality is the product of the activity of the Ego. But the finite ego is the product of the impersonal underlying ego, the Absolute. Fichte denies the personality of God. In his view an absolute personality is a contradiction in terms. In the place of God there is substituted the moral order of the world. Thus ethics is exalted to the supreme place. Religion is reduced to faith in the moral order of the universe. Despite Fichte's vehement denial of the charge of atheism he was expelled from his position at Jena. In the latter part of his career he approached Christianity, in appearance at least, in that he introduced a mystic element into his philosophy of religion. As he came to see the blessedness of life in the loving surrender of the whole soul to the All-Spirit, he liberated religion from the mere service of morality. But his metaphysical views remained unaltered. They exhibit the last results of unbelief and the nearest approach to absolute scepticism. Schelling (1775-1854) agreed in the main with Fichte as to the Absolute, the Ego and Non-ego, but he inverted the relation. While Fitchte allowed reality to the world only as the reflex of the spirit, Schelling saw in the spirit nothing else than the life of nature itself and consequently identified the spirit with nature. Schelling's "philosophy of identity" is essentially pantheistic natural philosophy. God is absolutely immanent in the world. Man is a reflection of God and a microcosm. Hegel (1770-1831) accepted Schelling's fundamental position, but transformed pantheistic natural philosophy into pantheistic mental philosophy. Starting from the principle: All that is rational is real, all that is real (or absolutely existent, substantial) is rational, he maintained that the Absolute manifests itself not so much in the life of nature, as rather in the thinking and acting of the human spirit. He thereby refuted the Kantian theory of man's inability to know things as they are by the intellect. The human reason is to Hegel a mirror of the eternal reason. The Bible is not a revelation but a record of it given by God to man. God is the concrete unity, the idea determining itself, the generating principle of immanence. The leading point in Hegel's theology is the idea of the trinity. According to Hegel the most elementary idea is not a unity, but a trinity. The very existence of the human mind is tri-une. To follow Hegel in his thought we have but to remember the Hegelian process of reasoning. It begins with an affirmation or thesis; this is met by denial or antithesis; and the conflict results in the blending into one thought or synthesis. The very act of thinking involves a trinity of thought according to Hegel. Self-consciousness itself is not a single idea, but the synthesis or union of two distinct and even contrary ideas, self and non-self. We come to know ourselves only by knowing that there is something not ourselves. As there is a trinity in human thought, there must also be a trinity in the Absolute Mind, for man is made in the image of God. The very conception of God as a Spirit involves a trinitarian distinction. The Father becomes object to himself in the Son, and in one Spirit, which is consciousness of self in another, the Father and the Son are united. Religion is the consciousness of the finite being of its identity with the infinite. In this general upward movement of the mind from the finite to the infinite, religion completed itself in Christianity, which is truth in popular form which it is the mission of philosophy to convert into knowledge.

Hegel aimed at a reconciliation of theology and philosophy assuming that the substantial content of the two are identical. In contradistinction to rationalism, which assailed the truths of Christianity, he professed to accept them "in their real, inner significance". At any rate he claimed that his system was in accord with Christian faith. By this claim some contemporary theologians were beguiled into an approval of Hegel's theology of development. Others could not endorse this theology without qualification. Still others were convinced that Hegel, had he lived longer, would have brought his philosophy at various points more definitely into line with Christian faith. Whatever may be thought of this new philosophy, its logical forms of thinking are capable of being applied in the most opposite ways. Some sought to interpret is as in harmony with the leading truths of Christian theology. They represent the so-called Right of the Hegelians. To it belong Hegel himself, Daub, Marheineke, Schaller and Erdmann. Others, the so-called Left, sundered their philosophy from the real life revelation of Christianity and turned it into a new form of Rationalism which showed the most radical hostility to all concrete and individual historical life. As the best known of the Left we mention Bruno Bauer, F. C. Baur of Tuebingen, Feuerbach, Hitzig and Strauss. Attempts to mediate between the Right and the Left were made by the "Evangelical Hegelians", such men as Goeschel, Dorner, Martensen, Rothe, Lange.

The theologians of the right wing of the Hegelians represent the would-be orthodox party. They held that in the Son of Man dwelt the fulness of the Godhead bodily. Those who belong to the left wing maintained that the Divine Spirit can never be embodied in an individual form, but can only find his abode in human nature as a whole. This process of becoming incarnate will not be completed until the last individual of the human race appears on earth. In this theology God is the creature of man, each individual of the human race helping to make God conscious of his own existence. God did not make us after his own image, but we are making God after ours. Hegelian pantheism here passed over into materialistic atheism which reached its baldest form in the philosophy of Feuerbach (d. 1872). After having studied under Hegel Feuerbach gave up the theological career and began to attack with great energy Christianity and religious ideas in general. In his first writing, "Thoughts on Death and Immortality", he disposed of immortality on psychological grounds. His later works on the relations of "Philosophy and Christianity" and on the "Essence of Christianity", in which he set forth his radical views, drew on the Hegelian system the reproach of being hostile to Christianity. Going beyond Hegel he denied the existence of an absolute mind and explained God as a subjective product of our conscious life. The Ego of the individual can neither think nor feel anything more elevated than itself. In man, the true ego, the only reality is nature. "Nature, or, in other words, animated matter, is higher than man. . . . . Man is what he eats". "Der Mensch ist, was er isst." Feuerbach carried out his theory to its final practical results by discarding God altogether from his system and proclaiming religion to be the worship of humanity: "We adore the great negation".

But why not discard religion altogether? How can humanity be to us an object of worship when that humanity is not yet completed, or has not yet found its head or culmination? In the year in which Feuerbach died, Strauss published, under the title of *The Old Faith and the New,* a curious book which aroused a storm of criticism for its sceptical views. He has himself entitled it, *A Con-*

fession. Adopting the Darwinian theory and taking his stand on the ground of natural science the author proposes to resolve successively the following four questions: Are we still Christians? Have we any longer a religion? What is our conception of the Universe? What is our rule of life? Of special interest to us are his answers to the first two questions. To the first one he answers bluntly, "No". To the second he replies "Yes or No", according to one's conception of religion. He does not hold the view that we must answer affirmatively. His answer to this question is, on the whole, in the negative, as he regards religion, in the common sense of the term, as something which man has outgrown. He heralds Darwin as one of the greatest benefactors of the human race, because he liberated men from the faith in miracles. Another champion of the extreme Hegelian Left, Bruno Bauer (d. 1882), denounced what he called "pectoral theology". No individual man can claim to be the recipient of divine impressions. So-called religious convictions are merely human imaginings of things unknown and unknowable. The goal to which all the speculations of the Left have led is the absolute negation of all knowledge of God.

If the infinite spirit cannot find manifestation in any finite individual form, it follows that history, being a mere finite manifestation, a collection of individual sentiments, cannot claim any authority whatever. The theologians of the Left were therefore opposed to historical Christianity and interpreted the Scriptures according to the distinctive doctrine of the Left. David Friedrich Strauss (1808-74), who had studied under Baur at Tuebingen, published, at the age of 27, his notorious *Life of Jesus* which rendered Strauss "famous in a moment". This work was directed against the traditional orthodox view of the Gospel narratives as well as the rationalistic treatment of them. In it Strauss advanced the so-called "mythical" theory of the Gospel narrative of the life of Christ. Assuming the impossibility of miraculous intervention he derived the whole story of the Gospel from the imagination of the primitive Christian community. According to Strauss the expectation of a Messiah, an imaginary personage, had grown gradually out of the legends of the Old Testament dispensation and was widely diffused in the first century. When there appeared a peculiar personage whose life and character rendered him conspicuous amongst his contemporaries, the early disciples simply ascribed to this personage words and deeds that should have been his according to the Old Testament legends, and the creative working of their thoughts invested him with miraculous power and divine authority until his original earthly life was altogether lost and obliterated. Strauss assigns all narratives of miracles in the New Testament to the category of myth not to that of legend. They were the product of unconscious inventions not that of intentional fabrications. The statements of the gospels are not legends or fables, but myths or parables of spiritual truths, but they are not historically true. Strauss uses the word mythical as a designation of spiritual as opposed to historical truths. But he does not only make Christ the product of the imagination of the early disciples, but he regards the idea of the Messiah as itself mythical, as a description of humanity itself. God becomes man in mankind collectively taken. Strauss' *Life of Jesus* aroused a storm of almost unparalleled fury. He lost his appointment as tutor in the seminary at Tuebingen. In his *Polemics for the Defence of my Writing on the Life of Jesus and for the Characterisation of Contemporary Theology,* 1837, and in an apology for his Life of Jesus, 1838, he answered his many critics. His Life of Jesus failed to give satisfaction, even to his teacher F. C. Baur.

In 1864, on the occasion of the appearance of Renan's Life of Jesus, Strauss published a new *Life of Jesus adapted for the German people,* which, he hoped, would serve for the German people just as Renan's did for the French. In this work he holds in general his former position, but prompted by the criticism of Baur upon his earlier work, he wishes to show how the legendary narratives of our Gospels were formed, relegating with Baur the Gospel of St. John to the middle of the second century. He also approaches to Baur's view that the Gospel narratives are deliberate forgeries. In his earlier work Strauss had regarded the Gospel Narratives as unintentional mythology. In his new *Life of Jesus* he essentially modifies his definition of a myth and makes room for conscious invention. In his latest work, *The Old Faith and the New* (*q. v.*), he proposes to substitute for the old a new faith which surrenders the name of Christian, substitutes for the ecclesiastical dogma and Christian tradition the assured results of researches into nature and history, and places in the room of a personal God an impersonal cosmos as the only object of worship.

Ferdinand Christian Baur, the founder of the Tuebingen school of Biblical criticism, and for more than thirty years (1826-60) professor of Historical Theology at Tuebingen, applied Hegel's philosophy of history to the New Testament writings and pushed forward their dates into the second century. To Baur Christianity gradually developed out of Judaism. With Strauss Christianity came forth undesignedly from the depths of human consciousness. With Baur it was created by the conflict of different tendencies, the opposing Schools of Peter and Paul. The legalism of Peter would make of Christianity only a purer Judism (thesis). The liberalism of Paul, transcending national bounds, would present a breach with Judism, the temple, and the law (antithesis). The alleged antagonism between the Jewish apostles, Peter, James and John, and the Gentile apostle Paul continued down to the middle of the second century. After the middle of the second century the fourth Gospel completed the process of reconciliation (synthesis). Of the New Testament writings only Galatians, I and II Corinthians and Romans are genuinely Pauline, according to Baur, because they clearly reveal Paul's antithesis, i. e., his struggle against Judaic Christianity. The rest of them are *Tendenz-Schriften*, created for the purpose of supporting different tendencies of thought or to obliterate the ugly feud of earlier days. None of them originated before 130 A. D. According to this theory we know nothing of what happened at the opening of the Christian era. The person of Christ retreats altogether into the background. The portraits of Christ contained in the synoptic Gospels simply represent different stages in the development of Christian belief and speculation. The account in John "does not possess historical truth, and cannot and does not really lay claim to it." We can therefore have no clear and definite conception of the actual person of Jesus. Schwegler who further developed Baur's theory voices the sentiment of the Tuebingen school concerning the person of Christ when he says, "We know not who he was". It is claimed that Baur as a critic has rendered a great service. This is true in so far as his revolutionary and extreme views compelled the scholars of the day to make a re-study of the New Testament canon and the history of the early Christian church. However, Baur's criticism was decidedly one-sided and subjective. He attempted to show wherein Paul differed from the original apostles. A fair critic could not have failed, as Baur failed, to show in what essential points Paul did agree with those apostles. But above all, Baur's radical views have done untold harm. They have undermined Christianity in the minds of many. Baur's theory, however, has had its day and his extreme views are no longer taken seriously by any one. His school, too, has long been on the decline. There arose within this school a series of dissensions, retractions, and retrograde movements. Chief representatives of this school were, besides Albert Schwegler, Eduard Zeller, Adolf Hilgenfeld who substituted the historical literary method for Baur's "tendency criticism", and Albrecht Ritschl who made an approach toward positive theology and may be regarded as a complete apostate from the school.

Before we take up the study of the Ritschlian school it will be necessary briefly to sketch the different contemporary theological schools or tendencies. At the beginning of the nineteenth cntury Germany was divided into three distinct schools which we may call (1) the old rationalistic and supranaturalistic, (2) the new orthodox, and (3) the liberal evangelical or mediating schools.

Prominent among the theologians who continued in the nineteenth century the primitive traditions of rationalism were Paulus, Wegscheider, Roehr and Bretschneider. The most active leader of extreme rationalism in the field of exegesis was Paulus (d. 1851), professor at Jena, Wuerzburg and Heidelberg. The religious sense is absolutely lacking in him. He made it his task to propagate a purely moral conception of Christ and of Christianity. He did away with the miracles of the Bible by performing miracles of exegesis. He referred the narratives of miracles to an unconscious exaggeration on the part of the witnesses. The angelic appearances to the shepherds were meteoric phenomena. In narrating miracles of healing the evangelists have omitted mentioning the natural remdies which Christ used. The raising of the dead took place only in the case of persons who had fallen into lethargy. Wegscheider (d. 1849), professor at Halle, wrote *Institutiones theologiae dogmaticae*, which is considered as the standard dogmatic work of rationalism. He declared the doctrine of immediate supernatural revelation unworthy of God, and reduces the gospel to a system of natural theism and of exalted ethical precepts. One of the most active defenders of rationalism was Roehr (d. 1848), chief court preacher and general superintendent of Weimar. *Letters on Rationalism* are a defence of vulgar rationalism. Reason as it is found in every human being is the last resort and the supreme authority in matters of religion. The final end of religion is pure morality. The deity of Christ is categorically denied. Bertschneider (d. 1848), prolific writer and general superintendent at Gotha, began as a moderate supranaturalist, but later approached to vulgar rationalism.

Side by side with the rationalistic school we find the supranaturalistic school. Though the two are separated from one another by shades that are often hardly perceptible we may distinguish two distinct types, rational and suprarational supranaturalism. Rational supranaturalism acknowledged a supernatural revelation in the Scriptures but regarded reason as a source of religious knowledge of equal authority with it, and consequently asserted that the Scriptures contain nothing which goes beyond the limits of our reason, or which is contrary to its affirmations. Among representatives of this type are Steudel (d. 1837) and Planck (d. 1833).

Supranaturalism proper (suprarational) maintained the necessity of revelation against rationalism, for reason without revelation could never have reached the results to which it has come. The Old Tuebingen School, in which the Lutheran orthodoxy had retained unbroken sway, was the centre of this Biblical supranaturalism. The school owed its Biblical trend especially to the influence of Johann Albrecht Bengel (d. 1752), prelate at Stuttgart, a man of eminent piety and vast and sound learning. When speaking of Bengel as scholar and critic we cannot commend his eschatoloical writings which are unfortunately marred with speculations regarding the end of the world and the millennium, which he predicted for the year 1836. These writings enjoyed for a time popularity in Germany. The works on which his reputation rests as a Biblical scholar and critic are his edition of the Greek New Testament with an *Apparatus criticus* based on a careful study of the text in various manuscripts, and his *Gnomon Novi Testamenti*, or Exegetical Annotations on the New Testament. The latter work, distinguished by brevity of expression and depth of comprehension, exerted considerable influence on exegesis in Germany and England and is most valuable even today. John Wesley made great use of it, incorporating many of Bengel's annotations in his *Expository Notes upon the New Testament*, (1755). In 1751 the university of Tuebingen conferred upon Bengel the degree of doctor of philosophy. A cycle of truly pious men gathered round him in private at Tuebingen and elsewhere, who became the disseminators of his teachings. The university of Tuebingen as well as the Church of Wuerttemberg remained true to their biblical trend. Even the Wolffian philosophy did not affect the Tuebingen school during that period. A new phase of theology, however, was introduced at Tuebingen toward the end of the eighteenth century when the Enlightenment began to assail all positive Christianity. It thus became necessary to defend Christianity against the then prevailing rationalism, especially the principles of Kant. One of the ablest defenders of the Christian faith, and the most worthy representative of Supranaturalism at that time, was Gottlob Christian Storr (d. 1805), the founder of the Old Tuebingen School of Theology. Storr made it his task to save the essential truths of salvation. He deemed it possible to lay a sure foundation for scientific theology and dogmatics on the attested authority of Scripture alone, ignoring altogether the accepted dogma of the church. Thus abandoning any material principle he insisted on a merely formal principle, making the Scripture the soul source, even the text-book of Christian teaching. From this sole source he attempted to derive the Christian truth through grammatical and historical exegesis and logical reasoning. In exegesis Storr combatted Semler's theory of accommodation. In dogmatics he does not always hold to the Lutheran position, but approaches Calvinistic, Semi-pelagian, and Socinian views. Storr's school continued in Wuerttemberg for thirty years, but its influence was from the beginning weak and feeble. These supranaturalists attempted to do the impossible: to prove Christian truth by Scripture and by reason. Kurtz has well described supranaturalism as "a dilution of the old faith of the church, effected by the water of the enlightenment."

One of the first and most influential representatives of the New Orthodoxy was Claus Harms (1778-1855), high consistorial councillor at Kiel. He grew up under rationalistic influences. The University of Kiel, where he studied theology, was dominated at that time by rationalism. But the reading of Schleiermacher's *Discourses* and the study of the Scriptures brought about his complete conversion. He passed from rationalism to positive Lutheranism. Being convinced that the church had left the faith of the Reformation, he published on the occasion of the three hundredth anniversary of the Reformation, 1817, together with Luther's ninety-five theses, ninety-five of his own against rationalism and the attempted union between the Lutheran and Reformed churches. The theses caused a tremendous sensation which brought forth no fewer than two hundred answers. Harms' influence continued to increase. He kept up close relations with the students of Kiel. In the University the spirit of rationalism began to disappear. The new orthodoxy found its way also into other universities. One of the most prominent among the leaders of the modern orthodoxy in the German universities and the staunchest defender against rationalism, unionism and the mediating theology of his day was E. W. Hengstenberg (1802-1869), professor at Berlin. In July 1827 appeared under his editorship the *Evangelische Kirchenzeitung*, which in his hands became a most powerful organ in defence of the truth, in attacking error without fear, and extirpating rationalism in all spheres. It aroused a violent controversy (the so-called Hallesche Streit) by publishing (1830) an anonymous article (by the jurist E. L. von Gerlach), which openly charged the professors Gesenius and Wegscheider with infidelity and profanity, and on the ground of these accusations advocated the interposition of the civil power. Hengstenberg's friend and co-laborer, August Hahn (1792-1863), also, defended, in an academic disputation at Leipzig, the position that the Rationalists ought to be dismissed from the church. To the same school belong the following: A. F. C. Vilmar (1800-68), most prominent Hessian theologian of the nineteenth century; Wilhelm Loehe (1808-72), pastor at Neuendettelsau from 1837, founder of the Deaconess Home at the inner mission institutions at Neuendettelsau, and a mission school to provide pastors for German emigrants to America and Australia. As pastor and theologian Loehe fearlessly bore testimony against the rationalism of his time and against the lax position of the state church. Both Vilmar and Loehe held Romanizing views with regard to the idea of the church and the ministry. Outside the church, according to their theory, there is no salvation, but the saving power of the church does not reside so much in the Word of God as in the sacraments as a source of forces which act on man in virtue of the proper efficacy resident in the baptismal water, and in the elements offered to the communicants in the Holy Supper. Approaching more or less nearly to the episcopal theory, Vilmar and Loehe, though holding fast to the parity of ministers, make the ministry the divine self-perpetuation of the pastor's office. Vilmar maintains that through ordination we receive powers which cannot be obtained in any other way, thus assigning ordination a high sacramental character. Adolf von Harless (1806-79), professor at Erlangen and Leipzig, and editor of the famous *Zeitschrift fuer Protestantismus und Kirche*, also belongs to this school. His "Christian Ethics" is still considered a classic. His friend, Heinrich Guericke (1803-1878), deposed from his professorship at Halle in 1835 on account of his opposition to the Prussian Union, was reinstated by Frederick William IV in 1840. In the same year he founded with Andreas Gottlob Rudelbach (1792-1862), of Copenhagen, the *Zeitschrift fuer lutherische Theologie und Kirche*. Guericke is known by several extensive theological works, especially his *Manual of Church History*. Johann Heinrich Kurtz (1809-90), professor at Dorpat and author of the well-known *Text-Book of Church History*, and F. D. Kliefoth (1810-95), superintendent at Schwerin and president of the superior ecclesiastical court, writer on church polity and liturgics, one of the most prominent theologians of his day and one of the most effective preachers of the nineteenth century, likewise, belong to this school.

Toward the latter part of the century the University of Erlangen exerted a far-reaching influence on the Lutheran Church. The leaders of this school have been J. C. K. von Hofmann (1810-77) and later F. H. R. von Frank (1827-94). The school claimed to represent conservative, confessional Lutheranism. For this reason it is, also, called the later "Confessional School". But it repudiated the principle that the Scripture alone is the source of theology and, attempting to develop a new "Scientific" theology out of the believing ego, the Christian consciousness, it followed Schleiermacher rather than Luther. "I, the Christian, am the proper material of my science as theologian", is Hofmann's own confession. Consequently, the Erlangen theologians differed to a very noticeable degree from each other in their teachings. Christianity, according to Hofmann, is the communion with God mediated, not by the Christ for us, but the Christ in us. Thus, he denied the vicarious atonement, and the charge of denying the atonement altogether was brought against him. Gottfried Thomasius (1802-75), professor of dogmatics and university preacher at Erlangen, in his work, *Christi Person und Werk*, advocated the modern theory of kenosis, or the self-limitation of the Divine Logos in the state of humiliation. Franz Delitzsch (1813-90), professor at Rostock, Erlangen and Leipzig, especially distinguished himself as an exegete. His commentaries on the Old Testament, prepared independently and in connection with Keil, are still the best of their kind. Delitzsch was at first a staunch Lutheran, but later, influenced by the new "scientific" theology, opposed the idea "of fencing theology off with the letter of the Formula of Concord". His theology was not free from theosophic influences, as is shown by his "System der biblischen Psychologie". He, also, advocated trichotomy. The most prominent exponent of the Erlangen theology was Frank, professor of systematic theology at Erlangen. Educated at Leipzig, under the influence of Harless, he passed from rationalism to confessional Lutheranism. At Erlangen, under the influence of Hofmann, he adopted "the new mode of teaching the old truths". In his *System der christlichen Gewissheit* he shows that the basis of belief is not the Scripture, but the positive assurance of the converted ego, the regenerate man. In his *System der christlichen Wahrheit* he sets forth, in their inner connection, the realities of Christian faith thus acquired. The leading point of view in this work is the evolution of the humanity of God. His third work on systematic theology is the *System der christlichen Sittlichkeit*, which represents the evolution of the man of God. Theodor Zahn (1892), professor of New Testament exegesis at Erlangen, is considered the leader of conservatives in New Testament criticism. Zahn's monumental work is his *Introduction to the New Testament*. In it largely the old views which the Church had entertained concerning the New Testament writings have been shown to be correct. Christian Ernst Luthardt (1823-1902), professor at Marburg and Leipzig, takes a high place among the theologians of the Erlangen school as a voluminous writer on dogmatics and apologetics. From 1868 he edited the *Allgemeine evangelische lutheranische Kirchenzeitung*. The Erlangen school has rendered the German church invaluable service by its uncompromising warfare against rationalism in its old form, as well as in its modern guise of liberalism, and by its valuable contributions to Lutheran theology.

Between the old rationalism and the new orthodoxy there arose at the beginning of the nineteenth century an intermediate tendency which counts among its members numerous and eminent theologians in Germany. The Liberal Evangelical school or the Mediating School, as it has been justly called, attaches itself directly to Schleiermacher. August Neander (1789-1850) takes his place by the side of Schleiermacher as the greatest of his disciples and as his friend and colleague on the theological faculty at Berlin. He exerted great personal influence in the church and especially upon the students of the University. He entered into Schleiermacher's theology of feeling and transformed it into a theology of the heart. His motto was: Pectus est quod facit theologum. He insisted on a heart theology against mere intellectualism, whether of a rationalistic or orthodox kind. His critics attempted to cast a reflection on his theology by calling it "pectoral" theology, because it ignored the rights of reason and of science and made too much of religious experience as a source of spiritual truth.

The theologians who attached themselves to this school differed widely from one another in their teachings. But they stood on common ground and had a common ideal. Accepting the conclusions of theological investigation and planting themselves firmly on the ground of supernatural revelation and the evangelical faith, they attempted a harmonious unity between the conflicting schools. They argued that if two opposing systems exclude each other by their false elements, they may be united by their true elements. It need not be said that this is an ideal which the mediating school has not attained.

The designation, mediating theology, Vermittlungs Theologie, has often been used as a term of reproach, and the theologians of this school have been charged with compromising truth. The mediating theologians have been honest in their efforts and independent in their thinking, but they attempted to do the impossible, to establish a true union without unity of faith. The same must be said of their "mediating" position in supporting the union of the Lutheran and Reformed Churches. Here they took their stand on the consensus of the two confessions in things deemed to be essential.

Among the principal theologians of the school of Schleiermacher there is not one who is not indebted to Schleiermacher for essential assistance; and there is, also, not one who agrees with Schleiermacher on every point of his theology. The one common element which unites them all is the starting point of individual feeling. It is evident that any theology which professes to have its foundation in feeling must break up into a multitude of divergent systems. This has been exactly the case with the theology of Schleiermacher. There are the "unbelieving" theologians, or the left wing, of the school of Schleiermacher, with Alexander Schweizer of Zurich, who has preserved the speculative and negative critical tendency of the master in its purest form, as chief representative. As to the "believing" theologians, or the right wing of the school, Tholuck represents the widest departure from Schleiermacher's theology, with which he has nothing in common beyond the starting point of pious feeling. Most of the theologians of this school, however, occupy an intermediate position between these extremes. It is impossible in a work like the present to enumerate and describe the different shades and diverse currents of thought which have met within the circle of this school. The following writers, in spite of their independence and individuality and the many differences among themselves, most exhibit the impress of Schleiermacher's genius. In the department of historical theology may be named Neander, the founder of modern church history, Hagenbach, Dorner, A. Schweizer, Baumgarten-Crusius. In systematic and dogmatic theology and ethics: Nitzsch, Rothe, Tholuck, Martensen, Koestlin, Beyschlag, Hess. In New Testament exegesis: Luecke Tholuck, Bleek, Olshausen, Meyer, and many others. In practical theology: Nitzsch, Ehrenfeuchter, Palmer, Brueckner. The only field in which Schleiermacher had not labored was Old Testament exegesis. Hence Schleiermacher's school has scarcely any distinguished Old Testament theologians. This discipline remained yet awhile in the hands of old orthodox scholars or rationalistic radicals. Karl August von Hase (1800-90), professor at Jena and writer on church history, dogmatics and polemics, belonged to no party or school, though he shared Schleiermacher's vital conception of religion. He held an independent position, standing "for the scientific investigation of the Gospels, an enlightened Christianity recognizing itself as Truth in the eternal laws of the Spirit, as opposed to the popular faith supported by external authority". His *Handbook to the Controversy with Rome* reveals his intimate acquaintance with the Roman Catholic religion. His polemical writings against Roehr, general superintendent at Weimar, made short work of the vulgar rationalism of Roehr and his clique.

In the latter half of the nineteenth century there arose in Germany a new school of theological opinion which, attaching itself to Kant, professed at the same time to carry on the work of Luther and Schleiermacher, especially in ridding faith of the tyranny of scholastic philosophy. The school owes its origin to Albrecht Ritschl (1822-89), first, professor at Bonn, and since 1864 at Goettingen. He studied at Bonn, Halle, Heidelberg, and Tuebingen. At Halle he came under Hegelian influences. In Tuebingen he was attached to the school of Baur which, however, he early abandoned. Since 1859, when he was promoted to a full professorship at Bonn, he became more and more the founder of a school of his own, influenced by Kant and Schleiermacher. The so-called "Ritschlian School", however, did not rise till nearly a decade after he had gone to Goettingen. Since then his school has grown with remarkable rapidity. His lectures drew to the university of Goettingen numerous and enthusiastic students. His writings exercised considerable influence on theological thought in Germany and other countries, while at the same time they provoked a storm of hostile criticism from the various camps of theology. His system of theology is contained in his large work on the Christian doctrine of justification and atonement, *Die christliche Lehre von der Rechtfertigung and Versoehnung*. His *Unterricht in der christlichen Religion* is a compend of his theological opinions. A brief thought-translation of Ritschl's theological views may serve to indicate the more essential features of his system.

Like Schleiermacher, Ritschl banishes all philosophy from the realm of theology. He criticizes the use of speculative philosophy in theology as being alien to the inmost essence of Christianity. He, also, excludes from theology mysticism because of its claim of an immediate communion with God unattainable by the natural intellect and incapable of being analyzed or explained. Over against metaphysics and mysticism he professes to give us an essentially religious conception of Christianity by means of the Biblical documents alone. The Scriptures of the Old and New Testament exclusively are for the Christian the fountain of religious knowledge. This holds true at once of the New Testament, the Old Testament being important mainly as supplying a means for understanding the New. And, as for the New Testament, allowance must be made for the fact that here and there, on subordinate points, it has been affected by the influence of apocryphal sources. The fourth Gospel, for instance, the genuineness of which is not questioned by Ritschl, is, nevertheless, said to be colored by subjective conceptions. The value of the Scripture as the rule and norm of faith is not founded on any theory of inspiration whatever, but on the fact that it alone makes us know the faith of the first Christian community in its primitive purity. In other words, Ritschl does not found his theology on the infallible, inspired and revealed Word of God but on the faith of the community as presented to us, especially, in the New Testament writings. Unlike Schleiermacher, who started from the believing individual and his Christian consciousness, Ritschl took up the standpoint of the believing Christian community and the historical testimony which it has deposited in the Biblical writings.

Christianity, according to Ritschl, is the monotheistic, completely spiritual, and ethical religion. It is spiritual, inasmuch as it consists in filial liberty which we enjoy as God's children through Christ, who by his life redeems us and founds the kingdom of God. It is moral, inasmuch as it includes the impulse to conduct from the motive of love, and has for its ideal the moral regeneration of humanity. The idea of the Kingdom of God is the centre of Ritschl's theological system. He defines it as "the highest good assured by God to the community founded by his revelation in Christ". Since the life of Christ is nothing less than the complete revelation of the love of God himself given to the community, it follows that the true Christian conception of God is that which defines him as Love. With God as "First Cause" or "absolute being" Ritschl would have nothing to do. Nor is he interested in the "speculative" problems indicated by the traditional doctrine of the Trinity. Nor would he allow any interference of natural science with theology. Miracles are striking natural occurrences to which the Christian attaches the experience of divine help, or of a special deliverance. Supernatural events, as recorded in the Bible, need not be considered contrary to natural laws. The same event may appear natural to science, and supernatural to faith. Faith regards miracles as direct interventions of Divine Providence with a view to the greatest good of the members of God's kingdom. Faith does not know God and divine things as they are in themselves, but only in their relation to the kingdom. Not what God is in himself, but what God means is the primary question of faith. This illustrates Ritschl's theory — in which he was anticipated by Lotze — of "value-judgments" (Werthurtheile). Considerations in religion are of moment only in so far as they are of *worth* in relation to our salvation. For instance, the thought of God must be treated solely as a value-judgment. God is to be regarded not as "self-existent", but solely in his active relationship to the kingdom, as spiritual personality revealed in spiritual purposiveness. Only in so far as Christ reveals to us the nature of God, which is love, has he the religious value of God to us. Through him we know that God is love, and that the purpose of his love is the moral organization of humanity in the Kingdom of God. His "righteousness" is his fidelity to this purpose. This is Ritschl's moral conception of the divine personality as opposed to the metaphysical and mystic conception.

Ritschl argues back from the experience of Christians to the person of Christ, who has for the religious life of the community the unique value of founder and redeemer. His founding and redeeming activity constituted his personal vocation, of which he was fully conscious. Being inwardly cognizant of the eternal purpose of love, Christ carries out that purpose in founding the kingdom of the redeemed and exercising his sovereign rule over all its members. Thus, the whole life of Jesus becomes the perfect revelation of the love of God himself. It may, therefore, be said that we see the Father in the Son. Even his sufferings and death have no penal character, but in them are perfected and evinced his absolute fidelity to his divine calling. His resurrection is, also, but the finishing of the complete revelation of God in him. By reason of his unity with God in love and purpose, he may be called and is an object of worship. Divinity, though not belonging to his essence, is, nevertheless, rightly attributed to him, since he reflects all the essential attributes that are decisive of divinity, namely, grace, fidelity and unlimited moral lordship over the world.

Ritschl denounces all attempts to make us understand how Christ became conscious of the eternal, divine purpose and of his vocation in relation to it. The eternal relation of the Son to the Father, as it is taught by John, Paul, and the writer of the Epistle to the Hebrews, is said to be their subjective conception. The "two nature" problem and the preexistence of Christ have no bearing on experience and, therefore, have no place in Ritschl's theology. The only real preexistence of Christ is in the redeeming purpose of God.

In the doctrine of sin and redemption all forensic ideas, such as law, punishment, satisfaction, atonement, are summarily rejected as foreign to God's purpose of love. God's attitude toward the world is not one of wrath, but one of love. Therefore, redemption can never be spoken of as a deliverance from wrath. The wrath of God denotes the divine retribution which will at the end befall those who have arrayed themeslves against God's Kingdom. But, whether any will actually continue to the end in wilful` resistance to the spirit of the good, we cannot know. Ritschl regards all sins, with a possible exception of this last, as mainly ignorance and weakness. The Biblical doctrine of original sin is discarded. There can be no redemption from sin and guilt in the accepted Biblical sense of the term. Here, too, everything is defined from the standpoint of the religious community. The governing idea is God's fatherly purpose for the Christian community (Gemeinde). "Sin" is the contradiction of that purpose, and "guilt" is alienation from the community. "Redemption" is the restoration of the broken community relationship. Christ revealed to men by his holy life and love-inspired suffering the love of God and maintained the filial relationship even to his death, and communicates it to the brotherhood of believers. This revelation of God's infinite love is said to kindle love in man's heart, so that he gives up his enmity against God and his distrust in God, and, thus, becomes reconciled to God. God is love, and as soon as man realizes this, he is redeemed and justified. The restoration of the broken community relationship, which may be described under the aspects of redemption, justification, regeneration, adoption, forgiveness, reconciliation, is in no wise conditioned by the direct and personal relation of the individual to Christ, but by a subjective enrolling of himself in the community of Christ's followers. The sinner who finds himself admitted to communion with God, must renounce his hostility to God and enter the kingdom of life and love which Jesus has founded on earth. Only in this way can he become a partaker of his filial relation to the Father.

Ritschl's theology is really not a dogmatic system, but rather a form of ethics, independent of and divorced from the positive doctrinal basis of Christianity. His school is, therefore, properly called the Neo-Kantian School. The members of this school, in which Julius Kaftan, J. G. W. Herrmann, and Adolph Harnack are the chief names, have greatly modified the master's position and marked out courses of their own. In his *Metaphysics in Theology* and *Religion in Relation to Cognition of the World and Morality*, Herrmann follows Ritschl closely in accentuating the opposition between the practical reason and the theoretical reason, between religion and metaphysics. Ritschl's idea of the Kingdom of God was further developed in Kaftan's work on the *Essence of the Christian Religion* and Harnack's *Essence of Christianity*. A more correct title of the two works would be Kenosis of Christianity. The Ritschlians with many differences among themselves are united with their teacher in denying the deity of Christ and reducing Christianity to a moral system.

CHAPTER XXIX

CHRISTIAN THOUGHT AND THEOLOGY IN GREAT BRITAIN

DURING THE NINETEENTH CENTURY

The Church of England claims to be a branch of the Catholic and Apostolic Church and as such distinguished from the Protestant churches, Lutheran and Calvinistic, of the European continent as well as from those bodies which have at a later date seceded from it. Since the British Reformation under Henry VIII it has been the chief champion of the principle of episcopacy against the papal pretensions, on the one hand, and Presbyterianism and Congregationalism, on the other. But as to the divine origin of episcopacy, Anglican opinion has been, and still is, considerably divided. The terms *High Church* and *Low Church* designate two parties within the Established Church who hold divergent views on this point. The term *High-Churchmen* is applied to those who take a high view of the exclusive authority of the Established Church, of episcopacy and of the sacramental system. High Church views assumed an extreme form in the reign of Charles I and his advisor, Archbishop Laud, who maintained that episcopacy was not only necessary to the well-being, but essential to the very existence of the church. In the nineteenth century, during the Tractarian or Oxford movement, the High Church party passed over into the New High Church, or Anglo- Catholic, party.

"The term *Low-Churchmen* is applied to those who, while accepting the hierarchical and sacramental system of the church, lay stress on the Bible as the sole source of authority in matters of faith and reject the peculiar tenets of the High-Church school, namely, episcopacy as essential to the constitution of the church, sacramental presence of Christ in the Eucharist and baptismal regeneration. In the latter part of the 17th century the name was used as the equivalent of a "Latitudinarian", i. e., one who advocated toleration of opinions as to authority, government and doctrine varying from those then generally received in the church as being matters of minor importance. In the days of Tractarianism "Low-Churchman" became the equivalent of "Evangelical" in contradistinction to the High-Churchman of the Catholic type. "Latitudinarian" gave place at the same time to "Broad-Churchman", a term applied to members of the Church of England or its daughter churches who hold liberal views as to doctrine and fellowship. They are a school of theological thought and hold a position aside from both the High-Church and Low-Church parties, but maintain no party organization. Such, with respect to parties, was, and still is, the state of the Church of England.

After this general characterization of the different parties within the Church of England, we shall now proceed to delineate the three great movements in their working through a great part of the past century: the Evangelical movement, the Tractarian or Oxford High Church movement, and the Broad Church or Liberal movement. The Tractarian movement was essentially an agitation within the Established Church, while the Evangelical and Liberal movements have been going on both inside and outside the pale of conformity to the English Church.

The Evangelical movement was largely, though not entirely, an offshoot of the great Methodist Revival. Its leaders were greatly influenced by the leading Methodists, especially by Whitefield. The movement was promoted from three important centres — London, Cambridge, Clapham. The most influential among the London Evangelicals were John Newton of Olney (d. 1807), best known to readers of English literature as the admired friend of the poet Cowper, and Thomas Scott (d. 1821), the successor of Newton at Olney, and the author of a spiritual autobiography entitled *The Force of Truth*, which made a profound impression on the mind of J. H. Newman, as it did on many others. Scott's *Commentary* on the Bible was, also, widely popular. He held the theory that the meaning of Scripture can only be learned from Scripture itself. He, therefore, dispensed not only with church tradition, but with all the resources of science and philosophy.

The palatial home of the wealthy and munificent Henry Thornton of Clapham became a kind of hospitable centre for all evangelical labors. Those Evangelicals who looked to Clapham as their headquarters were nicknamed by Sidney Smith "the Clapham Sect". The outstanding figure among them was William Wilberforce (d. 1833), orator, statesman and philanthropist, who turned from social applause to the service of Christ and humanity. He stated the case for evangelicalism in *A Practical View of the Prevailing Religious System of Professed Christians in the Higher and Middle Classes in this Country, Contrasted with Real Christianity*, which had a great influence both in Great Britain and America and was translated into several languages. To the Clapham group, also, belongs Mrs. Hannah More (d. 1833), authoress and philanthropist, who urged the necessity of improving the frivolous education of women, and gave her hearty support to the Sunday-schools established by Robert Raikes.

In Cambridge the most prominent exponents of the cause were the two Milners, Isaac Milner (d. 1820), who edited and completed the *History of the Church of Christ,* which his brother Joseph Milner (d. 1797) had issued in parts during the last years of his life. The work is written from a strongly anti-papal point of view, but with a sincere purpose of describing what good had been effected by Christianity, in order that readers might be edified by the narrative. Charles Simeon (d. 1836) had great influence at Cambridge as a preacher of the evangelical school.

CHAPTER XXX

THE CHRISTIAN DOCTRINE IN ITS MODERN SETTING

By: Prof. J. T. Mueller, Ph. D., Th. D.

The publishers requested the undersigned to set forth, in a brief overview, the Christian doctrine in its modern setting, which, roughly speaking, means the Christian doctrine within the period of the past thirty years.

The outstanding feature, perhaps, of this period is the almost universal revival of interest in Christian dogma, both within various church groups and differing schools, led by theologians of preeminent parts on the European continent in England, and America.

Because of the wide-spread and overpowering influence of religious humanism, dating from Schleiermacher, and continuing throughout the century (and beyond) after him, with Ritschl and the Comparative School of Religion developing and applying experientialism in their own, modified forms, the Christian dogma, in its traditional sense, was bound to be set aside for thought categories based almost exclusively on human reason, though these were oriented, in a general way, to the remaining doctrinal substreams which generation after generation had handed down as a sacred heritage. Rationalism, in its various manifestations, could thus jump over the fence of traditional religious restriction, but it could not altogether get away from the green pastures of the Christian doctrine so deeply implanted in the religious consciousness of Christendom.

Practically, however, religious humanism terminated not merely in the repudiation of fundamental Christian beliefs, but, in many cases, even in agnosticism and downright atheism. There was no more theology; everything had become *Religionsphilosophie*, religious philosophy.

From the disastrous stupor of this almost complete religious apostasy and revolt the cause of positive truth was saved by the throes and woes of the first World War, which, by upsetting the general scheme of human deification and causing nation-wide rethinking of spiritual values, revived conservative religious thought in Germany and from there spread it into other countries.

We can speak in this sketch only of a few manifestations of the modern revival of interest in Christian doctrine: 1. The Positive

Confessionalism in Germany; 2. The Barthian Movement; 3. The Scandinavian Response; 4. Church Group Interest in England; 5. The Russian Soul-Search; 6. Three Trends in America: a. The Revolt of Modernism Against Positive Truth; b. The Awakening of Neo-Thomism; c. The Neo-Orthodox Half-Way Challenge.

POSITIVE CONFESSIONALISM IN GERMANY

It could not be otherwise than that in the storm and stress period of the first World War, Lutheran re-affirmation of the Reformation heritage and Reformed emphasis on the Calvinistic fundamentals should occur, both confessional groups often working side by side and hand in hand against National Socialism, on the one hand, and Barthian Liberalism on the other. Neither orthodox Lutheranism nor orthodox Calvinism had quite disappeared from the rank and file of German's Christian population, no matter how far rationalistic pastors, university professors, and editors of church periodicals had departed from the truth. When therefore during and after the first World War, the religious masses of Germany hungered for the bread of life, it required no new message to offer them just that spiritual food which they so greatly needed and desired.

Among the Lutherans of this group, no doubt, the clearest and most direct herald of the Gospel truth was Professor Hermann Sasse, professor of theology at the University of Erlangen. His amazing book *Was heisst lutherisch?* (published first in 1934, and in a second, enlarged edition, in 1936) [Footnote # 1) *Here We Stand. Nature and Character of The Lutheran Faith.* Translated, with Revisions and Additions from the Second German Edition, by Theodore G. Tappert; Harper & Brothers, 1938] proved itself a clarion trumpet challenge on such fundamental questions as: What Does It Mean to be Lutheran? The Lutheran and the Reformed Churches; The Doctrinal Differences Between the Lutheran and the Reformed Church a. The Gospel; b. Faith; c. The Church; d. Justification and Predestination; e. Incarnation and Real Presence; Lutheran Doctrine and the Modern Reformed Theology of Karl Barth; The Lutheran Church and the *Una Sancta.* Here was pure Lutheranism, presented in a firm, though gentle and winning way, by an honest disciple of Luther with a view to presenting Lutheran "purity of doctrine" to such as might be won, and to testifying boldly against what the author believed to be unbiblical doctrine ("the Christianity of pious sentiments and subjective religious experiences"). Dr. Sasse's lucid, yet positive statement of Lutheran truth will remain, most assuredly, as an immortal witness to the scripturalness of Luther's great teachings.

Another prominent exponent of Lutheranism in this period was Werner Elert, who in his monumental work *Morphologie des Luthertums. Erster Band: Theologie und Weltanschauung des Luthertums, hauptsaechlich im 16. und 17. Jahrhundert; zweiter Band: Soziallehren und Sozialwirkungen des Luthertums (C. H. Becklsche Verlagsbuchhandlung, Muenchen,* 1931 und 1932) [Footnote 2) The Morphology of Lutheranism. The theology and World View of Lutheranism especially in the 16. and 17. Century; Social Doctrines and Social Actions of Lutheranism] demonstrated with overwhelming clearness and forcefulness that Luther, both in his doctrines and in his ethical tenets, had presented to the world that scriptural truth which alone could save the German churches in this period of almost universal doubt and despair. Elert's book, too, was not written merely for his age, but is a work of lasting value, one of the outstanding testimonies that will outlast its age and generation.

Another powerful witness to Christian doctrine, in its Lutheran presentation, was Adolf Koeberle, in his *Rechtfertigung und Heiligung* [Footnote 3) *The Quest For Holiness. A Biblical, Historical, and Systematic , Investigation.* By the Rev. Adolf Koeberle, D. D., professor at the University of Basel. Translated from the Third German Edition by the Rev. John C. Mattes, D. D.; Harper & Brothers, 1936]. The real subject of this book is the relation of justification to sanctification, and vice versa. This subject matter is presented under the following heads : Man's Attempt to Sanctify Himself in God's Sight; God's Judgment on Man's Self-sanctification; Man's Justification Before God Through the Word of Forgiveness. Sanctification as the Work of God in the Life of the Justified Sinner; Sanctification as the Answer of the Justified Sinner; The Significance of Sanctification in the Preservation or Loss of the State of Faith; The Relation of Justification and Sanctification. While Koeberle here speaks as a "conservative Lutheran," he does not always represent the true viewpoint of confessional Lutheranism. Nevertheless, the book, written with great charm and rare, deep insight into the essence of the Lutheran *articulus omnium fundamentalissimus (sola fide),* is an eminent witness to the lucidity with which men during this period interpreted to their age the meaning of the central truth of the Reformation.

It is impossible, of course, in this brief overview to mention the large number of learned and pious theologians, who offered to believing German church groups the Gospel of Christ with constant relation to the Reformation. The few to which we refer here are only representative of the many who confessed anew the ancient positive truth. Though not entirely in agreement with Luther, Dr.

Ernst Sommerlath in his short, but nevertheless profound study *Der Sinn des Abendmahls nach Luthers Gedanken ueber das Abendmahl*, 1527-29 [Footnote 4) Verlag von Doerffling & Franke, Leipzig, 1930, points out the fundamental difference between Lutheranism and Calvinism on the Lord's Supper. Dr. Paul Althaus, in his *Theologische Aufsaetze*, again concentrated his attention on the central doctrines of Luther's Reformation, especially the *sola fide*, as also the doctrine of justification in its application to ethical problems. [Footnote 5) Theologische Aufsaetze. Von D. Paul Althaus, Erlangen. Erster Band, 1929; Zweiter Band, 1935. Verlag von C. Bertelsman, Guetersloh.] To the same group belongs also K. Holl, who, though not correctly interpreting Luther's doctrine of justification [Footnote 6) "Das *propter Christum*, in dem die Ortho-doxie Gottes Heiligkeit und Wahrhaftigkeit gewahrt sieht, reicht im Ernste nicht aus. Gott betrachtet den Suender, als ob er ein Gerechter waere, nur weil es ihm beliebt, ihn in Christus zu sehen." Cf. Paul Althaus, Theologische Aufsaetze II, S. 33; so also Zur Verstaendigung ueber Luthers Rechtfertigungslehre, Neue kirchliche Zeitschrift 34, S. 165 ff.; also Die Rechtfertigungslehre im Licht der Geschichte des Protestantismus. 2. Aufl. abgedruckt in: Gesammelte Aufsaetze zur Kirchengeschichte. III. 1928. S. 525 ff.], nevertheless was among those who called attention to Luther's central teaching of the Reformation. Nor was the witness of this confessional group in vain. Hundreds of students were attracted to the lectures of these serious men, who were not afraid to discuss again the old positive truths (though not always in their full purity), even though humanists might accuse them of Biblicism. Men like Karl Heim (*Leidfaden der Dogmatik; Glaube und Denken; Zeit und Ewigkeit, die Hauptfrage der heutigen Eschatologie*), Karl Stange (*Christentum und moderne Weltanschauung; das Ende aller Dinge*), Adolf Schlatter (*Theologie des Neuen Testaments; das christliche Dogma*), Robert Jelke (*Religionsphilosophie; die Grunddogmen des Christentums*) found ready and grateful hearers and readers. Later, their voices were drowned in the tumult and din of war, and some joined the differing groups of German Christians (*Deutsche Christen*) who endeavored to combine the old faith with the radical, pagan religious principles of extreme National Socialism; but a strong confessional minority remained firm and suffered captivity and privation (also outside Germany) rather than deny what they regarded as their right and the truth. Here are indeed glorious chapters in the modern book of church history, great also in view of the fact that a man like Dr. Albert Schweitzer, noted critical theologian and Bach student, exchanged theology and endured the privations of Lambarene, French Equatorial Africa, as a medical missionary to right the wrongs done to the Negroes by the Caucasian race.

THE BARTHIAN MOVEMENT

The Barthian movement in Germany became so vocal that the confessional group has not always received due credit for its part in combating religious humanism. Barthianism [Footnote 7) Karl Barth; Emil Brunner, Rudolf Bultmann, Friedrich Gogarten; A. Keller; "Dialectic Theology," "Theology of Crisis," "Theology of the Word of God"] certainly was not confessional theology in the orthodox Lutheran or Calvinistic sense, though Barth's constant admonition, especially at the beginning of his theological career [Footnote 8) Pastor in Safenwil, Canton Aargau, Switzerland; professor of Reformed theology at the University of Goettingen; at the University of Muenster; at the University of Bonn, and now at Basel, Switzerland, expelled from Germany by the Hitler government which he opposed], was : Back to Luther ! Back to Calvin ! Neither Karl Barth nor his associates, however, returned to Luther and Calvin in acknowledging the *sola Scriptura* and the *sola gratia,* as these fundamentals were acknowledged by the Reformation. Barth intermingled Law and Gospel in a sense foreign to orthodox Christianity. His theology has been called a "theology of crisis," and this in the sense that man stands at the bar of divine justice, hearing God's verdict or judgment (crisis), and though hearing the condemning judgment of the sovereign, unknown God, he nevertheless ventures to confide in this condemning, unknown Unknowable. Here truly there is only Law, not Gospel, though the two are strangely intermingled, the Law being made a Gospel. Barth indeed spoke of faith, but to him faith was a leap into the unknown, and not, as orthodox Christianity has always taught, confiding trust in the Gospel promises of God's grace in Christ Jesus. Again, Barth's theology has been called "dialectic theology," which means a theology of paradoxes, of contradictions, a theology in which there is no objective truth, no dogmatic objectivity, but only intercourse between God and man, inasmuch as God addresses man in a subjective, immediate way and man reacts upon this divine address by an act of faith. Lastly, Barth's theology has been called a "theology of the Word of God;" but to Barth the Word of God is not the objective Word of Scripture (he welcomes destructive higher criticism and denies verbal and plenary inspiration), but merely the immediate address of God, the "word" which lies behind the written Word of Scripture and which is practically no more than what the individual believer recognizes as a revelation. Barth thus, though opposing the experientialism of Schleiermacher and all the experimentalists that followed him way down to Harnack and popular religious liberalism, was forced back, by his very rationalism, upon the empirical method as the source of man's assurance of salvation. Barth's theology was ultimately a strange blend of humanism, rationalism, enthusiasm, and mysticism, though in his *Dogmatik* he has become more moderate in his expressions and more conservative in his religious estimates. Barth's mystic enthusiasm is clearly noticeable especially in his doctrine of the reconciliation, for in the incarnation God (he says) took man's place and sinful man thereby took God's place, which exchange of God and man is our justification and sanctification. [Footnote 9) Cf. *Die kirchliche Dogmatik*. Die Lehre vom Wort Gottes. Prolegomena zur kirchlichen Dogmatik. Erster Halbband. Chr. Kaiser Verlag, Muenchen, 1932. Zweiter Halbband. Verlag der Evangelischen Buchhandlung Zollikon. 1938; *Credo*. Translated by J. S. McNab. Charles Scribner's Sons, New York, 1936.]

While Barthian Theology, therefore, has not proved itself a return to orthodox Christian doctrine, it has, nevertheless, made a valuable contribution to modern theological discussion. It was directed primarily against Comparative Religion, the predominant historico-religious theology of his age, in which he saw nothing else than mere history of religion, mere philosophy of religion, mere psychology of religion [Footnote 10) Cf. Chr. E. Luthardt, *Kompendium der Dogmatik*, 13. Auflage. Voellig umgearbeitet und ergaenzt von D. Dr. Robert Jelke, p. 53 f.] Of this bare historism and psychologism Barth wanted to free contemporary theology, leading it back to acknowledgment of the sovereign God, the helplessness and sinfulness of man, and the impossibility of the sinner's being his own savior. His theological method, of course, was wrong and unscriptural; but over against the religious humanists of his day, who undeified God (finite God) and deified man (pantheism), he proclaimed the cleavage between the two by nature and the necessity of union between the two by faith.

Barth's background was essentially Reformed or Calvinistic. In some respects he followed Luther; in more respects he remained true to John Calvin. It was natural, therefore, that in Reformed circles, looking for positive theological expression along liberal lines, his influence should become tremendous. Calvinistic fundamentalism, of course, disavowed Barth; but Calvinistic liberalism hailed him as a new prophet, first in Scotland and then in America, where at Princeton Theological Seminary he has found able and willing proponents of his tenets, some leaning toward the left wing (Brunner's following) and others to the right (O. Piper). In

Theology Today this school has found a fitting organ of expression and its circle of readers has been considerable from the start. The Westminster Press (Philadelphia) has been extremely busy publishing works along liberal Barthian lines. Through Barthianism the study of Soeren Kierkegaard's mystic enthusiasm has again become popular, since Barth, especially in the beginning of his theological career, leaned heavily on the Danish philosophizing theologian, borrowing from him not only theological terms, but also some basic speculative ideas, which he used with telling effect.

THE SCANDINAVIAN RESPONSE

In Scandinavia, particularly in Sweden, the revival of interest in positive theology gave rise to a peculiar movement known as the Swedish Lundensian Theology. At the Lund University in Sweden theologians have pointed to the motif back of the development of the Christian teachings. [Footnote 11) Cf. J. L. Neve, *A History of Christian Thought;* The United Lutheran Publication House, Philadelphia, Pa., 1943; pp. 13 ff.] This motif (not the teachings themselves) of the churches and theologians (they said) must be made the special object of investigation and discussion. Prof. Gustaf Aulen (now bishop) outlined a program of investigation in his book *Den kristna gudsbilden* (1927), which was translated into German under the title *Das christliche Gottesbild in Vergangenheit und Gegenwart.* [Footnote 12) 400 pages; 1930; C. Bertelsmann in Guetersloh.] Professor Aulen's colleague and friend, Dr. Anders Nygren, professor of dogmatics at the same university, has developed this program in three volumes under the title *Agape and Eros.* [Footnote 13) Cf. Agape and Eros; published in English by the Society for Promoting Christian Knowledge in London and New York (Macmillan).] By *agape* is meant primarily God's own love, manifested in Christ, who came to seek and save that which was lost, but it includes also the love which the Holy Spirit kindles in the Christian heart in response to God's love. By *eros* is understood the "upward movement of the soul to seek the divine," a thought borrowed from Plato. In this *eros* there is nothing sensual or vulgar, but it is entirely "heavenly," inasmuch as the soul seeks to escape the fetters of sense and to find satisfaction in the eternal truth. By *agape* and *eros* the author thus discusses nature and grace as two ways of salvation, considering them as antitheses. *Agape* is God's work of grace transforming nature into His image. Lundensian theology has been praised as an attempt to return to Luther and the New Testament and as a eulogy of the *sola gratia* in opposition to the humanistic perversion of the Gospel in modern liberal Protestantism.

There is no doubt that Lundensian theology still is in a stage
of development, and it is as yet too early to pass final judgment
on it. It must also be admitted that the presentation of theology
under the aspects of *agape* and *eros* has aroused considerable interest in fundamental Gospel doctrines, so that we may truthfully
speak of a Scandinavian response to the confessional movement in
Germany, which began in connection with the first World War.
But it is obvious that there is here also, just as in Barthianism,
not a true return to the simple Gospel preaching, of the Lutheran
Reformation but a new attempt at a religious philosophy which
may have very serious results for the preaching of the *sola fide* in
its purity. Even if the Lundensians should remain true to Lutheran
theology, they have added a speculative element to theology which,
as Luther so often complains, turns the human mind from the
fundamentals of salvation to peripheral things and thus causes it
to forget the first and vital objectives of theology. Every form of
speculative reasoning in theology will ultimately end in rationalism.
God certainly has not asked us to look for *motifs*, but to preach the
Gospel. Not *Motif-Forschung*, but *Evangeliumsverkuendigung* is
the business of the Christian Church and of the Christian
theologian.

Church Group Interest in England

We shall mention this subject in passing only, since it does
not properly belong into the discussion of our subject. Nevertheless, indirectly the church group movement in England will, no
doubt, have a bearing on the question of doctrine; for here Anglicans, Presbyterians, Methodists, Eastern Orthodox Churches, outspoken modernists, and scores of other affiliations are meeting to
plan an ecumenical movement which will unite the entire Protestant
church family (if possible, also the Roman Catholic and Eastern
Orthodox groups) into one very solid and substantial church union.
The movement has been somewhat hampered by the second World
War, but it is bound to manifest itself very soon after peace has
been restored, since there are so many postwar problems to be
solved, not only in the realm of the State, but also in that of the
Church, in which Continental theologians are deeply interested.

We shall not go into detail describing the various larger con-
ventions that have been held in the interest of this projected inter-
church union. We merely wish to call attention to the fact, that
while, according to the Reformed concept, church unions need not
be cemented by unity of doctrine, some platform of doctrinal agreement is nevertheless necessary to hold together the newly organized
international church body. In the United States the Federal

Council of Churches of Christ in America has had considerable trouble in finding a common doctrinal formula by which the various church groups can be satisfactorily unionized. The formula adopted is the general confession that Jesus Christ is the divine Savior of the world. This statement can be interpreted in different ways by the various groups that subscribe to it but it must be held in theory, no matter how it is actually regarded. Now, however, groups are requesting membership in the Federal Council which are professedly non-Christian or Unitarian and which therefore will not even go as far as accepting this simple formula. What interests the student of Christian doctrine is that these modern attempts at church union necessitate a re-study of the Christian doctrine, and that is of the greatest importance. Confessional Christians will, no doubt, have ample opportunity in the future to come out with a clear-cut, far-reaching confession of the Christian faith, unless they are willing to forego their duty and privilege and tolerate conditions to which their consciences certainly cannot agree.

The Russian Soul-Search

It is, no doubt, incorrect to assume that the Eastern Orthodox Churches (especially the Russian Orthodox Church) have been altogether inactive and stagnant during the long period when they became hardly more than a tradition. In his scholarly work *Contemporary Continental Theology* W. M. Horton [Footnote 14) Harper & Brothers; 1938; cf. the chapter on The Rediscovery of Orthodox Theology] shows that A. Harnack's judgment "the Church has since been at rest" (p. 3) is too severe. In Greece, for example, there has been the "New Life Movement" (Zoe), aiming to revitalize the clergy in their ministry of preaching and teaching and the laity in their ministry of reading Scripture and manifesting their faith by its earnest application to life. In 1936 there met at Athens the Conference of Orthodox Theologians (for the first time in two hundred and fifty years) for the purpose of "clarifying the right relations of the Orthodox Church with others Communions and of settling its international controversies" (p. 4). It was largely motivated by the penetration of the "western spirit" (secularism, materialism, capitalism) and the tragic state of the Russian Orthodox Church. There was thus revealed a new life in Eastern Orthodoxy with an aggressive policy.

Certain it is that the Russian Orthodox Church suffered immensely under Bolshevism. Some of the priests remained in the Soviet Republic, while others fled abroad, preferring exile to degradation. Some of these refugees founded the Russian Orthodox Theological Institute at Paris, where "there is liberty of theological research and expression unknown under the old Holy Synod" (p. 5). Out of this strange exile there came a group of prominent leaders and writers, who in opposition to Marxian revolutionism (which they regard as antichristian), have tried to construct a philosophy of life against the background of the ancient Orthodox faith, a sort of pessimistic philosophy of suffering, yet having, too, stamina for spiritual and ecclesiastical action. The "Orthodox Action" thus pursues, in the main, three aims: (1) missionary work through lectures and writing; (2) practical charities ("aiding every miserable soul asking for aid"); and (3) brotherly communion between its members. Two prominent Russian writers have become leaders in this "Orthodox Action," the talented layman, Nicholas Berdyaev, and the gifted priest, Father Bulgakov. There are, of course, many others, for example, the monk Cassian, Kartasheff, Troitsky, Ilyin, Florovsky, Fedotoff, Zernov, Smolitch, Zander, Evdokimoff, not to speak of Khomiakoff, Solovieff, the Troubetskoys, and Pavel Florensky. [Footnote 15) Cf. People, Church and State in Modern Russia. By Paul B. Anderson; Macmillan; 1944; pp. 174 ff.]

All these writers have been largely influenced by the Russian *Leidensphilosoph* Dostoievsky, whose influence on the Barthian school has been considerable. This profound and original author was revolutionistic over against the whole set-up of Russian (and western) society; he recognized no solution of the numerous social problems in its bourgeois, idealistic, and socialistic (revolutionary) forms (Contemporary Continental Theology, p. 11). He himself found no solution for the vexing problem, yet maintained the free human spirit in all of man's errings and sufferings. But Dostoievsky was not an apostle of unbridled freedom, for (as he saw) the misuse of freedom would produce only the more disastrous results for human society. The freedom of the human spirit must be sanctified through faith or free surrender to Christ, the God-man, in which man's desire for freedom will be satisfied and human love will be raised to such heights as will, in its perfection, culminate in the kingdom of God.

Berdyaev, of course, did not follow Dostoievsky in every detail, but he made his doctrine of man's freedom and destiny [Footnote 16) Berdyaev, The Destiny of Man; Scribners, 1937] the central thought of all his teaching, the leitmotif of his religious philosophy, though he recognized that in man's history there is also the principle of transfiguring grace, besides those of necessity and freedom. "The motion of human history toward God and eternity is a response to an eternal motion of God toward man; in Christ, the two motions merge, and the divine love for man finds its perfect response in 'freely given' love for God" (Contemporary Continental Theology, p. 16). There is found in Berdyaev's writings also a mystic, if not downright theosophic (pantheistic) note, and with all his emphasis on man's "free creativity" a proper stress on man's passivity over against God. "Man's self-affirmation leads to his perdition; the free play of human forces unconnected with any higher aim brings about the exhaustion of man's creative powers" (ibid., p. 19). Horton is much attracted by Berdyaev's religious philosophy, which he regards as "liberal" and much to the liking of western liberal thinkers. In criticism of Berdyaev's religious philosophy it may be said that a simple acceptance and interpretation of Scripture, as also of the ecumenical church creeds, which the Eastern Orthodox Church approves, would solve the problem of man's destiny much better than any human philosophy could do, which views the human problems only from narrow angles and forces into a preconceived system irreconcilable antitheses. As a matter of fact, the human being, just as human history, is hopelessly complex and contradictory, and it remains by God's dispensation our limitation that we "now see through a glass darkly" and "know in part" (1 Cor. 13 : 12). For all who accept this stubborn fact the solution of human problems, as given in Scripture, will suffice, and they will draw from its comfort and encouragement that sturdy faith which will give them the victory over the world with its bundles of distressing problems.

In the writings of Bulgakov his Orthodox theological background becomes ever obvious. There are many things which Berdyaev and Bulgakov have in common; but the differences are equally great. Bulgakov's religious philosophy centers in the two principles of *sophia* and *sobornost, sophia* standing for God's image in man, or "divine energy", or "divine wisdom", and *sobornost,* for man's (the Church's) "ecumenicity" or "conciliarity" (Cf. Contemporary Continental Theology, p. 37 f.). Man is thus intimately joined with God into a oneness of being (*sophia*) and at the same time also with his fellow-men (*sobernost*), in which unity his destiny and suffering as also human dignity and victory find their ultimate explanation. As in Berdyaev, so also in Bulgakov there is strain of pantheistic mysticism, which goes so far as to approve the apotheosis of "Our Blessed Lady" and the transfiguration of the Church, the "Bride of Christ", through which the "social order and the whole cosmic order are destined to be creatively transformed" (Ibid., p. 35). Orthodox religious philosophy may perhaps stimulate the study of Christian doctrine, but certainly it is not Christian doctrine in the traditional sense of the term.

Three Trends in America

The great religious movements in Europe could not do otherwise than greatly influence religious thought in America. We may divide the results of their impact upon American Theology into three distinct trends: (a) Modernism's revolt against positive truth; (b) an awakening of Neo-Thomism; (c) a Neo-orthodox half-way challenge. Each is worthy of careful study since each, no doubt, will greatly influence religious thinking in the United States.

The Revolt of Modernism Against Positive Truth

When John Horsch published the first edition of his revealing book *Modern Religious Liberalism*, modernism was in full swing in America and had the right of way everywhere, in theological schools, liberal pulpits, and "progressive" periodicals. But modernism as a revolt against positive truth destroyed itself by its very destruction of the idea of knowable positive truth. It became agnostic and finally atheistic (cf. the splendid analysis of John Horsch and his documented evidence). Modernism, however, is nothing else than the "spirit of denial and of opposition to God," deeply ingrained in the Old Adam, and so it persists despite the fact that it has no foundation upon which to rest its vague and hollow categories. [Footnote 17) Cf. the writer's article The *Sola Scriptura* and Its Modern Antithesis; Concordia Theological Monthly, Concordia Publishing House, St. Louis 18, Mo., Vol. XVI, No. 1; January, 1945]. Modernism may duck for a while until the storm is over; but while it ducks, it digs in. Works, like *The Eternal Gospel*, by Rufus Jones; *Theology in Transition*, by W. M. Horton; *What is Christianity?* by C. C. Morrison, and scores of others, still read avidly by hundreds who find scriptural truth indigestible, are basically modernistic, agnostic, and atheistic. We find in them shifts of thought, but no lessening of the enmity of the carnal mind against God, in particular, against the Gospel of the crucified Christ.

But the revolt of modernism against positive truth has not been without a blessing for the religious population of America. We cherish what we may lose; and upon the rubble, which modernism has left in the destroyed church areas, Reformed Fundamentalism and Lutheran Biblical truth have constructed new and greater spiritual edifices to the glory of God. Never has the sale of the Bible been greater than it is today, which proves that, when deceived by church leaders, the common man will take God's Book for his standard and rest his case upon the inspired truth therein set forth. Nor have there ever been so great and ardently supported radio hook-ups as there are today, with millions of hearers, forsaking the dead and comfortless modernistic churches and listening day by day, Sunday after Sunday to the fundamentals of Christian doctrine. Modernism has deceived man, but it has moved many also to forsake its barren desert and to seek comfort in the rich pastures of the Gospel of Christ. The preaching of the glad tidings of salvation by grace through faith in Christ has never been as welcome in the United States as it is now, when thousands of persons are looking for positive truth and certainty of salvation.

THE AWAKENING OF NEO-THOMISM

The Roman Catholic Church welcomes the spiritual destruction which atheistic modernism has caused in our country, and its program of Neo-Thomism offers to the spiritually hungry intelligentsia an opportunity for a supposed feast of good things for the soul. The movement began in Europe when pagan National Socialism (Rosenberg, Hauer, and associates) forced itself on the religious masses of Central Europe. Then Catholicism "returned from exile" (Peter Wust; Contemporary Continental Theology, p. 42) and through great and profound Catholic writers like Maritain, Gilson, Rousselot, Marechal, writing in French, and through Przywara, Wust, Carl Schmitt, Theodor Haecker, and others, writing in German (cf. also Hilaire Belloc and G. K. Chesterton, in England, and Irving Babbitt and Paul Elmer More, in America) set up a mighty defense of orthodox Romanism (Thomism), which pagan National Socialism was unable to check. These writers went back to Thomas Aquinas and applied his basic philosophical principles (reason and revelation in salutary cooperation) to present-day religious conditions, thus setting up a new regulative for religious thinking, which is becoming ever more popular in areas where Roman Catholic forms of thought find recognition. Neo-Thomism, however, is not Christian doctrine; for it rests not on Scripture, but fundamentally upon human speculation as set forth and defended by Thomas Aquinas and other scholastics, though what they wrote was written against the background of traditional theology. Neo-Thomism sees in Thomistic philosophy the real solution of man's spiritual problems, and through Thomistic philosophy directs men to the Roman Catholic Church, which never changes its tenets, but forever remains the same in doctrine and able to solve all human problems. It tolerates no anthropocentric humanism and no secularization of human nature. Philosophy (just as science, the arts, etc.) is not an end in itself, but merely a means to the end, leading men into the "Church", which offers peace and satisfaction, direction and guidance to all who appeal to her for aid. Neo-Thomism, therefore only desires to be a servant of the Church and merely interprets its doctrines in terms to which thinking men will listen. Ultimately, it offers to unify man's spiritual and intellectual needs and concerns and so to safeguard human thinking and striving by centering them in God, the author of all temporal and spiritual blessings. If Maritain speaks of an "integral humanism" he has this goal in mind. Neo-Thomism is acceptable to thinking religious persons, in the main, for two reasons: it offers to root them in revelation (the Church dogma), and at the same time it satisfies human reason by providing for it a proper place in religious thought, stating that reason and revelation are not in contradiction, but that the soul, guided by the Church, can comprehend God by inward meditation. With these claims (the unification of man's spiritual and intellectual interests in God; its foundation on divine revelation, which alone is able to direct the individual and human society; its recognition of human reason (Pelagianism) as mediating divine knowledge and understanding) it satisfies many moderns who find themselves lost in the maze of materialistic humanism. [Footnote 18) Cf. E. E. Aubrey, Present Day Theological Tendencies, Harper & Brothers, 1936; W. H. Horton, Contemporary Continental Theology; Jacques Maritain; Three Reformers, Scribners, 1929; The Angelic Doctor, Dial, 1931; Freedom in the Modern World, Scribners, 1936; Humanisme Integral, Paris, Aubier, 1936; Etienne Gilson, The Philosophy of Saint Thomas, Cambridge, Heffer, 1924; The Spirit of Mediaeval Philosophy, Scribners, 1936. A comprehensive bibliography, covering the entire field, is given in Horton's Contemporary Continental Theology].

THE NEO-ORTHODOX HALF-WAY CHALLENGE

Neo-Orthodoxy is Barthianism in its peculiar adaptation according to the proponent's personal orientation to the left or right of positive truth. It is inwardly related to Neo-Thomism, corresponding to it in its general recognition of church dogma, of reason as a means of understanding spiritual fundamentals, and of the unification of man's spiritual and intellectual concerns in God. While not a copy of it, it is, nevertheless, a sort of Protestant counterpart of Neo-Thomism. It challenges atheistic humanism to recognize spiritual values that lie beyond the comprehension of reason; and it challenges orthodox Christianity to recognize reason as a source and standard of faith. We may thus speak of a Neo-Orthodox half-way challenge; it professes relative orthodoxy and yet tolerates religious liberalism, just as does Barth's Crisis Theology, of which Neo-Orthodoxy is a development, though in many respects independent and original. Perhaps Reinhold Niebuhr has best given expression to its basic principles in his popular book *The Meaning of Revelation* (Macmillan, 1941) and, above all, in his still more popular work *The Nature and Destiny of Man* (2 vols., Charles Scribner's Sons, 1943). His almost violent emphasis on sin and his equally strong emphasis on the necessity of man's return to God, without, however, offering to him the Gospel means for such a return, well characterizes this Neo-Orthodox trend as religious liberalism with a quasi orthodox background. C. C. Morrison, in *The Christian Century,* champions Neo-Orthodoxy in his own special form, and in numerous periodicals an ever increasing number of prominent theologians are sponsoring this movement. But Neo-Orthdoxy is not fundamentally Christian, nor does it offer to men orthodox Christian doctrine. The voice is indeed that of orthodox Jacob, but the hands are those of liberal Esau. Christian orthodoxy and Neo-Orthodoxy can never merge. Christian orthodoxy speaks the language of faith; in Neo-Orthodoxy reason ultimately determines what shall go as truth. Reason, unable to comprehend the mysteries of faith, never bows to worship the Gospel mystery; it is always a foe of faith, though it may appear at times as an angel of light. Wherever it is accepted, there abides no *satisfactio vicaria* and no *sola fide* and no *certitudo salutis.* There is work-righteousness only, and philosophy, and endless speculation. "Ever learning, and never able to come to the knowledge of the truth" (2 Tim. 3:7).

The Christian doctrine in its modern setting! Indeed, the Christian doctrine is still in the world, for the gates of hell cannot prevail against it. It is of God and therefore imperishable, just as God is imperishable. It is His Word and so it must abide; for "it is easier for heaven and earth to pass, than one tittle of the Law to fail" (Luke 16:17). With this divine assurance in his heart, the Christian theologian, true to Scripture and to Christ, will go on and on, heralding the message of the cross without fear or favor, knowing that if he continues in the Word of Christ, he is His true disciple and he knows the truth and is free in the truth. (Cf. John 8:31, 32). If the history of the Christian doctrine has ever proved anything it is this: The speculations of men are bound to pass away, but the Word of God is in the world to stay. The well-known Lutheran motto is founded on scriptural truth: *Verbum Dei manet in aeternum.*

JOHN THEODORE MUELLER.

Concordia Seminary,
St. Louis, Mo.

CHAPTER XXXI

THEOLOGICAL DEVELOPMENTS SINCE WORLD WAR II

David P. Scaer, Th.D.

No period in the history of Christian thought has been as theologically complex and contradictory and as literarily productive as the period following World War II. The changes that occurred in these years (1945-1979) in another era would have happened over centuries. In respect to Christian thought previous centuries can be characterized by one major theme. The sixteenth was the century of the Reformation, the seventeenth the century of denominational orthodoxy and religious fervor, the eighteenth the century of Rationalism and the Enlightenment, and the nineteenth the century of the reputedly scientific quest for Jesus. Characteristic of the postwar years in the mid-twentieth century is the decline of Christianity, especially among larger churches. This time the enemy is not an external opponent like Mohammedanism in the Middle Ages or like Communism, but theological secularism spawned by the churches themselves. The church's own theologians have spread the seeds of its destruction, and a grim harvest is being reaped. In some cases these seeds bear devastating results. The church is losing its grip on the private lives of believers and its moral force in society. In other cases the church is responding with a vibrancy. Those who are committed to classical Christianity and who mourn its decline in the two decades after World War II are becoming more optimistic as the 1980s approach.

The years 1945 through 1979 will be covered under these headings: (1) neo-orthodoxy; (2) secular theology; (3) theologies in flux; (4) developments within Roman Catholicism; (5) the ecumenical movement; (6) Bultmann: his method and its influence on New Testament study; (7) the survival and revival of conservative theology; (8) English Bible translations; and (9) theology at the beginning of the 1980s.

NEO-ORTHODOXY

Karl Barth

Neo-orthodoxy originated right after World War I with

350

the publication of Karl Barth's *Commentary on Romans* (1919; English translation, 1933), but the rise of Naziism in Germany in the 1930s and the devastating global war in the early 1940s delayed the effects of neo-orthodoxy from being felt until the 1950s, especially in Britain and America. Only in the 1950s did English translations of the neo-orthodoxy theologians appear in quantity. Germany quickly rose from the defeat of World War II and with her remarkable economic recovery she also regained her prominent place not only in the intellectual world in general, but also in theology. More efficient means of travel and the high exchange rate for the American dollar made it possible for American theological students during the postwar years to sit at the feet of the German theologians. The reigning theology of those years was neo-orthodoxy. Its giants were Karl Barth, Emil Brunner, and Rudolf Bultmann. They provided the controlling direction on the theological faculties of the German universities. The effect of German theology on the English-speaking world was compounded by faster and more efficient means of translation, printing, and distribution. The quicker exchange of ideas meant that there could be no real pockets of theological isolation. The decline in the importance of denominational differences and distinctions among Christians continued. The important factor was the pace-setting theologians rather than any denominational heritage.

Neo-orthodoxy had moved into the vacuum caused by the collapse of nineteenth-century and early twentieth-century liberalism with its major tenet the fatherhood of God and brotherhood of man, and its major ethic expressed through the Social Gospel. This "minimalism" was best expressed by the Berlin theological professor, Adolf von Harnack, especially in his *What Is Christianity?* (1901). Before Albert Schweitzer earned his fame in Africa as a humanitarian, he had put together an anthology entitled *The Quest for the Historical Jesus* (1910), in which were collected essays of eighteenth- and nineteenth-century scholars whose conclusions contradicted each other. From the midst of the contradictions, Schweitzer produced only a shadow of the man Jesus sitting by the Sea of Galilee. To counteract the negative heritage of such men as von Harnack and Schweitzer, neo-orthodoxy had to rebuild a theological structure whose base had been eroded by "minimalism." The first distinguishing mark of neo-orthodoxy was that it would ignore rather than dismantle the dilapidated liberalism which it had inherited.

The publication of Karl Barth's *Commentary on Romans* (1919) inaugurated the neo-orthodoxy which remained the major theological influence into the early 1960s. Barth's commentary was less of an exegetical study than it was a vehicle for the German-speaking Swiss theologian to set forth his views. Barth's great work was his *Kirchliche Dogmatik,* which was put out in fourteen volumes (1932-1964). The English translation (*Church Dogmatics*) was put out in twenty-one volumes (1934-1969). Closely associated with Barth was another Swiss theologian, Emil Brunner of Zurich, whose *The Mediator* (1927; English translation, 1947) helped to popularize neo-orthodoxy. Both Barth and Brunner explicitly repudiated the experience-centered theology of the nineteenth century, and especially its founder Friedrich Schleiermacher. Brunner had even written his dissertation *Der Mystik und das Wort* (1924) as a refutation of Schleiermacher. Barth expressed a similar repudiation of Schleiermacher in his *Word of God and Word of Man* (English translation, 1957). Nineteenth-century liberal theology was under attack at its very roots, as is evident in Barth's *Protestant Theology in the Nineteenth Century* (1947; English translation, 1973).

Neo-orthodoxy, as the name implies, was the revival of the classically formulated theology associated with the sixteenth- and seventeenth-century Protestant orthodoxy of the European Reformation, but without clear and explicit repudiation of those historical methods of biblical research which originated in the eighteenth century and developed in the nineteenth. The neo-orthodox theologians were plainly discontent with the minimal results which had been produced and rejected Schleiermacher's concept that saw Christian consciousness as the source of religion. Such subjectivism could never serve as the basis of Christianity. Something more objective would have to be established as the basis of religion. Among unacceptable ideas in the older liberalism which were targeted for theological extinction were: (1) Jesus was only a man; (2) His death has only moral significance for men instead of being an actual atonement for sins; (3) His miracles, especially His resurrection, can be explained away; and (4) sin is a correctable defect in man.

Viewed from the perspective of the historical faith of Christianity, neo-orthodoxy's goals can be regarded in only a positive light. But it is here that neo-orthodoxy is of all the theological options the most deceptive. Neo-orthodoxy is not simply orthodoxy. It did indeed attempt to revitalize older theological concepts which had been discarded by nineteenth-century liberalism, but without any commitment to that understanding of the Bible which in previous generations had generated those views. The results of liberalism were repudiated but the methods were not. The substance of an older conservative theology was revived, but its approach which equated the Bible with God's Word was not. Barth's *Church Dogmatics* may be regarded as the most massive and serious theological production by one single man in the twentieth century. His dogmatics read with the same type of theological seriousness that marked the classical Protestant theologians of the Lutheran and Reformed traditions. In fact Barth not only was acquainted with them but incorporated them into his general theological discussion. Barth treats the pertinent biblical data with reverence and seriousness; he does not engage in the destructive textual criticism so typical of theological liberalism. It is here that Barth's method is deceptive. It ignores but does not repudiate the methods and results of those who adopted a critical position concerning the Bible.

Essential to Barth's position is his understanding of the Bible as the "Word of God." This understanding of the "Word of God" is hardly that of classical Protestantism with its interpretation of biblical inspiration. In his view all of theology is totally dependent upon a revelation from God; it does not depend upon nature (the view of the Enlightenment) or upon the human consciousness (the view of Schleiermacher and liberalism). Barth attempted to attach to his "Word of God" theology an objectivity which was rejected by the totally subjective approach of the older liberalism. But the objectivity which Barth so desperately desired, he denied by making the "Word of God" dependent on God's encounter with man. The encounter was the existential moment in which God's revelation became real or took place for each individual. Revelation was regarded always as a present event or happening rather than a past occurrence in history. The Bible's value was seen not as a historically revealed record of the past, but as occasion for revelation to the individual believer. The thorny historical problems raised by the nineteenth-century theologians were ignored. The key to the revelation was the encounter. The German word *Begegnung* was carefully chosen by Barth. "Encounter" means a meeting between two persons. Because of the popularity of neo-orthodoxy, *Begegnung* was adopted into the English theological vocabulary. Within the context of the encounter or *Begegnung* the Bible can *become* the "Word of God." Revelation is personal in the sense that the *Begegnung* happens between two persons and not between a person and a thing. Rejected as static was any permanent equation between the Bible and the Word of God. Barth would strongly affirm the priority of the divine in the encounter with the human, but without the human participant in the act of revelation he considered no word in and of itself to be revelation or the "Word of God." Barth had constructed his "Word of God" theology around the philosophy of Sören Kierkegaard, the father of modern existentialism. Kierkegaard's existentialism incorporated in Barth's idea of the encounter was as subjective as was the liberalism which Barth explicitly rejected.

Emil Brunner

Emil Brunner also developed neo-orthodoxy but was overshadowed by the more prolific Barth. Brunner opposed Barth's rejection of all natural theology. He was also willing to tie down Christ's atonement to the actual historical event of crucifixion. A not always friendly controversy was waged between the two Swiss theologians with Brunner defending nature as a source of theology and Barth denying it. Of the two, Barth has been the more influential and his views are still debated. The internal contradiction implicit in Barth's earlier theological views became explicit in his last years. He wanted to be understood as belonging to the Reformed tradition of John Calvin, but his endorsement of universalism makes this dubious. By combining his concept of grace and sovereignty with a Christomonistic view of revelation he concluded that all men are elected in Christ—universalism with a Calvinistic tinge. His original emphasis on the sovereignty of grace allowed him at first to accept infant baptism, which he later rejected because of his subjective understanding of revelation as an encounter involving both human and divine. He never wrote a volume on eschatology, which might have more clearly revealed his views as universalistic. The tenets of liberalism—with its emphasis on universal revelation and salvation—which were so repugnant to Barth, in the end became his own legacy to theology.

Rudolf Bultmann

Influential more as a New Testament scholar than as a proponent of neo-orthodoxy was Rudolf Bultmann. His contributions to exegetical research and methods will be discussed later. As a New Testament scholar he belongs to the nineteenth century, but as a theologian he belongs to the school of neo-orthodoxy. With Barth and Brunner he attempted to revive classical theological views. Bultmann could separate his exegetical studies and their results from his construction of theology. Ignoring his own negative exegetical conclusions, he like Barth could view the New Testament as God's revelation to man within his own existential situation. Within the context of the scriptural revelation God encounters man and makes a claim upon him. Bultmann is dependent for his expression of existentialism upon the philosopher Martin Heidegger, with whom he was associated at the University of Marburg from 1922 to 1928. He agrees with Barth in holding that outside of the encounter there is no real or authentic revelation or knowledge about God. Talking about God means talking about self. With Bultmann *theology* has in fact become *anthropology*. Preaching reaches its goal in a personal existential release from one's own predicament. Characteristic of Bultmann's theology is the view that this existential release from sins is in no way attached to or dependent upon any type of intellectual commitment to the factual history or accuracy of the life of Jesus as portrayed in the Gospels. His *Jesus and the Word* (1926) takes a virtually agnostic approach with regard to determining any real history about Jesus. The search for true self-authenticity within the Bible is not dependent on affirming the Bible's historical truthfulness. Bultmann's theology was as anthropocentric as was Schleiermacher's concept of Christian consciousness. As will be shown later, he reduced the nearly absolute "minimalism" of nineteenth-century exe-

getical research even further. He was really a product of that
century and more its child than he was willing to acknowledge.

Paul Tillich

Neo-orthodoxy had its representative in the United States
in the German-born theologian and philosopher Paul Tillich.
From 1933 to his death in 1965 he made his mark at such
prestigious American institutions as Union Theological Seminary, Harvard Seminary, and the University of Chicago. He
wrote his three-volume *Systematic Theology* (1951, 1957,
1963) in English, but he belongs to the German theological
movement of neo-orthodoxy. Like Barth, Brunner, and Bultmann, he was concerned about providing theology with a more
objective basis than had been left by the legacy of the older
liberalism. For Tillich revelation was seen as coming to man
in the form of "revelatory constellations." He spoke of the
transcendental as did Barth, but placed it within the human
situation. The transcendental is immanent. All things and
persons possess a potential for revelation, but certain groupings
are more conducive to bringing about actual revelation. Tillich's views understandably brought against him the not in-
frequent or unmerited accusation of pantheism or at least
panentheism, the belief that God is in all things. God was seen
not as a personal Being, but as ultimate reality; the way to Him
is man's "ultimate concern." This viewpoint might better be
described as "potentialism-panentheism": God *could* be revealed in all things.

Tillich attempted a marriage between philosophy and theology, the former asking the questions and the latter providing
the answers. He put it like this: "The questions of human
existence are answered by divine revelation." On the surface
this was an improvement over the older liberal theology in
which the situation provided both the questions and the
answers. But this seemingly positive contribution was negated
by locating the transcendental element within the structure
of immanence. God is symbolized for each man in that which
concerns him ultimately; but no single symbol, not even Jesus,
can exhaust the divine revelation, be the unique revelation, or
be identified with it. Branded as idolatrous would be any
identification between God and a manifestation of Him. This
principle would also forbid making any identification between

God and Jesus. God is not autonomous, but He Himself is Being. The uniqueness of Jesus lay in the way He incorporated Himself within this Being. Tillich's concept of a universal kind of incarnation is clearly dependent on Oriental thought. Like the others involved with neo-orthodoxy he adopted the very subjectivity which he wanted to repudiate, but in his case the subjectivity was more blatant. He was unwilling to place God above the world or to identify Him with any object or person in the world; nevertheless, in his view God is virtually entrapped in His own creation. No similarities between Tillich's theology and classical Christianity, especially the doctrines of God, incarnation, and atonement, remain. Tillich more than any of the other theologians we have discussed could speak favorably of Schleiermacher's contributions. It seems as if this was more than mere historical admiration and adulation; it may in fact have been real dependency.

Neo-orthodox theology was filtered down for the more pragmatic English mind in the mercifully (but perhaps forgivably) brief paperback *The Idea of Revelation in Recent Thought* (1956, 1964) by Scottish theologian John Baillie. Through this man neo-orthodoxy won converts in Great Britain and the United States and became the rage in most major theological schools.

Neo-orthodoxy, with its revival of classical theology and its attempt to understand the Bible as the "Word of God" (though this concept is given a special definition), had many side benefits. The eight mammoth volumes of *Theologische Wörterbuch zum Neuen Testament,* edited by Gerhard Kittel and generally designated simply by his last name, appeared from 1933 to 1969. By 1974 these volumes appeared in English, translated and edited by Geoffrey W. Bromiley. Each major New Testament word was traced from its etymological origins in the Greek language, and its use and meaning in the Old Testament (Septuagint), rabbinical literature, and the various sections of the New Testament were thoroughly reviewed. This was possible because neo-orthodoxy, unlike the liberalism of the previous century, appreciated the Bible for its theological value. A similar work for the Old Testament was published in German, edited by G. Botterwick and Helmer Ringen (1970-1972). It began to appear in English translation in 1974.

An appreciation of the classical Protestant theologians of the

Reformation and post-Reformation eras was another side benefit of neo-orthodoxy. Barth had set the tone in becoming theologically versed in the Reformation and post-Reformation writings which were appreciated for their historical value but received little real theological attention. A renaissance of Luther studies centered around such men as Werner Elert, Paul Althaus, Gustaf Wingren, Hermann Sasse, Edmund Schlinck, and Peter Brunner. A congress on Luther research began meeting at regular intervals. In the United States a fifty-four volume set of *Luther's Works* appeared in English, a gigantic scholarly activity. Neo-orthodoxy served as the key to opening up the older treasures of Protestantism. This was not unlike the repristination theological movement of the 1830s which had been inaugurated by Schleiermacher's appreciation for the expression of Christian consciousness in the classical Protestant confessional documents which had lain forgotten in the wake of the Enlightenment.

Secular Theology

Neo-orthodoxy was never permitted to come into full bloom before it was enveloped by secular theology in the 1960s. For theology these years were the most innovative in the revolutionary period after World War II and perhaps the most sensational since the Enlightenment itself. The first years of the decade of the 1960s are called the period of *secular theology* because theological study at that time was marked with a secularism which removed God as a viable option. Perhaps the secular theology attracted more attention than it merited; nevertheless, the nadir point to which it plunged was destined to become a turning point for theology.

The stage for secular theology had been set by Paul Tillich, who seriously questioned the existence of a God separate and distinct from the created universe. Tillich had made an equation between God and Being; the secular theologians dismantled the equation by removing "God." All that remained was existence, which no longer was equated with God. The third and final volume of Tillich's *Systematic Theology* appeared in 1963. By his death in 1965, the radical secular theology was reaching maturity.

John A. T. Robinson

The clarion for the movement was sounded by a Cambridge don, John A. T. Robinson, who was serving as bishop of Woolwich, when his shattering *Honest to God* was published in 1963. A sound theological contribution it was not, but it caught the headlines on both sides of the Atlantic. It popularized neo-orthodox thought for the people, having come to conclusions which remained only implicit in Tillich and Bultmann. Soon the battle broke out and the press, especially in Great Britain, carried it regularly on its pages. It is debatable how much of Robinson's thought was comprehended. But he did take full advantage of the situation.

Following the cue from Bultmann, Robinson saw the Bible as teaching a three-story universe, a view which he regarded as scientifically untenable for modern man. Without a heaven for God's habitation, a new home within human existence had to be found for God. Here the bishop relied heavily on Tillich's theology of immanence. God as ultimate reality could be reached through ultimate concern. Christology was reduced to understanding Jesus as the symbol of humanity. Sanctification was reduced to an ethic determined by the situation without any outside imposition of a divinely ordained code. Supernatural religion was dead. Secular theology had arrived. Robinson commented that his views were not sufficiently radical and would soon be regarded as conservative. He was right.

Thomas J. J. Altizer, Paul M. Van Buren, William Hamilton, Gabriel Vahanian

As sensational as the bishop's theology was, it did not last long; it was superseded by four theologians who bluntly and boldly proclaimed the death of God—Thomas J. J. Altizer, William Hamilton, Gabriel Vahanian, and Paul Van Buren. Their theological conclusions were stated in such radical terms that, though they were more sensational than substantive, they made an impression that could not be ignored. The "God is dead" slogan popularized by Altizer originally came from the nineteenth-century German philosopher Friedrich Nietzsche's *Thus Spake Zarathustra*. A spate of books appeared in the 1960s proclaiming in one form or another the divine demise: Gabriel Vahanian, *The Death of God* (1961); Paul M. Van Buren, *The Secular Meaning of the Gospel* (1963); Thomas J. J.

Altizer, *The Gospel of Christian Atheism* (1966); Altizer and William Hamilton, *Radical Theology and the Death of God* (1966). Though they all operated under the umbrella of the same slogan, the sloganeers had progressed to the one destination along different paths. Altizer saw the incarnation as the beginning of God's commitment to His own death, which finally takes place in the crucifixion. For his thought he was dependent on Tillich's stress that the transcendental looses itself in immanence. In this we see the influence of Oriental thought and ultimate dependence on Schleiermacher. Though God died, Jesus can still have redemptive influence in the world. Hamilton sees God's death as a gradual occurrence within the last centuries of Western culture. Vahanian's view is similar to that of Altizer, but he takes a more radical step in seeing absolutely no use for Jesus in theology. Van Buren, working from the base of analytical philosophy, finds the statement "God exists" to be a meaningless tautology.

Harvey Cox

A practical expression of secular theology was made by Harvey Cox in his *Secular City* (1965). For him God is removed from the sphere of the transcendental and placed within political and technological realms. The sacred had to be metamorphosed through the secular into the profane. Cox had given us hardly more than a popularized version of Tillich's thought by localizing God within the corners of the industrialized society. The effects of practical secularism on theology were immeasurable. Ministry was no longer viewed primarily as preaching the message of redemption to lost human beings, but as involvement in society and community. The boundary lines between church and society were removed.

Joseph Fletcher

Joseph Fletcher provided the ethical program (which really amounts to a lack of an ethical program) for the secular theology. His *Situation Ethics* (1966) made the Episcopal clergyman an overnight sensation. The book's subtitle *The New Morality* became a cliché adopted even by those who had no commitment to Christianity and little understanding of it. According to Fletcher, ethical decisions were made not in accordance with a divine code superimposed from the outside, but were made on the basis of particular needs and circumstances in the lives of particular individuals. There were no moral absolutes. Under certain circumstances lying, murder, stealing, and premarital sex could be legitimate. The last item caught the public's eye and imagination.

By the 1970s the sensation of the secular theology had evaporated. It left as quickly as it came. It can be debated whether it really had any effect on contemporary culture or whether it was in fact only a child of its culture. Its proponents will not be the theological leaders of the 1980s; their books are no longer best-sellers. The message of the "God is dead" theology is no longer shocking. Perhaps the theological world has moved to another plateau, a more conservative and traditional level. It might be more accurate to assume that the theological world has become accustomed to the message of secular theology and the shock factor has been lost. *Honest to God* and *Situation Ethics* were best-sellers probably for no other reason than that their message released people from responsibility to a personal God and His revealed will for their lives. At the end of the 1970s many thinkers regard Western culture as standing in a moral abyss. Francis Schaeffer and Malcolm Muggeridge interpret this as a real collapse of the Western world. The moral decline might have happened without the secular theology, but the secular theology must always bear the burden of having endorsed it. In the Western world religion has always played a prophetic role over against culture, society, and government. By endorsing the culture and identifying with society, secular theology abdicated this role. Therefore, it can no longer be identifiable as theology. It is theology without purpose.

Since the Age of the Enlightenment theology has moved without major obstruction and predictably to the conclusion of the "God is Dead" theologians. These theologians themselves trace their thought back two hundred years. A requisite of theological respectability is heritage and lineage. The conclusions of the "God is dead" theologians are regarded as the logical results of their theological predecessors. Some see this theology as the legitimate heir of fifteenth-century Renaissance humanism, a world view which put man into the place of God. The Enlightenment removed the boundary line between the natural and the supernatural. Then Schleiermacher ignored

the transcendental, seeing human consciousness and its deriva-
tives within the community as the only realities. This theology
of immanence reigned through the nineteenth century and into
the twentieth with only a slight but unsuccessful and deceptive
reprieve offered by neo-orthodoxy. While the neo-orthodox
theologians thought they had safeguarded God's existence in
their particular theology of the "Word," the theological world
moved past them to the ultimate conclusion that God no longer
exists. Theology which even entertains the thought of divine
demise, let alone proclaims it, is self-defeating, because theology
means the study of God. The "God is dead" saga is not a large
or the last chapter in the history of Christian thought in the
twentieth century, but it is one which will not be forgotten.

THEOLOGIES IN FLUX

At the end of the 1970s four theologies which stressed movement and change in God and in the world were flourishing:
the theology of hope, the theology of history, the theology of
liberation, and process theology. The first three belonged to
the theological development that can be traced back to the
Enlightenment and Schleiermacher. The fourth was clearly
contemporary philosophy transformed into a theology.

The theologies of hope, history, and revolution were reactions against the existential and antihistorical concept of God
put forth by neo-orthodoxy. They appeared in the middle of
the 1960s when the secular theologians had proclaimed the
death of God. Secular theology taken to its logical conclusion
would have meant the end of Christianity, religion in general,
church organizations, and established clergy. The decline of
the church's influence can be traced directly to secular theology,
whose major tenets negate the divine and see only the secular
as real. Two centuries before, the Enlightenment had in fact
dechristianized Europe; left unchecked secular theology would
have accomplished similar results. The instinct for survival
and the urge for success meant that theology had to adopt a
more positive direction.

Theology of Hope—Moltmann

A significant breakthrough in theology came in the person
of the German Reformed theologian Jürgen Moltmann of
Tübingen. His *Theology of Hope* had gone through its fifth

printing by 1965; an English translation became available in 1967. The title of this book provided the name for a movement that would still be flourishing at the dawn of the 1980s. As Bultmann had incorporated the philosophy of Martin Heidegger's existentialism as a result of their association in Marburg during the 1930s, so Moltmann came under the influence of the Marxist philosopher Ernst Bloch. Their paths crossed at Tübingen after Bloch had emigrated from the German Democratic Republic. Bloch, who was indebted not only to Marx but ultimately to Hegel, held that matter is the basis of a future unpredictable development. In contrast to neo-orthodoxy with its obsession on the present encounter or existential movement, the theology of hope anticipates real answers for theology in the future. All of theology is subsumed under the general overarching category of eschatology. This also provides the key to biblical interpretation. Since the future is open-ended with no restrictions, both God and man operate with perfect freedom. All questions search for their answers in a future which never fully arrives. Moltmann, who is both the popularizer and major exponent of the theology of hope, has shown a remarkable durability in the theological world. At the end of the 1970s he continues to publish and to be in great demand as lecturer not only in Europe but also in the United States. The success of his theology must be understood as a reaction against the quietism of neo-orthodoxy and the ultimate defeatism of secular theology. He has won converts from those who were previously devotees of both these schools of thought. Ultimately the theology of hope can never be finally satisfactory. Theological questions are seriously presented but never definitely answered. A large question mark clouds every point of the horizon.

Theology of History—Pannenberg

Equal to Moltmann in theological stature is Wolfhart Pannenberg, whose theology of history was set forth in his *Jesus—God and Man,* published in German in 1964 and in English in 1968. His position is similar to Moltmann's in placing God's revelation within history. This is a clear reaction against neo-orthodoxy, especially as it was set forth by Barth, which saw revelation approaching man from a dimension outside of this world. Neo-orthodoxy wanted to be understood as truly transcendental. Moltmann and Pannenberg share a similar perspective in designating history as the place of God's revelation to man. Jesus is understood as the appearance of the God of the future. Of the contemporary theologians who do not want to be regarded as being in the heritage of classical Christianity, Pannenberg may be considered the most conservative, because he comes closest to traditional Christianity in asserting the historical character of Jesus' resurrection as the basis of the biblical witness. But it is debatable just how historical the resurrection is for him. True, he does define the resurrection as the basis of history, but the unanswered question is, "Is it real history?" Pannenberg attempts to unlock history in order to obtain a revelation of God for salvation. This approach does not permit him to distinguish universal history from salvation history or universal revelation from special revelation. The historical objectivity for which Pannenberg strives is attractive, but unleashes several problems. Since faith must ultimately and inevitably make value judgments on events within world history, true objectivity remains elusive. Pannenberg as Barth before him falls into the very subjectivism which he explicitly attempted to avoid.

Liberation Theology

Liberation theology is a further development of the theology of hope and shares the same philosophical premise. It is eminently practical in calling for and working for the overthrow of society's structures. Philosophically it is related to Marxism and in practice it is frequently indistinguishable from it. Liberation theology is very popular among the Roman Catholic clergy of South America. Much of its literature is in Spanish and Portuguese. In January of 1979, at a special conclave of Latin American bishops, hardly into his pontificate, John Paul II, in his first trip outside of Italy, gave a special warning against liberation theology and the revolutionary clerical activity which this theology has spawned.

Process Theology

Process theology resembles the theologies of hope, history, and liberation in stressing the forward-going activities of God, who necessarily and essentially is involved with the world and its history; but process theology has a different set of philosophical roots. It is built upon an ancient philosophical principle of Heraclitus (500 B.C.), who saw all of reality in a state of flux. The impossibility of stepping into the same river twice is a famous illustration of this principle. Reality is described by such words as "becoming," "process," and "evolution." Much of the philosophical material for process theology was provided by Alfred North Whitehead, who defined the essence of a thing in terms of the process which brought it to its present condition. Process thought was further developed by Charles Hartshorne and John Cobb. In process philosophy a static view of reality is replaced by a dynamic one. Whitehead was not a professing Christian, but his views were adopted into a Christian framework by Schubert Ogden and Norman Pittenger. The latter developed a process Christology which defined Christ's divinity not as the Son's sharing in a static essence of the Father, but rather as God's activity in Jesus. Process theology sees God's being as so inextricably connected with the world that the world's suffering means suffering for God. Pittenger was admittedly dependent for his views on Whitehead's disciple Hartshorne, to whom he dedicated *Process Thought and the Christian Faith* (1968). Pittenger produced writings from the early 1940s into the 1970s. Though process theology uses traditional Christian terms, everything is redefined. Incarnation becomes little more than God's immanence in the world and resurrection dissolves into the making of a contribution to the world process. Personal immortality is no longer possible.

The theologies of hope, history, and liberation developed out of German thought. They are dependent on Hegel for their philosophical substance, but attempt to set forth their position within a biblical terminology. Process theology is hardly distinguishable from process philosophy. These two systems resemble each other in recognizing development, identified as "becoming," as the basic ingredient of reality.

Developments Within Roman Catholicism

Contributing to the theological strength of Roman Catholicism was its ability to acclimate itself culturally to different situations without surrendering its basic allegiance to the medieval tradition as it was codified vis-à-vis the Protestant Reformation in the Council of Trent (1545-1563). The Tridentine answers to the Reformation served as the classical expression of the Roman Catholic faith right down into the middle of the twentieth century. Nineteenth-century declarations of papal infallibility and Mary's immaculate conception were a perpetuation of this development rather than a rupture within this tradition. Though traditional Catholicism remained the church's official position, new theologies were being developed which were related more to developments within Protestantism than to the church's tradition. The declaration by Pope Pius XII in 1950 that Mary was bodily assumed into heaven belonged to another era and would prove strangely out of step with the developments of the next thirty years. The church in the last half of the twentieth century would settle issues by negotiation and compromise at assemblies of councils instead of by infallible papal decrees. Papal infallibility was the church's officially stated position, but theology by councils was being practiced more.

Politically the Roman Catholic Church was placed into a weakened position during these years. The Bolshevik Revolution which in 1918 dethroned the Eastern Orthodox Church from its favored place in Russia did not at first alarm the Roman Catholic Church. In fact many saw here an opportunity to extend the influence of Catholicism in Eastern Europe. But by 1948 Roman Catholicism suffered a similar fate when Soviet-controlled regimes were installed in Poland, Hungary, Czechoslovakia, and elsewhere. By the end of the 1970s Communist parties were major political forces in Western Europe and in fact posed real threats in such Catholic countries as France and Italy. The governments in Portugal and Spain were threatened by active Communist parties. The bastions of Catholicism in Europe were falling. Latin American Catholicism was not immune. Cuba was controlled by a Soviet-sponsored government. The organization of the church was weakened. Many of the priests in South America had adopted revolutionary theology, an ideology which was hardly distinguishable from Marxism. The church was suffering from internal problems.

The American church was still firm in providing financial support, but it suffered steep declines in the number of the faithful going to mass, men pledging themselves for the priesthood, and men and women taking monastic vows to serve in such institutions as hospitals and schools. The situation was reaching near crisis proportions. As the Roman Catholic Church approached the end of the 1970s it was a church internally and externally under siege.

The mid-century papal decree of the assumption of Mary would be the last exercise of the principle of papal infallibility, which was always an offense to Protestants and became increasingly unacceptable in Roman Catholic circles. The Second Vatican Council, known simply now as Vatican II, meeting intermittently from 1962 to 1965, changed church direction. It will probably be considered the most important event for the Roman Church in this century. The prime mover behind the council was John XXIII, an older cardinal who was regarded at first as a caretaker successor to the austere and tradition-bound Pius XII. The winds of change had already broken loose at the beginning of the century. George Tyrrell in Ireland assailed the doctrine of papal infallibility on the grounds that it contradicted and thus prevented the natural evolutionary development of doctrine within the church. William Sullivan in the United States and Baron Friedrich von Hügel in Germany joined in this opposition without placing themselves outside the church's boundaries. By the 1940s the movement to modernization centered around such theologians as Jean Danielou, Yves Congar, Marie Dominique Chenu, Karl Rahner, and Hans Urs Balthazar. Hans Küng questioned not only papal infallibility but all forms of infallibility in his *Infallible? An Inquiry* (1971). The antipapal feelings among Roman Catholic theologians cannot be interpreted as a late resurgence of sixteenth-century Protestantism. It was rather an attempt by theologians to adjust to what they considered new cultural realities and to find within these cultural realities authentic religious expressions. Right after Vatican II the Dutch Catechism (1965) caused a sensation in making these modern views available to the people (English translation, 1966). The move to modernization included both clergy and laity.

Vatican II tried to remove barriers between Roman Catholics and Protestants, Jews, Mohammedans, and even unbelievers. Some Roman Catholic theologians are suggesting that their church recognize the Augsburg Confession, considered the first formal expression of Protestant Reformation faith. Such recognition would be a positive step but within the

Catholic understanding of the development of doctrine and dogma. The anathema against Luther has not been lifted, but it would be no surprise to many if this happened. Some are predicting the establishment of communion between the pope and the patriarch of Constantinople. Officially the Vatican is holding discussions with major Protestant groups. Unofficially Catholic priests are participating with Protestant clergy in worship and even giving communion to Protestants.

As the Roman Catholic Church began stepping over boundaries turned into walls in the sixteenth century, she was admitting to the same type of internal diversity which was obviously characteristic of denominational Protestantism since its inception. The exegetical method (demythologizing and form criticism) of Rudolf Bultmann was adopted and applied by such Roman Catholic scholars as Raymond E. Brown. The publication of a collection of essays by Catholic theologians in *Rudolf Bultmann in Catholic Thought* (1968) attests to Bultmann's growing influence. The charismatic movement crossed over from Protestantism into Catholicism with the approval of church leaders as highly placed as Cardinal Suenens of Belgium. Sometimes Catholic charismatics were indistinguishable from Protestants, but in other cases they used their new experiences to honor Mary. In South America the clergy were associating themselves with theologies of hope and revolution. The Dutch theologian Edward Schillebeeckx was critical of the doctrine of transubstantiation and offered a view that might be acceptable to Calvinism. He offered an interpretation of the Lord's Supper which showed Karl Barth's influence in emphasizing the encounter and focusing attention on the congregation as the place of Christ's real presence. It is not surprising that in the Catholic-Reformed discussions in the 1970s there could be such wide agreement.

The internal developments within Roman Catholic theology were complex and even contradictory, but the developments within the worshiping life of the people were clear. The basis of these developments was the fresh understanding of the universal priesthood of all believers, so essential to the Protestant Reformation in the sixteenth century. The mass was no longer recited in Latin but in the vernacular, and individual bishops had the liberty to offer to the laity both the bread and wine, thus correcting abuses of long standing. Protestant hymns including Luther's "A Mighty Fortress" were sung and more attention was paid to preaching. Laymen and women were assisting in the church services by reading the Scriptures and distributing the sacrament. The ancient order of deacon was revived as a separate office and not merely as a step on the way to the priesthood. Deacons could preach, but were not allowed to say mass. Most important they could marry. Today movements exist calling for the permission of priests to marry and women to be ordained as priests. On these issues the official position of the church remains the same, but this has not blunted internal protest. Tension within the church clearly surfaces in the birth-control issue. The church remains officially opposed to birth control, but the official position is largely ignored by the laity.

The changes within Roman Catholicism have been real and internally disruptive. That church is simply not the same today as it was in 1945. Forces for change and modernization have been met by forces calling for a reinstitution of a more conservative Catholicism as it was known before Vatican II. Schism over this issue remains a distinct possibility. The future of Roman Catholicism in the remaining two decades of this century will be strongly shaped by Pope John Paul II. Having not yet reached sixty years of age, he is younger than most of his predecessors were at the time of their election. He may be expected to survive until the year 2000. His emphasis on installation as bishop of Rome instead of coronation as pope may indicate continued movement in the tradition of Vatican II away from the centrality of the papacy to a decentralized government of councils. Much of the decision-making may be given to the bishops. John Paul's sharp rebuke of the Latin American clergy for their revolutionary theology, however, shows a man committed to traditional Roman Catholic theology. John XXIII was the first pope since the Reformation to be recognized by Protestant theologians in a positive light. John Paul II may also be recognized as a theological factor in his own right. The denominational diversification and stratification of Protestantism have provided a release valve for its controversies which monolithic Catholicism does not have. The disruptive struggle which Roman Catholicism experienced between authority and freedom in the 1960s and 1970s still remains fundamentally unresolved. Catholicism previously demonstrated its ability at acculturation. Now it is faced with a widespread need for internal doctrinal accommodation.

THE ECUMENICAL MOVEMENT

Without exaggeration it can be said that there was more movement and formal and informal association among denominational groupings in the years following World War II than there had been in any previous period of church history. Frequent and successful attempts were being made to mend the millennium-long breach between the Roman Catholic Church and the family of Eastern Orthodox churches. Far-reaching were the endeavors to reconstruct some type of formal church unity in western Christianity. The sixteenth century experienced the fracturing of the monolithic countenance of western Catholicism first into divisions between Roman Catholics and Protestants and then among Protestants themselves. The fracturing process was never successfully contained. The currents within the ecumenical movement have been so massive that we can give only a brief sketch of the various forms and types which it took.

The philosophy behind the modern ecumenical movement in nearly all of its forms is based on the theology of Schleiermacher, who saw religion and Christianity springing up from the consciousness of the community. In his *Faith of the Christian Church* (1830), he recognized truths as Christian not because they were revealed by divine inspiration in the Bible, but because they were associated with certain Christian communities: Lutheran, Anglican, Reformed, and so on. The concept that objective truth is revealed by the Bible as the Word of God was foreign to his thinking. Communities demonstrated that they were Christian by their expression of religiously ethical behavior; and thus all such communities, including Unitarians, contributed to a widening circle of religious truth. In such a system there were no contradictions but only aspects of the same truth. Churches no longer stood in a polemical relationship with each other, contending for the truth. Each denomination was to be appreciated for its own contribution to the whole and its reflection of the one central truth. In the ecumenical age polemics was replaced by dialogue, that is, unprejudiced exchange of theological views, in order to reach the goal of truth.

The motivations behind the ecumenical movement were contradictory. In part it was a revival of the desire to make the twentieth century the Christian century, an older liberal idea that had not prevented the two cosmic conflicts of the century; but the movement was also motivated by fear and the various churches' instinct for self-survival. Christianity, which had been the major continuous influence in the world dominated by Europe and its culture since the fourth century, was being globally challenged by Communism, Mohammedanism, mystic religions originating in the East, and downright secularism. The decline of Western Europe as politically dominant hastened the failing influence of the church. No longer was the church the undisputed world conscience, but it was quickly finding itself a minority group even within Christian countries.

The major organizational expressions of the ecumenical movement were global and national associations of churches with differing beliefs, confessions, traditions, and heritages. The World Council of Churches (WCC), formed in Amsterdam in 1948, has since its inception incorporated the wide spectrum of world Protestantism and Eastern Orthodoxy. During the early years the WCC was inclined to present a forum for serious theological discussion. In 1961, due to pressure from the family of Eastern Orthodox churches, its constitution was adjusted in a conservative and classical direction by making more explicit the references to scriptural authority and the trinitarian belief about God. This direction has since been negated by including within the membership churches whose commitment to the Bible and the doctrine of the Trinity could not even be described as formal.

Through the 1960s and 1970s the WCC has become a forum for expressing political viewpoints and taking political action. It has been severely criticized for furnishing military aid to groups fighting for liberation in Third World countries. Some claim that the organization is strongly influenced by churches in the Soviet bloc which have served as mouthpieces for Communism. By the end of the 1970s very few remained optimistic about the WCC as an effective organization for theological discussion and real ecumenical unity. While some criticized it for its radical political involvement, others saw its structure simply as another form of the establishment. Conservative Christians refused to acknowledge the WCC as a legitimate expression of the church or ignored it entirely; revolutionary liberal Christians saw its organization as just another distrusted instrument of the establishment. The failure of global organizational ecumenism was expressed by one of the founders and architects of the WCC, William Visser 't Hooft, in the revealing title of his book *Has the Ecumenical Movement a Future?* (1976). The answers to this question on a global level was represented on lower levels by national have been increasingly negative. Worldwide interdenominational ecumenical organizationalism is being increasingly ignored.

The same type of organization represented by the WCC and local councils of churches. Their programs have sometimes depended on the particular situation and on the cooperative enthusiasm of their members. Frequently these councils have represented social and political concerns to their respective governments. Since church leaders' opinions have often been at variance with the rank and file, they have lacked wide support and have not made notable contributions to the total political process. Their impact politically has been minimal and theologically nil.

During the post-World War II period there was an increased global consciousness within the denominational families. The tone for this was set by Anglican bishops who, after the first Lambeth Conference in 1867, began meeting in ten-year intervals to express their own unity and to work for a wider unity among Christians. Eastern Orthodoxy has enjoyed a type of fellowship centering around the patriarch at Constantinople. Such groups as the International Congregational Council, the Lutheran World Federation, the Baptist World Alliance, the World Convention of the Churches of Christ, the World Alliance of Reformed Churches, and the World Methodist Council have provided denominational families an opportunity to work together with coreligionists on a global level. On the national level denominations splintered into smaller groups have been merging into larger groups, for example, Methodists, Presbyterians, Baptists, and Lutherans in the United States.

Also on the national level churches with differing beliefs and backgrounds have merged into one church organization. The Church of South India, formed in 1947, was closely watched as the first church to bring together such disparate groups as the Anglicans, Baptists, and the Congregationalists. Similar unions but with slightly differing denominational mixtures took place in the United Church of Canada and in the United Church of Christ in the United States. In Germany, Lutheran, Reformed, and Union churches were brought together in the loose affiliation of the Evangelical Church of Germany. The enthusiasm for organizational unity could not be maintained in all cases. A union in Great Britain between Methodists and Anglicans was aborted shortly before the scheduled birth, as was a union between Presbyterians and Methodists in Scotland. An American denominational union involving the Protestant Episcopal Church, the United Presbyterian Church, and the United Methodist Church, known as the Consultation on Church Unity (COCU), was suggested in 1960 by Eugene Carson Blake. After meetings throughout the 1960s and 1970s it was no longer considered a viable possibility. The Leuenberg Concord, a European Protestant fellowship still without organizational expression, saw the historic Lutheran and Reformed differences on the Lord's Supper (among other issues) glossed over and ignored. Sixteenth-century differences were no longer seen as obstacles for European Protestants in the twentieth century.

The Roman Catholic Church could not remain untouched by the currents of the ecumenical movement. Vatican II (1962-1965) referred specifically to a gathering of Roman Catholic leaders, but in a wider sense it was also ecumenical. It must be viewed as part of that massive movement which was bringing Christians from all over the world together to participate in decision-making. Though the decisions of Vatican II had to be papally approved, the worldwide resources of that church were being tapped. Without the ecumenical movement among the Protestants, Vatican II would have never happened. Protestants were invited to participate in Vatican II, but of course without vote. There have been other real signs of Roman Catholic ecumenical participation besides Vatican II. The pope has personally received leading patriarchs of the Eastern Orthodox communion, the Archbishop of Canterbury, and leaders of Protestant churches and ecumenical organizations. The Catholic Church is participating in officially sponsored dialogues with Anglicans, Methodists, Reformed, Baptists, and Lutherans. To express what seemed to some to be a growing unity of faith, Catholic and Protestant theologians produced *The Common Catechism: A Book of Christian Faith* (1975).

On the local level the participation of Roman Catholics in ecumenical endeavors is obvious. Though not officially permitted, participation of Protestant and Catholic clergy in each other's worship services is clearly ignored by church authorities. Not uncommon is the invitation of Catholics to Protestants to participate in communion. Clergy of both groups join together in a wide variety of services. It is debatable whether Catholics are actually accommodating themselves to Protestants or whether this ecumenical interest is an attempt to exercise control. With such wide diversification within the Catholic Church a clear answer may not be possible. Quite definite, however, is the commitment of the Catholic Church to the ecumenical movement. As the ecumenical movement at the organizational level faces disintegration among Protestants, Catholic participation is contributing a theological vigor which some Protestants seem to have lost.

The ecumenical movement at the end of the 1970s can hardly be judged a success. Such large churches in the United States as the Southern Baptist Convention and the Lutheran Church—Missouri Synod sat on the sidelines deliberately. The Church of Norway (Lutheran) was reevaluating its membership in the WCC. A committed but not overly effective challenge came from the International Council of Christian Churches formed by Dr. Carl McIntire in the same year as was the WCC (1948) as a protest against it, especially for its religious and political liberalism. As mentioned above, the WCC has already lost most of its romance as a possible harbinger of a great future for Christianity. The Lutheran World Federation was typical of many global denominational groupings in that it bogged down in political issues and left theological ones unresolved. In 1963 at Helsinki the Lutherans could not even agree among themselves on the doctrine of justification, the very point that made Lutherans distinctive and the heart of the Protestant Reformation.

Worldwide Anglicanism was suffering a similar disintegration. It had cast itself as the bridge to effect reunion of Protestantism, Eastern Orthodoxy, and Roman Catholicism. In the 1970s the issue of the ordination of women priests was tearing at the cords that held Anglicanism together. The daughter churches in Canada and the United States had officially accepted a practice which the mother church in England could not accept. In addition the American church was facing open schism in her own ranks on the issue. The Lambeth Conference, which once chartered the course in 1886 for Christian reunion, was concerned in its 1978 meeting whether there would be sufficient unity among Anglicans to come together for another meeting in 1988. Worldwide Christian reunion was far from their minds. Roman Catholicism now all flush with ecumenical enthusiasm is also not immune to wide internal dissension. Steps to outward unity are matched by countersteps of internal dissent.

Organizational ecumenism has proven ineffective and is approaching a state of hibernation. A personal type of ecumenism survives and thrives. Personal contacts between clergy and people largely ignore the older denominational boundaries. Organizational ecumenism is floundering because of a general apathy toward organizations; at the same time denominational boundaries are transgressed because of an apathy that sees all Christian expressions as valid. Schleiermacher's philosophy of community consciousness survives in both the successes and failures of the ecumenical movement. Any decline in ecumenical enthusiasm has not meant a restoration of the Reformation faith that recognizes the Bible as the source of truth.

BULTMANN: HIS METHOD AND ITS INFLUENCE ON NEW TESTAMENT THEOLOGY

Bultmann's Method

Rudolf Bultmann operated within the spheres of systematic and New Testament theologies. Like Barth and Brunner he was strongly influenced by existential philosophy, and together these three theologians were the major figures in the formation of neo-orthodoxy. Barth was the giant figure in neo-orthodoxy. His disregard for history (perhaps the most radical of the three) became the point of departure for systematic theology for the rest of the twentieth century. Systematic theology, however, did not occupy center stage in the world of theology. The spotlight focused on New Testament exegesis in general and on Rudolf Bultmann in particular. As a theologian he was not unlike Barth, but as an exegete he belongs to the nineteenth century.

Whereas other neo-orthodox theologians ignored and repudiated exegetical minimalism, Bultmann endorsed it by editing and republishing von Harnack's sensational *What Is Christianity?* (1950). Bultmann's exegetical method will long be associated with the terms *form criticism* and *demythologizing*.

Form criticism had been developed previously in Old Testament studies by Hermann Gunkel and in New Testament studies by Karl-Ludwig Schmidt and Martin Dibelius, but the method of form criticism will always be associated with the name of Bultmann. Form criticism identifies certain types of literature and classifies them in categories known as forms. Among the forms are tales, legends, myths, short stories, and the like. In New Testament times the gospel, that is, the basic Christian message, came into a community where it was clothed in a form. This message was called the *kerygma*. The New Testament scholar has the task of first identifying the form or category in which the message was clothed and then removing the form to get at the *kerygma*. This process is called demythologizing.

In Bultmann's view the Gospels as they exist today were the creation not of the apostles or even other individuals but rather communities made anonymous by history. The form which the *kerygma* took within the community was determined by that community's culture rather than by the conscious act of a particular author. Such miracles as the virgin birth and resurrection of Jesus Bultmann regarded as part of the form of Hellenistic rather than Jewish communities. He thought the Greeks would naturally express the *kerygma* in legendary forms. With this approach the only sure conclusion Bultmann reached was that there had been a Jewish rabbi named Jesus who was put to death under Pontius Pilate. About His real personality we know almost nothing. Bultmann's *Jesus and the Word* (1926; English translation, 1958) popularized these views. Some scholars were not even certain that he saw anything in the Gospels as verifiable. As a New Testament scholar Bultmann was a continuation of nineteenth-century exegetical minimalism. He had with a purpose republished von Harnack's *What Is Christianity?*, which had stripped Christianity of its history. It was not because of his exegetical approach, but in spite of it, that he was able to assert that in the scriptural revelation God makes a claim upon modern man. However, it was Bultmann's form criticism and demythologizing which would attract New Testament scholars. Some scholars have tried to identify with more precision the communities which formed each Gospel. Others repudiated the whole idea.

Post-Bultmann Era

Bultmann's methods were not left unchallenged or uncorrected by his own students who were favorably disposed to him. The quest for the historical Jesus which Schweitzer had pronounced dead and which Barth ignored was again a lively issue. Bultmann's own disciples were challenging their master. Ernst Käsemann asserted that there was a continuity between the preaching of Jesus and the faith of the Christian community, and thus the Gospels did preserve several authentic aspects of His preaching. The gap between the historical Jesus and the early Christian community made unbridgeable by Bultmann was being closed. Günther Bornkamm in his *Jesus of Nazareth* (1960) was willing to assert the authenticity of the accounts in which Jesus deals with demoniacs. Ernst Fuchs went even further and held that Jesus had a consciousness of performing a special mission for God, a type of messianic complex. These three theologians along with Bultmann were committed, however, to *Gemeindetheologie,* the belief that the community, rather than an individual (whether that be Jesus, an apostle, or a writer), was chiefly responsible for the final form of the Gospel. Attributing to the community the significant role in the formation of the Gospels was an application to New Testament theology of Schleiermacher's legacy of community consciousness as the source of Christianity. The fundamental basis of this entire method may be untenable. It could be challenged on the grounds that creative force is found in individuals, and not in communities, as Bultmann contends. Form criticism was offered as an objective standard to judge the Gospel material; however, such forms as legend, fairy tale, and myth were themselves subjectively determined categories.

Redaction Criticism

Redaction criticism, a reaction to form criticism's concentration on isolating, identifying, and classifying shorter materials known as forms, put the emphasis on determining the theological motives of the final editor or compiler of each Gospel, known in German as the *Redaktor*. In redaction criticism the editor is regarded as a writer and a theologian in his own right, who through selection, omission, and arrangement of materials attempted to teach the early church his theology. Scholars advocating this method use the traditional names for the Gospel writers, that is, Matthew, Mark, Luke, and John, but without suggesting that these men were the actual authors. Their names were used as handy and traditional labels to identify the editors.

THE SURVIVAL AND REVIVAL OF CONSERVATIVE THEOLOGY

A struggle between fundamentalist and modernist theologies raged in the United States during the first decades of the twentieth century. American modernist theology was essentially an import of German nineteenth-century liberal theology on which it was greatly dependent for its themes of religious experience as the source of truth, higher critical study of the Bible, the Social Gospel, and evolution. The Social Gospel was suited for the pragmatic American mind. Harry Emerson Fosdick, a defrocked Presbyterian minister, was at the center of the controversy. The views for which he was removed from office soon became those of the larger Protestant denominations. Fundamentalism found its foremost champion in J. Gresham Machen, also a Presbyterian clergyman, who left Princeton Theological Seminary to found Westminster Theological Seminary in Philadelphia in 1929. Fundamentalism's major themes were the virgin birth, the vicarious atonement, the physical resurrection, and biblical inspiration. Modernism won out in most of the major American Protestant churches because seminaries trained and placed in congregations clergymen who were committed to the newer theology. In the 1930s, as neo-orthodoxy was overcoming the older liberal theology in Germany, liberalism in America was winning out over fundamentalism, which had been dominant during the period of westward expansion. Schleiermacher's and Ritschl's theology was being transfused into the American scene at the same time that it was being rejected in Germany. Only after World War II were most works of neo-orthodoxy translated into English. Both American liberals and fundamentalists together with their respective allies would have to restate their positions over against the new overpowering force of neo-orthodoxy.

Neo-orthodoxy because of its many-faceted approach was appealing to both liberals and conservatives, but for different reasons. Conservatives could easily be attracted to Barth's peculiar brand of biblicism, which might be mistaken for a revival of the classical views. His opposition to hardcore liberal theology would find a ready welcome. Bultmann's method of demythologizing was recognized by conservatives as a clear threat, but was incorporated by those who followed in the nineteenth-century liberal tradition. With the importation of neo-orthodoxy to the United States, a conservative reaction, which was not merely a continuation of early twentieth-century fundamentalism, took shape. Since Barthian neo-orthodoxy in its dogmatic formulation so closely resembled traditional biblical theology, the challenge for the conservative theologians was greater. The rise of conservative theology was diversified rather than monolithic, American rather than European.

In 1949 the Evangelical Theological Society was formed by American theologians who together with their students became the conservative Protestant leaders for the next thirty years. The movement was identified as evangelicalism or neo-evangelicalism, though many associated with the movement would eschew the label. Among the founders were Carl F. H. Henry, Kenneth Kantzer, Harold Lindsell, Laird Harris, J. Barton Payne, and Walter A. Maier. The society's membership roll included the most prominent conservative theologians in America. In 1956, Henry, a Baptist clergyman, began publishing *Christianity Today* with the support of men like L. Nelson Bell, a Presbyterian layman and father-in-law of this century's most significant preaching evangelist, Dr. Billy Graham. The biweekly periodical soon hit a circulation rate of around 200,000, surpassing the *Christian Century*, liberal theology's floundering publishing beacon. Its declining circulation rate was little helped by attempted transfusions through publishing mergers. *Christianity Today* minimized differences among conservative Protestants in order to organize them more effectively against the common enemy of neo-orthodoxy. The conservative Protestants had been excluded from leadership roles in most major Protestant denominations, but they had not silenced their voice. Though not written with the usual scholarly apparatus, *Christianity Today* was able to attract writers who had solid credentials.

With major denominational and historically prestigious seminaries under liberal control, conservative Protestants moved to establish and reinforce independent seminaries. Trinity, Dallas, Fuller, Asbury, and Reformed, all with strong enrollments, were overnight success stories in preparing ministers committed to conservative theology and at the same time aware of the newer theological methods. Conservative theology was determined to be intellectually acceptable and in this it succeeded. The message of the postwar conservative revival was carried by such publishing houses as Baker, Zondervan, Eerdmans, Inter-Varsity, Tyndale, and Moody. Older classics were reprinted and the works of the new generation of scholars were published. Mainline denominations, especially in their administrations and seminaries, however, remained mostly untouched by the upsurge of conservative theology. They showed a continual decline in such vital signs as membership, accessions, and stewardship. At the end of the 1970s denominations not recognizable as conservative in theology were facing a crisis in surplus clergy and a shortage in congregations available for them.

Two exceptions to the general picture were two large denominations, the Southern Baptist Convention and the Lutheran Church—Missouri Synod, both of whom projected conservative images throughout the twentieth century. The Missouri Synod remains the one church which did not succumb when confronted and seriously threatened by neo-orthodoxy.

This church body of nearly three million was dependent for its conservative theology on its strong confessional Lutheran heritage of sixteenth- and seventeenth-century Germany. It did not belong to the mainstream of American Reformed Protestantism, but shared nevertheless an equally determined commitment to biblical inspiration and inerrancy. Since it had not been completely Americanized by the first part of the twentieth century, it had sat on the sidelines during the modernist-fundamentalist controversy. As the process of Americanization accelerated in the 1930s, the Missouri Synod began assimilating the life of American Protestantism. When the process was completed at the end of World War II, neo-orthodoxy, popular among American Protestants, was warmly received by many in the Missouri Synod. Its clergymen—at home in English now, but no longer competent in German—were drawn into the currents of American theology and neglected the major classical Lutheran works. The language change had cut the church off from its historical moorings and it was floundering without specific direction. By the 1950s Concordia Seminary, the synod's school in St. Louis, was swiftly moving in the direction of neo-orthodoxy, a phenomenon occurring in many American seminaries. By the 1960s the form-critical methods popularized by Bultmann were being taught as accepted procedures in this seminary's classrooms. The synod administration had committed itself to wider ecumenical participation. In the mid-1960s it appeared that the Missouri Synod was set on the same course which befell most of American Protestantism. During this period conservatives within and without the Missouri Synod, in America and then Europe, were aware of these developments. Herman Sasse, a conservative German theologian living then in Australia, had prophesied the nearing end of this last large conservative Lutheran body and with it the demise of conservative Lutheran theology.

Forces were moving within and without, however, which would prevent the Missouri Synod from becoming liberal. A conservative movement within the Missouri Synod began to take shape during the late 1950s and 1960s. One theological motivation for the revival of conservative theology within the Missouri Synod was provided by Robert D. Preus. He had made available sixteenth- and seventeenth-century Lutheran thought through his *Inspiration of the Scriptures* (1957). Sixteenth- and seventeenth-century theology had always been the foundation of the Missouri Synod, but it was funneled down in nineteenth- and twentieth-century writings. Preus became recognized for his scholarly expertise in early Lutheran thought. Though not trained by the synod, he was called to its seminary in St. Louis at the time when this institution was coming under the influence of neo-orthodoxy. His brother, J. A. O. Preus, later to become synod president, came in 1959 to the synod's other seminary in Springfield, Illinois, now relocated in Fort Wayne. Chosen as seminary president in 1962, he also demonstrated his scholarly expertise in sixteenth-century theology by his translation of Martin Chemnitz's *Two Natures of Christ* (1971).

A critical juncture for the Missouri Synod was reached in 1969 when a pastor explicitly committed to the new theological directions was selected president of the St. Louis seminary, and J. A. O. Preus was elected synod president. In 1971 the synod authorized its president to conduct a theological investigation of the St. Louis faculty; in 1973 the theological views of the seminary president and majority of the faculty were found unacceptable. The suspension of the seminary president in January, 1974, precipitated a near total walkout of faculty, staff, and students, and the establishment of a counterseminary. Since then the synod has experienced a further conservative theological shift. The crisis in the Missouri Synod in those years captured the nation's attention as few religious occurrences do. It was also discussed in European theological circles. In historical perspective the conservative survival and revival in the Missouri Synod may be viewed as a felicitous exception to or a reprieve from what seemed to be the unchallenged progress of Rationalism born in the eighteenth-century Enlightenment. The conservative movement within the Missouri Synod was parallel to, but not dependent upon, the general conservative revival in American Protestantism. Yet it cannot be overlooked that *Christianity Today,* the voice of conservative Protestantism, flourished in this period of confessional Lutheran revival and was read by Missouri Synod pastors. Non-Lutheran conservative scholarly-exegetical works provided the basic materials for conservative Missouri Synod theologians, professors, and their students.

In Germany and Scandinavia conservative opposition evoked by the radical conclusions of Bultmann crystallized in the "No Other Gospel" movement. A more distinctly Lutheran opposition appeared in the "Church Assemblies for the Confession and the Church." The state-related churches and theological faculties at the universities showed little or no conservative leanings. At the end of the 1970s Enlightenment theology and its heirs still controlled the European situation— with a few rare, but bright exceptions. These exceptions can best be understood as reactions against or repudiations of Bultmann's exegetical procedure.

The conservative reaction against Bultmann was chiefly concerned not with any denial of biblical inspiration or inerrancy, but rather his dismantling of biblical history through demythologizing. The denial of the historical resurrection of Jesus was seen as the crucial item. Bultmann's opponents saw as absolutely necessary the connection between the historical Jesus and the resurrected Christ as one person. Repudiated was the understanding that the resurrected Christ was an invention of later Christian communities. Joachim Jeremias, a New Testament scholar at the University of Tübingen whose father had been a pastor in Jerusalem, isolated certain phrases that could be attributed only to Jesus and not to an early Christian community (*The Central Message of the New Testament,* 1965). At the University of Lund in Sweden, Harold Riesenfeld (*The Gospel Tradition and Its Beginnings,* 1957; *Gospels Reconsidered,* 1960) and Birger Gerhardsson (*Memory and Manuscript,* 1961; *Tradition and Transmission in Early Christianity,* 1964) defended the view that the Gospels contain the actual words of Jesus and were not fabrications of later communities. Essential to their argument was the thesis that Jesus employed rabbinic methods of having His disciples commit His message to memory. Karl-Heinrich Rengstorf, New Testament and rabbinical scholar at the University of Münster, established the link between Jesus and His apostles on the basis of the Jewish understanding of "apostle" (*Apostolate and Ministry,* 1969). F. F. Bruce at the University of Manchester and I. Howard Marshal at the University of Aberdeen led the way in establishing the link between Jesus and the Christian church. Conservative scholars regarded as intolerable the chasm which modern theologians had posited between the historical Jesus on one side and the resurrected Christ and the early Christian community on the other. These conservatives demonstrated that such a chasm was a philosophical invention without any New Testament support. English-speaking scholars became eminently influential among American conservative Protestant scholars by using scientific exegetical methods within a framework which did not threaten the basic assumption that the Bible is God's Word. Bruce is particularly noteworthy for his *Traditions—Old and New* (1970), which handles the problem of sources behind the New Testament, and for his *Paul and Jesus* (1974), which tackles the old liberal separation between Epistles and Gospels.

ENGLISH BIBLE TRANSLATIONS

Since the *King James Version* of the Bible was produced in 1611, it has served as a standard of the English language and biblical orthodoxy wherever it was used. The post-World War II years experienced a remarkable interest in producing new

English translations of the Bible. There was a general agreement that the Elizabethan English preserved in the *King James Version* was beautiful but was becoming more and more incomprehensible in each generation. These newer translations were not, however, without their own theological motivation. The general theme sounded by all the versions was that the Bible in English translation should be as easily understood as were the original languages in their time. Along with the desire to update the language was an awakened interest in utilizing extant manuscripts and early translation of the biblical books. Behind the *King James Version* there stood only one text.

J. B. Phillips, an Anglican divine, translated the Epistles (*Letters to Young Churches,* 1947), *The Gospels* (1952), and then the Acts (*The Young Church in Action,* 1955). His translation was so contemporary that in certain passages it was clearly a paraphrase. "Phillips" became a household word in Bible translations. The *Revised Standard Version,* which aimed at both preserving the dignity of the revered English of the *King James Version* and conforming to recent manuscript discoveries and to what were considered scientific exegetical studies, appeared in completed form in 1952. Certain key passages supporting Christian doctrines were revised; and, as a result, this translation came under heavy criticism.

Two other translations attempting to incorporate the general exegetical developments of the nineteenth and twentieth centuries were *The New English Bible* (1961), which was intended for Protestants, and *The Jerusalem Bible* (1966), intended for English-speaking Roman Catholics. Scholars committed to newer critical views played prominent roles in their production. Other translations were to come from the United States. The American Bible Society finished its *Today's English Version* in 1976. Quite contemporary in its expression, it also was criticized for making use of certain modern critical opinions. *The Living Bible* (1971), a paraphrase, was immediately recognized for its vibrant style, but it soon became associated with millennial and neopentecostal views. *The Berkeley Version* (1959), the *New American Standard Bible* (1960), *An American Translation* (1976), and the *New International Version* (1978) provided up-to-date translations and incorporated recent manuscript evidence, but made every attempt to preserve basic Christian doctrines. Among conservative Protestants the general trend is to give the *New International Version* the revered position held so long by the *King James Version*. English-speaking Protestantism will not, however, ever have again such unity of biblical expression as the *King James Version* provided up until recent times.

THEOLOGY AT THE BEGINNING OF THE 1980s

Since the middle of the 1960s the theological tradition which began with Rationalism and can be traced through Schleiermacher, Ritschl, von Harnack, and Barth has reached a plateau in the theologies of the future, history, and liberation. At the beginning of the 1980s there seems to be little direction, up or down, from this plateau. The two-hundred-year-old theological tradition rooted in the Rationalism of the eighteenth-century Enlightenment has always been strongly imprinted by culture, rather than by a biblical commitment. World culture in general during the last two decades of the twentieth century is almost sure to bear the mark of political activism, especially among the emerging Third World countries. Parallel to activism in politics are the philosophy of continual change and the program of revolution offered in the theology of liberation. Liberation theology is a child of its own culture and is only a poor disguise of the prevailing *Weltgeist*. Its theology is attractive because it not only calls for but requires universal participation in the changing world political process. Not unlike the Social Gospel, it substitutes societal change for individual conversion, but of course it demands that these changes come quickly and outside the established means wherever necessary. Since with liberation theology the theological science reaches a pinnacle and then dissolves into raw activism, it is questionable how long liberation theology can be recognized as theology.

Theology since the end of World War II has literally burned the bridges behind it. The "God is dead" theology has created what appears to be an unfordable chasm, so that a return to the comfortable liberalism of the nineteenth century and the contemplative, autonomously self-sufficient neo-orthodoxy of the first half of the twentieth century seems impossible. In terms of theological production Pannenberg and Moltmann still do not measure up to Karl Barth, the giant

of neo-orthodoxy, but without any new imaginative luminaries
on the horizon they may have very well by default occupy the
center stage for systematic theology at least until the dawn of
the twenty-first century. Into that century no prophetic eye
looks.

Denominational theology has done very poorly and does
not seem to have much of a future except among conservative,
traditional bodies which take seriously the heritage of the
sixteenth-century Protestant Reformation. Here denominational
theology will remain internally influential, but will not really
contribute to the general theological flow. Such groups where
denominational theology is successful are with but a few exceptions small in comparison with other churches.

Though liberation theology and denominational theology
will not be exceptionally productive, a great deal of activity
can be expected in the area of biblical studies. Bultmann, by
distinguishing between the historical Jesus, about whom he
was virtually agnostic, and the Christian community, opened
the question of the relationship between the actual words of
Jesus and their inscription in the Gospels. This is a historical
quest which has attracted scholars who are not necessarily committed to Bultmann's philosophy. The same question is being
asked concerning all parts of the Holy Scriptures. Since this
type of research is very individualistic, great schools of thought
centering around one person should not be expected. The great
contributions will be those of separate individuals working
alone. Recent archaeological finds may have a greater effect on
theology than can be determined or even imagined now.

Conservative Protestantism suffered severe blows in the
loss of major denominational seminaries and then the denominations themselves to liberalism. By the middle of the century
this was an accomplished fact. The rise of neo-orthodoxy,
Bultmann's radical dehistoricizing exegesis, and theological
secularism from 1945 to 1980 might have spelled the end for
those who build on the foundation of the Protestant Reformation. But the facts prove the contrary. As the end of the
twentieth century approaches, conservative theologians are indeed more optimistic than they were twenty years ago. There
seems to be little hope that the older denominational structures
will again become effective and there seems to be little desire
to establish any type of conservative organizational structure.

Conservatives, without in any way surrendering the Reformation principles which have caused serious divisions among them, have had to defend such basic Christian doctrines as God's personal existence, the historical character of Jesus in particular and the Bible in general, and the church's chief mission as God's agency for world conversion. In defending these doctrines they found and are still finding a unity which transcends the importance of the older Reformation divisions without denying them. The effectiveness of conservative biblical theology will depend largely on how the challenge posed in contemporary questions is met.

David P. Scaer, Th.D.

twin brooks series BOOKS IN THE SERIES

THE ACTS OF THE APOSTLES .... Richard B. Rackham
APOSTOLIC AND POST-APOSTOLIC TIMES (Goppelt) .... Robert A. Guelich, tr.
THE APOSTOLIC FATHERS .... J. B. Lightfoot
THE ATONEMENT OF CHRIST .... Francis Turrettin
THE AUTHORITY OF THE OLD TESTAMENT .... John Bright
BACKGROUNDS TO DISPENSATIONALISM .... Clarence B. Bass
BASIC CHRISTIAN DOCTRINES .... Carl F. H. Henry
THE BASIC IDEAS OF CALVINISM .... H. Henry Meeter
THE CALVINISTIC CONCEPT OF CULTURE .... H. Van Til
CHRISTIAN APPROACH TO PHILOSOPHY .... W. C. Young
CHRISTIAN PERSONAL ETHICS .... Carl F. H. Henry
COMMENTARY ON DANIEL (Jerome) .... Gleason L. Archer, Jr., tr.
THE DAYS OF HIS FLESH .... David Smith
DISCIPLING THE NATIONS .... Richard DeRidder
THE DOCTRINE OF GOD .... Herman Bavinck
EDUCATIONAL IDEALS IN THE ANCIENT WORLD .... Wm. Barclay
THE EPISTLE OF JAMES .... Joseph B. Mayor
EUSEBIUS' ECCLESIASTICAL HISTORY
FUNDAMENTALS OF THE FAITH .... Carl F. H. Henry, ed.
GOD-CENTERED EVANGELISM .... R. B. Kuiper
GENERAL PHILOSOPHY .... D. Elton Trueblood
THE GRACE OF LAW .... Ernest F. Kevan
THE HIGHER CRITICISM OF THE PENTATEUCH .... William Henry Green
THE HISTORY OF CHRISTIAN DOCTRINES .... Louis Berkhof
THE HISTORY OF DOCTRINES .... Reinhold Seeberg
THE HISTORY OF THE JEWISH NATION .... Alfred Edersheim
HISTORY OF PREACHING .... E. C. Dargan
LIGHT FROM THE ANCIENT EAST .... Adolf Deissmann
NOTES ON THE MIRACLES OF OUR LORD .... R. C. Trench
NOTES ON THE PARABLES OF OUR LORD .... R. C. Trench
OUR REASONABLE FAITH (Bavinck) .... Henry Zylstra, tr.
PAUL, APOSTLE OF LIBERTY .... R. N. Longnecker
PHILOSOPHY OF RELIGION .... D. Elton Trueblood
PROPHETS AND THE PROMISE .... W. J. Beecher
REASONS FOR FAITH .... John H. Gerstner
THE REFORMATION .... Hans J. Hillebrand, ed.
REFORMED DOGMATICS (Wollebius, Voetius, Turretin) .... J. Beardslee, ed., tr.
REFORMED DOGMATICS .... Heinrich Heppe
REVELATION AND INSPIRATION .... James Orr
REVELATION AND THE BIBLE .... Carl F. H. Henry
ROMAN SOCIETY AND ROMAN LAW IN THE NEW TESTAMENT .... A. N. Sherwin-White
THE ROOT OF FUNDAMENTALISM .... Ernest R. Sandeen
THE SERVANT-MESSIAH .... T. W. Manson
STORY OF RELIGION IN AMERICA .... Wm. W. Sweet
THE TESTS OF LIFE (third edition) .... Robert Law
THEOLOGY OF THE MAJOR SECTS .... John H. Gerstner
VARIETIES OF CHRISTIAN APOLOGETICS .... B. Ramm
THE VOYAGE AND SHIPWRECK OF ST. PAUL (fourth edition) .... James Smith
THE VIRGIN BIRTH .... J. G. Machen
A COMPANION TO THE STUDY OF ST. AUGUSTINE .... Roy W. Battenhouse, ed.
STUDIES IN THE GOSPELS .... R. C. Trench
THE HISTORY OF THE RELIGION OF ISRAEL .... John Howard Raven
THE HISTORY OF CHRISTIAN DOCTRINE (revised edition) .... E. H. Klotsche
THE EPISTLES OF JUDE AND II PETER .... Joseph B. Mayor
THEORIES OF REVELATION .... H. D. McDonald
STUDIES IN THE BOOK OF DANIEL .... Robert Dick Wilson
THE UNITY OF THE BOOK OF GENESIS .... William Henry Green
THE APOCALYPSE OF JOHN .... Isbon T. Beckwith
CHRIST THE MEANING OF HISTORY .... Hendrikus Berkhof